Value Quest

Driving Profit and Performance by Integrating Strategic Management Processes

C.J. McNair and The CAM-I
Cost Management Integration Team

*A Performance Model
for Today's
Competitive Challenges*

THE COST MANAGEMENT
INTEGRATION TEAM

James Cypher, DaimlerChrysler

Mark Ferguson, Honeywell International

Tom Freeman, Arthur Andersen LLP

Keith Hallin, Boeing Commercial Airplane Group

Randolf Holst, Arthur Andersen LLP

George Millush, DaimlerChrysler

Tom Roberts, CNH Global N.V.

Charles Ross, Eastman Kodak Company

Peter Zampino, CAM-I

Contributors:

Joseph Donnelly, Arthur Andersen LLP

Alan Verico, IBM

CAM-I
3301 Airport Freeway
Suite 324
Bedford, Texas 76021 USA
Tel: 817/860-1654
Fax: 817/275-6450
www.cam-i.org

Library of Congress
ISBN 1-890783-03-X

Table of Contents

PART III:

PART IV:

FOREWARD

Over the last several decades we have witnessed what has been labeled the "information age". Never before in the history of mankind have we possessed the ability to gather and process data as rapidly as we do today. Has this new ability changed the way we conduct business? Absolutely! However, while this new processing power allows management to collect and analyze reams of data – it does not guarantee we will successfully utilize the data to create information and knowledge.

How often have we heard the frustrated cry, "If only I would have had the information I needed, I could have made a better decision!". While new information processing technologies have given us the ability to rapidly gather data to be interpreted, they only deliver the data and not the information and knowledge an organization needs to optimize decision capabilities. The ability to make optimum decisions, therefore, rests on an organization's ability to convert data into knowledge. What does this mean exactly? It means that organizations must learn to harness the new power of data processing and develop mechanisms to expedite the creation of knowledge.

This is what the Consortium for Advanced Manufacturing-International's Cost Management Systems Program set out to accomplish when it launched the Cost Management Integration Team. Recognizing the changing nature of business and the extreme advancements in information technology, this CAM-I interest group set out to develop a framework to facilitate collecting the "required data" to enable rapid information and knowledge development.

It has been stated that knowledge creation and its appropriate utilization will provide organizations the greatest competitive advantage. Given this statement, organizations must learn how to rapidly create knowledge. *Value Quest – Driving Profit Performance by Integrating Strategic Management Processes* attempts to help the business practitioner simplify the decision complexity that every manager faces. Value Quest begins by presenting a model of the firm's decision making needs and demonstrates how the utilization of seven Strategic Management Processes (SMPs) can expedite a firm's ability to develop and deploy strategy, design products and services, optimize process ability, and leverage resource consumption.

The CAM-I SMP Model is the foundation of an organization's *Value Quest.* This model will help organizations focus on what information is required for key strategic decisions, and how to compile this information through the utilization of the appropriate SMPs.

Value Quest encompasses the work of CAM-I's Cost Management Systems (CMS) Program over the last fourteen years. It represents the collective learning of more than three hundred leading companies and is based on the applied research conducted by the Program over this time frame. This model details the integration of numerous improvement initiatives and outlines a process for creating critical information and knowledge for firms competing in this new millenium.

It is not the intent of *Value Quest* to provide a "silver bullet", but rather to provide an understanding of how to integrate key Strategic Management Processes to create competitive knowledge and a competitive position. Today's leading companies have mastered parts of this integration – tomorrow's leaders will be those that master it all.

May your journey lead you to your desired outcome.

Peter A. Zampino
Director of Research
CAM-I

ACKNOWLEDGEMENTS

It would be extremely difficult to identify each individual that contributed intellectually to this project. Due to the nature of CAM-I, many individuals share their knowledge and experiences on an ongoing basis. This constant interchange provides a fountain of ideas, many of which never develop individual ownership.

It is this spirit of "group development" that enables CAM-I members to develop and deliver leading edge thinking. Contributors are less concerned with idea ownership, but rather more focused on creating new solutions. Many individuals contributed ideas and "sweat equity" over the two and a half years of our pursuit. While too numerous to mention them all, I thank and recognize each of them.

It is critical, however, to identify those that pushed us forward. The CAM-I Strategic Management Process (SMP) Model was based on the concepts presented by Alan Vercio of IBM. His thinking provides the foundation for our work. Sven Kalve of The Boeing Company provided a management overview to keep us realistic and Keith Hallin of Boeing Commercial Group recorded our thoughts and gently reminded us of our commitments. Professor C. J. McNair performed the incredible task of deciphering our ideas, integrating her knowledge, and producing a document that hopefully provides value to the reader. Mark Ferguson of Honeywell and Randolf Holst of Arthur Andersen organized each meeting and provided the leadership and facilitation required to deliver this project.

It is also extremely important that we acknowledge the experts that reviewed our work and validated our thinking: Robert Miller of Boeing (retired), Frank Reynolds of Eastman Kodak, Ross Thompson of Case Corporation, Joe Donnelly of Arthur Andersen, Ken McIntyre of Honeywell International, Alan Stratton of Stratton Associates and Mike Roberts of MEVATEC Corporation. CAM-I is also grateful for the support and encouragement provided by the Institute of Management Accountants to carry out this aggressive project.

The dedication of the CAM-I Cost Management Integration Team was phenomenal. These individuals gave countless hours and shared their lifetime of experience to the development of the concepts presented in this book.

Lastly, how can a project be managed without "Managers"? Nancy Thomas of CAM-I kept us all on track while Mary Ann Cockrell, also of CAM-I, helped bring this project to a timely closure. Ron Bleeker, Cost Management Systems (CMS) Program Director, provided the resource support for undertaking Value Quest.

As a final note, thanks to all who helped, those who finished, and even those who suggest we never do it again!

Peter A. Zampino
Director of Research
CAM-I

Chapter 1

Transformation

To change and to improve are two different things.
– German Proverb

Key Learnings:

- Managing interdependencies and linkages throughout the value chain has the greatest impact on entity performance

- Introduce the CAM-I SMP Model and benefits

- Imperative—That traditional forms of information are insufficient for managing the business

- Industry focus on Process Improvement

We live in challenging times. The profits of most Western organizations are reaching the highest levels ever recorded and productivity gains are outstripping expectations. Yet, there is a constant pressure to get even better. The relentless master—the global economy and the customers who comprise it—are constantly in search of ever better products and services at competitive prices with mass customization and rapid delivery guaranteed. It is indeed both the best of times, and the worst of times, for businesses everywhere. These challenges are leading to rapid innovation in products and in the management processes that support their delivery. Change without improvement is not an option in this demanding market.

In every organization, every walk of life, the rules of the game are shifting. Gone is the ability to recover costs in price; price is driven by its own set of rules. Gone is the ability to improve profits by making more of the same product faster; effectiveness has replaced efficiency as the driver.   Gone is the ability to manage performance with traditional financial statements and performance dimensions (for instance, quality, cost, and delivery) must be actively balanced and managed to ensure strategic objectives are attained.

As the challenges facing management multiply, there is increasing recognition that traditional forms of information are falling short of the mark—they provide too little insight or support for today's complex decision needs. While profitability remains a key results measure, it is a lagging indicator.   It may make individual managers pleased or dissatisfied, but in the end they are no smarter about how best to manage the company's performance drivers. Gaining and sustaining a competitive edge requires forward-looking data and analysis—not hindsight.   It is this new demand for action-oriented, future-focused information that the emerging cost management systems are designed to meet. Supporting the firm in the search for excellence — the *Value Quest*—is the ultimate goal of advanced cost management systems.

Looking back over the last ten years, the available cost management information has grown in response to new management models and business practices. The first of these initiatives, Activity-Based Cost Management (ABCM), set the stage for challenging existing forms of financial information and their relevance. Redefining cost in terms of the resource consumption *caused by* specific activities and processes, ABCM   laid the groundwork for questioning what was measured by the cost management system, when it was measured, where measurements were taken, how they were used and why they were used.

While ABCM provided new insights into the management of the firm, it rapidly became bogged down in the details of general ledger closings and accounting routines.   In its initial implementations, ABCM was unfocused   in nature—the resulting new form of information was "better" than prior data but it seemed unlikely to reach its true potential.   What was needed was a purpose for creating and sustaining the activity-based information that went beyond improved product cost accuracy.

Developments in areas outside of the finance function provided the focus and urgency required to put activity-based information, and supporting data, to work. Specifically, process management initiatives, supply chain management efforts, and the *voice of the customer* combined with other new or existing management tools to create a need for economically-sound estimates of the impact of decisions and improvement efforts on company performance. Enabling technologies began appearing and multiplying, providing a flexibility and responsiveness that had always been missing in financial reporting systems. Most importantly, a new breed of finance managers came onto the scene, individuals driven to become part of the operations management team. These forces combined to create a new vision, and structure, for the business.

Today, managers are beginning to understand that it is managing the interdependencies and linkages within the organization and throughout the value chain that has the greatest impact on entity performance. Managing interdependencies effectively requires an integrated information system that spans the multiple levels and management processes of the enterprise. Integration is the key to harnessing the power of information to leverage and focus a company's resources and to maximize value creation—to transform problems to opportunities, challenges to success.

In the pages that follow, a new vision of information and its role in the modern business enterprise will be developed. Starting from its humble beginnings as an inventory valuation device, the development of cost management systems that integrate with other forms of data to create holistic, comprehensive, flexible sources of information to support strategic, tactical and operational decision-making will be explored. Part of a unique, bold initiative undertaken by leading firms to harness the power of information to identify, exploit, and sustain competitive advantage, the resulting **Strategic Management Process Model** provides a blueprint of the decision and data flows that define the *value equation* for the twenty-first century enterprise.

The Challenge

The only things that evolve by themselves in organization
are disorder, friction, and malperformance.
– Peter Drucker

Developing an understanding of the factors behind the drive to create new forms of information and analysis begins with exploring changes that have taken place in business structures and strategies over the last several decades. These core features of the organization shape its reality, define its information demands, and create the assumptions and constraints under which management operates. As these core features have changed, so has the definition, and demand for, information.

A CHANGING FOCUS

The structure of a business is a fluid concept, defined more in abstract terms and through channels of communication than in concrete, unchangeable features. The daily operational aspects of an organization can be transformed into a new shape through a change in focus and a shift in underlying communication and reporting patterns. Over the last 25 years, numerous organizations have evolved to become matrix, platform-driven, or virtual structures[1] as companies seek to finds ways to become focused, responsive, lean competitors in the global market.

It used to be that the focus in organizations was functional in nature (see Figure 1.1). The shaded bars, representing such areas as engineering, operations, finance, logistics, and procurement, were the dominant structural feature. Top management assigned individuals to manage each functional area, evaluated individuals within their functional silos, and emphasized the performance of each function separately from the entity and any related area.

Figure 1.1   A Functional Perspective

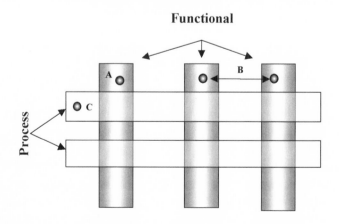

Within this functional structure, improvement efforts emphasized optimizing the performance within the functional silos (see Point A in Figure 1.1). For example, Engineering might be incented to improve its schedule release performance, to reduce the cost in manufacturing, or to work on creating better inspection techniques for quality control. Engineering would be asked to develop these improved techniques, but once designed, they would be "tossed over the wall" to the next function in line.

The numerous horror stories accompanying these functionally-defined improvement efforts include such events as an R&D organization at a major producer of perfumes and toiletries substituting a propellant within the firm's aerosol products that transformed simple bottles of perfume into "bombs." Having no responsibility for line testing the new propellant under actual operating conditions, the R&D function received a bonus for finding a cheaper propellant while manufacturing was left to deal with the cost, danger, and delay caused by the propellant on the plant floor.

The costs, in terms of lost production, scrap, and retrofitting of production machines in order to make the new propellant work far exceeded the savings claimed by the R&D function for material savings. R&D received its bonus, though, while Manufacturing Management was put to the test and failed. Did the entity win? No. In the end, no one was better off except the supplier of the new propellant and the R&D managers that had received bonuses. The firm experienced lower profits, reduced quality, higher scrap, and delays. The final customer? No one even thought about this part of the business equation.

Situations like the one described in this example led to the realization that management needed to work on "managing the white spaces" between functions (see point B in Figure 1.1).[2] Understanding that the intense focus on optimizing the performance of the functional silos had actually led to sub-optimization of the entire organization, attention turned to bridging the gap between functions through new forms of measurement and control.

Facing poor results from early attempts to bridge the white spaces between functions, companies turned to cross-functional process techniques. Here the focus became performance improvement along process lines (see point C in Figure 1.2) – **Process Management.** Each process was given performance targets and objectives. The result was improved process performance, but the failure to modify the functional structure made these improvements difficult to sustain.

In many companies, competing process and functional improvement efforts began appearing. In others, a new form of "white space" emerged—between processes. Having failed to emphasize integration at the entity level, the conflict between what was best for "parts" of the organization versus what was best for the whole company continued. Individuals remained incented to improve only those areas and results bundled into their own performance package, regardless of their impact on the downstream customer or the other parts of the organization.

The evolution of structure has led to the growing recognition that any performance improvement effort, and the information system that supports it, must emphasize the integration of both functions and processes. As suggested in Figure 1.2 (see point D), to meet the entity's needs, the new forms of information have to focus on bridging the white space between the two key dimensions of the organization: functions and processes.

Figure 1.2   The Drive for Integration

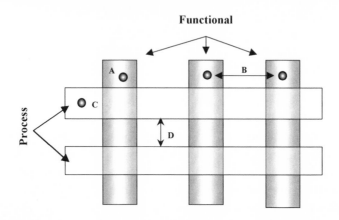

The bridges being built across the white space at point "D" in the above diagram are defined and shaped by forces outside the organization. Only at the end point of the entire value creation process can the entity be evaluated. This realization is driving companies to develop customer-defined measurements of current and desired performance that emphasize the performance of the entire value chain, not just one function, one process, or one company. Understanding what customers want, what value they place on various features of the value chain's delivered product/service bundle—the value proposition—is essential. These value perceptions translate into the revenue, cost and market share results that define strategy and survival in the global market.

A QUESTION OF VALUE

Only in recent years have companies really begun to focus on understanding, and evaluating, their performance from the perspective of the customers they serve. While customers have always been a key part of the business equation, defining and meeting their needs has not been a consistent element in a business strategy. For instance, a firm may talk of pursuing a "cost-based" or "differentiation" strategy without really coming to grips with the underlying customer value profile the targeted product/service bundle should address.

These traditional strategic terms reflect an internal perspective, a positioning of existing product/service bundles to gain maximum returns—not optimal value creation for customers. A failure to understand value from a customer's perspective may cost a company significant sales and market share. It is critical that each company understands the value a potential customer places on particular features and functions of a product or service.

For many years, in fact, business has operated from the maxim that revenues from existing products and services had to "cover the cost" of doing business. "Covering cost" as a goal has led to the reliance on full cost accounting models to define inventory values and measure product profitability, standard costs to set limits on the resources used, allocations to spread incurred costs around, and variances to measure success and failure. Spreading costs around, then absorbing them based on "earned hours" or some related activity metric, is at the heart of this traditional business performance measurement model. Reflecting the internally focused, product-based view of strategy and performance, these traditional reporting systems met the needs and matched the assumptions of the managers who used them—but failed to capture the value equation.

In pursuing a "cover cost" objective, companies argued that price (e.g., revenue) had to be related in some logical way to cost. Value and cost were one and the same—what it cost a company to make a product or provide a service was believed to be the baseline measure of its value (hence price) to the customer. If the customer didn't agree, the search was on for other customers who were more appreciative of what the company had to offer and were willing to pay the requisite price for these goods and services.

The downward cycle of performance created by the emphasis on covering costs is being reversed today by a new set of rules and objectives. Placing the customer first in everything they do, successful companies are recognizing that value only exists in the eye of the customer. Cost, or what is spent to meet customer requirements and complete basic business transactions, is no longer seen as a direct road to revenues and profits. Price is set by the perceived value embedded in the product/service bundle in the customer's mind. Price is what the customer is willing to pay a company for its outcomes, not its efforts.

A value-based perspective, one that begins and ends with identifying and satisfying customer requirements, uses customer-defined product/ service attributes as the key input to its competitive strategy. Price is set, not based on cost, but rather on management's best estimate of the value delivered by the targeted product/service bundle. Managers need information to support this *Value Quest*...to achieve growth and profits by better understanding and meeting customer requirements.

Added to this shift in strategic focus is the evolution of organizational structure from traditional vertically integrated firms to today's networked or virtual corporations. These changes have transformed the manager's job from one of managing internal activities to managing transactions and relationships. These changes have led to the growing recognition in leading edge firms that any performance improvement effort, and the information systems that are designed to support it, must emphasize the integration of activities and outcomes across functional, process and organizational boundaries.

In this new world, cost is what companies have to control to ensure profit. This isn't a new concept, but it is very different to strive to cover costs than it is to seek to earn them. Severing the link between price and cost has made it clear that a firm cannot afford to waste resources–waste will not be recovered in price. The "cost plus" world that made this economic anomaly a reality for businesses during much of the twentieth century has faded away, yielding to the relentless demand of increasingly sophisticated customers for optimal value, excellent service, and customized solutions, all delivered at a reasonable price.

The Response

Perhaps it is a sense of history
that divides good economics from bad.
– John Kenneth Galbraith

What these changes in the structure, strategy, and focus of business mean for today's managers is that understanding the relationship between activities, outcomes, and value creation has become the key to achieving profitable performance. Gaining this understanding requires an integrated flow of knowledge, information, and decisions from the top to the bottom of the organization and across all functions and processes—a new, yet common, language.

In the past, this commonality of language and concept was easy to attain through the financial reporting system. The general ledger contained the basic information used to guide decision analysis and to summarize the general economic condition of the firm. As the competitive arena shifted, though, the adequacy of the traditional financial reporting system was increasingly called into question.

With the back-to-back publications of the book Relevance Lost by Johnson and Kaplan in 1987[3] and the first CAM-I Conceptual Framework in 1988,[4] the questioning of existing accounting models intensified. Responding to these challenges, the finance profession began to experiment with and develop a number of new cost management tools. The development of each new tool, though, further eroded the underlying integrity and cohesion of the core databases used to support decisions—the assumed cohesion of the financial reporting system became more myth than reality. What were the signs that the cost management system was in need of re-integration? Some of these were:

- Managers received conflicting information from financial and operational performance measurement systems;

- Different decision makers would come to the table with very different cost and performance estimates and projections;
- Cost management information system implementations would flounder, although everyone agreed that new forms of data and information were needed;
- New product costing efforts (such as Target Cost Management) were difficult to connect to ongoing reporting and performance tracking systems;
- Every new management initiative resulted in a new database or a new set of reports that could not be tied to other information;
- Requests for ad hoc analysis increased even as data warehouses grew and information processing costs skyrocketed.

Reconnecting the fragmented pieces that are the reality of modern financial systems is a challenge that cannot be avoided. Regaining a shared vision of the organization, its current and future economic structure, as well as the chosen strategic and tactical objectives its managers should strive to achieve is the key to success for firms engaged in the global market.

THE CAM-I CONCEPTUAL DESIGN

The recognized need for an integrated approach to the cost and performance management system led to the creation of the Conceptual Framework project at CAM-I (Consortium for Advanced Manufacturing – International). Collaborating with member firms and subject matter experts, CAM-I developed a comprehensive model of the firm, its information requirements and its decision challenges. This model has been used to integrate the diverse tools in the management toolbox into a powerful, reinforcing, and supportive storehouse of information and ideas.

The resulting model, called the **CAM-I Strategic Management Process Model** (the SMP Model), is detailed in Figure 1.3. The key to the integration portrayed in this diagram lies in understanding the relationship between the core decisions made by managers within the firm, their impact on the total value delivered by the entity/value chain to customers, and related information needs. Information within this model is depicted as a resource flowing throughout the organization's value chain, linking individuals and teams together to create a coordinated stream of actions and results. Information flows to each decision domain and is directed by the various SMPs as depicted by Figure 1.3. The CAM-I SMP Model provides a logical framework to understand what critical high level decisions an organization must make and how to get the required information. Synchronized actions and results, so critical to the success of the global enterprise, cannot be achieved through the use of fragmented information systems or disjointed tools and techniques – integration is required. It is this concern with integration that underlies the model, examples, and discussions in this book.

Figure 1.3 The CAM-I Strategic Management Process Model

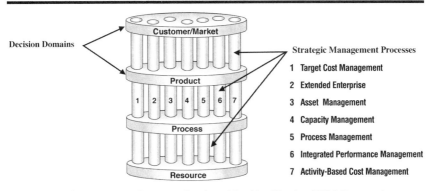

Source: Based on an original concept developed by Alan Vercio of IBM Corporation.

Two primary dimensions of information integration are encompassed in the structure detailed above: decision-making and information flows. Both of these dimensions of the SMP Model require the use of a common language. In terms of decision-making, the model emphasizes the four primary decision domains where an entity can act upon, or change, its ability to meet customer needs: customer/market, product, process/activity, and through the core factors of production (resources). The driving force of the organization, the answer to why it exists at all, is found at the customer/market level. Products and services are what the company is offering to meet customer needs and deploy its strategy. Processes and their capacity are the "how" of the management equation. They are the means to the desired ends – value creation and profits. All of these levels draw upon and define the resource requirements of the firm.

Decision-making within each decision domain requires a different type of information and a unique emphasis on how the available information is compiled. For instance, at the top level of the firm, the driving force is the design, development and distribution of a product/service bundle that meets customer needs better than any competitive offering. While the information required to make decisions at the customer/market level draw upon many different sources and perspectives, the Target Cost Management Strategic Management Process (SMP; explained in detail later) is the one that emphasizes this relationship between price, market share, and allowable costs to achieve desired profit levels.

To execute the plans developed during target costing efforts, the defined strategies and objectives have to be communicated from the customer/market decision domain to product, process and resource levels. A strategic management process, such as Target Cost Management (TCM), serves a second key role in achieving information integration—it is a conduit of vital data, objectives, and decisions from one decision domain to another. The individual SMPs do not play an equal role at all times or in all situations, but each is a critical part of the information and communication network that knits the enterprise together. Each SMP provides a unique set of data which may be useful, or not, depending on the type of decision that needs to be made. Understanding which SMP provides the best match between the primary decisions and competitive challenges faced by the enterprise in each decision domain is the key to designing an information system that optimizes the firm's ability to create value for its customers.

The required integration of a firm's information system cannot be accomplished through fragmented efforts or poorly coordinated improvement projects. Regaining the simplicity and effectiveness of the small, entrepreneurial firm requires active and effective deployment of modern management tools, a shared language and vision that reflect the core value preferences of the chosen customer base, and a responsiveness achieved through flexible, instantaneous sharing of ideas, issues, decision, and results.

INTEGRATION OVERVIEW

The integration challenge is clear, but the solution to the problems it represents can be more difficult to see. What are the tools available to help link the layers and rings that make up the Strategic Management Process Model? To date, the tools and techniques developed under this information umbrella include:

- Target Cost Management (TCM);
- The Extended Enterprise (EE);
- Asset Management (AM);
- Capacity Management (CM);
- Process Management (PM);
- Integrated Performance Management (IPM); and
- Activity-Based Cost Management (ABCM).

These strategic management processes serve as "rods" that lock the "layers", or decision domains, into synchronous action.

For instance, Target Cost Management and related forms of strategic analysis link the goals and objectives of every level, and every individual, to customer requirements. Target Cost Management is a system of profit planning and cost management that is price led, customer focused, design centered and cross-functional. It incorporates profit, cost and value-based management concepts at the earliest stages of product development and applies them throughout the product life cycle by actively involving the entire value chain, or Extended Enterprise. The Extended Enterprise SMP brings trading partners together in order to leverage cross-organizational competencies and knowledge to better meet customer requirements, both during the design and execution of the strategic plan.

Aligning resources to meet specific customer requirements, and ensuring that execution of plans is not impaired or prevented by inadequate or improper resources, is the overarching objective of Target Cost Management as well as the two related SMPs: Asset Management and Capacity Management. The Capacity and Asset Management SMPs combine to create a life cycle focus on identifying and evaluating technology, equipment, people, systems, and related opportunities that could be used to improve performance. They are extensions of the capital investment process that emphasize decisions that add value to the company and benefits its stakeholders, zeroing in on the capacity of resources to create value, as well as the causes of idle, excess, and ineffective capacity utilization. Emphasizing communication, the Capacity and Asset Management SMPs make the many different types of asset capacity and capability visible, understandable, and discussable   across the levels of management.

Another concern that has to be addressed before total integration can be achieved—the ongoing actions across the many different layers and areas of the firm have to be knit together into a stream-lined, seamless whole. It is this arena of integration that Process Management addresses. Process Management emphasizes the horizontal linkage of activities from core work flow management through business and enterprise process integration. It aligns organizational actions with customer values.

Having dealt with the integration of efforts from strategic through operational levels of the firm, attention now turns to locking everyone into the established game plan. Defining strategies and planning for their execution are necessary but not sufficient to ensure success. Results depend on two factors: the motivation of individuals to achieve the goals and the actions they take to make plans a reality. Integrated Performance Management (IPM) is the vital link between plans and results. Motivated people, individuals and teams that have goals in line with those of the organization and its primary stakeholders consistently outperform the competition.

The final SMP, Activity-Based Cost Management, emphasizes the effective combination of resources to create unique organizational capabilities. It helps analyze specific actions and their tie to processes, costs, performance and results. One of the earliest of the new cost management tools, Activity-Based Cost Management fills a basic information void by providing cost and operating information that mirrors the process view. Emphasizing opportunity costs and value analysis, Activity-Based Cost Management creates an economically-rich basis for supporting decision analysis.

As each of these tools come into use, they serve to integrate the efforts of management at specific levels of the firm as well as coordinating actions up and down the organization, flowing between decision domains to coordinate action at multiple levels. Combined into an integrated information system, these tools and techniques can help transform a company into a customer-driven, profitable enterprise.

Benefit

Knowledge of means without knowledge of ends
is animal training.

– Everett Dean Martin

The question that remains is a simple "why?" Why should any company use any or all of these specific strategic management processes, let alone undertake the effort to integrate them? While the benefits are many, several specific advantages dominate. Specifically, the integration of the strategic management processes can help a company to do the following:[5]

- Anticipate and react to environmental changes before a firm is affected by them. This means avoiding problems before they occur rather than correcting them after they happen.

- Continually improve the operations and not merely seek a temporary equilibrium.

- Create an external focus on customer requirements and competitive threats. Customer requirements drive the organization.

- Systematically relate all elements, internal and external, so problems are solved holistically rather than incrementally through cross-functional integration. This facilitates the problem being viewed and solved as a whole by building long-term relations with the suppliers and other members of the extended enterprise.

- Link current improvement tools, activities, and initiatives.

- Optimize profits by ensuring that resources remain focused on value activities, that waste is identified and removed, and process improvements result in reductions in nonvalue-added efforts.

- Avoid duplication of information collection, storage and generation.

- Link individual, group, and organizational incentives to ensure that everyone in the organization understands, and is motivated to achieve, strategic and operational objectives.

- Communicate across all levels, all processes, and all units the needs of the customer, the results achieved, problems encountered and solved, and remaining challenges to be met.

An organization that is just beginning down the path toward a responsive, customer-driven structure and strategy may not be ready or even need to use the entire set of SMPs immediately. Even so, management should understand and be ready to seamlessly integrate these related SMPs when the problems at hand warrant their implementation.

The evolution of the cost management system toward the ideal depicted in the SMP Model is a journey (see Figure 1.4). To create an effective, integrated system, a company has to understand what information it needs when, where and why. Steps that can be taken to support this effort are:

1. Isolate the firm's key decision requirements, or most critical decision domain (e.g., customer/market, product, process or resource);

2. Identify which SMP is the best source of the information needed by the chosen domain;

3. Map out the data requirements for the SMP to operate effectively;

4. Implement the dominant SMP;

5. Implement all or part of the supporting SMP's required to feed data to the dominant SMP;

6. Expand the cost management system implementation to reflect the identified flow of information from the most critical decision domain to the key secondary domain.

Repeating these steps as each new challenge or need is identified, a company can logically build an integrated SMP framework around its core business information needs, expanding the system as communication requirements grow either across a specific decision domain or between these primary areas of analysis and action. Choosing a communication strategy – a logical design and development of the information flow – is the key to effective, efficient implementation and utilization of the SMP Model.

As the figure suggests, the implementation and utilization of the SMP Model is part of an overall migration of the information system

Figure 1.4   The Migration of Information Systems

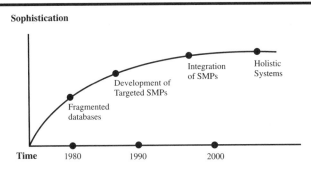

capabilities of a firm from early financially-driven, fragmented database structures to a seamlessly integrated system that can be accessed within a virtual office structure. The culmination of the migration path is the use of information as a strategic weapon. Companies such as Frito Lay are relatively far along in integrating their operational data streams, instantaneously collecting and responding to information obtained at the point of sale. Tight linkage of this operational information to financial, marketing, logistics, development, and related databases would enhance the strategic value of information even in this best practice firm.

Integrated information systems facilitate the creation of a sustainable competitive advantage. It is a goal that is rapidly becoming a reality for leading edge companies. For other firms, who are earlier in the migration path, the challenge is simpler: to choose the one or two SMPs that will yield the optimal improvement in performance for dollar invested in information. For each firm the choice of the "right" sequence in which to implement current and future SMPs will depend on the primary business challenges being faced, the existing information capabilities of the firm, and the nature of its competitive arena. There is no one best migration path to be followed. That is the message embedded in the SMP Model.

In the chapters that follow, the key issues in achieving integration will be more fully developed. Part I will provide an overview of the CAM-I Strategic Management Process Model. Specifically, Chapter 2 will summarize the basic features of the information provided and used by each SMP, while Chapter 3 will develop the framework by exploring the integration within decision contexts. A diagnostic to aid a company in understanding what tools it needs most to meet the firm's key integration challenges will then be presented in Chapter 4.

Part II will emphasize the various SMPs, presenting them in much more depth, including a full description supported by a process template, defined benefits, primary obstacles or issues in their use, and future trends. Specifically, Chapter 5 will develop Target Cost Management and strategic analysis in more depth, while Chapter 6 will explore the Extended Enterprise SMP. Chapter 7 details core Asset Management concerns, while Chapter 8 examines Capacity Management issues. Chapter 9 turns attention to the Process Management SMP. Chapter 10's discussion focuses on Integrated Performance Management, which is then linked to managing actions through Chapter 11's review of Activity-Based Cost Management.

These SMP-focused discussions will give way in Part III to detailing the implementation and integration issues within and between each decision domain. Beginning with an integration of the SMPs at the customer/market level, Part III will progress through the information integration issues faced within the product, process level and resource decision domains. Attention will then turn to putting the model into motion through a series of case studies of companies that are facing, or have successfully dealt with, the information and communication challenges either within a specific decision domain or between domains in Part IV.

Taken in total, the concepts and information contained in this book should help solve the puzzling dilemma of what Strategic Management Process to use when, where and why. By providing an integration framework, it will help a company pinpoint key areas where change needs to be made, where benefits can be gained from improved coordination, and waste eliminated by better communication and focused action. Implemented in its entirety, the CAM-I Strategic Management Process Model can become a competitive weapon that can support strategic and operational analysis, decision-making and results by integrating the levels of the organization into a holistic, synchronized and effective system.

Ideals are like the stars: we never reach them,
but like the mariners of the sea, we chart our course by them.

– Carl Schurz

Endnotes

---

[1] A virtual organization, for the purposes of this book, will be defined as one that has outsourced all but its defined core competencies, using electronic commerce and other enablers to complete transactions and manage the operational aspects of the business. Nearly asset free, these firms have minimal structure in place and have permanent employment relations with a minimal number of employees.

[2] This term originates in the work of G. Rummler and A. Brache, Improving Performance: How to Manage the White Space on the Organizational Chart, 2nd edition, San Francisco: Jossey-Bass Publishing, 1995.

[3] H.T. Johnson and R.Kaplan, Relevance Lost: The Rise and Fall Management Accounting, Boston, MA: The Harvard Business School Press, 1987.

[4] C. Berliner and J. Brimson, eds., Cost Management for Today's Advanced Manufacturing: The CAM-I Conceptual Design, Boston, MA: Harvard Business School Press, 1988.

[5] This list originally appears in the CAM-I publication Target Costing: The Next Frontier in Strategic Cost Management by Shahid Ansari, Jan Bell, and the CAM-I Target Cost Core Group. Chicago: Irwin Professional Publishing, 1997: 6.

Chapter 2

Information and Communication

Communicating is one of the most difficult challenges in any business, because people hear what they want to hear.

– Jack Stack
The Great Game of Business

Key Learnings:

■ A company that fails to develop a rich, integrated database of economic and non-economic information, accessible by individuals across the organization and within partnering organizations, will not be able to learn fast enough to sustain itself in the future.

■ The key criteria for assessing the effectiveness of information integration efforts within a firm include: consistency, compatibility, objectivity, relevance, uniqueness and customer-driven.

■ Integration of the Strategic Management Processes (SMPs) is the best way to ensure that all of the information that is needed by the firm's decision-makers resides somewhere in the organization, that these data points are accessible across the various levels and functions within the firm, and that duplication is avoided in the acquisition, storage, and provision of information.

Communication is the lifeblood of the organization. The development of an open, unambiguous communication network is essential if everyone in the organization is to know what needs to be done and how their efforts influence the performance of the entire system. This knowledge empowers each individual involved in the firm's *Value Quest*. The CAM-I Strategic Management Process (SMP) Model provides individuals with the integrated information needed to support the knowledge creation and decision-making process. The CAM-I SMP Model is part of the emerging "Information Society." Yoneji Masuda, a well known expert in the field of management information systems, describes this new world in the following way in his recent book, Managing in the Information Society:

> If the goal of industrial society is represented by volume consumption of durable consumer goods or realization of heavy mass consumption, the information society may be termed a society with highly intellectual creativity... which will embody the principle of synergy and social benefit with a European or American orientation towards the self-actualizing individual.[1]

The development of an information infrastructure plays the dominant role in Masuda's view of the global future. The Internet, as well as internal company Intranets, are examples of information infrastructures. The CAM-I SMP Model is another form of information infrastructure that emphasizes the core data elements needed to support analysis and decision-making in organizations.

The power of information to enable and empower individuals to learn and act in a coordinated fashion builds on the self-multiplying nature of information.[2] Information is not consumed when it is used, it remains. It is non-transferable – in the transfer of information both giver and receiver can access it. Information is indivisible; it can only be used as a set. Finally, information is cumulative.[3] The SMP model builds upon these core features of information to create an information infrastructure.

Companies are beginning to utilize information flows as the basis to create new structures. Virtual corporations are nothing if not a coordinated information system that spans organizational and geographic boundaries. The Extended Enterprise SMP is a structuring information flow that has been described as "Infopartnering"[4] by many of its proponents. It is an approach that can help a company implement an "Efficient Consumer Response" system. What is ECR and how does it affect organizations?

The ultimate goal of ECR is a responsive, consumer-driven system in which distributors and suppliers work together as business allies to maximize consumer satisfaction and minimize cost. Accurate information and high-quality products flow through a paperless system between manufacturing line and checkout counter with minimum degradation or interruption both within and between trading partners.[5]

What is interesting about this description of ECR is the dominant role played by information flows in improving the communication between, and performance of, the trading alliance. It would seem that Masuda's vision of the Information Society is an emerging reality within the world of business.

In the pages that follow, the role of information and communication in coordinating and improving the performance of the modern organization will be explored. Specific attention will be paid to the seven SMPs (Target Cost Management, the Extended Enterprise, Asset Management, Capacity Management, Process Management, Activity-Based Cost Management, and Integrated Performance Management) as conduits of information. Each SMP will be introduced in terms of the information it provides both to the organization and to the other SMPs. Serving as one of the two primary dimensions of SMP integration, the creation of information infrastructures can create the opportunity for quantum improvements in performance. It is to these issues that the discussion now turns.

Information and Knowledge Creation

Knowledge is the small part of ignorance that we arrange and classify.

– Ambrose Bierce

The drive to gain knowledge about external events and to tame and control nature is an essential human trait. To avoid being simply arranged ignorance, this knowledge must focus on improving understanding. Knowledge is, after all, *"cognitive information that has been generalized and abstracted from an understanding of the cause-and-effect relations of a particular phenomenon occurring in the external environment?"*[6] Knowledge, and knowledge creation, uses information to improve the nature of life, whether in business or society at large.

In what way does the concept of an information society bear upon the creation of the CAM-I SMP model? The answer is quite simple: the evolutionary path toward the information society demands the integration of information flows, the creation of shared knowledge networks, as its core dimension. Integrated information is not an option for a company within this setting – it is a requirement for survival and prosperity.

Shoshana Zuboff,[7]a Professor at the Harvard Business School and proponent of the emerging information age, suggests that there are three primary trends that will influence business as this age develops: informating technology, learning as the key driver of business, and the development of concentric organizations. Informating is described as follows, "when the technology also informates the processes to which it is applied, it increases the explicit knowledge content of tasks and sets into motion a series of dynamics that will ultimately reconfigure the nature of work and the social relationships that organize productive activity."[8] At the heart of this reconfig- uration is learning, which serves a pivotal role. To Zuboff, the informating manager "assumes that, through making the organi- zation more transparent, valuable communal insight will be gained."[9] Sharing, not hoarding information, is the goal.

Figure 2.1   Concentric Responsibility

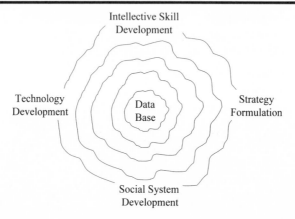

Intellective Skill
Development

Technology
Development

Data
Base

Strategy
Formulation

Social System
Development

In this informating world, personal gain is based not on private knowledge, but rather upon mastering the interpretation and utilization of information and communication networks. In direct contrast to the control of information to gain power within organizations, informating places learning and communication in this pivotal role. Knowledge is made public, shared through information systems that support learning. This learning further increases the pace of change. One only has to turn to the first pages of most business publications to find proof that the accelerated pace of change suggested here is a reality; learning extends the frontiers of the possible at ever-increasing rates.

As knowledge becomes the key resource of the firm, organizational structures need to change in order to reflect the developing concentric rings of responsibility (see Figure 2.1). At the core of these new structures lies the data warehouse and its supporting information systems. Personal influence within this emerging structure depends on the ability to learn and to support learning by others, as the following comment suggests:[10]

> *The activities arrayed on the responsibility rings at a greater distance from the core incorporate at least these four kinds of managerial activity: intellective skill development, technology development, strategy formulation, and social system development. This means that some organizational members will be involved in both higher order analysis conceptualization as well as in promoting learning and skill development among those with operational responsibility. Their aim is to expand the knowledge base and to improve the effectiveness with which data are assimilated, interpreted, and responded to. They have a central role in creating an organizational environment that initiates learning and in supporting those in other managerial activities to develop their talents as educators and learners.*

If one were to describe the role of the SMP Model, and the individuals who develop and maintain it, it would in almost all respects reflect the concentric responsibility framework.[11]

The driving force behind the movement to integrate business processes and information systems is the ever-expanding demand for knowledge, a knowledge which captures the key value attributes of the consuming public and then transforms this information into a system of management that optimizes organizational performance. A company that fails to develop a rich, integrated database of economic and non-economic information, accessible by individuals across the organization and within partnering organizations, will not be able to learn fast enough to sustain itself in the future.

Integrated information flows are the key to starting the knowledge creation engine. Through integrated information approaches, such as the SMP model, learning spreads rapidly through the organization. The result is often quantum improvements in performance that could not be attained in any other way. Breaking down the communication barriers that have inhibited performance, the CAM-I SMP Model helps build a knowledge network that can be leveraged to optimize the creation of value for customers.

What are the core features, or criteria, for assessing the effective integration of information within the informating environment? Some of these factors would include:

- *Consistency*: The measurements and data used within the information system need to be defined consistently across all databases and all users to ensure that communication is ungarbled and that analysis throughout the firm is based on the same set of facts.

- *Compatibility*: The various components of measurement should be defined in such a way as to ensure that a measurement of one performance dimension will yield information that is compatible, and therefore capable of integration, with other measures and information sources.

- *Objectivity*: The information, measurements, and data points need to be objectively stated and obtained, minimizing bias in the overall information system and the decisions it supports.

- *Relevance*: The data contained should have high applicability to the decisions made within the organization. Information content is a core requirement to ensure relevance.

- *Uniqueness*: The information flows should all provide unique information and insights into key management and organizational issues.

- *Customer driven*: The information should be focused on key performance indicators that capture primary value attributes. Reporting formats built from the information should support assessment and analysis of value creation efforts.

As these criteria suggest, creating an integrated information system is not the accidental outcome of collecting, then merging, multiple sources and types of information. Avoiding a "Tower of Babel" requires careful analysis of currently available information, identification of what data is needed to support decision-making within the firm, and the development of an information infrastructure that carefully links disparate data sources into one consistent, objective, relevant source of knowledge. The SMP Process Model meets these requirements, as do the individual SMPs that comprise it. It is to the details of this model that the discussion now turns.

Strategic Management Processes – An Overview

It is a capital mistake to theorise before one has data. Insensibly one begins to twist facts to suit theories, instead of theories to suit facts.

– Sir Arthur Conan Doyle

There are many new management techniques and information systems being developed and used in companies today. These are normally fragmented efforts, popping up in different areas of the business as need, and knowledge combine with resource availability to pave the way toward implementation. This scattered, unfocused development of capability and knowledge wastes valuable, scarce information resources. The CAM-I SMP Model seeks to overcome these problems by creating a system of hierarchical relationships and processes that provide a communication platform to tie performance measurements and global drivers to the daily efforts of individuals across the organization. The model's goal is to extend the concept of "open book management" to the entire range of information and knowledge available to the firm (see Figure 2.2).

As the diagram suggests, there are different performance measurements and tools at use across the various decision domains. At the top level, growth, profit and market share combine to define optimal customer/market strategies. Driven by external forces, including wage shifts, environmentalism, and expansion in customer expectations, the top level of decisions shapes the downstream actions and information requirements of the organization.

Figure 2.2 CAM-I Strategic Management Process Model Details

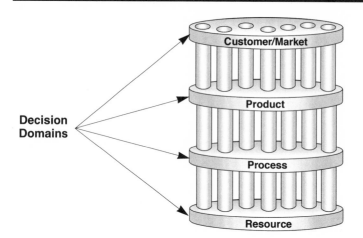

The high level strategic decisions made at the top level of the decision hierarchy emphasize customer requirements, strategies to provide value, and determine the products and services to be offered within specific markets. These decisions set off a chain of events that begins with the development of the product/service bundle to be provided. The product/service decisions then drive the need to obtain required processes and capacity to meet these demands. Resources are then marshaled to support process efforts.

Implicit in this natural hierarchy of decision-making is the free flow of information through communication channels that create a shared vision and common knowledge of the relationship between the desired results (ends) and the organizational efforts needed to reach them (means). This fact is captured in the conceptual model as the "rods" that flow through the various decision layers, carrying consistent, objective information about current and planned performance (see Figure 2.3). The "layers" cannot stand on their own. What unifies the decision layers into an efficient business is the information and processes that flow across as well as up and down through the layers. It is the information contained within the SMPs that links the organization together, facilitating open communication and decision-making.

The SMP Model highlights key areas of the business where things must go right if strategic objectives are to be met. In so doing, it also identifies areas where integration of the SMPs must take place. For

Figure 2.3 The "Rods" within the SMP Model

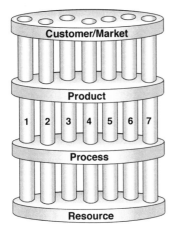

1 Target Cost Management

2 Extended Enterprise

3 Asset Management

4 Capacity Management

5 Process Management

6 Integrated Performance Management

7 Activity-Based Cost Management

instance, it is critical that customer value assessments be used to guide the development of a new product/service bundle. This information, gathered by marketing and through the efforts of the Extended Enterprise SMP, has to be communicated to Target Cost Management. If it is not, the new products and services will only meet customer requirements by chance, not design. Target Cost Management takes the input from key external sources, such as information on customer requirements (the voice of the customer) and transforms it into a range of potential product/service bundles. Target Cost Management cannot be relied upon as the sole source of analysis as the effort to narrow the range of potential candidates for development down to one or two specific products continues. It needs to draw upon information available in each of the other SMPs.

To effectively meet the demands placed upon it, the CAM-I SMP Model has to meet the following requirements:

- *Balanced*: the measurements used and available data have to provide a balanced view of actions and results, incorporating both financial and non-financial metrics from all functions and areas of the firm.

- *Owned*: the system and its measurements must have a clear ownership structure, beginning with the customer and extending throughout the firm with clear accountability and responsibility for specific outcomes and performance levels.

■ *Actionable*: the data provided must be current and timely, understandable, meaningful, and serve to improve decision-making.

■ *Simple*: the data and information system must be easy to access and use.

■ *Accurate*: the data must be entered correctly and validated for input accuracy at the source according to standard operating procedures. This is the key source of the system's data integrity. Single data sources are preferred. Data should be chosen if it is directionally correct, even if it is not precise.

■ *Predictive*: the system should identify and use measures that capture key business drivers of outcomes and performance.

■ *Aligned*: the goals, objectives and actions promoted by the system must be consistent, or aligned, from corporate headquarters down to the actions on the plant floor.

■ *Flexible*: the system needs to be able to accommodate future needs, satisfy local requirements, and be extendable to enterprise-wide use, all within an effective platform that minimizes the total amount of data required to meet organizational information needs.

■ *Cost effective*: it has to have reasonable up-front and ongoing resource requirements. The benefits must be balanced off against projected and incurred costs.

■ *Promotes knowledge/best practice sharing*: effective capture and sharing of knowledge is at the heart of the SMP model.

How well do each of the separate SMPs reflect these objectives, and how do they factor into the integrated model? It is to answering these questions that the discussion now turns.

THE SMPs

The seven core SMPs bring unique forms of information to the use of managers across the organization.

Specifically:

■ *Target Cost Management*: emphasizes the relationship between the value embedded in a product/service bundle, customer requirements, and the maximum amount of resources/costs that can be consumed to meet these needs. It identifies the right products, prices and features to optimize the value created by processes and activities.

■ *Extended Enterprise*: encapsulates the horizontal flow of products and services that makes up the industry value chain. Identifying core relationships and creating system solutions to performance shortfalls, the Extended Enterprise is the primary source of external information about customer satisfaction, changes in buying patterns, supply chain capability, and system performance against customer requirements.

■ *Asset Management*: serves as the organizing system for all asset investment and management efforts. Monitoring investments against their planned results helps pinpoint areas that may become "hot spots" for performance downstream. It also helps ensure that value creation, not the politics of self-interest, lies behind the request for and use of scarce organizational resources.

■ *Capacity Management*: When the organization is aligned to customer requirements, actions are effective, incentives lead to desired results, and investments reflect and support goals and strategies. With these achievements in place, attention can turn to ensuring that the resources are yielding as much value as possible. New investments should never be undertaken unless it is clear from sound capacity management-based information that existing resources cannot meet projected demand.

■ *Process Management*: Whether implemented through Total Quality Management (TQM) or as a free-standing management initiative, Process Management systems emphasize the linkage of activities within an organization into a seamless, coordinated, effective whole that experiences minimal disruption due to errors or miscommunication. Process Management provides unique information on the side-to-side, value creating flows of activities that combine to provide the products and services customers require.

■ *Integrated Performance Management*: Measurements must be developed to complete the communication and control loops required to make ongoing adjustments to processes and outcomes,   as well as to perform ongoing evaluation of organizational effectiveness.

■ *Activity-Based Cost Management*: Captures the core activities and the resources they consume. These measures can be linked to the other SMPs through the creation of trended estimates, waste measures, and related indicators of financial performance.

The information contained in one SMP is interdependent with that stored in another. For instance, Capacity Management stores information on physical asset capabilities and current utilization levels. To place an economic value on the utilized versus wasted components of capacity, Capacity Management turns to the Activity-Based Cost Management SMP, where key economic facts are recorded.

Capacity Management also turns to the Extended Enterprise to identify potential sources for surge or unplanned production, and to Target Cost Management to place the limits on the total costs that can be incurred to provide specific types of capacity. Asset Management, on the other hand, provides the baseline measures of performance and defines the hurdles to new investment in concise, consistent terms. Process Management details the impact of capacity problems on organizational throughput. Finally, Integrated Performance Management details non-quantitative metrics, such as quality, throughput time, first past yields, to note just a few. Effective Capacity Management cannot take place without the support and insights ensuing from the other SMPs.

Integration of the SMPs is the best way to ensure that all of the information that is needed by decision-makers resides somewhere in the organization, that these data points are accessible across the various levels and functions within the firm, and that duplication is avoided in the acquisition, storage, and provision of information. One source of data reduces the potential for error, inconsistency, and

confusion. Integration of these disparate data sources helps to enhance decision-making and communication.

Summarizing the discussion, the six core features that define a
well-integrated, effective information system are: consistency, compatibility, objectivity, relevance, uniqueness, and customer-driven.
This list of generic attributes of the information system is expanded
within the SMP model to ten measurement criteria: balanced, owned,
actionable, simple, accurate, predictive, aligned, flexible, cost effective,
and promotes knowledge sharing. In other words, within business it
is not enough for the information to contain compatible data elements,
it must ensure that the underlying measurements provide a balanced
view of operations and results that allows responsible individuals to
take action.

The evaluation of the information system along the dimensions
noted here creates a form of benchmark baseline that can provide
insight into areas where improvement efforts need to be directed. An
information system that scores low on consistency may rate high on
simplicity. Simple, inconsistent data, though, is not good data – it does
not pass the information content threshold. Similarly, information that
is highly objective, but that fails to be actionable or is not owned by
anyone, cannot result in organizational learning. As progress is made
on each of the information system and measurement dimensions, the
quality of the information system grows and its ability to support
effective decision-making is enhanced.

The CAM-I SMP Model, when completely implemented, earns a
high score on each of the six core information system criteria and the
ten measurement characteristics. It does so because it is, by design,
shaped by one clear, unambiguous goal: to optimize the value created
for customers. Information is obtained and organized around this
central theme, first within the individual SMPs, and then within the
knowledge sharing infrastructure that is the natural outcome of the
linkage of the SMPs into one cohesive model. While no company
today has all of the SMPs in place, integrated fully across all of its
decision domains, many companies (e.g., Caterpillar, DaimlerChrysler
and Case Corporation) have gone further on this journey than others.

As with all aspects of business, achieving integration of the
various SMPs and related management techniques is a journey, not a
destination. Each time a new element is added to the integrated
information system, its ability to support knowledge creation and

improvements in the value delivered to customers increases. Each new piece of information fills in the gaps in the knowledge puzzle, improving the firm's ability to predict down-stream events and ensure that these goals are reached more often than not. The integration and sharing of knowledge embedded in the SMP Model are the keys to superior performance in the dawning Information Age.

Summary

Social advance depends as much upon the process through which it is secured as upon the result itself.

— Jane Addams

This chapter has reviewed the basic issues surrounding the emerging Information Age and its implications for business information systems. Three factors combine to create the knowledge rich environment of the future: informating, learning as the key driver of business, and the development of concentric organizations. At the center of these new organizations lies the data warehouse, the repository of historical information and knowledge as well as the source for new ideas and strategies.

The SMP Model resides at the core of the informating organization, providing consistent, compatible, relevant, objective information that can be used to shape actions and results to optimize the value created for customers. Each of the SMPs within the Model provides a unique form of information, capturing data flows up and down the organization and organizing them into a seamless, real-time database of facts, figures, and results on core performance dimensions. The SMPs also share information, linking together to provide multiple perspectives on the problems facing business and the multiple opportunities to turn challenges into successes.

The level of integration achieved by an information system can be assessed against sixteen core dimensions. Six of these dimensions deal with the degree of compatibility and shared vision present within the information system. The remaining ten features expand on the concept of "relevance" and "informativeness" to suggest a framework for actionability within organizations.

Gauging where a company is on each of these sixteen dimensions today helps identify where improvements are needed, which changes should take precedence, and why. Improving the effectiveness and value delivered by the information system is not an option if, as the preceding discussion has suggested, the Information Age is truly upon us. In the emerging environment, knowledge will be the basis for sustainable growth, information its fuel. Creating a transparent, actionable, communication network and information system is a challenge that must be embraced and met.

> The "information society" will be completely different from the one we know today…the production of information values and not material values will be the driving force behind social and economic change. More specifically, computer technology will not only substitute and amplify the mental labours of man but the mass production of systematized knowledge will ensue; the information utility, consisting of information networks and data banks, will replace the factory as the society symbol, and become the production and distribution centre for information goods; the knowledge frontiers of tomorrow, as opposed to the physical frontiers of yester-year, will yield the potential markets of the future; and the leading industries will be intellectual industries.

> – Ronnie Lessem
> Foreward to Managing in the Information
> Society, pg. xxv. Latin Proverb

Endnotes

[1] Y. Masuda, *Managing in the Information Society*, Oxford: Basil Blackwell, 1990: 131-2, 9.

[2] R. Lessem, "Foreward: Business in an Information Society," in Masuda, op.cit., pg. xxvii. This entire paragraph draws heavily from this work, including the direct quote cited here.

[3] Op cit.

[4] A. Martin, *Infopartnering: The Ultimate Strategy for Achieving Efficient Consumer Response*, Essex Junction, VT: Omneo, 1994.

[5] This paragraph appears in Martin, op.cit., pg. xiii, where it is cross-referenced to Kurt Salmon Associates as a copyrighted brand name for the application of Extended Enterprise concepts.

[6] Masuda, op.cit., pg. 32.

[7] S. Zuboff, In the Age of the Smart Machine, London: Heinemann, 1988.

[8] Ibid, pg. 11.

[9] Attributed to Zuboff, this exact quote appears in the foreward by Lessem, op.cit., pg. xxi. This entire section draws heavily upon Lessem's insights in the development of the discussion and its key comments.

[10] Ibid, pg. xxiv.

[11] Lessem's introduction to Masuda's book on Managing in the Information Society contains a concise, and informative, examination of the issues faced by organizations as the information society emerges.

Chapter 3

Information for Decision-Making

The SMP Model Perspective

*He who chooses the beginning of a road chooses the place
it leads to. It is the means that determine the end.*

– Harry Emerson Fosdick

Key Learnings:

- The CAM-I SMP Model is defined around a hierarchy of decision contexts that are common to all types of firms, regardless of the product or service they provide or the industry they operate within.

- Each data stream, or strategic management process, organizes data to fit the unique needs of its users—the underlying structure and nature of decision-making, the firm's decision architecture defines the integration effort.

- Data integration is not a software issue — *it is a process issue.*

- The CAM-I SMP Model adds structure, consistency, predictability and focus to the decision-making process.

Information and decision-making are intricately linked within the web of organizational life. One of the primary roles of management is to make decisions, to choose among competing alternative uses for the scarce resources of the firm. Choice is guided by multiple goals, including creating the optimal amount of value for customers.

Decisions set the limits on organizational performance, establishing the means that will be used to attain the stated ends.

One of the major problems in organizations today is the proliferation of data while available, reliable, accurate information becomes increasingly difficult to find. Management's role in organizations is to make the decisions that improve performance and value creation. If they have to drudge through volumes of data to find needed insights and information, or wait for someone in another area to pull the required data together in usable form, time is lost. In the rapidly changing global market, time truly is money. Opportunities lost due to delays and missed deadlines cannot be regained.

What is information? It is data with a purpose, aggregated to provide a comprehensive, objective view of events and their impact on the organization. An information system should provide this purposeful summary of data in a flexible format, one that meets the needs of multiple users. If an information system does not meet this basic requirement, it cannot possibly stand up to the primary demand placed on it by management—the effective support of decision-making.

Figure 3.1 The Decision Domains

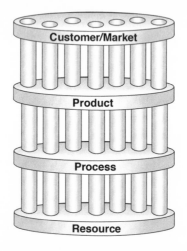

The CAM-I SMP Model is defined around a hierarchy of decision contexts that are common to all types of firms, regardless of the product or service they provide or the industry they operate within (see Figure 3.1). The four primary decision contexts that make up the SMP model are: customer/market, product/service, process and resource. The customer/market level deals with the "why" a company is in business. The issues considered include market segment development, business plans, product development and order fulfillment, all centered around the customer. Relatedly, the product/service decision domain emphasizes the "what" that is delivered to customers. Processes, then, represent the "how" of providing the products and services, while resources define the "how much" or executional elements of the business process.

To be effective as an information system, the SMP model must be able to deploy strategy and support decisions at all levels of the firm. Supplying information that is relevant to such a broad number of contexts and users is a challenge that can best be met if the underlying information is knit together effectively to create a solid knowledge base capable of supporting analysis, choice and organizational learning. Only if integration is designed into the system, in the structure and definition of the data, can the information system perform as a seamless whole. Data integration is not a software issue, though—*it is a process issue.* Understanding how and where information can be used to improve communication and coordination across the organization is a process-driven concern.

The luxury to recreate all of the databases within the firm simply does not exist for many companies. Enterprise Resource Planning (ERP) systems, such as SAP and PeopleSoft, provide an architecture for knitting together diverse data streams, but as anyone who has implemented these approaches knows, it is not a simple task. Integration, ex post, at the data level, requires a re-doing of most of the firm's data input routines, a reordering of the data that exists, and the redevelopment of detailed definitions for each data element. A "re" means that something has been done once, and for some reason, is now being done again. "Re's," in almost all cases, waste scarce resources.

The CAM-I SMP model takes a different approach to data integration. Each data stream, or strategic management process, organizes data to fit the unique needs of users of the specific SMP. The underlying structure and nature of decision-making, the firm's decision architecture, defines the integration effort. When decisions are the focus, only shared data and its compilation, information, needs to be consistent across the various data platforms (operational databases, financial databases, and marketing databases are three unique data platforms).

A decision-making emphasis helps focus attention on the 20 percent of shared data that is necessary to support the 80-90 percent of decisions made. It identifies the essential 20 percent — the information that is used in multiple decisions and by multiple users. If Pareto's law holds in this setting, as one would expect, this should also mean that only 20 percent of the total resources required for a comprehensive, integration initiative will be consumed by the effort.

The type of integration suggested by Figure 3.2 starts with understanding the decision architecture of the firm, then builds the information linkages based on the shared needs of each SMP. The SMPs complement each other through the provision of *unique* forms of data and information, reducing the integration challenge even more. Unique data, resident in SMPs that as free-standing systems support a wide range of decisions, is combined with unique data from other sources within other SMPs to create a pool of data capable of creating information and increasing knowledge. The result is that not all data must be integrated.

Figure 3.2   The Logic of SMP Model Integration

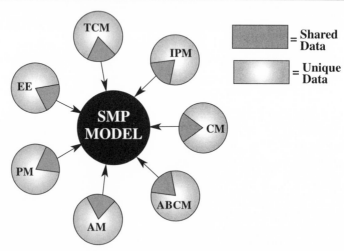

In the discussion that follows, the key concepts defining decision-making, information's value in supporting these decisions, and a design framework for identifying the core list of decision requirements will be presented. The SMPs will then be explored as decision support tools, including the development of a "short list" of common decisions and the identification of the SMP most likely to fill that need.

Basic Issues in Decision-Making

The executive exists to make sensible exceptions to general rules.
– Elting E. Morison

Decision-making is, in essence, a choice between alternatives. A decision not to choose is also a decision—to accept the status quo and whatever fate it holds. Decision-making in organizations is focused on the pursuit of defined goals and objectives. It is a complex process because it affects more than one individual and often calls for the concerted efforts of multiple individuals to turn the decision into actions and results.

There are five major phases in the decision-making process: threshold, analysis, design, choice, and implementation.[1] The *threshold* phase is a pre-analysis of a situation to determine whether or not a decision is required. A decision has to make it onto the firm's and management's radar screen if it is to be actively addressed. If errors are made during this phase, they can create downstream crisis requiring disaster recovery efforts. One of the functions of a good information system is that it gets key events and potential risks on the company's radar screen, providing assessments of the potential impact of the alternative outcomes the event suggests.

Having made its way onto the radar screen, a decision opportunity is analyzed. During *analysis,* problems and opportunities are identified and information about them is gathered. These problems and opportunities are defined within the context of the goals and objectives of the firm. The information system plays a key role during analysis. If the information system is fragmented or poorly integrated, it may not be able to provide the right information at the right time to support analysis. This unfortunate fact does not relieve the manager from the responsibility to make a decision, it just moves the analysis out of the arena of facts and into the realm of intuition and experience.

During the *design* phase of decision-making, attention turns to generating alternative courses of action to deal with the problem situation. Brainstorming is often useful at this stage, as it opens up a free discussion of potential solutions that may yield a low cost, high benefit approach that lies outside the normal approach used by the organization. It is these sensible exceptions to general rules that often provide for quantum improvements in performance.

With the pros and cons of each decision alternative assessed, using both quantitative and qualitative assessment tools, decision-making moves on to the fourth phase: *choice*. Choice is the reason behind analysis and design; choice is the outcome of using information to understand current and future implications of the alternatives open to the firm. During choice, evaluation criteria need to be developed. The most likely of these is that the course of action satisfies the requirements leading to the need to make a decision, and does so within the constraints of available time and resources. Choice criteria can include such items as minimization of total costs, optimization of value created for customers, greatest improvement in delivery and responsiveness, or highest total quality delivered. These criteria reflect the core dimensions of performance for the entity. Choice is guided by the same set of rules, measurements, and objectives that define daily activities and results.

Implementation takes place once a decision has been made. Of the five phases, implementation takes the longest and is most fraught with danger. As the decision moves from plan to reality, the political and behavioral issues multiply in number. Decision-making is never a purely rational, objective process. There are always biases, self-interest, politics and other forms of "ambiguity" that transform the decision from a concrete abstraction to a real-life event.[2] In the end, though, a decision does get made, and it does shape the future actions and results of the organization. However concrete and objective a decision is, or is not, it will lead to very real outcomes.

The process of making a decision, therefore, is not goal free. Circumstances (e.g., complex situations) can complicate the decision-making effort. There are three general characteristics of complex situations:[3]

1. (a) Two or more values are affected by the decision.
    (b) There is a trade-off relationship between the value such that a greater return to one can be obtained only at a loss to the other.
2. There is uncertainty (i.e., imperfect correspondence between information and the environment).
3. The power to make the decision is dispersed over a multitude of individual actors and/or organizational units.

The key issue is that choice, in the end, is driven as much by values as it is by objective data and rational facts. Does information still play a role if the decision process itself contains elements of "irrationality" and ambiguity? It most definitely does. For one thing, information can help reveal the assumptions, irrationalities and biases that are operating behind the scenes, shaping the analysis and choice process. Information makes events and outcomes *visible*. This is one of the most valuable roles played by information.

In looking at the very real list of factors that transform decision-making from a straightforward, objective exercise in reason to the messy, complex, reality that they are, the role for integration of information becomes evident. Trade-offs can only be assessed if an analysis can be completed that incorporates key elements of the trade-off in terms that everyone agrees to. Uncertainty is reduced as the data is reassessed through a series of "what-if" or sensitivity analyses that explore the impact of changing assumptions on the apparently "optimal" choice.

Integrated information systems help bridge the gaps in communication caused by time and space. If everyone can access the same information, do their own targeted analysis, and explore potential results, the debates over which course of action is preferable can move away from politics to a more objective setting. Politics, bias and tradition can never be eliminated in the decision process, but an effective, integrated information system can mute their effects.

The CAM-I SMP model adds structure and focus to the decision-making process. Driven by an ongoing concern for customers and optimizing the value created for them, the SMP Model organizes information to support the attainment of common objectives and values through the decision-making process. It also provides for a more structured, defined approach to decision analysis, as the information used and the type of analysis completed become regularized. This regularity and predictability in the decision process plays out through the decision domains, where the common de-cisions made at the customer/market, product/service, process and resource levels are structured within the dominant SMP. Each SMP has evolved from a need for information to support unique groups of decisions or analyze specific types of opportunities and issues.

Target Cost Management, for instance, defines the data requirements, objectives, and evaluation criteria for the design process. Customer requirements, translated into product/service value attributes, become the dominant measure used to evaluate and choose one alternative over another. Capacity Management, on the other hand, focuses attention on the choice and utilization of an organization's resources and processes. Current production requirements, as well as planned products and services, serve to define the amount of resource capability needed. In both cases, the design of the cost management information (e.g., SMP) plays a key role in defining its downstream ability to support decision-making. Given the key role played by design in the establishing information relevance, key information system design principles will now be addressed.

The Design of Information Systems

As there is design and symmetry in nature, I believe there is also design and symmetry in human experience if we will learn to yield ourselves to our destinies.
– Katharine Butler Hathaway

Destiny is a large concept, and perhaps less than common in the vocabulary of business. In fact, business sets itself up to change destiny, to modify results, through decisions and the actions they generate. To be in business is to believe that a concerted effort can change the course of events, that results can be attained even if there are obstacles in the way to their achievement.

Information plays a vital role in defining the "destiny" pursued by an organization. This role is so important that it is imperative that the design of the information system be consciously conducted, and carefully executed. As with all efforts that impact the operation of a system, the design process defines 80-90 percent of the costs (resources) that system will consume when used to attain its defined objectives. Whether the design is for a product, a process, or an information system, its effect is the same. Design decisions set the limits on what will be possible in the future.

The recognition that there are principles guiding the design of information systems is not a new concept. In fact, R.J. Chambers, a noted expert in all forms of accounting information systems, wrote of the role of information in decision making in 1964.[4] What principles did this expert identify?

- An information system is a system for supplying information to users who must take coordinated action. If effective communication is to take place, the language used must be such that response will be identified by all members of the organization. If action is to be coordinated, the information system cannot be treated as a group of independent subsystems.

■ The information system must remove all doubt about data; that is, the system must be so reliable that the user will depend upon it rather than upon his own observations.

■ There is a point at which the marginal cost of differentiation of information and comprehensiveness of information exceeds the marginal utility of information to the receiver; i.e., an individual's capacity for making sound judgments about a complex situation may be seriously impaired by supplying him with a lot of information which he believes would be relevant but whose influence on the situation is not clear to him.

■ Thus, the information system is an abstracting system. Its justification lies in the reduction of the information available to the information that is relevant to action. But abstraction should not be carried to the point where differences in the significance of data are obscured.

■ An information system is a device for continually bringing under notice new facts and new knowledge. It must provide not only the premises of decisions but also a feedback so that decisions may be reaffirmed or abandoned in favor of others. The development of an organization and the development of the judgment of its agents alike depend on this feedback.

■ Since both the capacity and the time available for observation are limited, an information system must provide a formal record to guard against misinterpretation of past experiences. The records of an organization are its memory. Therefore, all records and communications at any time serve not only their immediate function but also the function of memory.

■ The information system must be regarded as a continuously developing instrument, in much the same way as an organization is continuously developing.

■ It is a matter of experience that information processing is done according to habitual modes far more commonly than according to deliberate assessments of the user's requirements.

Chambers' insights may have been initially set down 35 years ago, yet they could be used even today as a list of the symptoms of a broken information system. What would this list include?

- Information exists in separate databases that are difficult to integrate.
- Inconsistent signals and information are given by different parts of the system.
- Users complain of information overload.
- Users complain that while there is lots of data, there is little usable, relevant information available.
- Feedback about the impact of decisions is not regularly provided.
- Prior results are not maintained in usable format (e.g., trends, etc.).
- The information system has not been adjusted as the organization has changed.
- The information system does not support "what-if" analysis, so most decisions are guided by the "we've always done it this way" theory.

To avoid these problems, the information system must be designed around the decisions made within the firm, support a wide range of analysis, and provide reliable, consistent details and information to users.

The achievement of these objectives begins with a sound design. Five general steps are followed to ensure that an information system meets its decision requirements:

1. Analysis of the decision system.
2. Analysis of information requirements.
3. Aggregation of decisions.
4. Design of information system features.
5. Design of internal control processes to ensure data integrity.

Each of these five design steps is explored in more detail below, providing the basis for analyzing the decision relevance of the CAM-I SMP Model and to guide its downstream implementation in a firm.

Analysis of the decision system. Developing a decision flow chart is the first step in gaining an understanding of the requirements facing the information system. Each key decision type made in the organization, as well as the relationship between decisions, should be detailed. This exercise often reveals that some important decisions are being made by default based on established "routines". Still other decisions emerge as interdependent efforts, even though only one department or manager may have been involved in actually making them in the past. A decision made in the purchasing department, for instance, has an effect on the work done on the plant floor. The quality of the final output, the operation of the production process itself, and the number and type of defects that are encountered are just three of the operational issues raised by the procurement decision.

Decision flow charts are useful devices for analyzing the firm's decision set. These charts should detail what type of decision is being made, who is responsible for it, what other departments, activities or processes are affected, problems with the decision or its outcome, and related factors. In other words, decision flow charts lay out the sequence of events and individuals that make up each unique type of decision in a format that supports analysis of problem spots and assists in identifying interdependence .

These charts should contain enough detail, to ensure that all key decision clusters and their information demands are included. As noted by Russell Ackoff, renowned author and Professor at MIT, "It is easier to introduce finer information into an integrated information system than it is to combine fine subsystems into one integrated system.[5]

Analysis of information requirements. There are three very different categories of decisions made within the organization, each with its own unique information requirements: routine, complex but capable of being modeled, and complex/ambiguous. The first type of decision is one that is concrete, is easily modeled using existing tools, and for which an optimal solution can be found. This is a decision made under relative certainty. Any decision that falls into this class should be built directly into the information system, transforming it from an ongoing decision to an automatic one that is revisited only when problems occur or periodic reviews are undertaken. For this type of decision, such as the need to replenish stock on a low value inventory item such as toggle bolts or copy paper, the information needed is easy to identify (stock levels, lead times, demand patterns). MRP systems transform many procurement decisions into automatic replenishment routines, reducing the effort and analysis required.

The second class of decisions incorporates some of the reality of everyday life. For these decisions, the "right" model or approach to use is known, but it is difficult if not impossible to identify an optimal solution. This is often the case when there is a very complex set of variables impacting the decision. For instance, scheduling production within a large factory needs to factor in a large number of issues, such as available capacity, routings, ship dates, raw material inventory levels, and labor availability. There may be some theoretical optimum for this complex decision, but it cannot be directly identified. Instead, a series of simulation-based analyses are performed that narrow down the range of potential schedules to the set that meets all performance requirements. If during the day problems not originally in the scheduling analysis occur, the plant may need to be rescheduled to ensure that promised delivery dates are met. While these decisions rely on simulation and scenario analysis to identify potential solutions, the information requirements of the decision models are fairly concrete.

Yet a third class of decisions is faced by organizations. For these decisions, models do not exist to structure the analysis. In this case, not only do optimal solutions not exist but information requirements are also unknown. Only affected managers can have insight into the information and analysis they believe needs to be done. To the extent that the decision-makers can identify what information they need, it can be incorporated in the information system. If they are less sure of these facts, then judgment in the choice of data and information is needed. This area is where design and use of information systems becomes the most challenging. While many managers know what output they need, and the issues of concern in the decision process, they do not have the knowledge (nor should they) of the detailed data requirements these needs represent.

If the information is integrated around the SMPs, it by definition is more apparent what data is available, what criterion will be used in the decision process, and how best to capture currently unavailable data bits. In an unstructured setting, the entire responsibility for defining the decision and its information requirements falls to the affected manager. This can lead to short-term stress and long-term gaps in the information database.The CAM-I SMP Model helps reduce the ambiguity and problems that can be experienced in this type of decision setting by creating a framework for data and analysis that is consistent across key decision settings faced by the firm.

Aggregation of decisions. Finding a logical way to group the decisions being made and the information they require is a difficult process when the decision models are not uniformly defined. Perhaps one of the greatest benefits of the SMP Model is that it is built around the natural hierarchy of decisions within an organization. Aggregation is not a task that needs to be done, it is a built-in feature of the Model. As such, the issue becomes one of identifying the types of decisions made at the customer/market, product/service, process and resource levels, then matching the information capabilities of the seven SMPs against these decisions. The result is a table similar to that presented in the next section of this chapter.

Design of the physical system. Clearly, the information and decision analysis yields a demand pattern for the information system, but there are a wide variety of ways to configure the physical assets that make up the information system. Should a company use a relational database and a Local Area Network (LAN) structure, or a mainframe-based client server system, or any number of other approaches? This is not a question for this book, but clearly is a concern as the information system is configured and implemented. The advantage of the SMP Model is that it allows for the separation of the SMPs in daily functioning, only accessing these sources of data as needed by other SMPs. The shared data is minimized, and can be handled in any number of cost effective ways, including the use of a relational database on a PC platform. The key is to remember that the more tightly integrated the databases are in the integrated system, the more costly the system will be to configure and sustain.

Control processes. One of the major issues in the creation of any information system is the integrity of the underlying data entering the system. If input errors are made, the information system cannot provide accurate information to users. Internal control procedures need to be designed to address these potential problems. The CAM-I SMP Model is not as prone to input errors because data is unique to each data set and therefore is not being reentered in multiple sites. Even so, input errors can occur, and within the integrated system will actually be less likely to be detected. They will also have more far-reaching implications for decision analysis.

All of these factors combine to create a reliable information system that can be used for decision-making. These benefits arise from the fact that the SMP Model emphasizes the 20 percent of shared data that supports 80-90 percent of the common decisions, and as such represents 20 percent or less of the total potential effort for achieving integration. A second source of benefit comes from the unique nature of each SMP, which serves as an infrastructure for organizing the data to all but eliminate redundancy in the database. The Model also results in a more logical basis for aggregation of the decision requirements of the firm and for structuring the data gathered into bundles that meet the needs of specific users. The complete Model provides a logical, consistent basis for collecting, sharing, and using data to create relevant information and reports. It is to the specifics of the relationship between the SMPs and the various decision domains that attention now turns.

Decision-Making: An SMP Approach

The block of granite which is an obstacle in the pathway of the weak becomes a stepping stone in the pathway of the strong.
                                                                    – Thomas Carlyle

The key to creating the CAM-I SMP Model was the need to ensure that the information needed for decision-making, wherever it occurs in the firm, would be available in a consistent, easily understood format. To accommodate this need, a decision hierarchy was created to encapsulate the four primary areas where clusters of decisions could be developed. The four levels, or *decision domains*, have been described earlier. At this point attention is turned to the specific types of decisions found within each domain and the role the SMPs play in providing information to these decisions.

These relationships are depicted in Tables 3-1 through 3-4, each corresponding to a specific decision domain. Within the tables, a dark solid circle below an SMP denotes a primary source of information, a shaded circle a supporting SMP, and an unfilled or empty circle suggests that the SMP plays a minimal role in providing information to the decision.

At the customer/market level, the decisions made emphasize the choice of customer segments, geographic areas, value creation strategies, core competencies, and the optimal markets to choose to optimize the match between firm strengths and customer needs in a competitive setting. The most commonly used SMP for these decisions is Target Cost Management, which by definition emphasizes these issues. Supporting SMPs include the Extended Enterprise, Asset Management, Capacity Management, and to a lesser extent, Activity-Based Cost Management. Integrated Performance Management is the source of information on core competencies, but otherwise plays a minimal role in this decision domain. As Table 3-1 suggests, then, the application of an SMP to a decision begins with matching the information content of the SMP with the primary information requirements of the decision itself.

Table 3-1 Customer/Market Platter

	TCM	EE	CM	AM	PM	IMP	ABCM
1. What markets do we want to be in?	●	◐	○	◐	○	○	○
2. What customer segments do we want to be in?	●	○	○	○	○	○	○
3. What geographic regions?	○	●	○	○	○	○	○
4. Assessing market size?	●	○	○	○	○	○	○
5. Profit potential of customer/market segments?	●	○	◐	○	○	○	●
6. Industry/competitive trends?	●	◐	◐	○	○	○	○
7. What strategies to address customer needs/value requirements?	●	○	○	○	○	○	○
8. What are our core competencies?	○	○	○	○	○	○	○
9. What time frames/windows of opportunity?	●	○	◐	◐	○	○	○
10. What distribution strategies?	○	●	○	○	○	○	●

● Primary source of information   ◐ Supporting information   ○ Minimal information

As attention turns to the Product decision domain, Target Cost Management is asked to serve dual roles. First, it is the dominant structure used to feed information from the Customer/Market decision domain to the Product Decision domain. It is this linkage of core decisions and information *through* the SMP Model that ensures that decisions and their supporting information are consistent across the many affected dimensions of the firm (e.g., horizontal, vertical, entity, team and individual). The passage of SMPs through all of the Decision domains ensures that the unique information they contain is uniformly provided, displayed, used, and updated.

Table 3-2 Product Decision Domain and the SMPs

	TCM	EE	CM	AM	PM	IMP	ABCM
1. What are the product or service features required by each target market?	●	◐	○	○	○	○	○
2. What are the competitive offerings?	●	◐	○	○	○	○	○
3. What is the optional product mix?	●	○	◐	○	○	○	○
4. Quality/functionality requirements?	●	◐	○	○	○	○	○
5a). Pricing strategy vs. core competencies?	●	○	○	○	○	○	○
5b). Distribution strategy vs. core competencies?	○	●	○	○	○	○	○
6. Capacity investment requirements?	○	○	●	○	○	○	◐
7. Are we meeting our return on sales objectives?	○	○	○	○	○	●	◐
8. What product technology is available?	●	◐	○	○	○	○	○
9. Supplier capabilities?	○	●	○	○	○	◐	○

● Primary source of information   ◐ Supporting information   ○ Minimal information

Target Cost Management also serves as one of the dominant SMPs for decisions made within the Product domain (see Table 3-2). As can be seen, though, there is increasing diversity in the dominant SMPs within this domain—multiple issues are faced across multiple functions and resource clusters. Product level decisions are also more detailed in nature than customer/market analysis, creating a greater role for Activity-Based Cost Management and Integrated Performance Management. Whether the decision is to define specific product or service features, identify capacity requirements, or how to best manage the product life cycle, the issues and concerns of the Product domain rely on information embedded in, and integrated through, the SMPs.

The passage of information from the Product domain to the Process domain is the next major concern faced by the SMP Model. At the Process level, the decisions emphasize sensing and reacting to outside factors and creating smoothly aligned work flows to meet specific, tightly defined customer requirements. The transition from product features to the way the organization intends to execute these customer/market and product strategies is a key shift made in the migration down through the decision domains to the Process level.

Table 3-3 The Process Decision Domain and the SMPs

	TCM	EE	CM	AM	PM	IMP	ABCM
1. Organizational structures?	○	○	○	○	●	○	●
2. How well maintaining core competencies?	○	○	○	◉	●	●	○
3. Process cost drivers?	○	○	◉	○	●	○	○
4. Capacity – internal/external?	○	◉	●	◉	○	○	○
5. How are the processes performing (cycle time, quality, process, yield, flexibility, dependability, downtime, bottlenecks, scheduling)?	○	○	○	○	○	●	○
6. What process technology?	○	○	○	◉	●	○	○
7. Process capability assessments?	○	○	◉	○	●	○	○
8. What are the performance gaps?	○	○	○	○	◉	●	○
9. What are the activities in the process? Value/nonvalue-added?	○	○	○	○	●	○	○
10. Are they value/ nonvalue-added?	○	○	○	○	●	○	○
11. What are our process improvement targets?	○	○	○	○	●	◉	●
12. What is our shared services strategy?	○	○	◉	◉	●	○	●

● Primary source of information   ◉ Supporting information   ○ Minimal information

Process Management plays a key role in taking the information from Target Cost Management at the Product level and structuring the Process domain to ensure that defined performance requirements are capable of being met by the organization. (see Table 3-3) Identifying process asset requirements, capacity management issues, performance gaps, and the degree of value-added in each major process and activity are key to effective process design and execution. Process Management, though, is not the only SMP to shape Process decisions. Asset Management, Capacity Management, and Integrated Performance Management all enter into Process domain analyses at some critical point.

Supporting SMPs are quite varied at the Process level. Activity-Based Cost Management now takes on a richer role, serving as a primary source and recipient of Process domain data. Process Management, Asset Management, Capacity Management and Integrated Performance Management are constantly interacting within this domain, serving either as the dominant or supporting SMP in almost every case.

Why is this so? Simply put, the six SMPs (Process Management, Extended Enterprise, Asset Management, Capacity Management, Integrated Performance Management, and Activity-Based Cost Management) provide detailed information on the current processes, their capability to meet customer requirements, and their ongoing performance levels. Each of these SMPs focus management's attention on different tactical and operational issues, as different subsystems and their characteristics are explored. For instance, the Extended Enterprise draws attention to the performance of the entire supply chain, its ability to meet customer requirements, and the total time and cost of meeting these needs. Capacity Management provides similar data on the internal resources of a single firm, linking with the Extended Enterprise to provide end-to-end analysis of capabilities and performance of key processes and resources.

As the passage is made from the Process to the Resource Decision domain, then, there is no longer one information flow or SMP providing critical linkages. All but the Target Cost Management SMP are called upon to provide smooth information flows from the Process domain, where the interdependence of SMPs, customer requirements, resource needs, and other issues are dominant (see Table 3-4). A vast majority of the firm's decisions take place within the Process or Resource Decision domains—they are the arenas of daily action and results. At the Resource level, though, the SMPs are not required to be as integrated as they were at the Process domain level. Resource decisions affect subsystems that make up the Process domain.

As the Table suggests, there are clusters of SMPs that work together to support various decisions at the Resource level. For instance, resource capability is a question that requires information on internal assets (Asset Management) and external support (Extended Enterprise). In a related manner, understanding what the utilized resources cost in economic terms brings Activity-Based Cost Management and Capacity Management into the foreground of analysis. There is much greater heterogeneity in the dominant SMP at the Resource level than at any other point in the Model. This is because resource decisions focus on so many different dimensions of performance.

The need to link the Resource level back to the higher level decision domains is reflected in the feedback and control effort that is the heart and soul of the Activity-Based Cost Management and

Table 3-4 The Resource Decision Domain and the SMPs

	TCM	EE	CM	AM	PM	IMP	ABCM
1. What is our resource capability?	○	◐	○	○	○	●	○
2. What is our resource utilization (people, plant, equipment)?	○	○	●	○	○	◐	○
3. Scheduling?	○	◐	◐	○	●	○	○
4. Resource mix?	○	◐	○	○	○	○	●
5. Cost of resources utilized?	○	○	◐	○	○	○	●
6. Should we buy or lease, etc.?	○	◐	◐	●	○	○	◐
7. What resources are needed to support our core competencies?	○	◐	○	◐	●	○	◐
8. Inventory policies?	○	◐	◐	○	●	○	○
9. What would be optimal asset management practices?	○	◐	◐	●	◐	○	○
10. What R&D investments should be made?	○	○	○	●	◐	○	○

● Primary source of information   ◐ Supporting information   ○ Minimal information

Integrated Performance Management SMPs. The primary role of these two SMPs, in fact, is not to support one specific class or level of decisions, but rather to provide detailed data on prior and current performance to all the various decision domains. These two SMPs are the primary source of integrated performance information, serving to link the past with the present and future plans and results accomplished by the firm. They tie the SMPs and decision domains together over time as they track progress against entity and individual goals, such as return on investment, profitability trends, and customer loyalty. Taken together, the SMPs and the decision domain structures create an information infrastructure that provides solid support to decision analysis because they are integrated around decision needs. Infusing the information system integration effort with a purpose, the CAM-I SMP Model seeks to reduce the complexity of information system integration by focusing attention on those few issues and data requirements that are needed to support the majority of internal analyses performed and decisions made.

The SMP Model structure has one other advantage, as will be explored in more depth in Chapter 4. It allows a company to identify, based on its most critical information requirements, which SMPs would provide the optimal support, and hence should be implemented first, as well as the most logical sequence of additional SMP implementations to follow. This does not come from a "cookie cutter" analysis, but rather from the firm being able to match its decision needs against the most useful SMP. Many different migration paths can be followed in the implementation of the various SMPs. An overview diagnostic is developed in Chapter 4, and extended in the Appendices, to help a firm or practitioner choose a migration path that best meets their needs for information.

Summary

What we need most is not so much to realize the ideal as to idealize the real.

– H.F. Hedge

Information is not a free good. It consumes scarce resources, and as with any activity, must be put to the test—the benefits it provides must exceed its costs. The CAM-I SMP Model integrates information around the key decisions of the firm. This idealization of the real world provides a logic for the design, implementation, and use of information for decision-making. Reflecting the 80-20 rule, the SMP Model emphasizes integration of only those data elements needed to support the key decisions of the firm. This idealized system has an added benefit—it provides a company with the means to create a migration path for its information system investments that ensures that the optimal value is created with the affected resources.

The CAM-I SMP Model creates a logical structure for information that reflects key decision requirements because it: 1) analyzes the decision system of the firm through the diagnostic structure suggested here and detailed in Chapter 4; 2) analyzes information requirements for the decision system; 3) aggregates these decisions into Decision domains; 4) designs information system features to reflect the Decision domains; and, 5) embeds internal control processes to feed information back through the system.

By organizing information into logical structures that reflect the nature of decisions made, the interdependence of data flows and analysis, and the relevance of a decision type or Strategic Management Process to the organization, the CAM-I SMP Model helps attack the information Tower of Babel. It supports the ever-present need to understand and meet customer requirements that lies at the heart of the firm's *Value Quest*.

Endnotes

[1] The comments in this section draw heavily from M. Murray, *Decisions: A Comparative Critique*, Marshfield, MA: Pitman Publishing, 1986: 10-11.

[2] The discussion here has reflected what is called the "rational choice" model. In the modern world, there is little belief that decision-making is really this tidy an exercise. Politics, power, and bias can transform objectivity into irrationality. The dominant belief is that most decisions have at least some grain of the irrational in them, and to understand organizational decision-making this "irrationality" has to be dealt with.

[3] This list appears in Murray, op.cit., pg. 11. It originally can be found in J. Steinbruner, *The Cybernetic Theory of Decision*, Princeton: Princeton University Press, 1974: 6.

[4] R.J. Chambers, "The Role of Information Systems in Decision Making," *Management Technology*, IV, No. 1, June, 1964. As with many issues in modern business, good thinking and analysis have gone on before the current date. While some might argue for a more "modern" view of this topic, the two writers used in this section represent some of the best thinking that has been done in the area of information system design.

[5] This list and the discussion that accompanies it is draws heavily from R. Ackoff, "Management Misinformation Systems," in *Information for Decision Making*, A. Rappaport, ed., Englewood Cliffs, NJ: Prentice-Hall, 1970: 32-34.

The SMP Model Diagnostic

*Perhaps the greatest impulse to trying to foresee and plan the
future comes from the combination of having new tools with which
to do it and the growing realization that every technological and
social innovation has repercussions which spread like a wave
through the complex interlocked sessions of society.*

– Ward Madden

The value of any model is its ability to make the world a little
easier to understand or the appropriate actions to take in a given
situation easier to see. The CAM-I SMP Model is focused on facilitating the information system analysis and choices made within an
organization. Emphasizing the type and frequency of decisions made,
or dominant Decision domain, for a firm, the CAM-I SMP Model helps
identify an information system migration path that fits the unique
needs of each firm.

Determining which Strategic Management Process (e.g., Target
Cost Management) is the most important to a specific firm at any
point in time is the key to creating a successful implementation path
toward information system integration. Every SMP has its unique
uses—no one dominates in every situation. Which begs the question—
what should be done first and why? It might be possible to determine
the answer to this question by simply thinking through, and debating,
the pros and cons of the various SMPs using the descriptions found
in Part II. Or, a careful reading of the way the SMPs interact with each
other in each of the four Decision domains (Part III) might provide a
clue as to what a firm's implementation migration path should look

like. But then again, this might be a difficult way to reach a conclusion.

In reality, there is no one right way to implement the entire range of available management tools. The SMPs each have a very different focus. While complementary, in reality they overlap only in philosophy and intent—to maximize ability of the firm to create value for its customers by continuously improving performance and abilities. The value of the CAM-I SMP Model is that it details and separates the information and capabilities of the available cost management tools, emphasizing the unique forms of knowledge embedded in each one. No one company has mastered all of the SMPs, but those that are further along the migration path (e.g., DaimlerChrysler and Caterpillar, Inc.) are reaping the benefits of improved communication and decision-making.

To aid the reader in their journey through *Value Quest,* two sets of diagnostic tools are provided. The diagnostic tools can be used as a roadmap for developing a cost management system implementation or an integration strategy. Not every chapter is critical for every reader. The diagnostics can help direct the reader to the area most critical to his or her organization.

Exhibit 4.1 provides a diagnostic tool based on issues/concerns that may be faced by a company within a Decision domain, along with the key SMP that is best suited to analyzing that issue/concern. As can be seen, Target Cost Management is the primary SMP in the Customer/Market and Product Decision domains. Emphasizing customer requirements as a key to unlocking company performance and profits, Target Cost Management is one of the most powerful cost management techniques developed in the last 10-15 years.

Within the Process Decision domain, it should be of little surprise that Process Management becomes a critical SMP. Just as interesting, though, is the fact that it is not the only SMP needed. As with the Customer/Market and Product Decision domains, the issues faced in the Process domain call for a range of information and analyses. Process Management may be the pivotal SMP, but others (e.g., Integrated Performance Management) serve an equally important role in supporting process-based decisions.

Appendix A, as well as the accompanying diskette, provides a "Practitioner's" diagnostic tool that focuses on the core decision and information needs within each of the Decision domains. Computer based, the answer to the series of questions is either a simple "true" or "false". Your responses, weighed as noted, are cumulated by Decision

Exhibit 4.1   The Value Quest Navigator

VALUE QUEST DIAGNOSTIC TOOL

If your major concern or issue is:	Key Strategic Management Process	Key SMP Chapter	Supporting Strategic Management Processes
Customer/Marketing Decisions			
Aligning product strategies to create highest customer value.	Target Cost Management	5	Extended Enterprise, Integrated Performance Mgmt.
Performing market analysis and and understanding customer requirements in order to make market segmentation decisions.	Target Cost Management	5	Extended Enterprise, Integrated Performance Mgmt.
Optimizing the match between the firm's competencies and chosen customer/ market segments.	Target Cost Management	5	Extended Enterprise, Capacity Mgmt., Process Mgmt.
Linking tactical and operational decisions to the chosen market segment.	Target Cost Management	5	Extended Enterprise, Integrated Performance Mgmt., Process Mgmt.
Missing key product targets, ie, timing, quality, investment or costs.	Integrated Performance Mgmt.	10	Asset Mgmt., Capacity Mgmt., Process Mgmt.
If your major concern or issue is:			
Product Decisions			
Design evaluation criteria that meets customer requirements.	Target Cost Management	5	Integrated Performance Mgmt.
Choosing product alternatives that are aligned with customer requirements.	Target Cost Management	5	Integrated Performance Mgmt.
Developing effective product service and support strategies.	Target Cost Management	5	Integrated Performance Mgmt., Extended Enterprise
Understanding core competencies and effective utilization of the supply chain.	Target Cost Management Extended Enterprise	5 9	Integrated Performance Mgmt., Capacity Mgmt, Activity Based Cost Mgmt.
Lacking information to effectively monitor market intelligence.	Integrated Performance Mgmt.	10	Extended Enterprise
Transitioning to high performance products from current product.	Integrated Performance Mgmt. Target Cost Management	10 5	Asset Mgmt., Extended Enterprise, Activity Based Cost Mgmt.

Continued on next page.

Exhibit 4.1   The Value Quest Navigator

VALUE QUEST DIAGNOSTIC TOOL

If your major concern or issue is:	Key Strategic Management Process	Key SMP Chapter	Supporting Strategic Management Processes
Process Decisions			
Optimizing internal processes to minimize or eliminate non-value added/wasteful activities.	Process Management	8	Capacity Mgmt., Integrated Performance Mgmt.
Creating flexible and responsive processes that minimize idle capacity while leveraging technology.	Process Management	8	Extended Enterprise, Capacity Mgmt.
Linking sourcing and capacity decisions to ensure optimal use of extended supply chain capabilities.	Extended Enterprise	9	Integrated Performance Mgmt., Process Mgmt., Activity Based Cost Mgmt.
Information that allows proactive (feedforward systems) rather than reactive responses.	Extended Enterprise Process Management	9 8	Integrated Performance Mgmt., Capacity Mgmt., Activity Based Cost Mgmt.
Managing your performance gap to quickly identify issues and develop corrective actions.	Process Management	8	Integrated Performance Mgmt., Extended Enterprise
If your major concern or issue is:			
Resource Decisions			
Determining the optimal resource choice or mix (people, material and equipment).	Integrated Performance Mgmt. Activity Based Cost Mgmt.	10 11	Extended Enterprise, Process Mgmt., Capacity Mgmt.
Development and continuous improvement of policies.	Process Management	8	Activity Based Cost Mgmt., Integrated Performance Mgmt.
Balancing competing demand for existing resources.	Activity Based Cost Mgmt.	11	Integrated Performance Mgmt., Extended Enterprise
Meaningful management reporting on your factors of production.	Integrated Performance Mgmt. Activity Based Cost Mgmt.	10 11	Extended Enterprise, Capacity Mgmt., Process Mgmt.

domain and then plotted on a Spider graph. This graph visibly illustrates the areas where your company is weak, and where its use of the Strategic Management Processes is moving toward maturity.

The reader is encouraged to complete either of the two following diagnostics before continuing through the book: 1) Exhibit 4.1 should be reviewed if your focus within the company is from an issues/concerns perspective. 2) The "Practitioner's" diagnostic (Appendix A) will assist you if you are interested in focusing on the core decisions and information needs of each Decision domain. Completion of the diagnostics will guide you in determining where you need to direct your attention.

THE VALUE QUEST JOURNEY

Parts II and III of the book present various perspectives on the CAM-I SMP Model. Picking up where the diagnostics leave off, Part II presents each SMP in detail, along with its key information and decision characteristics. Chapters 5 through 11 provide a summary description of the various SMPs, focusing on what they are and how they are used to support decision-making in an organization. Each serves as a review of the topic for an experienced reader and an introductory level discussion for the novice.

The completion of the diagnostic may suggest that the focus of the information integration effort needs to be at the Decision domain level (almost all decisions of current critical nature fall into one domain). If so, then Part III can be used to gather more insight about the way the SMPs interact within the Decision domain. Specifically, Chapter 12 details the integration and SMP issues at the Customer/Market level while Chapter 13 emphasizes the challenges faced in the Product decision domain. Chapter 14 goes on to focus on Process Domain issues, while Chapter 15 emphasizes the major challenges faced at the Resource level. Part III, then, turns its attention toward how the tools work together to support decision-making at various levels of the firm. If one decision type, or set of decisions within a domain, is of major importance to a firm, it should first master the SMPs that directly support these efforts.

Part IV provides three case studies of how different organizations are utilizing the SMPs to improve their performance. Chapter 16 details the experiences of Case Corporation as they begin to utilize Target Cost Management to drive their product design and development efforts. Chapter 17 describes a very different situation— the City of Indianapolis' use of Activity-Based Management and Integrated Performance Management to improve its decisions with the Resource decision. Finally, Chapter 18 illustrates DaimlerChrysler's experiences with the Extended Enterprise SMP and Target Cost Management in its drive to design and launch the Neon model. Chapter 18 also discusses the performance improvements the firm has reached through the integration, coordination, and improved cooperation of internal teams and the entire supply chain are significant.

As this discussion suggests, then, the choice of a migration strategy for the CAM-I SMP Model will depend on several key factors:

- SMPs information and decision support content versus the set of current critical decisions facing the organization;

- The organization's dominant Decision domain, or the area where the majority of its decisions are made or need to be made; and

- The primary interdependencies between SMPs given the list of critical decisions currently facing the firm.

As in any major change initiative, there is no one easy or best way to approach the development of a cost management competency within an organization. Learning to turn data into information, and information into knowledge, requires not only improved data integration — it entails a mindset change that makes experimentation and learning the norm, not the exception. Integration of the SMPs, both in terms of information and perspective, creates a strategic arsenal of knowledge that can be used to leverage the resources and competencies of a firm to gain a competitive advantage. In the coming millenium, it is knowledge, not mechanics, that will dominate.

Chapter 5

Target Cost Management

An ideal is often but a flaming vision of reality.
– Joseph Conrad

Key Learnings:

■ Target Cost Management (TCM) is defined as *a system of profit planning and cost management that is price led, customer focused, design centered and cross functional.*

■ The purpose of TCM is to ensure the achievement of profit goals for a specific product or service.

■ The strategic profit and cost management processes that make up TCM are based on six key principles:
    1) price-led costing;
    2) customer focus;
    3) focus on design of products and processes;
    4) cross-functional teams;
    5) life cycle cost reductions; and
    6) value chain.

■ Each participant of the Extended Enterprise brings a unique insight and ability to contribute to TCM based on both their position within the value chain and their ability to influence upstream and downstream costs and activities.

Within a competitive market, price is determined by the value a product or services provides to its customers. To ensure that profit goals are reached, a company facing a competitive market for its products and services has to actively and effectively manage its costs relative to the market prices these product offerings command. **Target Cost Management** provides a company with the insights and information required to manage the complex puzzle of costs, value, price and profit.

Target Cost Management is defined as *a system of profit planning and cost management that is price led, customer focused, design centered and cross functional.*[1] Emphasizing the application of cost consciousness and sound cost management principles at the earliest stages of product development, Target Cost Management also applies throughout the product life cycle by actively involving the entire value chain in the decision process. The purpose of TCM is to ensure the achievement of profit goals for a specific product or service. These goals are reached through the simultaneous use of customer awareness, profit and planning tools.

A fundamentally different way of looking at the relationship between prices and costs is at the heart of TCM. Building from the basic equation of "Price — Desired Profit Margin = Allowable Cost," TCM[2] embeds the discipline of the market within the structure and culture of the firm. It is this discipline, and its application to the development and management of a firm's product and service offerings, that ensures long-term business survival, growth, and prosperity in today's rapidly changing, competitive market.

While the TCM logic, or the need to contain costs before they are incurred, can be applied to many different settings, its primary focus is on shaping the decisions and efforts undertaken during the design and development of products and the processes that support them. It is during the design phase that a company locks in a majority of the costs of its products and services along with the potential levels of customer satisfaction. Downstream, very little can be done to eliminate cost and improve profits if the initial design is flawed or if excessive resource needs have been built into the structure and operations of the product, and hence the firm.

The strategic profit and cost management processes that make up TCM are based on six key principles:[3] 1) price led costing, 2) customer focus, 3) focus on design of products and processes, 4) cross-functional teams, 5) life cycle cost reductions, and 6) value chain involvement. Taking place during the strategic planning and product development cycles of the firm, TCM can be broken down into two main phases: *establishment and attainment.*[4]

The establishment phase takes place at the product planning and concept development stages of the underlying product development cycle. It involves setting a target cost for the product as well as limits for allowable cost. Attainment, on the other hand, is centered in the design development and production stages. Here the emphasis shifts to transforming the *allowable cost* into an *achievable* cost. The steps involved include computing the current cost gap, designing costs out of the product, and the release of the design for manufacturing and assembly. Once the product is released, continuous improvement goals are set to ensure that downstream cost and performance improvements are attained.

TCM normally emphasizes those costs that are most directly affected by product level decisions, including:[5] material and purchased parts, labor/conversion costs, tooling costs, development expenses, and depreciation. Comprehensive in nature, though, TCM should not stop with these items. If it is to achieve the optimal benefits for the firm, TCM should emphasize all of the cost and asset implications of the product and its design. Areas of concern would include indirect overhead charges, transaction costs, service costs, capital expenditures, and inventory holding costs. TCM should also look beyond the boundaries of the firm to include the concerns of the Extended Enterprise and the customer throughout the product life cycle. When TCM is applied to the complete system of inter-dependent processes and entities, it can help a company create a competitive advantage that is difficult to overcome.

One of the messages embedded in TCM, then, is that the key to overall cost reduction and achieving the optimal level of profitability within the firm is to bring costs down across the entire Extended Enterprise and throughout the life cycle of a product. A company that simply passes on its need for cost reductions to its suppliers, dealers, or recyclers is not engaged in Target Cost Management. TCM relies upon the active involvement of every member of the value chain. Each participant of the Extended Enterprise brings a unique insight and ability to contribute to TCM based on both their position within the value chain and their ability to influence upstream and downstream costs and activities.

In the discussion that follows, the integration of TCM within the

CAM-I Strategic Management Processes SMP Model will be developed and key details and issues in the utilization of TCM in an organization will then be presented. Basics in place, attention will turn to the application of TCM to the Extended Enterprise and the information technology issues this extension suggests. Next, implementation of TCM and its related challenges and opportunities will be presented. Finally, a case study of a firm using TCM will be detailed, followed by a set of references for further reading on this topic. By the end of the chapter, readers should be able to determine whether TCM is applicable to their business, how, when, where and why, as well as the potential profit and performance improvements that may be reaped by its application.

Principles of Target Cost Management

Everything should be made as simple as possible, but no simpler.
– Albert Einstein

Target Cost Management is, in essence, a simple concept. It defines the allowable cost of a product or service that ensures that required rates of return are earned by the company that provides it. The TCM process, though, is multi-faceted, spanning the entire value chain and the range of activities that take place to meet customer requirements over the product life cycle. Driven by competitive market forces that make traditional cost-plus pricing models all but obsolete, TCM lies at the heart of creating a modern, globally competitive, profitable organization.

Viewing TCM within the broader framework of the CAM-I SMP Model (see Figure 5.1), the role played by TCM within the Customer/Market and Product Decision domains is clear. Providing the basic structure and logic for the design, development and use of the other core SMPs. Target Cost Management emphasizes the creation of product/service bundles that provide superior value to customers while ensuring that enterprise economic goals are attained.

The flows depicted within Figure 5.1 show the integrating exchange of information from Target Cost Management to the other SMPs, which is the essential element tying the SMP Model together. The flow arrows indicate areas where TCM is generating information to be used by other SMPs, such as the target cost estimate that is used

Figure 5.1   Target Cost Management Integration

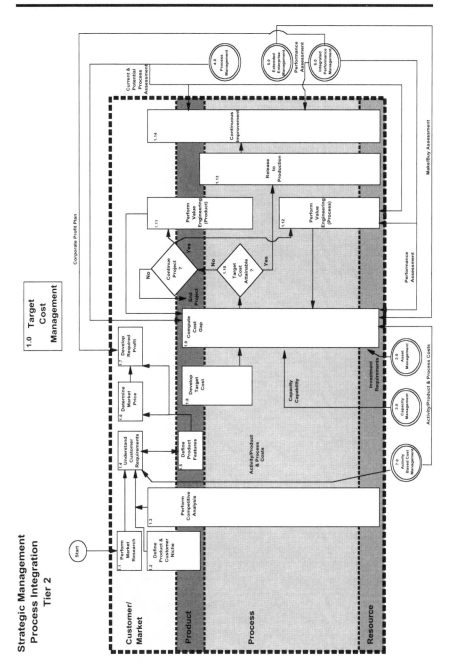

by Process Management and the Extended Enterprise to set tactical and operational objectives. In a related way, information flows from each of the other SMPs to Target Cost Management serve to inform the analysis of the existing cost gaps and identify areas where cost improvements or performance enhancements are needed. The use of Activity-Based Cost Management estimates for various core business activities affected by the proposed product/service bundle would be an example of this information sharing. TCM would use these estimates to assess the cost gap and identify areas where reductions are needed.

Within the Customer/Market and Product Decision domains, TCM integrates the information available from a variety of sources to support management's analysis of current and potential future product/service bundles. It is also used to identify potential profitability problems prior to product launch and to track the impact of the new products and services on the enterprise. Specifically, the steps completed during TCM-based analyses are:

- Perform market research to determine customer requirements, share and price data;
- Define product and customer niche;
- Perform competitive analysis;
- Define and detail internal understanding of customer requirements;
- Define product features;
- Determine market price required to attain desired share; and
- Develop required profit projections.

TCM relies on information from the supporting Strategic Management Processes to complete the profitability projections.

Dropping down into the Process Decision domain, TCM focuses attention on developing target costs, computing current projected cost gaps, and ensuring that the target cost is attainable. If it is not, value engineering and process reengineering is performed until target costs are reached. The related SMPs (Extended Enterprise, Process Management, Capacity Management, Asset Management, and Activity-Based Cost Management) are active partners in the development and use of information at the process level as this iterative cost analysis is completed. For instance, the Extended Enterprise provides make/buy assessments, including supplier capability, supplier cost assessments and risk analysis, and supplier cost conversions to in-house equivalent costs. Relatedly, Process Management provides process cost capability data, potential current process cost improvements, process cost leverage areas, and long-range process cost reduction information. At this point, the product is released to production and continuous improvement efforts are put into motion.

At Boeing, the cost analysis effort is based on a four-dimensional evaluation matrix that requires a simultaneous evaluation of cost element, work breakdown structure, level of product commonality as well as a projection of potential cost impacts of process improvement initiatives. The uniqueness of the work statement must be played against available cost history, recognizing that the cost of detailed component level costing would be prohibitive. On an airplane the size of a 777, for instance, there are over 100,000 unique part numbers and over three million total parts. Costing each of these unique parts would be very expensive in the early design phases.

While still in the early stages of integrating TCM into the company's management framework, Boeing has recognized that this integration must be multi-dimensional. Information flows across time, functions, and SMPs combine to create a flexible basis for applying Target Cost Management to the design and development of new product/service bundles. TCM uses data from multiple sources to complete its analysis of current and potential profitability. Once a target cost has been set for a product and its core components, TCM feeds the other Strategic Management Processes the required levels of cost and functionality required to meet target profit and performance objectives. TCM drives the voice of the customer into all of the elements of the SMP Model, as a review of the following principles suggests.

TARGET COST MANAGEMENT PRINCIPLES

Price led costing. Gaining an understanding of TCM begins with knowledge of its six guiding principles—price led costing, customer focus, focus on design of products and processes, cross-functional teams, life cycle cost reductions, and value chain involvement.[6] *Price led costing* means that the competitive market price is the starting point of analysis. Subtracting the required profit margin from the competitive market price needed to attain the desired market share for the product or service results in the cost objective, or allowable cost, for the product/service bundle. Price-led costing can be summarized by a simple equation:

$$C = P - \pi$$

Where C = Allowable cost
      P = Competitive market price for desired share attainment, and
      π = Target profit.

Price is controlled by market conditions, such as the degree of competition, presence of substitute products, and barriers to entry, while the target profit is determined by the financial requirements of the firm within its industry. If a firm needs a 15 percent profit margin to remain financially viable, and the competitive market price for the product being developed is $100, the allowable cost is $85 ($100 less the $15 target profit). Two important sub-principles complete the price led costing principle:[7]

- Market prices serve to define both product and profit plans. These plans should be analyzed frequently to ensure that the firm's product portfolio provides resources only to those products that yield acceptable, reliable profit margins.

- Ongoing competitive intelligence and analysis drive the TCM process. It is crucial to understand what is behind a market price (e.g., service, quality and functionality) if it is to be used in a meaningful way for meeting or preempting competitive threats and challenges.

Not all companies can be the low cost producer within an industry. Establishing the firm's allowable cost for a product/service bundle and a related target profit margin that is attainable begins with understanding the firm's competitive position and related cost structures.[8]

Focus on customers. The customer lies at the heart of TCM, a fact that is the basis for the second TCM principle. Customer requirements, or the *voice of the customer,* for quality, cost and delivery have to be simultaneously incorporated into the product and process decisions that guide the firm. Meeting these requirements is not an option; allowable cost objectives cannot be achieved by sacrificing features customer wants, lowering performance or reliability of a product, or delaying its introduction or delivery to customers.

Product feature and function decisions must ensure that the final product/service bundle meets three basic goals: (1) they meet customer requirements, (2) customers are willing to pay for them, and (3) the additions to features/functions enhance market share or sales volume. At Texas Instruments, the voice of the customer drove planning and design decisions for its new Digital Light processing products, including better definition of large-screen requirements for customer-used video graphics and text displays.[9]

Focus on Design. TCM is driven by the fact that most downstream costs, and potential customer satisfaction levels, are determined by early product and process design decisions. Removing costs from a product once it has been fully designed, or adding features that address overlooked customer requirements, is quite difficult. That means product design, material choices, specifications and tolerances, sourcing decisions, process designs, customer service levels and asset investment issues all need to be carefully thought through prior to finalizing product and process designs. Time spent early on to reduce time to market by eliminating expensive and time consuming changes downstream can reap significant benefits for the firm. Four sub-principles are embodied in the design focus:[10]

- TCM emphasizes managing costs before they are incurred rather than afterward. Figure 5.2 details the typical relationship between committed and incurred product costs. Specifically, most of the costs are committed during the design stage but incurred during the production stage. As the design is finalized, material requirements become fixed, assembly configurations and costs are set, and the fixed asset requirements are defined—future performance is limited by the design of the product and the processes it uses. TCM focuses attention on the design phase because that is when the maximum impact on life cycle costs and profits can be made.

- TCM challenges engineers to look at the cost impacts of product, technology and process designs. Relative customer value impact assessments are used to filter engineering decisions to result in "State-of-the-market" rather than "State-of-the-art" solutions.

- TCM encourages all participating functions of the firm to examine designs. Product or engineering changes are made before the product goes into production.

- TCM encourages simultaneous engineering of products and processes rather than sequential approaches, reducing the time and cost necessary to launch products.

Figure 5.2   Comparison of Committed and Incurred Costs

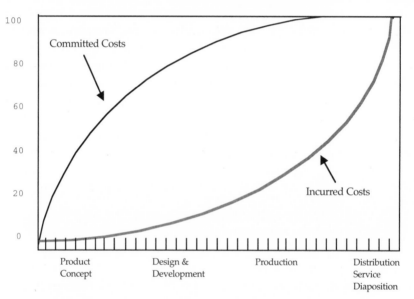

Source: Adapted from depicition in Cost Management for Today's Advanced Manufacturing Systems, Arlington, TX: CAM-I, 1991: 140.

Cross-functional Involvement. Achieving the objectives of TCM requires the active support and involvement of multiple functions within an organization, including design and manufacturing engineering, production, sales and marketing, materials procurement, cost accounting, service and support. Cross-functional teams provide the optimal means of attaining the necessary cooperation from initial concept through production as functional goals are replaced with product and process goals. These teams often need to include outside participants, such as suppliers, distributors, customers, dealers, service providers, and recycling firms.

Cross-functional involvement cuts the time to market for a product/ service bundle by reducing design reviews and engineering changes, resulting in reduced total costs and increased quality levels as problems are caught and corrected early in the development cycle. Finally, a cross-functional TCM team is not a group of specialists who contribute their expertise and leave; they are responsible for the product across its entire life cycle. At Chrysler, the development of the Neon included the decision to have the financial analysts assigned to the design team travel to Nova Scotia in the winter to observe "crash testing." This was done to help them understand how the product works, to take ownership of the product, and to appreciate how their recommendations impact overall product performance.[11]

Life cycle orientation. TCM efforts encompass the entire life cycle of a product/service bundle, from initial conception through analysis of purchase price versus operating, maintenance, and disposition costs. Two sub-principles underlie the life cycle orientation of TCM:

- From a customer's viewpoint, a life cycle focus means minimizing the total costs of ownership of the product, from purchase through disposition.

- From the producer's viewpoint, a life cycle focus means minimizing the total development, production, marketing, distribution, support, service and disposition costs.

Failing to consider costs from both the company's and customer's perspective over the life cycle of the product/service bundle can leave the company open to competitive threats from firms more aware of the total cost picture. Gaining customer loyalty requires that the company make a concerted effort to improve the total value created over the life of the product so that downstream purchase decisions are in the firm's favor.

Value Chain Involvement. TCM spreads cost reduction efforts throughout the value chain by developing collaborative relationships with all members of the Extended Enterprise. While in the short run target costs and profits might be attainable through less cooperative efforts, in the long run an effective competitive strategy depends on the total support of every organization and individual affected by the product. TCM is a long-term, strategic initiative whose ultimate success depends on the identification and implementation of a win-win approach.

Figure 5.3 The Target Cost Management Process

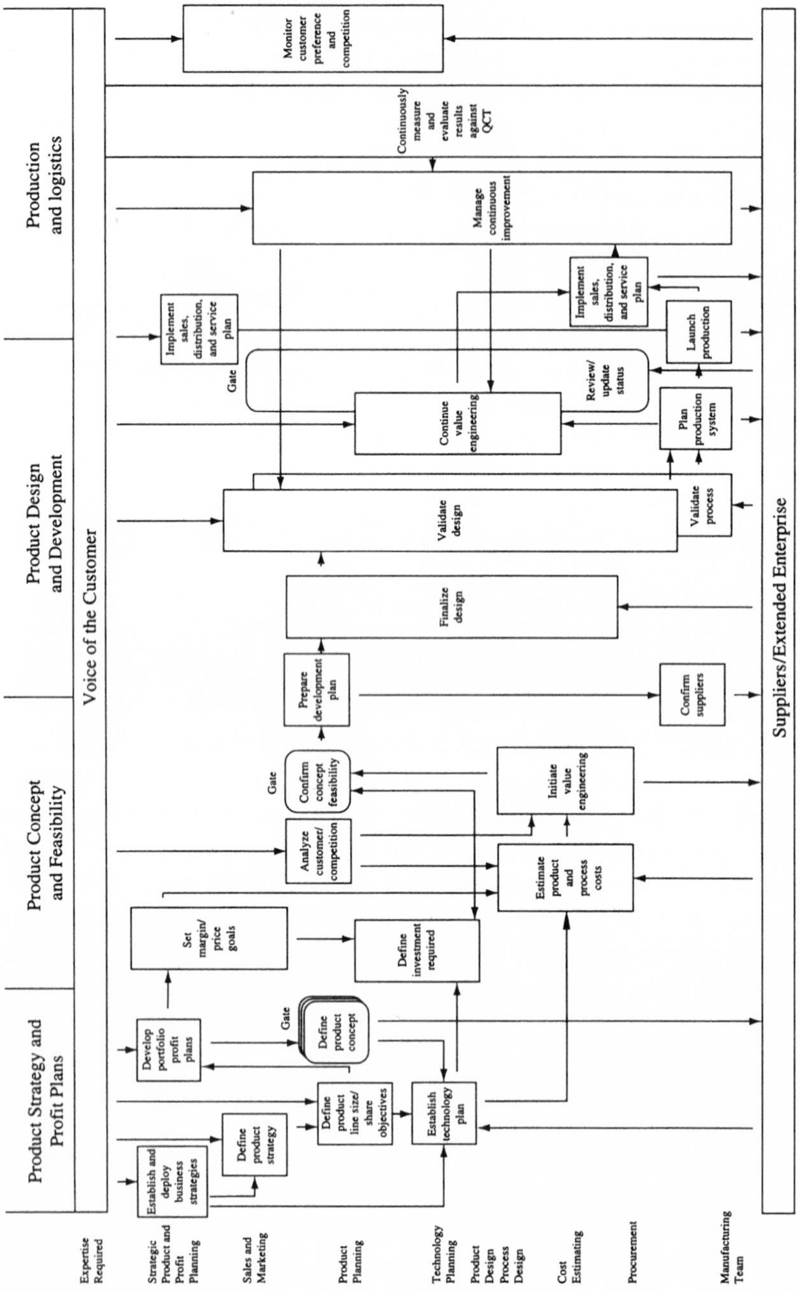

Note: This flowchart has been adapted from Arthur Andersen's study of global best practices in the area of new product development processes.

These six basic TCM principles combine to paint a conceptually unique approach to the design, development, and long-term management of a company's product and process investments. Combining design-to-cost principles and tools, accurate and structured cost estimating, and the implementation of cost/price analysis buying principles yields a proactive, customer driven organization that achieves its desired profits goals by maximizing performance against customer expectations for the entire value chain. Figure 5.3 summarizes the Target Cost Management process.

As Figure 5.3 suggests, TCM is multi-faceted, spanning the strategic planning and product development cycles of the firm. Competitive strategy defines the goals that an organization must attain to satisfy market demands and remain profitable; TCM provides the means for achieving these goals. TCM helps a firm actively balance the needs of customers, market share requirements, profit expectations, and costs within the strategic context facing the firm. As has been noted, TCM occurs in two phases that roughly correspond to the two halves of the product development cycle: the establishment phase and the attainment phase. Attention now turns to these two critical phases in the TCM process.

CORE TOOLS AND TECHNIQUES

Target Cost Management requires several core tools, or management methods, techniques and technologies that work in tandem with other process tools already available in many organizations.[13] Using the right support tools and techniques greatly increases the effectiveness of the TCM process. Where core tools are not already being used, the process owner and top management both need to assess the trade-off between the cost and benefit of investing in the various tools.

There are nine core target costing tools that are used at various stages in the target costing process (see Figure 5.4):[14] value engineering and value analysis[15], quality function deployment, design for manufacturing and assembly and design to cost, cost tables, feature to function costing, component cost analysis, process (operations) costing, multi-year product and profit planning, and benchmarking.[16] Supporting tools include capacity measurement, supplier ratings, process testing, waste and yield analysis, CAD/CAM, activity-based management, Pareto analysis, failure mode and effect analysis, make

Figure 5.4   Target Cost Management Core Tools and Product Development

	Product Strategy	Concept and Feasibility	Design and Development	Production and Logistics
Planning	Multiyear Product Plan			Multiyear Product Plan
Marketing	Benchmarking QFD			
Costing	Cost Tables	Function Cost Feature Costing QFD	Component Cost Process Costing	
Engineering		Value Engineering DTC QFD	Value Engineering DFMA, DTC QFD	Value Analysis
Procurement		Supplier Based Value Engineering	Supplier Based Value Engineering	

Product Development Cycle (when tools are used) →

Functional Expertise for Tools (left axis label)

Source: *Target Costing: The Next Frontier in Strategic Cost Management,* Ansari, Bell and the CAM-I Target Cost Core Group, Chicago, IL: Irwin Professional Publishing, 1997: 128.

or buy models, regression analysis, net present value analysis, and discriminant analysis.

The level of investment for the core tools ranges from low (process costing and component costing), to medium (feature to function costing, design for manufacturability and assembly, benchmarking and multi-year product/profit plan matrices), to high (cost tables, value engineering, quality function deployment).[17] The level of investment required, and difficulty of implementation, will vary for each firm. While having the right tools is critical to complete implementation, a balance between tools, benefits, and the overall costs they represent should be maintained. This balance is an essential part of the Target Cost Management philosophy.

Target Cost Management and The Extended Enterprise

Planning and competition can be combined only by planning for competition, not by planning against competition.

– Friedrich August von Hayek

TCM incorporates the voice of the customer into the business, shifting attention from internal operations to the value chain and its performance against customer requirements. It is a shift that drives the organization into explicit recognition of its value chain partners, their abilities, and the need to balance short-term objectives for internal performance with the well-being of trading partners and the long-term satisfaction and loyalty of consumers. It is often possible to leverage the value chain to reduce total delivered costs, improve quality, or enhance responsiveness. Moving from a conflictual relationship into the framework of the Extended Enterprise begins with understanding how to capture and incorporate customer input in the TCM process.

A CUSTOMER PERSPECTIVE

TCM systems are market driven. They must build customers' wants, desires and needs into all four stages of the product development cycle. That means that the voice of the customer is needed throughout the product development cycle as an input to set prices and profit targets, to guide design decisions, and to make function and feature trade-offs. The process of monitoring the voice of the customer includes asking the right questions, absorbing the answers into a proper mental model of the market, communicating that information to other members of the management team, and then acting on it. A customer-focused firm will exhibit the following traits:[18]

- It uses state of the market technology in its products, which means it introduces product features because customers, not engineers, want them.

- It conducts open-minded inquiries to gauge current market needs, shifts in those needs, and to respond to specific customer requests.

- It has a coherent and systematic way to make customer and market information available throughout the organization.

- It shares information through teams to reduce interpretation bias, better understand customer needs, and develop shared perceptions of their requirements.

- It challenges all assumptions to prevent existing mindsets and implicit assumptions from becoming self-fulfilling prophecies.

- It makes underlying data assumptions explicit so that the models used to understand and analyze data can be scrutinized and challenged.

Customer input can take many forms, and is available at many different points in the purchase decision. Forward-looking data about what the customer perceives he or she wants is the basis for determining customer attitudes.[19] These attitudes reflect what customers want and what they would be willing to pay for. It is most useful in the profit strategy/profit planning, product concept, and feasibility stages of the product development cycle. Feedback information, on the other hand, reflects the actual choices made by customers and their post-purchase attitudes. Data collected at this stage includes purchase patterns, returns, complaints, and product failures. Since customer actions do not always follow expressed attitudes, it is important that both feed-forward and feedback information be used to garner customer values and trends.

Customer information can be gathered through focus groups, surveys, customer service records, and sales feedback. The data that is collected should be used to understand such things as: brand groupings and segmentation, features demanded by customers versus current product functions (a *quality table*), company product qualities and price versus those of competitors (*quality and price profiles*), and customer choice criteria and perceptions of a product (a *customer value map*). Other data used by TCM include: 1) an analysis of competitive bidding performance (a *won/lost analysis*); 2) a *Pareto chart of complaints* that shows the most frequent cause of customer complaints about the company's products; and, 3) market trend data (*time plot of market share trends and a plot of customer retention rates over time*).

Different types of customer input information is used at various stages of the product development and design process, shaping the Target Cost Management analysis and its efforts (see Figure 5.5). For instance, in the case where the direct customer is an intermediary for the ultimate consumer, key representatives from the direct customer should be included throughout the design and development phases. At Boeing, the development of the 777 brought airline pilots, mechanics, flight attendants, and other knowledgeable or affected individuals in to sit on cross-functional teams, while focus groups were used to tap into final consumer concerns and preferences.

As at Boeing, the key objective at this stage of the TCM effort is to understand what information is needed, the most efficient and effective ways to collect it, and once collected, to ensure that it is acted upon. Customer values and perceptions are the key, perhaps only, determinants of a product's price and demand patterns. To fail to turn to the customer whenever possible, in whatever way possible, is to miss out on a vital piece of information that can shape the future of the firm. For this reason, if no other, a firm should think carefully before outsourcing any activity (core or nonessential) that has direct connection with customers and their needs. Gaining the advantages of customer-driven knowledge is the first step in managing the Extended Enterprise effectively.

Figure 5.5 Collecting and Using Customer Data

Product Development Cycle	What Data?	How Collected?	What Analysis?	Limitations
Product Strategy and Profit Planning	Market Segmentation Data. Customer Need Survey. Competitor Product Profile.	Focus Groups. Ethnographic Interviews. Surveys.	Segmentation Matrix. Repeat Feedback from Focus Group. Head to head Comparisons.	Hard to define unfilled spaces for new products that have no history.
Product Concept and Feasibility	Needs, Wants, Delight Factors	Surveys Focus Groups Direct participation on teams.	Value Quality Map. Value Quality Matrix. Price Map.	Customers often don't state a need but are dissatisfied if it is not provided.
Product Concept and Feasibility, Continued	Quality Characteristics	Brainstorming by team members. Direct customer participation on teams. From customers' own evaluation process.	Correlation between product characteristics and needs, wants, and delight factors. Value Quality Matrix.	
Product Design and Development	Feedback data from test user groups.	Interviews. Participant-observer data. Beta Tests. Customer Previews. Prototype Testing.	Value Profile. Price Profile. Quality Profile.	Customer input may not be completely indicative of purchase preferences.
Production and Logistics	Feedback data on actual decisions or purchase returns, complaints, warranty repairs, post purchase satisfaction.	Data on returns, warranties, complaints. Follow-up Interviews. Customer Analysis	Progress Charts. Warranty Repair Costs. Defect rates. Product Recalls.	Usually too late for existing products.

Source: *Target Costing: The Next Frontier in Strategic Cost Management*, Ansari, Bell and the CAM-I Target Cost Core Group, Chicago, IL: Irwin Professional Publishing, 1997: 77

TARGET COST MANAGEMENT IN THE EXTENDED ENTERPRISE

Reaping the total benefits of Target Cost Management requires the involvement of the entire value chain. Beginning with research and development and continuing through manufacturing, delivery, servicing, and disposing of a product, many different firms with many different capabilities are needed to provide required products and services to an increasingly demanding market. The resulting *network of firms* is what is meant by the term **Extended Enterprise.** Whether formally integrated through partnership agreements, or simply locked into daily conflict by the very nature of business itself, the network of firms that make up the value chain has joint control of cost, quality, and the satisfaction of customer requirements.

The key to total cost reduction is to reduce costs in the entire value chain. Passing on cost reduction targets to suppliers, dealers, and recyclers is not target costing. Every firm in the value chain must remain economically viable if the chain itself is to continue to function effectively. To ensure that customer expectations are met, the complete network of value chain members has to be involved at each stage of the product development cycle. This involvement provides benefits to all parties, as more durable and reliable products using more efficient production processes are developed and delivered in ways that better meet customer requirements, creating a cycle of growth.

Value chain members provide valuable support throughout the TCM process. For instance, in the product strategy and profit planning stage, value chain members contribute information about technology and its capabilities, changing use patterns for products, changes in lifestyles that affect demand for services, and cultural patterns such as environmental awareness.[20] Relatedly, at the product concept and feasibility stage, value chain input is critical to ensure that suppliers can make required parts and that distributors can actually sell the output. The product only makes sense if it meets the needs of the customer and can be provided by the value chain in a cost effective, value-ensuring manner.

Moving to the product design and development stage, value chain members need to coordinate their products and services so they fit together to yield the product desired by customers.[21] Finally, in the production logistics and support stage, ideas from value chain members can lead to continuous improvement in products and processes through cooperative efforts that lead to improved yields and quality.[22] Diffusing TCM throughout the value chain leads to many benefits. Gaining these benefits requires creating nontraditional, nonconflictual relationships with trading partners which ensure that all parties win because the customer needs drive the process. Only with this level of cooperative effort can the customer focus truly be said to be at the heart of the business enterprise.

What benefits can an Extended Enterprise approach provide?[23] First, it can support a better focus on customer requirements because it brings multiple perspectives about customer needs and how best to bring them to the table. Second, it can enhance technological solutions as each member of the value chain brings different specializations and technology frontiers in both products and processes to the entire network. Next, collaboration can provide input and ideas early in the concept formation stage where ideas are best tested, refined, and incorporated into product specifications.

Total value chain involvement can also help to eliminate nonvalue-added activities as process analysis and improvement begins to span organizational boundaries. The resulting win-win solutions can permanently eliminate waste and nonproductive transactions. In a related way, unnecessary features and parts can be eliminated earlier in the design process as value chain partners brainstorm for ways to make the entire productive process more efficient and effective. In these discussions, alternative materials often emerge as a means to trim costs without impairing the quality or value of the product to customers.

While managing the entire value chain is a critical goal, there is increasing evidence that managing the supply chain is the most critical relationship for the market maker seeking to use advanced management approaches to secure optimal market share and a sustainable growth pattern. So important is the concept of supply chain management (e.g., the Extended Enterprise) that a chapter will be used to explore its complexities, challenges, and opportunities. To be completely effective, TCM needs to incorporate key Extended Enterprise axioms, such as: [24]

- There is a shared specific focus on satisfying the common end customer.
- There is an alignment of vision.
- There is a fundamental level of cooperation and performance to commitment (trust).

- There is open and effective communication.
- Decisions should emphasize the maximization of the competencies and knowledge within the supply chain.
- All stakeholders are committed to generate long-term mutual benefits.
- There is a common view of how success is measured.
- All members are committed to continuous improvement and breakthrough advancements.
- Whatever competitive pressures exist in the environment are allowed to exist within the extended enterprise.

Only by developing cooperative relationships with partners within the Extended Enterprise can a company come to understand how upstream decisions influence downstream costs, and how downstream decisions influence upstream efforts and costs. Much like Henry Ford's River Rouge plant, the goal is to create a seamless, rapid flow of material through the value chain that is focused totally on meeting customer needs in the most effective, efficient manner for all involved parties. Target Cost Management deployed throughout the Extended Enterprise is a win-win solution that creates profits by maximizing customer value creation.

ESTABLISHING TARGET COSTS, PRICE AND PROFIT MARGIN EXPECTATIONS

Target costs are defined within the parameters of the firm's product strategy and its long-term profit plans, which specify the markets, customers, and products that the company intends to develop. Seven major activities take place during the establishment of target costs within this strategic framework:[25]

- *Market research* provides information about the unrecognized needs and wants of customers and identifies market niches the firm can successfully exploit.
- *Competitive analysis* determines what competitors' products are currently available, how customers evaluate these products, and the reactions of potential competitors to the firm's entry to the market.

- *Customer or market niche* determination entails the analysis of market and competitor information to determine which customer segment to target.

- *Customer requirements* are attained at the product-specific level both before design is undertaken and throughout the development and production phases.

- *Product features* are established based on customer requirements to ensure that quality, reliability, dependability, and frequency and ease of repair expectations are met.

- *Market price* is determined based on a competitive analysis of the market, trends, and desired share projections. It should be acceptable to customers and capable of withstanding competition.

- *Required profit* targets are set based on company-defined rates of return for this type of investment.

At Toyota, the planning stage begins with a product concept about three years before a new model is introduced. Target profit is determined by a long-run profitability analysis, then applied to the unit level. Allowable cost is the difference between target price and profit. The new product concept is usually released 36 months before production begins, and the allowable cost is typically agreed to 33 months before production. [26]

Establishing the target profit and allowable cost is the first step in TCM, but achieving them is the key to successful implementation. There are three key steps in attaining TCM objectives:[27] (1) compute the cost gap, (2) design costs out of the product, and (3) release the design for manufacturing and continuous improvement. The identified *cost gap* is the current estimated difference between the total cost to manufacture, market and distribute the product and the related allowable cost based on the established market price. The cost gap is closed by designing out costs both at the product level and within the entire value chain that supports it. A design is released for production only when its projected actual cost equals its allowable cost target. Finally, continuous improvement objectives should be pursued once the product has been launched to ensure that costs track downward over time as competitive forces lead to price reductions in the marketplace.

Four key recursive problem-solving activities are used to close the cost gap through focused product and process design: product design, cost and value analysis, value engineering, and cost estimation. Many times the core business processes (development, production, etc.) must be reengineered to ensure target process costs are met. At Boeing, the 777 Program turned to digital product definition (computer design) and digital pre-assembly (electronic mock-ups) in order to reduce the cost associated with mock-up construction and engineering changes, while reducing flow time and overall engineering cost and time spent on derivative models. TCM looks at every cost, wherever it is incurred or designed into a product/service bundle, seeking to reduce or eliminate resource requirements that do not directly support meeting customer needs.

The establishment of price and profit margins, essential to the TCM process, is shaped by several key issues:[28]

- Traditional pricing methods, such as cost plus, marginal, volume, and premium pricing, are inappropriate in the competitive environments where TCM is employed.

- Physical and aesthetic properties of the product as well as customers' acceptable prices, competitors' product offerings, and the market share goal of the firm determine product prices under TCM.

- Setting target profit requires combining product mix information and required return on sales or other profitability measures (NPV, IRR, MIRR, etc.) from the business level plan, with the projected sales volume (assuming market size, share and price) from the product level plan.

Price in this context is the realized price net of discounts, payment terms, and any other off-invoice adjustments.[29] It should be developed within the boundaries of the total cost of ownership for a customer from initial purchase (invoice plus transportation), repair and maintenance, service and support, and disposal costs.

Four primary factors influence the price set in TCM:[30] (1) consumer needs/wants/tastes related to physical features and aesthetic functions of the product; (2) acceptable price, or what customers are willing to pay for these features; (3) competitive analysis that determines relative price and functionality of competitors' products, and (4) market share goals and price required to achieve them over the product's life cycle. For existing or moderately innovative products, current product prices can be used as a baseline. If a product is markedly new, it is much more difficult to establish optimal pricing strategies. In this case, trends for similar products or innovations should be used to support the analysis of the product's value and price profile. For instance, when Sony first introduced the Walkman, it was difficult to evaluate the features customers desired or determine the price they would be willing to pay for these features. Strategic and competitive factors played a greater role than customer requirements in setting the initial target prices in the early days of this product. [31]

Figure 5.6 Setting Target Profit

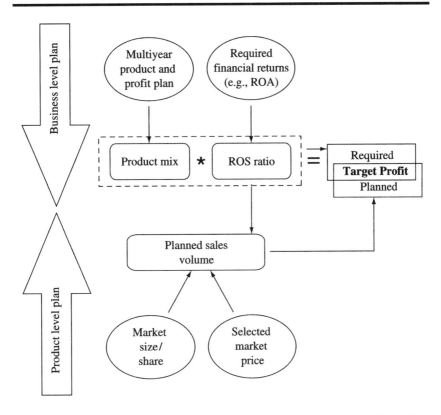

Source: *Target Costing: The Next Frontier in Strategic Cost Management*, Ansari, Bell and the CAM-I Target Cost Core Group, Chicago, IL: Irwin Professional Publishing, 1997: 37.

Setting target profit margins is based on the profit requirements for the business as a whole. Combining the product level plan and business plan, the resulting margin should be based on the estimated lifetime sales of the product and may vary over the product's life cycle. It is quite likely that target margins will need to be revised during the product development process as well as over the product's life cycle as market conditions change or continuous improvement cost reduction targets are met. The steps used in setting target margins are summarized in Figure 5.6.

FROM ALLOWABLE TO ACHIEVABLE TARGET COST

Setting a target cost is an essential first step, but without a well-defined plan for achieving this goal, the promised benefits may not be realized. Turning an allowable cost into an achievable target cost utilizes three basic tools: cost analysis and estimation, value engineering, and continuous improvement. The purpose of cost analysis is to focus cost reduction and design efforts so that product costs are aligned with customer values.[32] This requires a flexible cost system that can be used to analyze, calculate, and summarize costs on multiple dimensions under diverse assumptions. The cost estimating system should allow for increasing levels of accuracy as the product goes from a concept to a design ready for manufacturing. Regardless of whether the costs are newly caused costs, or embedded in legacy systems and procedures, they are open to challenge and improvement during the TCM process. At NEC this recursive process is used to continually manage the costs of new products downward based on learnings from prior product launches and production efforts.[33]

Five steps underlie the cost planning process:[34] (1) computation of the overall cost gap, (2) decomposition of this gap by cost element, (3) assignment of cost targets to designers, (4) estimation of revised costs, and (5) deciding on a treatment for unattainable cost targets. Initial estimates of the actual costs for a product should incorporate all resource uses driven by it. Whether costs are incurred in production, R&D, sales, distribution, service, support or downstream disposal of the product at the end of its life, the affected resources are relevant in setting the allowable cost target and estimating projected actual spends. Where market forces determine allowable cost, the initial cost estimate is driven by current structures and processes both within the firm and throughout the industry value chain.

Figure 5.7   Multiple Views of Typical Elements of Allowable Target Cost

	In-House				
	New	Legacy	Suppliers	Dealers	Recyclers
Design-Driven Recurring Cost					
Manufacturing					
Raw Material					
Purchased Parts					
Processing Costs					
Material Handling					
Quality Assurance					
Sales and Marketing					
Sales Training					
Additional Sales Salaries					
Distribution					
Packaging Materials					
Shipping and Handling Costs					
Service and Support					
Warranty Repairs					
Customer Training					
Recycling					
Waste Disposal					
Clean-up Costs					
Design Driven One Time Cost					
Product Development Costs					
Research, Development and Testing					
Test Marketing					
Capital Costs					
Machinery, Equipment, Tools and Dyes					
Special Training					
Allocated Activity Driven Costs					
Manufacturing					
General Purchase Support					
Grounds and Parking Lot					
General Property Taxes					
Sales and Marketing					
Sales Management Salaries					
General Advertising and Promotion					
Distribution					
Transportation					
Shipping Clerk Salaries					
Service and Support					
Salaries					
Supplies and Travel					
General Overhead					
Divisional Salaries					
Corporate Overhead Allocations					
Total Allowable Target Cost					

Source: *Target Costing: The Next Frontier in Strategic Cost Management,* Ansari, Bell and the CAM-I Target Cost Core Group, Chicago, IL: Irwin Professional Publishing, 1997: 50.

Once the gap is identified, it is important to decompose the overall product cost to increase understanding of where design-based improvements can be attained. Using a multi-dimensional perspective is useful here as it can shed light on unique ways to remove costs from the product or process (see Figure 5.7). Each perspective emphasizes a different element of the cost puzzle and suggests different means for eliminating excess cost and creating improvement goals. The decom-position of cost supports the assignment of cost targets to design and build teams.

Five key elements define this stage of the TCM process: [35]

- Customer features are translated into functional cost targets.

- Seasoned judgment is applied to translate features into product functions.

- Indirect methods for assigning functional targets can be used when a direct feature-function mapping is not possible.

- Functional cost targets are decomposed into cost targets for major components and parts.

- Cost targets are assigned to design teams throughout the value chain.

An example may be useful at this point. Let's say a PC is being designed and it has been determined that customers value the speed of software operations to be fully half of the total defined value of the product. If the total allowable cost for the PC is $1,000 then $500 should be targeted to this value attribute. Translating this amount into functional cost targets requires determining how each function of the PC contributes to this feature (such as the microprocessor, power supply, case, memory, hard disk and bus) as well as their relative impact on overall speed. The result is a weighting factor for the product functions that can be used to set their cost targets.

Setting cost targets by function and feature is a complex task, one that requires a significant number of estimates, assumptions, and iterations. [36] Once accomplished, these targets can be used to develop specific cost reduction goals for each team. The next step is to then develop actual cost estimates for the revised feature and function options devised by the design teams. Cost estimation models for TCM need to be related to the physical attributes of the product or the process and detail how these attributes affect a product's cost.[37] A *parametric* cost estimating model can be used that focuses on the impact of a few salient features on product cost, such as square footage of finished versus unfinished space in construction.

Simulation models using cost tables and the output of parametric cost models can often be used to refine the product design options. Finally, a *detailed* cost estimation model that includes a complete bill of materials, bill of activities, investment demands, and transaction costs should be developed as the design process moves to its completion. Only when the final detailed costs meet preset targets should the product be released to production.

Clearly, there may be some cost goals that are going to be un-attainable, even with the most conscientious and innovative attempts to reach them. Non-attainment is a serious problem, because it is in violation of the basic principles of the TCM process. At the overall product level, non-attainment can be addressed by:[38] (1) evaluating the possibility that targets can be met with kaizen or continuous improvement; (2) keep the target costs in place and reduce the features; (3) postpone launch until target costs are met; (4) raise the target cost (only in rare cases for specific strategic reasons); and, (5) as a last resort, abandon the product.

If the non-attainment problem resides at the function, component or parts level, there is a high probability that savings in other areas will offset the problem at the product level.[39] There are several ways to address non-attainment at this level: (1) transfer savings from other components and products to meet the shortfall in components that do not meet target costs; (2) transfer savings but attach stigma to subsidies, assigning problem solving teams to address them; and, (3) do not transfer savings, a solution that may create behavioral problems if the targeting process is subsequently perceived to be too rigid. It is the attainment of the target cost which is important, not the progress of an individual team or individual. Only if everyone focuses on achieving target cost objectives, every team and individual provides needed insights and support, can the enterprise succeed. The key is to ensure that the discipline of TCM is preserved within a positive culture where improvement is achieved and rewarded.

Bringing Target Cost Management to Life

*Thunder is good, thunder is impressive; but it is the
lightning that does the work.*

– Mark Twain

Attaining the benefits promised by Target Cost Management
depends on its effective deployment and use. TCM principles need to
be employed as soon as possible in the design and development process. Unless the gap analysis identifies specific "show stoppers," the
deployment of TCM throughout the organization should begin even
if all of the gaps have yet to be closed. Several core issues make up
the range of factors to be considered as target costing is brought to life
in the enterprise:TCM organization and participants, deployment
assessment, information demands, and integration with supporting
tools and techniques. This final section will review these areas.

TARGET COST MANAGEMENT ORGANIZATION
AND PARTICIPANTS

Target Cost Management initiatives are deployed by using a
variety of cross-functional teams.[40] As such, TCM needs a strong
program manager to effectively coordinate teams during the product
development cycle and to spell out exactly what is expected of team
members, including the seamless transition of the initiative from
one team to another. Underlying the cross-functional target costing
structures is a deep body of functional knowledge and expertise. The
skills of an active process owner, as well as the ongoing support of top
management, are required to ensure that the target costing process
meets its objectives.

Four types of teams comprise the TCM infrastructure (see Figure 5.8).[41] The first of these is a *business planning team* of senior
executives from all major functions that sets the long-term strategic
plan, defines core competencies and key technologies, details product
strategies and plans, and develops the deployment plan. A second
team, the *product team* includes the product team program manager,
sales and marketing, product planning, manufacturing, cost analysis,
procurement, and representatives of key suppliers. Its goal is to
develop product level profit plans, a defined product concept, product
feasibility, perform value engineering, set cost targets, and develop
capacity and investment plans.

Figure 5.8   Team Structures in Target Cost Management

Team	Membership	Major Team Output
Business planning team	Senior executives from all major functions including program managers	Long-term strategic plan, core competencies and key technologies, product strategy and plans, deployment plan
Product team	Product team program manager, sales and marketing (including international), product planning, manufacturing, cost analyst, procurement, key suppliers	Product level profit plans, product concept, product feasibility, value engineering (VE), cost targets, capacity and investments plan
Design team	Design engineering, prototype development, product planning, manufacturing, cost analyst, procurement, key suppliers, service and support, sales/ marketing/distribution, recycling	Product concept, VE, detailed product and process design, validated product and process
Product manufacturing team	Design engineering, plant manufacturing, quality control, cost analysis, procurement, key suppliers, service and support, sales/marketing/ distribution	Production plan, capacity requirements, final make/buy decisions, training on new processes, supplier management, continuous improvement

Source: *Target Costing: The Next Frontier in Strategic Cost Management,* Ansari, Bell and the CAM-I Target Cost Core Group, Chicago, IL: Irwin Professional Publishing, 1997: 99.

The third team involved during TCM is the *design team,* which includes members from design engineering, prototype development, product planning, manufacturing, cost analysis, procurement, key suppliers, service and support, sales/ marketing/distribution, and recycling. The goal of this group is to define the product concept, support value engineering, develop detailed product and process design, and validate the product and process. Finally, *the product manufacturing team,* made up of design engineering, plant manufacturing, quality control, cost analysis, procurement, key suppliers, service and support, and sales/ marketing/ distribution. It is called upon to finalize the production plan, define capacity requirements, make final make/buy decisions, conduct training on new processes, and engage in ongoing supplier management and continuous improvement initiatives.

The coordination of these teams and their efforts falls to the process owner and top management. Best practice TCM firms use an organi-zational unit, called the *Target Cost Management office* or *kaizen unit* to deploy and promote TCM throughout the organization. The key roles of this office include:[42]

- Coordinate target costing efforts at the business unit level.
- Maintain manuals and distribute information about best practices and value engineering successes.
- Maintain cost estimation models and cost tables.
- Monitor progress toward targets.
- Help address problems in the process.
- Maintain and distribute improvement ideas.
- Promote the target costing activities companywide.
- Provide cost estimation and modeling.

Nippon Denso is an example of a firm using this approach.[43]   It co-ordinates its activities with both the central planning and policy deployment units as well as the Target Cost Management offices within each business unit. The business units have the primary responsibility for meeting cost targets. The Target Cost Management office's role is to support these efforts by promoting value engineering ideas, providing training, and maintaining cost tables.

Whether or not a process owner or Target Cost Management office is used to coordinate the TCM process, it is critical that the goal of achieving required integration, coordination, and objectives be assigned to a specific individual or organizational unit. Second, it is crucial that the efforts of the process owner be sanctioned by active, visible top management support. Without the latter, the TCM process will not reach its potential due to the unavoidable political and behavioral challenges that emerge during organizational change efforts. Target Cost Management is strategic: its effective deployment requires visible authority and consistent top management support.

DEPLOYING TARGET COST MANAGEMENT

The deployment of Target Cost Management will not happen just because management thinks it is a good idea. It requires organizational readiness, a conceptual plan, and an action plan. Before proceeding with deployment, one must create acceptance for TCM, provide a common understanding of it, and use it to link daily action with organizational strategies. In addition, TCM deployment requires determining the technical and structural changes needed, the behaviors desired, the cultural value, symbols and mindsets to be employed, and the political issues that need to be resolved.

The starting point for TCM deployment is the agreement of all affected participants regarding the nature, purpose, and need for target costing. Seven basic questions can guide the assessment of the firm's readiness for TCM:[44]

1. Have we made the reason for TCM clear? Is its connection to business strategy clear?

2. Does top management support TCM?   Without this support, the required cross-functional cooperation may be hard to attain.

3. Is this the right time to introduce TCM? TCM should not simply be added to a plethora of other initiatives; it should represent a clear strategic priority for the firm.

4. Are people ready for change? Without an imperative for change, it may be difficult to institute TCM's rigor in product design and operations.

5. Is there a readiness to embrace the key principles of TCM? The core principles defined earlier must be in place, or capable of being instituted, if TCM initiatives are to be successful.

6. Is the organization ready to commit the necessary resources? Most organizations have a product development process and the talent to form cross-functional design teams, but will find a need to grow expertise and/or acquire the nine core tools and techniques defined earlier.

7. Are all management levels ready to respond quickly and do their part in the TCM effort?

The answers to these questions determine whether an organization is ready for TCM deployment as well as setting the scope, breadth and speed of deployment. If the answer to any of these questions is no, there may be a need for significant upfront preparation before TCM is pursued.

Figure 5.9   A Sample Gap Analysis for Target Costing Deployment

Deployment Requirements (Enablers)	Marketing		Design	
	Should	Does	Should	Does
Technical Requirements:				
1. Do we have clearly delineated product line objectives?				
2. Do we have a ranking of customer needs?	Φ	Yes	λ	No
3. Do we have VE training?			λ	Yes
4. Do we have a cost breakdown of components used?			λ	No
5. Have we set up cross-functional teams?				
6. Have we identified a list of critical suppiers?			λ	No
Behavioral Requirements:				
7. Are all functions ready to participate in design activity?	λ	No	λ	No
8. Do our engineers use cost data?			λ	No
9. Is marketing willing and able to do feature trade-offs?	Φ	Yes	λ	No
10. Are we willing to share information across functions?	λ	No	λ	No
11. Is accounting ready to act as business advisor?				
Culture/Symbolic Requirements:				
12. Does target costing have a positive meaning for us?	λ	Yes	λ	Yes
13. Does our culture support open sharing of information?	λ	No	λ	No
14. Is target costing consistent with our organizational culture?	λ	Yes	λ	Yes
15. Do we value customer input in our culture?	λ	Yes	λ	No
16. Do we value cross-functional teamwork?	λ	No	λ	No
Political Requirements:				
17. Does it preserve our vital interests?	λ	Yes	λ	
18. Will the target cost initiative reduce our power?	λ	No	λ	No
19. Will those who have formal power support target costing?	λ	No	λ	
20. Will target costing adversely affect our resource base?	λ	No	λ	

Key: Φ = Functional area primarily responsible for or affected by a deployment requirement.

Source: Target Costing: The Next Frontier in Strategic Cost Management, Ansari, Bell and

Functional Area Involved

Manufacturing		Service		Accounting		Procurement		Top Management	
Should	Does	Should	Does	Should	Does	Should	Does	Should	Does
								Φ	No
λ	No								
λ	No			λ	No	λ	Yes		
								Φ	Yes
λ	No					Φ	No		
λ	Yes	λ	No	λ	No	λ	No		
					No				
				λ	No				
λ	Yes	λ	Yes	λ	No	λ	No		No
				Φ	No				
λ	No	λ	No	λ	Yes	λ	Yes	Φ	Yes
λ	Yes	λ	Yes	λ	No	λ	Yes	Φ	No
λ	Yes	λ	No	λ	No	λ	Yes	Φ	Yes
λ	Yes	λ	Yes	λ	Yes	λ	Yes	Φ	No
λ	Yes	λ	No	λ	Yes	λ	Yes	Φ	Yes
λ		λ		λ				λ	Yes
λ		λ		λ				λ	Yes
λ		λ		λ				λ	No
λ		λ		λ				λ	No

λ = Area affected by deployment requirement.

the CAM-I Target Cost Core Group, Chicago, IL: Irwin Professional Publishing, 1997: 230-31.

Taking deployment from planning to action requires attention to four specific steps:[45] (1) gap analysis; (2) determine the scope and depth of deployment; (3) develop an action item list; and, (4) execute and follow-up on actions. TCM spans many functions. Therefore, to ensure effective gap analysis a cross-functional team needs to be deployed. A cross-functional team will view each performance gap from a different perspective and will subsequently act as an ambassador for a well-defined process within their area of expertise. During the gap analysis shortcomings in the current capabilities of the firm to implement TCM need to be enumerated, defined, located within the organization, and assigned to an individual or group for resolution. Major performance or cost gaps can be quickly identified using an interactive flowchart for the company's current product development process, which can then be benchmarked against a best practice firm. Figure 5.9 suggests one way this gap analysis can be performed for the organization.

Having identified the gaps and assessed where they reside, the scope of the deployment can be determined. Four choices shape the scope of deployment:[46]

1) selected business unit deployment can be used when there are differences in the readiness and gaps across business units;

2) program-based deployment can be used to test deployment when there are multiple programs and not all of them are ready for deployment;

3) company-wide deployment will force change, but brings with it considerable risk and turmoil; and,

4) value chain deployment, which extends the implementation to the entire value chain and can once again be costly and risky. This latter option is the final objective, but it may not be achievable in the early stages of implementation.

The last planning step in deployment is to convert the "gap analysis" into a detailed action item checklist that specifies the many tasks or activities needed to address each gap area. These tasks are then assigned to individuals and sub-teams using a "who-when" matrix that clearly delineates who is responsible for completing the task and by what date. Finally, planning is complete and attention can turn to target costing execution. Here actions must be monitored to ensure that deadlines and targets are met. The steps outlined earlier shape the execution, which can begin as soon as identified performance and capability gaps are closed. Picking teams, gaining required information capabilities, and integrating related tools and techniques are important during both planning and execution.

FILLING THE INFORMATION GAP

Target Cost Management is heavily dependent on information during planning and execution. Five major organizational databases are utilized during TCM[47]: competitive intelligence, marketing data, cost data, procurement data, and engineering data. Not all of the required information for TCM is routinely collected within these five databases, leading to the need for an organization to invest in information to fill the identified gaps (see Figure 5.10). Sound judgment needs to be exercised to determine whether the lack of information creates an impassable "show stopper" or if the organization will make a quantum leap forward by enhancing current systems, implementing the Target Cost Management process, then developing or purchasing a complete database over time. For an organization, speed to implementation is as important in adopting a new process as it is in bringing new products to market.

Figure 5.10 Typical Information Gaps in Target Cost Management

Product Development Cycle				
Type of Data	Product Strategy and Profit Plans	Product Concept and Feasibility	Product Design and Development	Production Logistics and Support
Competitive intelligence		Competitor's prices and features	Competitor's price structure	
Customer and marketing	Product life cycle	Features/price data and attribute/price data		Improvement ideas
Cost		Features/cost data	Attribute/cost data and function cost data	Improvement ideas
Engineering	Technology life cycle		Components/sub system interaction, VE case studies	Improvement ideas
Procurement			Supplier cost data	Improvement ideas

Source: *Target Costing: The Next Frontier in Strategic Cost Management*, Ansari, Bell and the CAM-I Target Cost Core Group, Chicago, IL: Irwin Professional Publishing, 1997: 114.

Another issue to consider in the information arena is that data needed for TCM must be easily assessable to the Target Cost Management teams. To support TCM in this way, databases should have an open architecture that allows multiple views of data, uses consistent definitions, and provides user defined reports. TCM participants should also have transparent connectivity that can make access and information sharing easy. Finally, recognizing that acquiring information is costly, organizations may need to consider networked and distributed "parallel" databases as viable alter-natives to more costly data warehouses. The key is to identify what information is needed, when, where and by whom to ensure that information gaps are closed efficiently and effectively.

Implementation Enablers

Man's highest merit always is, as much as possible,
to rule external circumstances and as little as possible
to let himself be ruled by them.

– Goethe

Four cultural attributes combine to enable the successful deployment of TCM in an organization:[48] (1) customer focus; (2) cross-functional teamwork; (3) open information sharing; and, (4) trust. Shared organizational values, symbols, mind-sets and world views underpin this type of culture. Where these shared perspectives do not exist, political challenges will likely emerge. The three political objectives when this latter situation occurs are:[49] (1) accommodate legitimate interest; (2) obtain "buy-in" from major groups; and, (3) avoid turf battles. Achieving these goals requires careful attention to protecting individual and group reputations, preserving resource control, compensation for lost knowledge or power, and respect for formal authority.[50] In the end, TCM strives to get organizational participants to think holistically, setting aside individual goals and objectives to ensure that customer requirements are met effectively and profitably.

Meeting the technical and structural requirements of TCM means examining four core enablers: (1) information, (2) tools, (3) organizational structure, (4) and value chain relationships (see Figure 5.11). The gap between current capability of the enablers and required status results in a deployment gap that needs to be bridged. For instance, component cost data is a critical piece of information for TCM Accounting is primarily responsible for, and should have, this data. Design and manufacturing need to have access to this same data. Unfortunately, in most organizations the only place this data can be found is in procurements, which has no direct responsibility for the data.

Figure 5.11 Key Structural Enablers

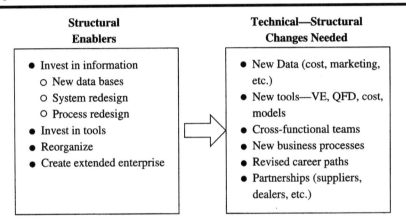

Structural Enablers	Technical—Structural Changes Needed

• Invest in information
  ○ New data bases
  ○ System redesign
  ○ Process redesign
• Invest in tools
• Reorganize
• Create extended enterprise
	• New Data (cost, marketing, etc.)
	• New tools—VE, QFD, cost, models
	• Cross-functional teams
	• New business processes
	• Revised career paths
	• Partnerships (suppliers, dealers, etc.)

Source: Target Costing: The Next Frontier in Strategic Cost Management, Ansari, Bell and the CAM-I Target Cost Core Group, Chicago, IL: Irwin Professional Publishing, 1997:

A second major concern in deployment is getting the desired behaviors from organizational participants. TCM is a new way of doing things. As such it may require significant behavioral changes including:[51] (1) early involvement of all functional areas rather than sequential support; (2) engineering needs to take cost ownership; (3) marketing must evaluate trade-offs, not just sell; (4) targets must be seen as commitments, not negotiable standards; (5) cross-functional cooperation is essential; and, (6) accountants must be business partners. These desired behavioral changes are enabled by active communication through newsletters and policy manuals or through general as well as specific, training.

Motivational influencers can also be used to gain desired behavioral changes, such as process and output performance measures and extrinsic or intrinsic rewards for achieving target goals. Rewards relating to target achievement should be focused at the product level to avoid "gaming" and sub-optimization. It is important to remember that if 99 out of 100 product teams meet their target decomposition exactly and one team fails....then everyone fails.

A failure to address behavioral changes and issues during TCM deployment can lead to dysfunctional consequences, such as longer development times, employee burnout, market confusion and organizational conflict. Avoiding these problems starts with open communication of the goals and methods of TCM, how the system will affect individual activities, performance, and rewards, and a clear linkage of the effort to the strategic initiatives and customer requirements facing the firm. Wherever possible, "win-lose" scenarios should be explored to find a "win-win" approach that will encourage everyone to support the effort. Failing to deal with the politics and impact of legacy systems on the target costing initiative in this way can lead to a "lose-lose" outcome—TCM does not get implemented and the company fails to achieve its strategic goals. Enabling change begins with disabling the barriers to change.

Target Cost Management: A Case Study [52]

Example is not the main thing in life—it is the only thing.

– Albert Schweitzer

In response to intense competitive challenges from Japanese companies, Caterpillar Inc. turned to Target Cost Management. Competitive issues included product reliability, after-sales services, and the demand for increased value from customers. For Caterpillar's customers, value is determined by elements such as the customer's cost to own and operate the product, the mix of features and functions in the product, and the relative quality of these elements.

To meet these competitive challenges, Caterpillar turned to its multi-functional New Product Introduction (NPI) teams. These teams are responsible for delivering reliable, quality products on time, within target costs, and achieving sales as well as market-share goals. Frequently, cost comparisons across product lines are conducted to identify solutions and evaluate cost drivers in the design of products and processes. The results of such analyses can provide important advantages in terms of quality, cost, and time-to-market.

Caterpillar's TCM process is, in essence, a management-by-policy program. Instead of delegating responsibility and "just steering the ship," as one executive puts it, the firm provides true leadership in terms of deciding what is important in products, when things need to be done, etc. Strategy for the entire company is focused on delivering new products on time and meeting quality, cost, and price targets while achieving research and development and capital targets. Members of the teams responsible for those products focus on these goals.

At Caterpillar, the need to continue to enhance target costing techniques was driven by a number of factors, including the company's emphasis on:

- providing outstanding customer service;
- meeting the competition's high-quality, low-cost product innovations;
- developing new manufacturing strategies;
- focusing on quality in terms of competitive designs as well as ongoing product and process improvements;
- creating new relationships with suppliers; and
- implementing changes throughout the company in every area from managerial perceptions to understanding the value of data and information in running the business.

In the process, Caterpillar expanded its emphasis on TCM to include achieving return on investment goals, targeting capital investment levels, and improving supplier alliances and engineering commitments.

The Target Cost Management initiative allowed Caterpillar to introduce a new way of thinking and reshaped corporate culture. New Product Introduction became essential to Caterpillar's long-term strategy. New products and major updates to existing products now occur about every three years. Such changes are planned and coordinated within a nine-year planning horizon and driven by the new product managers, who incorporate changes in customer expectations and competitive pressures into new products.

One of the critical issues the company faced in breaking with tradition was how to decompose target costs. For example, in building an earth mover, the planners had to determine how much of the total cost should be designated for the drive train, the hydraulic, or any other particular part. Planners looked at these proportional costs as a study of major functions across product lines to find the best engineering solutions.

As it sought best-design solutions, Caterpillar management took this idea a step further. In addition to creating multi-functional product development teams, the company also organized specialty teams across product lines. The specialty teams focused on particular function and feature aspects of the products. Because design decisions can influence a significant percentage of the total cost of a product, Caterpillar set up joint meetings in which these groups could exchange ideas and talk about design elements across product lines.

Individuals throughout the organization working with the products, also had to be kept fully informed about the overall project. They needed to understand that all members were part of a cross-functional team that designs, builds, develops and decides on changes for various products. Another innovation applied by Caterpillar was the integration of strategic business objectives with Quality Function Deployment (QFD). Relative weights within QFD provide the indicators for determining where to spend time designing better features and implementing the features customers really want in their products.

Cost ownership, namely assigning responsibility for expenditures to those who actually do the work either on the plant floor (e.g., production cells) or in the back office (supply chain management), is another key element of Caterpillar's successful cost management program. Accountability and cost ownership are assigned to the lowest possible levels of an organization. In the deployment of cost ownership and cost management objectives, the company spends hundreds of hours making sure everyone understands the importance of cost management; for example, the company provides regular training programs. Caterpillar's TCM process has five key elements:

1) target cost establishment, satisfying customer needs and achieving enterprise financial goals;
2) cost management organization, or cost ownership and commitment by those who do the work;
3) cost management communications;
4) target cost maintenance, or negotiation and adjustment by process owners; and

5) access to cost and target cost data, where finance provides financial analysis as well as current historical and projected costs for in-plant and out-plant suppliers through the business analysis function.

As a result of these efforts, Caterpillar has been able to maintain its market leadership position. For instance, annual sales in 1994 rose to $14.3 billion, 30 percent above their 1989 level. The lessons learned by Caterpillar in implementing TCM include:

- TCM is a competitive and strategic weapon.
- The TCM process requires managers to go beyond delegating responsibility to lead the company.
- TCM requires cost awareness, cost accountability, and cost ownership on the part of everyone in the firm.
- TCM requires a method for generating the kind of information necessary for managing the Target Cost Management processes. Targets can and should be established for all facets of a business, whether service organizations or products.
- New information gaps and communication breakdowns developing between processes and product teams must be constantly identified and addressed. Ensuring that local optimization (sub-level product or process team) does not overwhelm enterprise objectives and efforts, or cause costs to increase in other areas of the firm, is a key element of effective TCM.
- TCM is essentially a process to achieve customer satisfaction and profitability by simultaneously managing quality, cost and delivery/timing of new products and services.

Meeting the challenges inherent in implementing and utilizing TCM is the ongoing goal of the Caterpillar organization. Identifying and avoiding the pitfalls of TCM implementation is the key to reaping its long-term benefits.

References

Ansari, S., J. Bell and the CAM-I Target Cost Core Group, *Target Costing: The Next Frontier in Strategic Cost Management*, Chicago,IL: Irwin Professional Publishing, 1997.

Baker, William N., "The Missing Element in Cost Management: Competitive Target Costing," *Industrial Management*, Inst. of Industrial Engineers, Inc., March, 1995, Vol. 37, No. 2, pg. 29-35.

Bayou, Mohamed E., and Alan Reinstein, "Formula for Success: Target Costing for Cost-Plus Pricing Companies," *Journal of Cost Management*, Sept/Oct., 1997: 30-34.

Brausch, John M., "Target Costing for Profit Enhancement," *Management Accounting*, November, 1994: 45-49.

Collins, Jay, "Advanced Use of ABM—Using ABC for Target Costing, Activity-Based Budgeting, and Benchmarking," in *Activity-based Management: ABM Arthur Andersen's Lessons from the ABM Battlefield*, eds. S. Player and D. Keys (New York: MasterMedia, Ltd.), 1995: 153-160.

Cooper, Robin and W. Bruce Chew, "Control Tomorrow's Costs through Today's Designs," *Harvard Business Review*, Jan/Feb, 1996: 88-96.

Dutton, John J., and M. Ferguson, "Target Costing at Texas Instruments," *Journal of Cost Management*, New York: Warren, Gorham and Lamont, Fall, 1996: 33-38.

"Target Costing at Caterpillar," in *Activity-Based Management: ABM Arthur Andersen's Lessons from the ABM Battlefield*, eds. S.Player and D. Keys (New York: MasterMedia, Ltd.), 1995: 173-181.

Charles A. Marx and W. Scott Baker, "Target Costing," *Handbook of Cost Management*, Release 4, New York: Warren, Gorham and Lamont, 1996; D2-1 - 26.

Kato, Yutaka, "Target Costing Support Systems: Lessons from Japanese Companies," *Management Accounting Research*, March, 1993: 33-47.

Monden, Yasuhiro and Kazuki Hamada, "Target Costing and Kaizen Costing in Japanese Automobile Companies," *Journal of Management Accounting Research*, Fall, 1991: 16-34.

Sakurai, Michiharu, "Target Costing and How to Use It," *Journal of Cost Management*, Summer, 1989: 39-50.

Society of Management Accountants of Canada, *Implementing Target Costing*, Management Accounting Guideline #28, Hamilton, Ontario, 1995.

Endnotes

1   This entire chapter draws very heavily from S. Ansari, J. Bell and the CAM-I Target Cost Core Group, Target Costing: The Next Frontier in Strategic Cost Management, New York: McGraw-Hill, 1997 as well as from the Management Accounting Guideline #28, Implementing Target Costing, Hamilton, ON: The Society of Management Accountants of Canada, 1995. This definition appears on page 11 of the Ansari text noted.

2   This paragraph, as with several others in this summary chapter, draws upon the logic and arguments in Implementing Target Costing, The Society of Management Accountants of Canada, Management Accounting Guideline #28, Hamilton, Ontario, 1995. These comments reflect the discussion on page 2.

3   Ansari, et.al., op.cit., pg. 10-11.

4   Ibid, pg. 23.

5   MAG #28, op.cit., pg. 9.

6   This entire section draws almost exclusively from Ansari, op.cit., pp. 11-18.

7   Ibid, pg. 12.

8   Ibid, pg. 12.

9   J. Dutton and M. Ferguson, "Target Costing at Texas Instruments," Journal of Cost Management, Fall, 1996: 34.

10 Ansari, op.cit., pp. 12-14.

11 Ibid, pg. 15.

12 Ibid, pg. 15.

13 Ibid, pg 127.

14 Ibid, pp. 128-139.

15 These supporting tools are defined within the attached CAM-I glossary.

16 For a detailed discussion of these tools, please refer to the CAM-I Dictionary or the description in Target Costing: The Next Frontier in Strategic Cost Management, op.cit., pp. 129-138.

17 Ibid, pg 139.

18 Ibid, pg 68.

19 Ibid, pp. 70-71.

20 Ibid, pg 81.

21 Ibid, pg 82.

22 Ibid, pg 82.

23 These benefits are drawn from Ansari, op.cit., pp. 83-86.

24 Ibid, pg 86.

25 Ibid, pp. 24-26.

26 "Implementing Target Costing at Toyota," Journal of Cost Management, Summer, 1995: 56.

27 Ansari, op.cit., pg. 26.

28 Ibid, pg. 29.

29 Ibid, pg. 30.

30 Except where noted, the majority of the remaining discussion in this chapter draws heavily from Ansari, op.cit.. Specific pages will be noted where the comments are a minor reparaphrasing of the original work. For instance, this list appears on page 32.

31 Ibid, pg. 34.

32 Ibid, pg 42.

33 This comment is paraphrased from Implementing Target Costing, Society of Management Accountants of Canada, 1995: 27.

[34] Ibid, pg 44.

[35] Ibid, pg 51.

[36] The reader is asked to review the material in the CAM-I Target Costing book referenced below for further insights on this complex element of target costing, as there is inadequate space for a complete development of the topic in this summary chapter.

[37] Ibid, pg 57.

[38] Ibid, pg 60-61.

[39] Ibid, pg 61.

[40] Direct quote from ibid, pg 98. This entire paragraph is based on comments on the cited page.

[41] Ibid, pg 99-100. This entire section draws heavily from this source, pp. 99-110.

[42] Ibid, pg 106.

[43] Ibid, pg 107-108 is source of this example.

[44] Ibid, pg 162-163.

[45] Ibid, pg 176-178.

[46] Ibid, pg 176-177.

[47] Ibid, pg 112.

[48] Ibid, pg 171.

[49] Ibid, pg. 176.

[50] Ibid, pp. 174-175.

[51] Ibid, pp. 165-166.

[52] This case illustration is taken from the discussion of "Target Costing at Caterpillar". The entire discussion of Caterpillar draws very heavily from this reference, using paraphrasing and bullet points from the original work. For a more comprehensive example, the reader is referred to the CAM-I publication, *Target Costing: The Next Frontier in Strategic Cost Management*, op.cit., pp. 140-158.

Chapter **6**

Asset Management

The importance of money essentially flows from its being a link between the present and the future.

– John Maynard Keynes

Key Learnings:

■ There are a broad range of *assets,* or tangible and intangible resources, that can be used to create future value for customers.

■ Creating value for customers requires three distinct types of assets or "capital": financial capital, physical assets, and intellectual capital.

■ Asset Management details the requirements for, and tracks the progress of, new resource acquisitions that are often critical if strategic and tactical objectives are to be met.

■ The five principles guiding asset investment decisions are:[1] (1) Relate investment decisions to the strategic plans and operating goals of the company; (2) Evaluate the investment alternatives consistently; (3) Evaluate investment alternatives using multiple decision attributes that include both financial and non-financial criteria (4) Assess risk in evaluating investment alternatives; and (5) Establish a management system that provides the cost and performance data needed to evaluate investment decisions.

Every organization has at its command resources that can be used to create value for its stakeholders. Varying widely in their capacity to support work over time, these resources are as diverse in nature as they are in their use. To reduce the complexity surrounding resources, categories have been created, such as those resources classified as "assets" on a balance sheet of a firm. Assets are traditionally considered to be those resources which can have a reasonably accurate economic value placed on them, and that this value-creating capability can be stored. Resources that cannot be stored or accurately valued become either expenses or are ignored in the accounting model altogether.

The traditional view of assets and their management has reflected these rather narrow definitions and treatments. Today, though, companies are increasingly becoming aware that there are a broad range of *assets*, or tangible and intangible resources, that can be used to create future value for customers. Not every one of these can be measured in economic terms either at their purchase or their use, but they are critically important to the long-term viability of the organization.

The *Value Quest* begins with the directed transformation of all forms of assets, or resources at the firm's command, into the value-enhancing product/service bundles that lead to competitive strength. Once obtained, these assets must be actively managed to ensure that their value-creating capacity is utilized. Creating value for customers requires three distinct types of assets or "capital" (see Figure 6.1): financial capital, physical assets, and intellectual capital. It is the latter of these which poses the greatest challenge, and holds the greatest promise of benefit, for modern management. The three forms of assets (physical, financial and intellectual) are constantly interacting to create new opportunities and challenges for management. A sound information strategy, built around key decision contexts, such as that embodied in the CAM-I Strategic Management Process (SMP) Model, can help a firm accelerate its learning.

Asset Management plays a pivotal role in the CAM-I SMP Model. Asset Management details the requirements for, and tracks the progress of, new resource acquisitions that are often critical if strategic and tactical objectives are to be met. Asset Management moves beyond the purchase of new physical resources, though, to examine the competencies of the human resources of the firm. Investments in human capital can often spell the difference between success and failure of new programs and strategies.

Figure 6.1 The Assets of the Firm

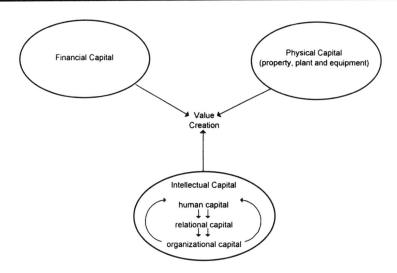

Source: *The Management of Intellectual Capital: The Issues and the Practice,* Hamilton, Ontario: The Society of Management Accountants of Canada, 1998: 15.

A recent publication on knowledge management, the emerging discipline that emphasizes the creation and application of new tools to the intellectual capital area, notes:[2]

Sustained value creation and long-run corporate survival involve a dynamic exchange among all forms of corporate capital.

The assets of the firm, whether easy to see and measure or not, work together to create value. It is a dynamic process, where shifting customer demand and changes in both the internal and external environment make effective Asset Management difficult. Difficult though it may be, effective asset management is the cornerstone of the *Value Quest.*

To cover this broad topic, this chapter will only briefly delve into the issues and concerns for each of the three classes of capital, or assets, that the firm has at its command. This is not to downplay the importance of the financial or intellectual capital aspects of this SMP, but is rather a practical reflection of the current progress in these areas as well as their impact on the overall information system that the SMP Model embodies. Things that cannot be measured or seen are difficult to include physically in the information system. While some suggestions for measuring the relative value of these less traditional assets will be made, it is a field that is just beginning to take shape— a future challenge to be met.

Managing Physical Assets

Put not your trust in money, but your money in trust.

– Oliver Wendell Holmes

One of the primary obligations of managers is to create value for the shareholders of their organization. While simple in concept, achieving this goal presents significant challenges. Investments in new products, processes, or human and physical assets requires management to make estimates of current and future direct cash flows from the investment. Separating the promised improvements of one asset from the complex actions and interactions that it is embedded within, let alone precisely assessing the risk of these investments, is a challenge that might lead some, as it does Oliver Wendell Holmes, to put their money in trust.

The issues facing managers attempting to make these trade-offs and assessments, include estimating the dollarizable benefits, quantifiable benefits (tangible, measurable benefits such as improved quality or cycle time that may be hard to dollarize), and qualitative benefits of an opportunity given the level of investment required. If indirect and intangible benefits are ignored, strategic investments may not be made. Conversely, if these potential benefits are overstated, investments that do not ultimately increase shareholder value may be undertaken. Since Asset Management[3] is by definition charged with attempting to part the veil that separates today's events and tomorrow's possibilities, it requires significant analysis, estimating, sensitivity testing, risk assessment, and integration with other core SMPs to perform optimally.

Asset Management goes beyond the assessment and choice of investments to include tracking investments after implementation to ensure that promised benefits are achieved. Asset Management interacts directly with Capacity Management and Integrated

Performance Management to complete these post-purchase tasks. While not involved in the daily decisions that assign acquired assets to specific uses, Asset Management remains in the foreground as an ever-present reminder that every investment must increase the value-creating ability of the firm. Assets are not acquired for convenience or their intrinsic beauty by organizations. They are expected to support performance improvements and achievement of strategic objectives.

Placing Asset Management within the SMP Model framework that was introduced in Chapter Five, ten basic steps emerge (see Figure 6.2):

1. Determine the product portfolio plan.
2. Determine core competencies.
3. Identify technology requirements.
4. Identify process requirements.
5. Develop technology and process capability acquisition plan.
6. Establish strategic sourcing/outsourcing plan.
7. Establish internal/external investment performance metrics.
8. Implement acquisition plan.
9. Perform investment post audit.
10. Perform continuous improvement.

As this list suggests, Asset Management is intricately tied to the product/service bundle offered by the firm. It is the choice of specific products and services that defines the nature and number of resources needed by the firm. Not all resource needs, though, should be addressed by investments in specific assets or capabilities. It is often more logical to outsource non-core areas so that scarce internal resources can be directed to areas of the business that will yield a competitive advantage.

Having determined which assets will be acquired and which needs will be addressed through the Extended Enterprise, attention turns to crafting a specific technology and process capability acquisition plan. This plan should include details on potential sources of the asset, key features the asset must possess, lead time, limits on total costs for the asset, and expected returns from the investment. As the acquisition plan is being crafted, investment performance metrics for the asset will need to be developed. These metrics serve a dual

114

Chapter 6   ASSET MANAGEMENT

Figure 6.2   The Asset Management SMP

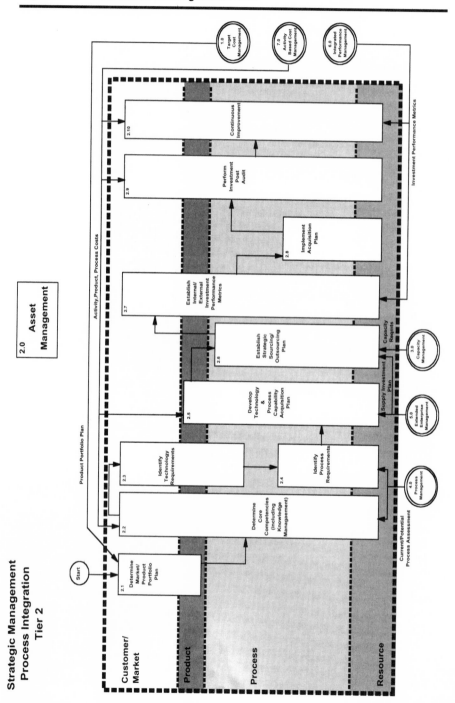

purpose: to help prioritize investment options prior to their acquisition and to support downstream efforts to ensure that promised benefits are realized.

This complex setting implies that applying Asset Management techniques to current and potential business opportunities is a principle-driven rather than routine process decision process. The five principles guiding asset investment decisions are:[4]

1. Relate investment decisions to the strategic plans and operating goals of the company. Set up performance measures that compare the results of the decision with the company's strategy.

2. Evaluate the investment alternatives consistently.

3. Evaluate investment alternatives using multiple decision attributes that include both financial and nonfinancial criteria.

4. Assess risk in evaluating investment alternatives.

5. Establish a management system that provides the cost and performance data needed to evaluate investment decisions.

These five principles combine to create a framework for asset investment decisions that result in a natural linkage to operational and strategic objectives and initiatives.

An asset investment strategy is driven by current and planned product/service bundle offerings and shaped by the changing business environment. It is a long-term business issue that has significant implications for a firm's overall manufacturing strategy, its sourcing/partnering strategy, the cost competitiveness of the Extended Enterprise, the level of customer service provided, human resource management, manufacturing flexibility, and product line management.[5] As noted by Howell and Schwartz, "If capital investment decisions within a firm are handled on a short-term, annual basis, the decisions over time are likely to conflict. They may, therefore, become counterproductive and dysfunctional."[6]

In a traditional asset investment analysis, the capital budget is developed once the strategic plan is approved. Having set investment limits, top management is then presented with a potpourri of engineering and operations investment options, all "justified" with the hurdle rates or payback policies of the firm. These investments are

Figure 6.3 Asset Management—A Problem Solving Approach

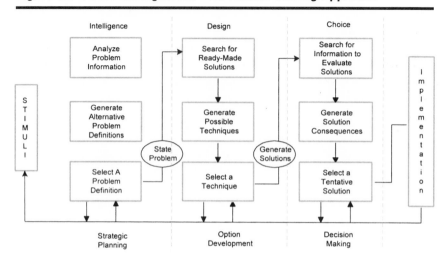

Source: Klammer, *Managing Strategic and Capital Investment Decisions*, Homewood, IL: Irwin Professional Publishing, 1994: 55.

not coordinated in any meaningful way. The end result is that a piecemeal approach to investment management may emerge that can actually lead to sub-optimal performance over time. While individual departments may show improved performance, the entity may actually experience reduced levels of shareholder and customer value creation. In fact, excess capacity, purchased on the basis of projected labor savings that quite likely never get achieved at the entity level (labor is transferred, not eliminated), gives the impression of improvement that is in reality a new form of waste.

To counteract this problem, a four stage asset investment approach can be followed (see Figure 6.3).[7] By tightly linking the strategic planning process to the list of options considered for acquisition analysis, an organization can combat the tendency to make piecemeal investments that do not yield long-term strategic benefit. Having created a list of options that reflect strategic concerns, the actual decision process to choose one specific asset or resource solution is undertaken, executed and monitored. Of the steps in this diagram, traditional Asset Management approaches have only emphasized the decision-making to execution activities. Having overlooked the essential ingredient—the strategic focus of the firm—these traditional models can lead to a confused asset strategy and open the way for gamesmanship and politics in the investment decision. Of course, there are tremendous hurdles facing a firm attempting to implement a strategic approach to Asset Management. Not the least of these challenges is the very real fact that not all key variables are measurable, and not all investments are equally complex. These realistic challenges to the development of an effective asset investment and management approach require the development of innovative measurement and evaluation approaches, such as that detailed in Figure 6.4. As this example suggests, intangible concerns and issues can be included in the assessment and choice of an asset investment option based on what benefits the asset offers compared to defined strategic objectives and how well it meets those objectives. Serving to add structure to the qualitative aspects of the decision, scoring models such as these can lead to a balanced investment strategy. Since the qualitative aspects of investment decisions are as important as their quantitative, or cash flow impacts, creating models that help highlight relative benefits of asset investment options is a critical step in the crafting of an effective asset strategy.

There are a number of ways that a firm can conduct its formal asset investment analysis on definable, quantitative benefits. Traditionally, three primary methods have been used: (1) the years' payback method; (2) the accounting rate of return method; and, (3) the discounted cash flow (DCF) method. Surveys indicate that these three techniques are widely used, with some 58 percent of 1,000 surveyed major companies using payback methods, 39 percent using DCF, 32 percent using a form of cost/benefit analysis, 10 percent employing strategic methods, and a final 10 percent using other approaches.[8] Since these results sum to more than 100 percent, it is clear that some companies use multiple quantitative approaches.[9]

Such traditional methods have been under increasing criticism because they fail to take into account the interdependence between various investments and the potential to reap significant performance improvements by melding together a portfolio of investments.[10] To gain enhanced benefits, the asset investment process must be tightly aligned to overall business results rather than being conducted as an independent financial analysis.

Several new forms of investment measurement are emerging to create a strategic perspective. These models emphasize increases in

Figure 6.4 Strategic Benefits Profile

Strategic Objectives	Relative Weight	Current Operations Rating	Current Operations Score	CIM Implementation Rating	CIM Implementation Score
Cost Reduction					
Minimize Direct Labor	20	1	20	8	120
Minimize Indirect Labor					
Reduce Material Costs					
Reduce Inventory Costs	25	2	50	9	225
Minimize Set-up/Lead-time					
Minimize Scrap/Rework					
Maximize Equipment Utilization					
Reduce Floor Space	15	5	75	5	75
Increase Throughput Time					
Minimize Capital Expenditures	3	8	21	2	6
Productivity Involvement					
Increase Design and Manufacturing Productivity	10	3	30	6	60
Increase Production Control					
Minimize Forecasting Lead-time					
Reduce Paperwork	5	2	10	7	35
Provide Real-time Information	5	2	10	7	35
Increase Employee Morale					
Meet Increased Capacity Needs	2	1	2	8	16
Competitive					
Increase Market Share					
Increase Product Growth					
Maximize Customer Satisfaction	5	3	15	8	40
Develop Flexibility to Meet Demand					
Reduce Unit Cost					
Improve Response to New Market Opportunities					
Increase Competitive Advantage	10	2	20	7	70
Total	100		248		682
Rating: 10 -- Objective fully met 1 -- Objective not met					

Source: R. Howell and W. Schwartz, "Asset Deployment and Investment Justification," *Handbook of Cost Management*, New York: Warren, Gorham and Lamont, 1997: D4-22.

shareholder value as the basis for initial investment and ongoing evaluation of capital projects. The key principles of the shareholder value perspective for Asset Management include:[11]   (1) increasing returns from existing assets (profitability); (2) making incremental investments that have a return above the firm's cost of capital (growth); and, (3) freeing up cash to return it to investors when profitable investments are not available (use of free cash flow for regular dividends and other cash distributions). The factors driving shareholder-based value measurement reflect these principles and include the following:

- cash flow generation is more indicative of value creation than accounting earnings;
- capital has a measurable cost and must be deployed efficiently;
- financial performance at all levels of the business must be measured consistently;
- objective evaluation criteria should be sought over subjective, negotiated criteria; and
- performance measures must be tied to shareholder value creation.

The resulting shareholder value measurements provide a significant number of benefits to the firm and its stakeholders. Whether analyzed in terms of their Economic Value-Added (EVA)[12] or Market Value-Added (MVA)[13] or both, the goal of these new metrics is to ensure that the investment results in a positive cash flow effect that benefits the firm's primary stakeholders. The basic logic underlying the shareholder value framework is summarized in Figure 6.5, which depicts the relationship between strategic decision-making, the value drivers of the business, and the resulting Asset investment criteria used by a firm.

The alternatives available for identifying, assessing, and choosing among various asset investment options vary widely in how well they incorporate risk into the decision analysis, their entity – versus unit-focus, and their support for ongoing improvement and evaluation efforts. This suggests that more than one method of appraisal should be used. Specifically, a multi-dimensional investment analysis and appraisal system should be developed that:[14]

- emphasizes both short - and long-term goals;
- ensures that new investments are assessed within a total entity perspective;
- adjusts for the risks faced by the firm in making the investment;
- incorporates both income and cash flow requirements;
- adjusts for the time value of money or required rates of return to ensure that the investment creates a positive return for shareholders;
- includes adequate checks and balances to minimize gamesmanship;
- incorporates multi-period audit, review, and assessment to ensure that promised benefits are gained; and
- is integrated into the performance management and cost management systems in an explicit manner that encourages managers to take a long-term, shareholder-focused, entity-enhancing approach to asset acquisition and deployment.

Figure 6.5 Shareholder Value Framework

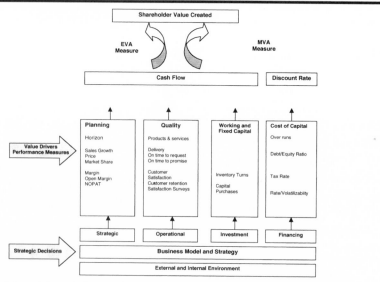

Source: Adapted from Arthur Andersen's, *Shareholder Value Creation Measures Primer*, Arthur Andersen LLP, 1998: pg. 3. Presented with permission

Of these requirements, the need to integrate the investment measures and decision models into the incentive system remains one of the most critical elements in transforming the culture of the firm to reflect a value creation perspective. As has been noted in the preceding pages, this integration will not happen by chance. Integrating information flows, and the Strategic Management Processes (SMPs) that structure them, is the key to crafting an effective Asset Management strategy that creates a positive growth trend for the firm.

Without a sound human and financial capital strategy, though, the benefits promised by physical asset investment proposals cannot be attained. It is to these other aspects of the Asset Management effort that attention now turns.

Financial Asset Management

There are no intrinsic reasons for the scarcity of capital.

– John Maynard Keynes

A recent book on capital structure strategies by Davis and Sihler[15] notes that, *"Financial decisions are very simple in structure—the judgments get complex."* These authors make an interesting comment that serves to tie the discussions in this chapter together:[16] *"Assets, once predominantly physical but now increasingly of an intellectual nature, generate the stream of cash that attracts investment."* Choosing an optimal capital structure, the essential concern in crafting an Asset Management strategy for financial resources, is no exception to this rule. Four components make up the capital structure decision: asset selection, debt-equity proportion, new equity issuance, and dividend payout policies. These four components interact (see Figure 6.6), creating the need to simultaneously make the decisions on these factors if a firm's financial value is to be optimized.

The capital structure decision in the organization is tied to the "2" in Figure 6.6. Here, the proportions of the firm's capital that will be raised from the debt and equity market is determined, which drives the split between interest and after-tax earnings for the firm. A third decision, namely whether or not to issue new equity, can affect the debt/equity ratio as well as the value of the equity in the hands of current investors. It may not always make sense to acquire new equity funding, even if the assets that would be acquired with these funds would provide a positive return to investment. In reality, current owners face dilution of their interests if new equity is raised. Lastly, the dividend policy is set. If the firm needs more financial resources, and it has decided to forego new equity, then dividends may be reduced to provide needed funds. If new funds are raised, then the decisions about dividend policies become more complex.

Figure 6.6 Components of the Capital Structure Decision

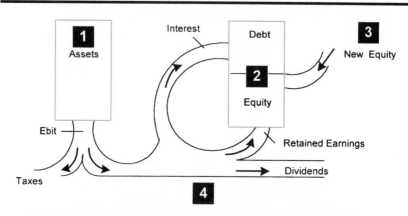

Source: Adapted from H. Davis and W. Sihler, *Building Value with Capital-Structure Strategies*, New York: Financial Executives Research Foundation, 1998: pg. 7.

Some firms, such as Marriott International, Monsanto and Oracle are repurchasing stock when the price seems favorable to offset the potential dilution of value created by employee stock-option programs. Others use stock repurchases to return cash to investors in ways beneficial for tax purposes. Monsanto also uses stock repurchases to make capital structure adjustments whenever excess funds remain after designated R&D and capital expenditures have been made. In each of these cases, firms are actively managing their debt-to-equity ratios and the value of shares of individual investors to increase their ability to gain new funds when needed or retain investments already in hand.

Managing the organization's financial assets means more than choosing a specific debt-to-equity structure or applying for new funds from the market. It includes the active management of financial assets by the firm. For instance, no well run treasury function today would dream of leaving cash sitting idly in any account, even overnight. At the end of each business day cash is invested in liquid securities that can yield significant returns over the course of a year. The distribution between long- and short-term investments, the structure of working capital (cash versus short-term investments versus inventory) and the use of off-balance sheet financial solutions are all ways that firms manage their financial resources to stretch their benefits.

Effective Asset Management policies for financial resources are intricately tied to the physical and intellectual assets that are purchased with these funds. If poor investments are undertaken with raised capital, there will be inadequate funds for shareholder payments. If debt becomes too large a share of the firm's financial assets, then hurdle rates for new asset investments will be raised and fewer funds will be available for new ventures. The three forms of assets of the firm—physical, financial and intellectual—represent a dynamic mix of past results and future opportunities. They serve to both constrain and support the creation of value for customers.

The choices made to pick one financial strategy or resource option over another need to incorporate global effects, such as exchange rate hedging, the placement of manufacturing or distribution to optimize costs, or the operation of facilities to attain global capacity management or cost goals. The study by Davis and Sihler[17] suggests that companies tend to set the policies that shape their capital structures based on management's perceptions of business needs and risks as well as what investments truly lead to enhanced shareholder value. These policies are seldom changed unless there are significant changes in the circumstances facing the firm, such as a major shift in the exchange rates for key trading partners/countries.

Financial asset decisions are fairly routine in nature, reflect overall management goals and control concerns, and serve to shape the opportunities open to, and pursued by, the firm. A firm that follows conservative policies in its capital structure will not grow at the same rate as more aggressive firms. High growth, though, comes at increased risk as fixed interest payments become a greater drain on the firm.

For the Asset Management Strategic Management Process, these issues come down to just a few points:

- the feasibility of customer/market and product strategies is driven in no small part by the available financial assets of the firm;

- if financial resources are scarce, there will be few opportunities to improve overall firm performance against customer requirements;

- performance evaluation and investment audit requirements should reflect the financial asset strategy of the firm;

- changes in the capital structure of the firm should be minimized because of their impact on the other decisions of the firm as well as its perceived value in the market; and

- new forms of asset investment management, such as EVA and MVA, provide a clear linkage between the financial and physical asset decisions, practices, and performance of the firm.

Financial assets are both the source, and the outcome, of effective Asset Management. Whether on the shop floor or in the development laboratory, the assets of the firm must work together to create new value for stakeholders. As Keynes suggests in the opening quotation to this section, there are no intrinsic reasons for scarcity of capital. If assets are managed effectively, they increase in value. If they are managed poorly, no amount of new debt or equity can be obtained that will undo the loss of value—the waste—that emerges. Knowledge Management, the last of the primary asset categories, is the key to ensuring positive results.

Knowledge Management

Undertake something that is difficult; it will do you good.
Unless you try to do something that is beyond
what you have already mastered, you will never grow.

– Ronald E. Osborn

Knowledge Management is an area of intense study as company after company comes to realize that many of its key value-creating assets walk out the door every evening. Failing to find a systematic way to catalogue, share, build, and sustain knowledge capital can expose a firm to significant business risks that can undermine the effectiveness of a chosen strategy. A company that cannot find a way to structure and manage its knowledge creation efforts cannot become a "learning organization". It is people, not organizations, who learn. Organizations can, though, systematize individual learning to create shared knowledge.

At the World Bank, Knowledge Management is being defined and developed to ensure that key business strategies are addressed, as the following suggests:[18]

> *Knowledge Management is……. "an interrelated set of knowledge creating, capturing, distilling, and dissemination processes aimed at increasing individual capabilities, and transferring information and knowledge to the organizational level from, between, and within the organization and outside such that individuals can take more effective action."*

Five primary roles and responsibilities have been defined by the World Bank in its development of a Knowledge Management system: knowledge leaders, knowledge architects, knowledge coordinators, regional knowledge advocates, and knowledge workers (see Figure 6.7).

Figure 6.7 A Knowledge Management System Framework

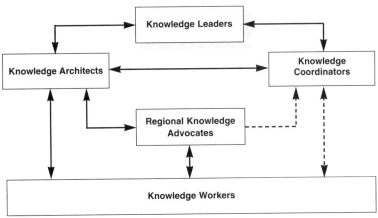

Source: Adapted from the World Bank Knowledge Management Working Paper, 1996: pg. 32. Provided by, and used with permission of, Arthur Andersen LLP.

Knowledge leaders in the emerging Knowledge Management system at the World Bank will be responsible for developing knowledge strategies that are linked to the bank's strategic objectives and that allow it to capture key knowledge within the organization.

Coordinators, on the other hand, are assigned responsibility for working with internal and external sources to develop and maintain knowledge system content, develop a common classification scheme for this knowledge, and organize non-technology based knowledge sharing forums. Knowledge architects in the World Bank knowledge management system provide the technology and management infrastructures to maintain the system, while knowledge advocates champion the Knowledge Management concept within the organization. Knowledge workers, then, are responsible for using and contributing to the Bank's knowledge base.

Knowledge Management is most useful if it results in revenue producing products and customer solutions—the desired end of the knowledge chain. Data, organized into information, leads to knowledge. The addition of experience and commercialization to knowledge helps transform this intangible into products and services for the market. While knowledge may be an intangible, the results of its application can be defined and measured.

Information plays a key role in the development of knowledge in an organization.[19] Information that has been internalized and structured by the organization becomes the basis for its knowledge system. When knowledge is made valuable it becomes intellectual capital. Intangible by nature, this progression from data to capital can result in an exponential growth curve for the firm as ideas are transformed into reality. Ideas are intellectual assets, as are the physical and intangible databases that generate them.

Some proponents of Knowledge Management suggest that the difference between a firm's market value and the present value of its physical and financial assets is the value of its intellectual capital.[20] If this is so, it would suggest that knowledge creation is the key to sustainable growth. No other form of asset can earn exponential returns per dollar invested. It is new ideas, funded by the financial assets and deployed through physical assets, that leads to new products, new markets, and new forms of competitive advantage. It is a lesson that has been leveraged time and again by 3M Corporation to create long-term growth and superior profits and performance.

The goal of Asset Management in the area of intellectual capital is to link Knowledge Management to financial and nonfinancial outcomes of value to customers and shareholders. In other words, Asset Management helps a firm leverage its intellectual capital in a reliable, measurable way—to take the luck out of gaining exponential growth through innovation.

Figure 6.8 Elements of Intellectual Capital

Human Capital	Relational (Customer) Capital	Organizational (Structural) Capital	
		Intellectual Property	Infrastructure Capital
• Know How	• Brands	• Patents	• Management Philosophy
• Education	• Customers (names, purchase history)	• Copyrights	• Corporate Culture
• Vocational Qualifications	• Customer Loyalty	• Design Rights	
• Work-related Knowledge	• Customer Penetration and Breadth	• Trade Secrets • Trademarks	• Management Processes
• Occupational Assessments		• Service Marks • Trade Dress	• Information Systems • Networking Systems
• Psychometric Assessments	Company Names		• Financial Relations
• Work-related Competencies	• Backlog Orders • Distribution Channels		• Corporate Strategies
• Models and Frameworks	• Business collaborations(joint ventures)		• Corporate Methods
• Cultural Diversity	• Licensing Agreements • Favorable Contracts • Franchising Agreement		• Sales Tools • Knowledge Bases • Expert Networks and Teams • Corporate Values

Source: *The Management of Intellectual Capital: The Issues and the Practice,* Hamilton, Ontario: The Society of Management Accountants of Canada, 1998: 14.

Not all intellectual capital is the same. To date, three classes of intellectual capital[21] have been identified in the literature:[22] human capital, structural capital and relational (customer) capital (see Figure 6.8). Human capital includes the human skills, capabilities, and expertise of employees, while structural capital is the systems, networks, and other management control systems that bridge the gap between market requirements and the available intellectual property of the firm. Finally, relational capital captures the connections of external agents to the firm, whether in the form of backorders or loyalty.

What forms of non-financial measures are being developed to assess the effectiveness of Asset Management policies in this area? Each of the three categories of intellectual capital is being measured in unique ways that reflect their inherent nature and the challenge of quantifying their costs and benefits.[23]

Organizational capital. Of the three forms of intellectual capital, organizational capital is the easiest to identify and measure. Measurements that have been developed for patents and related intangible assets include R&D expense per sales dollar, number of patents, income per R&D expense, cost of patent maintenance per sales dollar, and the project life cycle cost per sales dollar. Each of these metrics has in common its focus on matching today's dollars of investment to a yield that has occurred over time. While not perfect in nature, these metrics do provide insight into the historical yield of investments in these forms of intellectual capital by the firm. Not one, but several of these metrics should be used in tandem to evaluate the effectiveness of the intellectual capital investment efforts.

Innovation and Structural Capital. If Knowledge Management is effective, the firm should outperform its competitors in innovations identified and implemented per dollar of capital invested. Leveraging and sharing knowledge should create a culture where new ideas flow freely and reliable methods for identifying potentially high performing innovations can be created. Specifically, *"useful innovation, an item of value, arises from the interaction of human, relational and organizational capital when IC is properly managed."*[24] Indicators that can be used to track this relationship include:

- the ratio of new ideas generated to new ideas implemented;
- the number of new product introductions;
- the number of products retired;
- the proportion of income from new product introductions;
- the number of repeated mistakes per new product introduction; and
- the average length of time for product design and development.

Trended over time, each of these metrics can capture the increases in intellectual capital and the benefits it provides to the firm. A learning organization should expect to see improvements on each of these metrics over a reasonable period of time (one to five years).

Human Capital Indicators. One of the major concerns in any organization is retaining the services of key employees who are free to sell their time and knowledge to the highest bidder. While efforts have been made in the past to create a form of accounting that captures the human resource component of the firm's asset base, the transitory nature of this resource (human capital can be neither stored nor guaranteed to return tomorrow) makes any formal treatment of its value questionable. Even so, there are ways that the human capital of the firm can be tracked:

- employee training and development expenses as a percentage of total costs;
- the reputation of company employees with headhunters;
- years of experience in the profession;
- the rookie ratio (percent of employees with less than two years experience);
- employee satisfaction;
- the proportion of employees suggesting new ideas;
- value-added per employee or salary dollar;
- the number of knowledge builders; and
- the number of knowledge silos (e.g., organizational units closed off from sharing knowledge), which means the organization cannot leverage this knowledge.

Tracking the involvement of employees in new initiatives, their overall motivation, and the retention of key individuals are just a few of the ways the firm can ensure that its human capital policies are yielding positive returns.

Relational Capital Indicators. Maintaining customer loyalty may be one of the single most important things a company can do to ensure its long-term viability. Similarly, it is becoming increasingly clear that good supplier relationships, such as those created by the Extended Enterprise, can lead to performance and profitability improvements. Customer/supplier relationships are part of the intellectual capital of the firm, and can be monitored in a number of ways, including:

- growth in business volume;
- the proportion of sales by repeat customers;
- brand loyalty (preference) metrics;
- customer satisfaction;
- product returns as a proportion of sales;

- the number of supplier/customer alliances;
- the number (and value) of supplier/customer shared systems, such as electronic data exchange;
- the proportion of a customer's (supplier's) business that your product represents;
- customer referrals and recommendations; and
- the number of cross-sales.

As the value of the customer/supplier relationship grows, so does the effectiveness of the firm to leverage its investments in these relationships as well as all other forms of assets under its control. Reflecting the basic philosophy of the CAM-I SMP Model, the effective management of intellectual capital requires an integrated perspective that leverages every potential opportunity for performance improvement.

While a number of metrics have been suggested for intellectual capital, the embodiment of knowledge creation efforts, it remains an unavoidable fact that few of these metrics can be included in the financial reporting system. That simply makes it more important than ever that they be estimated and incorporated in the information system created by the integration of the SMPs into the CAM-I SMP Model. Where financial systems may fall short, the SMP Model can extend far beyond the boundaries of convention. The linkage of core data between the SMPs that comprise the Model also ensures that trends in performance can be correlated and that a multi-dimensional assessment of Asset Management effectiveness can be conducted.

Summary

That which seems the height of absurdity in one generation often becomes the height of wisdom in another.

– Adlai Stevenson

There are probably a few individuals who were solid proponents of human resource accounting in the 1960s[25] and 1970s who feel that Stevenson's quote may have been written specifically for them. In no area has new models and approaches become so common as in Asset Management. Whether physical, financial, or knowledge-based, constantly improving the utilization and leveraging of a firm's assets is the basis for its continued innovativeness and growth.

This chapter has provided a brief overview of the key Asset Management issues. Much of the material presented draws from sources outside of CAM-I, but as has been seen, the insights and focus of the information conveyed has been consistent with the CAM-I SMP Model. As each new SMP is added to the set of tools in the information system, management can effectively leverage more and more of its assets in interdependent ways that create exponential growth and sustainable competitive advantage.

The three forms of assets (physical, financial and intellectual) are constantly interacting to create new opportunities and challenges for management. A sound information strategy, built around key decision contexts, such as that embodied in the SMP Model, can help a firm accelerate its learning. The *Value Quest* begins with the resources of today, transforming them into the value-enhancing product/service bundles that lead to competitive strength. Once obtained, these assets must be actively managed to ensure that their value-creating capacity is utilized. It is to the Capacity Management SMP that the discussion now turns.

References

Arthur Andersen LLP, Shareholder Value Creation Measures *Primer, 1998.*

Arthur Andersen LLP, *Knowledge Services*, 1999.

Chang, J., "Spreading EVA," *Chemical Market Reporter,* July 14, 1997: SR3-7.

Coca-Cola Company, The, *Accountability for EVA,* 1994.

Davis, H. and W. Sihler, *Building Value with Capital-Structure Strategies,* New York: Financial Executives Research Foundation, 1998.

Evans, P. and P. Skov, *A Guide to Risk Analysis and Management of Manufacturing Investments,* CMS Research Report, CAM-I, 1990.

Howell, R. and W. Schwartz, "Asset Deployment and Investment Justification," *Handbook of Cost Management,* New York: Warren, Gorham and Lamont, 1997: D4-1 to D4-32.

Klammer, T., *Managing Strategic and Capital Investment Decisions,* Chicago, IL Irwin Professional Publishing, 1994.

Kroll, K., "EVA and Creating Value," *Industry Week,* No. 7., Vol. 246, April 7, 1997: 102-106.

Reeve, J. and W. Sullivan, *Strategic Evaluation of Interrelated Investment Projects in Manufacturing Companies,* CMS Research Report, Bedford, TX: CAM-I, 1988.

Society of Management Accountants of Canada, *The Management of Intellectual Capital: The Issues and The Practice,* Hamilton, Ontario: 1998.

World Bank, The, *Knowledge Management Concept Paper: A Practical Approach,* November, 1996

Endnotes

1 This list, and much of this opening section, draws heavily upon comments, observations, and discussions in *Managing Strategic and Capital Investment Decisions,* T. Klammer and CAM-I Investment Management Core Team, Homewood, IL: Irwin Professional Publishing, 1994. This list appears on page 4 of this text.

2 The Society of Management Accountants of Canada (SMAC), *The Management of Intellectual Capital: The Issues and the Practice,* Hamilton, Ontario, 1998: 15.

3 Throughout this chapter the term "asset management" will be used to incorporate the traditional, more limited concepts of capital budgeting. Capital budgeting, which refers to the quantification and analysis of investment opportunities for major asset purchases, is only a part of the effort and focus of the asset management SMP.

4 This list, and much of this opening section, draws heavily upon comments, observations, and discussions in *Managing Strategic and Capital Investment Decisions,* T. Klammer and CAM-I Investment Management Core Team, Homewood, IL: Irwin Professional Publishing, 1994. This list appears on page 4 of this text.

5 Ibid.

6 R. Howell and W. Schwartz, "Asset Deployment and Asset Justification," *Handbook of Cost Management,* New York: Warren, Gorham and Lamont, 1997: D4-16.

7 This figure and the related discussion draw heavily from Klammer, op.cit., pp. 54-59.

8 Howell and Schwartz, op.cit., pg. D4-9.

9 It is beyond the focus of this text to go into depth on specific investment assessment approaches. Readers are directed toward Klammer, op.cit. and P. Evans and P. Skov, *A Guide to Risk Analysis and Management of Manufacturing Investments,* CMS Research Report, Bedford, TX: CAM-I, 1990 for more detailed discussions.

10 These insights draw heavily from Klammer, op.cit.

11 The discussion of new forms of asset investment measurement is drawn from comments and discussion in Arthur Andersen's *Shareholder Value Creation Measures Primer,* Arthur Andersen, LLP, 1998.

12 EVA is a registered trademark of Stern, Stewart.

13 EVA is assessed using a formula such as: Economic profit equals net operating profit after taxes less capital charges. MVA, on the other hand, is calculated as: [(shares outstanding x stock price) + market value of preferred stock + market value of debt] less total capital. Many firms use a combination of these two metrics in their asset investment analysis.

14 These insights and comments draw from the three primary sources noted here: Andersen, op.cit., Klammer, op.cit., and Howell and Schwartz, op.cit.

15 H. Davis and W. Sihler, *Building Value with Capital-Structure Strategies,* New York: Financial Executives Research Foundation, 1998: 6-7. This entire part of the chapter draws from this work. Specific page citations will be used where appropriate.

16 Ibid, pg. 7-8.

17 Ibid, pg. 58.

18 World Bank knowledge management working draft, November, 1996, page 3. Used with permission through Arthur Andersen LLP.

19 This section of the discussion draws heavily from *The Management of Intellectual Capital: The Issues and the Practice,* Hamilton, Ontario: The Society of Management Accountants of Canada, 1998: 4-10.

20 Op.cit., pg. 7.

[21] Knowledge management and intellectual capital are not used interchangeably in this document. Knowledge management refers to the organizational processes that serve to transform information into knowledge while intellectual capital is value-imbued emodiment of knowledge.

[22] SMAC, op.cit., pg. 13.

[23] The rest of this discussion on Knowledge management is based upon the SMAC document, op.cit., pp. 41-46. No exact quotes are used, but the discussion itself is an abbreviated paraphrasing of this original work.

[24] Ibid, pg. 43.

[25] The repetition of a footnote from the SMAC document (pg. 10) is relevant here. Specifically, *Human resource accounting has a long history dating back to Hermansson's work in 1968 and Flamholtz's numerous publications in the area in the 1970s and 1980s.* It is not a new idea, but rather one whose time has come.

Chapter 7

Capacity Management

It is not enough to be busy; so are the ants.
The question is: What are we busy about?

– Henry David Thoreau

Key Learnings:

■ Capacity Management provides information on how assets are currently being used, what resources are being wasted, and where potential improvements may be reaped.

■ Capacity sets the baseline measure for every cost estimate used in a firm. It is the denominator in the cost equation used to measure resource use and determine profitability.

■ Capacity Management is constantly interacting with the other SMPs to identify optimal production strategies under changing market conditions.

■ Six key issues combine to create the language of capacity: resource capability, baseline capacity measures, capacity deployment, capacity utilization measures, time frame of analysis, and organizational focus

The survival, let alone prosperity, of an organization depends upon the effective and efficient deployment of its physical assets, people and processes. It is not enough to have the right resources at hand—they must be put to use in ways that increase the value delivered to customers and other stakeholders. Understanding resource capability and capacity, the amount and type of work the resource can support, is the basis for a large majority of the process design and operational decisions made within a firm. Strategies and tactical plans are established based on the firm's ability to deliver promised products and services to customers. Resource capacity is a primary constraint in these deliberations.

Capacity Management provides information on how assets are currently being used, what resources are being wasted, and where potential improvements may be reaped. The objective of Capacity Management practices, therefore, is to support the profitable management of the value-generating competencies, processes, and capacities of an organization. Effective utilization of the firm's resources means more than simply putting them to work—it means using them wisely in ways that directly lead to customer value and increased company revenues.[1]

Over the past five years there has been increasing recognition that existing Capacity Management practices have allowed high levels of waste to be built into products and processes. In a recent study[2] it was determined that up to 75 percent of the available capacity of the firms visited went unused. Womack and Jones,[3] in their recent book *Lean Thinking,* suggest that total systems level waste may reach up to 98 percent when all forms of resources (including time) are factored into the analysis. Any company, or value chain, that simply wastes less than the norm can outperform another organization where these forms of waste are more rampant.

Having painted a fairly gloomy picture of the state-of-the-art in Capacity Management, it is important to note that company after company is beginning to increase their capacity utilization rates. Whether driven by economic necessity or management expertise, the fact remains that Capacity Management has gone from relative obscurity to become a major leverage point for many organizations seeking to remove waste and improve their value creation to cost ratios.

Capacity Management practices are a microcosm of business history over the past century. As the focus of business has changed, so have the Capacity Management practices in vogue. The reason behind this close relationship is simple—capacity sets the baseline measure for every cost estimate used in a firm. It is the denominator in the cost equation used to measure resource use and determine profitability. As the purposes served by cost estimates have changed, so have capacity practices. For instance, in the early 1900s, the primary emphasis in business circles was on efficiency. This was the era of Scientific Management, of the search for the "one right way" to perform work. In this search for absolutes, capacity measurements were set at their theoretical limits—their peak efficiency. Any capacity not utilized was reported as idle capacity (waste) on the firm's *published* income statement.[4]

A modern manager would find this treatment difficult to comprehend. In fact, during the 1930s, as the country's attention turned away from efficiency to ensuring that everyone had a job, the message embedded in idle capacity was undesirable. The goal in this second major era in U.S. economic history of the 20th century was to keep people busy. While Thoreau may have relegated this goal to that of the ants, the societal impact of idle human and physical resources made any other solution unacceptable. So, the "best" way to measure capacity became to focus on how much work the firm intended to do (normal or budgeted capacity), not on what work it could do.

As with so many aspects of business practice, this treatment of capacity gave way to renewed concern with waste as the impact of the global economy began to be felt in industry after industry. Today, though, companies do not simply seek efficiency, they desire effectiveness—doing the right things the right way. In this world, idle capacity is preferable to using resources to build inventories or perform busy work. While theoretical capacity is once again the preferred method of setting baseline capacity levels, the reason for its use has changed. Specifically, if idle capacity can be utilized to create value-added products, services and activities, it should be. If the use of the resources is not driven by customer needs, then its use is not a good economic decision.

It is beyond the scope of this book to go into any more depth on the trends that have shaped the Capacity Management Strategic Management Process (SMP) over the last century.[5] The goal is, instead, to detail how Capacity Management interfaces with the other core SMPs to create a reliable, accurate, and relevant database of information for management's use in making strategic, tactical and operational decisions. Subsequent sections of this chapter will detail the various issues that affect Capacity Management and the models

Figure 7.1 Capacity Management SMP Framework

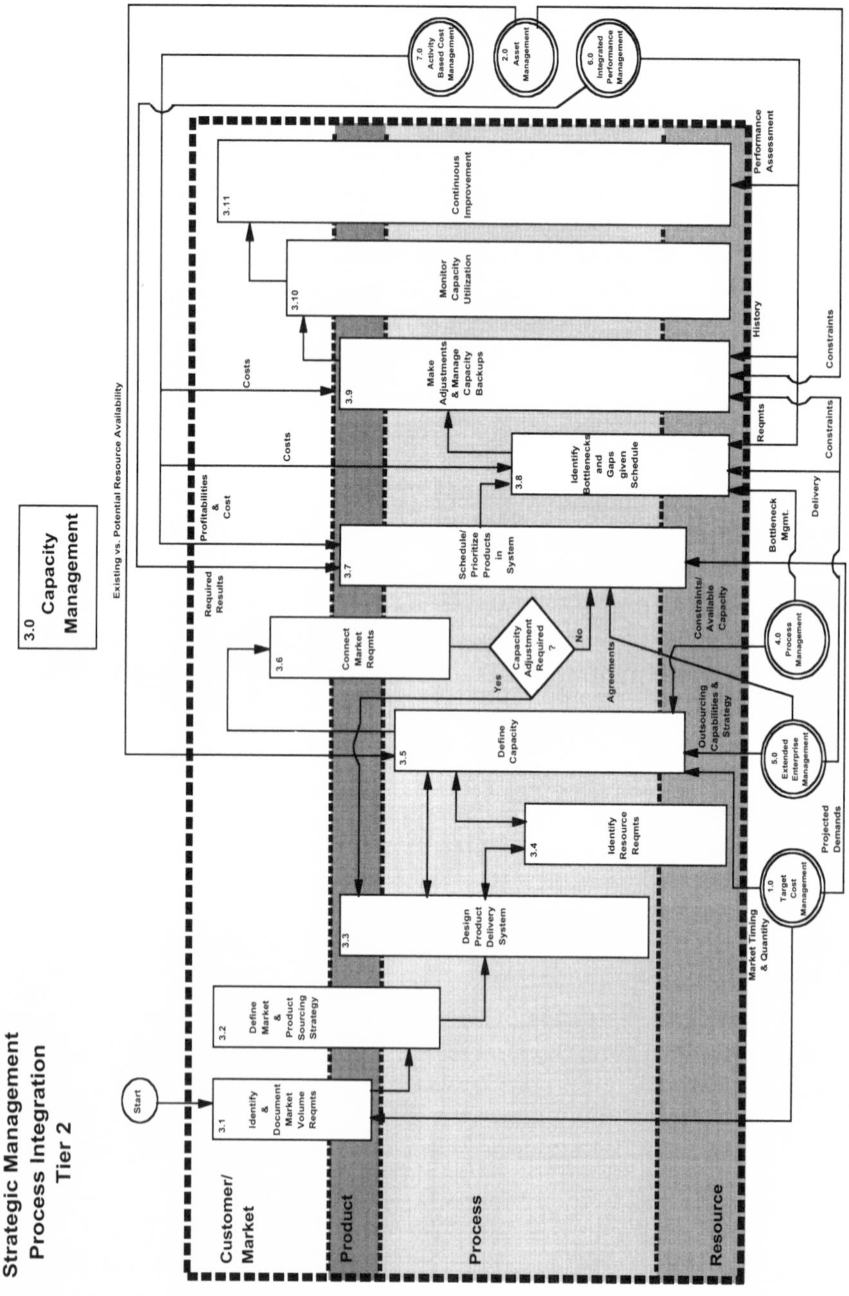

that have been developed to provide information for use in a variety of settings and database applications. The chapter ends with a case study of a company that is using Capacity Management to improve its performance—to shape its *Value Quest.*

Capacity Measurement and Management

Obviously, the highest type of efficiency is that which can utilize existing material to the best advantage.

– Jawaharlal Nehru

Capacity Management is a pivotal supporting SMP. It seldom is the first type of data needed to make a decision, but rather provides information to other SMPs more central to resolving the issues at hand. Even so, this is a major SMP in the CAM-I SMP Model because it provides data integral to so many different types of decisions. Every time a cost estimate is used, some judgment of potential capacity has to be made—it is an unescapable fact of business life. Whether the capacity estimate is made actively (by observation), or passively (using historical data), it affects the economics of a decision. Spreading costs over more (or less) units has a major effect on the estimated cost of a product, service or activity. Choosing a capacity baseline sets the cost limits *perceived by the management of the firm.*

As with each of the SMPs, there is a sequence of steps that are undertaken to implement and use Capacity Management (see Figure 7.1). The first step is the identification and documentation of market requirements for specific product/service bundles. Taking place within the Customer/Market and Product decision domains, Capacity Management turns to Target Cost Management to gain insights into what types and amounts of capacity the firm will need in the next one to five years.

Capacity needs, though, cannot all be met with direct company investments. In fact, once market requirements have been established, attention turns to the current investment strategy of the firm. Are assets being purchased only for core processes, with outsourcing of any non-core effort? Can the needed capacity be obtained by using currently idle resources elsewhere in the firm or value chain? If an asset is to be purchased, what level of capacity must it have? What investment requirements (e.g., returns) must it provide? Working in tandem with Asset Management, Capacity Management seeks to identify an optimal resource strategy that will ensure that the cost and performance requirements set during Target Cost Management will be met.

As the product/service bundle is moved from concept toward execution, it becomes important to begin to design the processes and support systems that will be used by the bundle. Capacity Management now links with Process Management as various solutions to performance requirements and potential problems are analyzed. Understanding what capabilities the process, and its key resources, must have is critical if an effective process design is to be attained. Part of the system's design is the designation of specific resources and capabilities that will be embedded within the design. Since over 80 percent of the total costs for operating a system—its cost limits—are set during process design, it is essential that adequate time be spent to ensure that excess capacity, or waste, is not embedded in the design of the system (see Figure 7.2).

After the system has been designed, the actual limits of the system, based on planned bottleneck and constraints, can be explored. How much work the system needs to be capable of is determined during Target Cost Management. The key information used to set capacity limits is market timing and quantity as well as approximate times when initial and peak demand levels are expected. Setting the system's capacity limits requires a complete analysis of demand patterns, competitive data, product portfolio impacts of the new launch, and market constraint data. The goal is to design the system to meet peak demand with little or no excess or wasted capacity.

Having connected the market requirements to the design of the system and established its capacity requirements over time, attention turns to managing the capacity. The first task completed here is the scheduling and prioritizing of specific products or services. Where TCM provides projected demand data, the Extended Enterprise details outsourcing and supply agreements affecting the schedule. Process Management, on the other hand, details constraint utilization and available capacity, while Activity-Based Cost Management helps identify the optimal mix of products for the given period. As can be seen in this description, Capacity Management is constantly interacting with the other SMPs to identify optimal production strategies under changing market conditions.

Figure 7.2 System Capacity—Design

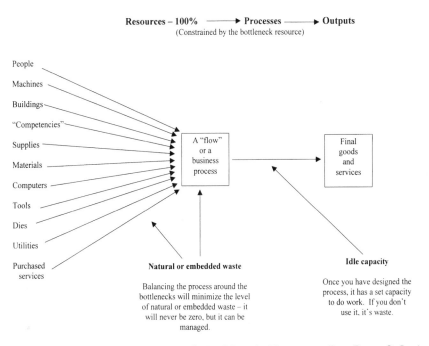

Source: C. McNair and R. Vangermeersch, *Total Capacity Management*, Boca Raton: St. Lucie Press, 1998: pg. 33.

As the schedule is set, the need to identify bottlenecks and gaps, given the schedule, emerges. Before any product is run, it can be estimated where potential problems may occur due to the projected mix or volume of output required to meet customer requirements. Interacting with Process Management to identify and assess changeover times, process flexibility, constraints, quality limits, and surge capacity, Capacity Management turns the projected demand into a physical production schedule. The Extended Enterprise validates lead times, raw material quality levels, quantity limits given the capabilities of trading partners, and the availability of surge capacity. Activity-Based Cost Management helps set priorities once again, as process costs per minute, outsourcing costs, costs of using "off process" assets to bridge output gaps, and bottleneck costs are analyzed to identify the optimal output profile for the process. Finally, Integrated Performance Management details the required performance levels for the system in terms of profitability, quality, delivery and related customer-defined metrics.

Even though schedules are developed in some detail, there is the need for ongoing adjustments to the actual flow as capacity back-ups due to unscheduled or unanticipated problems occur. The inputs from the same SMPs that support the initial scheduling effort are once again combined within the Capacity Management SMP to support analysis and decision-making in real time. Having completed a period of operation, the system's performance (whether people- or machine-based) is evaluated, reports are completed, and continuous improvement targets set. Coming full circle, the management of capacity leads to the identification of new forms of idle, available, and required capacity that must be considered as higher level decisions at the customer/market and product domains are made. Effectively managing capacity is both a long-term and short-term challenge spanning the entire set of decision domains. It incorporates and provides information to all of the other SMPs, as the firm's performance limits are set and met. Understanding capacity is to know the total value-creating potential of an organization.

Of course, these steps are more challenging to complete when the product under consideration is actually a service. While it is possible to develop estimates for different aspects of an engagement in a professional service firm, or demand for specific activities in other service settings, it is much more difficult to identify capacity limits. As will be noted in the following pages, it is often necessary to use benchmark standards or internal limits on the total cost and per occurrence costs of a service area to set capacity "limits" in these situations. While it may be more difficult to do, the effective management of human capital is at least, if not more, important than setting and meeting theoretical limits on the plant floor. Human capital is the source of the products and services that will utilize existing capacity, identify downstream process needs, and fill the gaps that emerge. Capacity is a concept for all systems, whether people- or machine-based, one firm-centered or as part of an Extended Enterprise.

Capacity Management is a process that begins when a product or process is first envisioned, and continues through the subsequent disposal or reassignment of resources downstream. Effective

Capacity Management requires that a firm pursue the following goals:[6]

- in the short run, optimize capital decisions and the effective and flexible use of investments that have already been made;
- maximize the value delivered to customers;
- help minimize requirements for future investments;
- support effective matching of a firm's resources with current and future market opportunities;
- close any gap between market demand and a firm's capabilities. At times the firm may have excess capabilities; at others, shortages may exist. These capabilities may be physical (i.e., bricks and mortar), labor, technology or capital;
- eliminate waste in the short-, intermediate- and long-run;
- provide useful costing information on current process costs versus those proposed in current or future investment proposals (e.g., the opportunity cost of not investing in a new asset which could provide better capacity utilization/cost results);
- support the establishment of capacity utilization measurements that identify the cost of capacity and its impact on business cycles and overall company performance;
- identify the capacity required to meet strategic and operational objectives, and to estimate current available capacity;
- detail the opportunity cost of unused capacity and suggest ways to account for that cost;
- support change efforts, providing pre-decision information and analysis on the potential resource and cost implications of a planned change; and,
- create a common language for, and understanding of, capacity management.

The last point, specifically the need to develop a common language, is at the heart of developing an effective Capacity

Management system. Available, utilized, and idle capacity are just a few of the core concepts that frame a capacity discussion. Specifically, six key issues combine to create the language of capacity: resource capability, baseline capacity measures, capacity deployment, capacity utilization measures, time frame of analysis, and organizational focus.[7] Attention now turns to defining capacity and related management challenges.

The Language of Capacity

One of the difficulties in the language is that all our words from loose using have lost their edge

–Ernest Hemingway

A business depends upon enabling resources and their effective deployment to create value for their stakeholders. The flexibility of resources as well as the firm's ability to match them to the specific needs of the organization and its customers sets the limits for Capacity Management. A *resource*, or purchased material, labor, activity, or support cost, has a capability to do work that may or may not be storable. The combination of resources into a system or subsystem defines the *cost of preparedness*,[8] or the initial and continuing cost of having resources in place to do required work. Some of these costs will be nonstorable, their consumption varying with units of time (such as rent or labor) while others can be held for downstream utilization with actual consumption varying directly with output (assets).

Combining the issues of how resources are used per unit of completed work results in the *behavior of cost* formula. While related to the concepts of fixed and variable costs that underlie most of management practice, capacity costs focus on the *committed* versus *managed* costs for a system or sub-system. A committed cost is one that will not go away whether or not the system is used to create products and services for customers. The rent or depreciation for a building that houses equipment is one example of a committed cost of capacity. Managed costs, on the other hand, are those that are needed to enable the system to operate. The people who run machines are managed costs; if the system is left idle these costs will not be incurred.[9]

The importance of separating resource requirements into these two categories becomes clear as the *baseline capacity measure* is added to

Figure 7.3 Capacity Measurement

Rated Capacity	Summary Model	Industry-Specific Model	Strategy-Specific Model	Traditional Model
Rated Capacity	Idle	Not marketable	Excess Not Usable	Theoretical
		Off-limits	Management Policy	
			Contractual	
			Legal	
		Marketable	Idle But Usable	Practical
	Non-productive	Standby	Process Balance	Scheduled
			Variability	
			Scrap	
		Waste	Rework	
			Yeild Loss	
		Maintenance	Scheduled	
			Unscheduled	
			Time	
		Setups	Volume	
			Changeover	
	Productive	Process Development		
		Product Development		
		Good Products		

Source: Klammer, T. and the CAM-I Capacity Management Core Team, *Capacity Measurement and Improvement,* Chicago, IL: Irwin Professional Publishing, 1996: 17.

the equation. Specifically, there are five different baselines, or total expected work, that can be applied to a system (see Figure 7.3): theoretical capacity, practical capacity, normal capacity, annual budgeted capacity, and actual capacity utilization.[10] *Theoretical capacity* is the optimal amount of work that a process or plant can complete using a 24-hour, seven day operation with zero waste. Theoretical capacity by definition is the only capacity baseline in which productive capacity could *theoretically* equal 100 percent of total capacity. All other definitions of capacity consist of both productive and nonproductive capacity.

Practical capacity is the level of output generally attainable by a process, or the theoretical capacity adjusted downward for unavoidable non-productive time, such as idle but usable or marketable idle time. Three factors are important in understanding practical and theoretical capacity. First, it is clearly impossible to utilize the theoretical capacity of a system for any extended period of time in productive ways. That does not make the measurement meaningless; theoretical capacity is the only baseline that provides information on the system's limits and how close current operations are to those limits. Avoiding unnecessary capacity investments depends on keeping the theoretical capacity of the system within current constraints, constantly in front of management.

The second factor of concern is that only practical and theoretical (e.g., rated) capacity measures emphasize the system's ability to do work. All other measurements focus on current utilization of the capacity, not on the amount of capability the system has. To fail to measure theoretical and practical capacity levels is to permanently ignore an at-times quite significant portion of the firm's ability to create value for its stakeholders. Finally, the appropriate baseline or denominator for the committed capacity cost pool is either theoretical or practical capacity.[11] Regardless of whether the system is manned to support production or not, the meter is running on committed capacity costs. Best practice firms, including Motorola and Texas Instruments, utilize theoretical capacity as their baseline measure.

Having moved beyond system capability, attention in the capacity measurement area turns to current or average utilization of the system. *Normal* capacity is the average, expected utilization of a machine, process or plant/unit over a defined period of time (e.g., three years). The affected asset or system is normally scheduled for use, and may be productively deployed or not. Normal capacity requires the addition of new resources (managed capacity costs) to be ready for use. Only a system in a state of readiness to produce, with all required resources in place, would qualify for the definition of normal capacity. In a related way, *annual budgeted capacity* is the current monthly or annual plan for utilizing the system. The actual size of the managed capacity cost pool should reflect its budgeted or normal utilization patterns. Managed capacity costs, therefore, use normal or budgeted capacity to develop a per unit of time or output "charge" for capacity utilization.

As suggested by Figure 7.3, scheduled capacity can be sorted into two primary categories: nonproductive and productive. *Nonproductive* capacity includes such things as standby capacity, wasted capacity, time spent on maintenance, and set-up time and costs. Finally, *productive* capacity is that amount actually utilized in process development, product development, or the actual provision of the product/service bundle. Nonproductive and productive capacity are the most expensive forms of resource capability; the system is in place and all of the resource required to make it productive have been secured (see Figure 7.4).

Figure 7.4 Capacity Cost Build-up

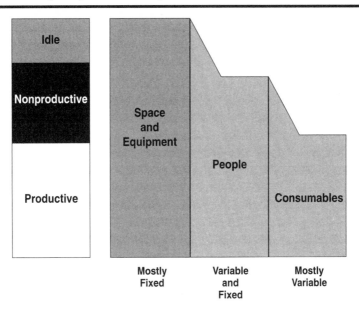

Source: Klammer, et.al., op.cit., pp. 51.

Capacity reporting uses these categories and definitions to provide management with a snapshot of current utilization, levels of waste, opportunities for improvement, and other areas of concern in improving the effectiveness of asset deployment. Some of these reporting templates will be developed in detail in subsequent pages. Summarizing the capacity cost equations:

- **Committed** capacity costs are the systems-based resources that cannot be avoided regardless of whether the capacity is idle, nonproductive, or productively deployed. Its cost equation is:

$$\frac{\text{Total Committed Capacity Costs}}{\text{Theoretical Time}}$$

- **Managed** capacity costs are the resources needed to bring the system into a state of readiness to make products or provide services. Incremental or variable in nature, these costs can be avoided if the system is purposely idled. The related cost equation is:

$$\frac{\text{Total Managed Capacity Cost}}{\text{Scheduled Capacity Time}}$$

- **Idle** capacity receives a per minute or percentage of total time charge for committed capacity costs only.

- **Nonproductive and productive** capacity utilization is charged for both the committed and managed costs per minute (or output level).

Capacity cost reports utilize these two components of resource costs and uses to develop a comprehensive analysis of the level of utilization, the effectiveness of the system's use, and to identify areas where improvements can be gained. Clearly, nonproductive capacity is the primary focus of improvement efforts because it is expensive (causes both committed and managed costs) and is not producing anything the customer or market will pay for today or downstream (e.g., new product development). It is waste that is both avoidable and actionable. Making this fact visible is the essence of the capacity reporting process.

Capacity Management Reporting Models
All of our knowledge has its origins in our perceptions.
–Leonardo da Vinci

Capacity Management reporting models seek to bridge the gap between operating information and financial information.[12] The language of operations is time, units, pounds and throughput. The language of management is profit from operations and cash flows. If the communication gap between these two different perspectives is not bridged, resource allocation decisions can become arbitrary. Given that the primary business process measures in best practice firms are cost, time, quality and delivery, it is critical to link the financial metrics to these process measures in order to provide the basis for informed analysis of trade-offs.

Time is the common denominator used to link the various issues and reporting formats in capacity measurement and analysis. A second core issue shaping capacity reporting practices is the recognition that focusing on the sources and costs of nonproductive capacity is the key to improving performance; efficiency-based measurements do not have this power.[13] Adding capacity is an easy, but expensive way, to address a *perceived* capacity shortfall. Converting nonproductive or idle capacity into productive capacity may require effort, but will provide greater economic benefit than new asset purchases or outsourcing because it avoids excess costs and wasted internal resources (e.g., idle capacity).

A second building block of capacity reporting models is an **activity**. Activities, or defined units of work performed within sub-units or processes that have a defined, measurable output, allows a company to link its capacity efforts to the management system of roles and responsibilities. In the traditional view of capacity, plant management was given sole responsibility for all forms of capacity costs.[14] As idle, nonproductive and productive capacity become more clearly identified and reported, the impact of the business team, manufacturing team, and support teams on capacity utilization becomes visible. For instance, idle capacity is the responsibility of the business team or top management. Only management or marketing can find business to fill this available time with productive efforts. In a related way, the support team is responsible for delays in set-up, for lost time due to material shortages, and related support process failures.[15]

A series of drill-down templates within the CAM-I Capacity Management reporting model provide the basis for communicating the current status of capacity utilization and the impact of

Figure 7.5 CAM-I Capacity Model Templates

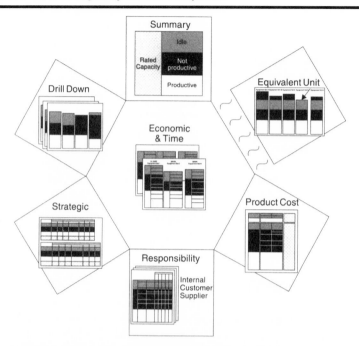

All templates are economic except the equivalent unit template.

Source: Klammer, op.cit., pg. 48.

improvement efforts (see Figure 7.5). All of the templates are economic in nature except for the equivalent unit template that transforms time into output measures such as number of activities completed or number of units made to support product or service costing efforts.[16]

The time and economic template is the core set of measurements within the CAM-I Capacity Management reporting model. The time used in each state of capacity varies for each equipment set or process, as does the cost to obtain the system and deploy it. Only three options are available for capacity use: produce products or services for sale today, produce products for inventory, or be lost/wasted,[17] the development of an organizational strategy must ensure that capacity utilization is optimized.[18] Wasted capacity will never generate revenues or profits, and may ultimately drive the costs of doing business to unsustainable, future-damaging levels.

The measurement and communication of the states of capacity are important to the entire enterprise.[19] Manufacturing teams need to understand, and take actions to reduce, nonproductive capacity costs and to actually *create* idle capacity for redeployment by the management team. While this may seem counter-intuitive at first, the best way to create "new" capacity is to eliminate waste or reduce current time demands by current output. Cellular manufacturing methods, which eliminate move, queue, and other forms of capacity waste from the system, create idle capacity. Unused, this idle capacity

Figure 7.6   CAM-I Capacity Responsibility Template

(Hypothetical percentages)

			Business Team	Manufacturing Team	Support Team Human Resources	Support Team Finances	Others
Idle	Not marketable	Excess Not Usable	70%		20%		
	Off-limits	Management Policy	80%		20%		
		Contractual	100%				
		Legal	80%		20%		
	Marketable	Idle But Usable	80%		10%	10%	
Non-productive	Standby	Process Balance	10%	30%	10%	40%	10%
		Variability	20%	30%	10%		40%
	Waste	Scrap	10%	60%	10%		40%
		Rework	10%	60%	10%	10%	10%
		Yeild Loss		40%	20%	20%	20%
	Maintenance	Scheduled		80%		20%	
		Unscheduled		60%	20%	10%	10%
	Setups	Time		40%	20%	10%	30%
		Volume		60%		10%	30%
		Changeover	50%			20%	30%
Productive	Process Development		70%	20%		10%	
	Process Development		80%		20%		
	Good Products			100%			

Source: Klammer, op.cit., pg. 65.

becomes waste; utilized it can lead to improved profitability with minimal additional resource requirements. Management teams, therefore, are responsible for finding ways to reduce idle time and increase productive capacity. Figure 7.6 suggests how responsibility concepts can be built into the Capacity Management reporting model.

The CAM-I Capacity Management reporting model is a sophisticated communication and capacity analysis tool that can provide significant benefits to a company. Its implementation should include nine basic activities: [20]

- organize the implementation team;
- determine the management objectives for the capacity reporting model;
- select a model presentation template;
- review element definitions;
- select the measurement period;
- identify and access operational data;
- identify and access financial data;
- summarize to level of required presentation model; and,
- monitor for results.

To serve as an effective communication tool, a capacity reporting model should be based on a common language applied across the multiple business units and levels of the organization. It needs to effectively integrate the short-, intermediate- and long-term perspectives in order to support the multiple needs of the organization. Serving as a mirror of existing capacity and its deployment, the model identifies activities that influence decisions. This emphasis is a natural tie to the CAM-I SMP Model framework of information integration within decision domains, all focused on improving communication and decision-making within the firm.

Data within any capacity reporting model should be summarized at the level needed for each user. In other words, the reporting model should be designed in a flexible format that allows users to enter the database, analyze and prepare reports, and assess current performance on an as-needed, ad hoc basis. The templates or data files that make up the complete model should be built to ensure that they are easy to access, use and understand. Data should also be consistent with the definitions and structures in other SMPs in use by the firm.

Texas Instruments' (TI) Dallas-based semiconductor plant was one of the first sites to deploy the CAM-I capacity reporting model.[21] The TI model was developed to answer three specific questions: "What product should we build?"; "What equipment should be buy?"; and "Which people should we hire?" Using the language of capacity commonly across multiple units and groups, the firm has found that the model has provided insights into Capacity Management and ways to enhance the utilization of assets and firm profitability. Examining both operational and run-time efficiencies, as well as overall asset utilization, the model provides a detailed view of current performance against plans, opportunities for improvement, and supports efforts to ensure that everyone in the organization is striving toward the same goal: optimizing capacity utilization. It is an approach that embodies many of the strong points of related Capacity Management approaches.

Related Capacity Management Approaches

For of course the true meaning of a term is to be found by observing what a man does with it, not by what he says about it.
– P.W. Bridgman

While the CAM-I Capacity Management reporting model is one of the most comprehensive and sophisticated tools available in Capacity Management, there are many different approaches that have been developed and used by firms to deal with this complex yet vital area of business (see Figure 7.7).[22]

For instance, the resource effectiveness model is used by Hill's Pet Food Company to tie capacity utilization to four specific operating measures: resource effectiveness, asset utilization, operating efficiency, and run-time efficiency.[23] Each of these measures builds up from the standard run-time for a specific type and batch size of pet food and then divides it into the varying types of capacity baseline measures affected. The resource effectiveness model looks at standard run-time as a percent of total resource available time (theoretical capacity), while its measure of operating efficiency compares the standard run-time to production available time (managed capacity).

Figure 7.7   Comparison of Capacity Cost Management Reporting Models

Features \ Model	Baseline Capacity Measure Emphasized	Primary Focus of Model	Suggested Treatment of Idleness Costs	Other Programs Supported
Resource Effectiveness Model	Theoretical Capacity	Resource Utilization	Charge to Profit & Loss	Continuous Improvement TOC & ABC
Capacity Utilization Model	Theoretical Capacity	Capacity Utilization	Charge to Profit & Loss	Continuous Improvement & ABC
Capacity Variance Model	Theoretical Capacity	Analysis of Performance	None Suggested	Continuous Improvement
CAM-I Capacity Model	Theoretical Capacity	Communication	Charge to Profit & Loss	Continuous Improvement & ABC
CUBES Model	Theoretical Capacity	Process Utilization	None Suggested	Continuous Improvement & ABC
Cost Containment Model	Implicit Theoretical Capacity	Total Cost/Activity	None Suggested	Continuous Improvement & ABC
Gantt Idleness Charts	Practical Capacity	Efficiency	Charge to Profit & Loss	Continuous Improvement
Supplemental Rate Method	Practical Capacity	Supporting both internal & external reporting	Charge to Product	Continuous Improvement
Theory of Constraints Capacity Model	Practical (Marketable) Capacity	Throughput	None Suggested	Continuous Improvement
Normalized Costing Approach	Normal Capacity	Decision Analysis	Charge to Profit & Loss	Continuous Improvement & ABC
ABC and Capacity Cost Management	Normal Capacity	Resource cost per activity	Charge to Profit & Loss	Continuous Improvement
Integrated TOC-ABC Model	Various	Minimize marginal cost	None Suggested	Continuous Improvement & ABC

Source: *Measuring the Cost of Capacity,* Management Accounting Guideline #42, Society of

Required I/S Capabilities	Data Requirements	Resources Required	Planning or Control?	Strong Tie of Financial and Operational Suggested?
Moderate	Moderate	Moderate	Planning	Yes
Moderate	Moderate	Moderate	Both	Yes
Minimal	Low	Minimal	Control	Yes
Sophisticated	High	Moderate to High	Both	Yes
Sophisticated	High	Moderate to High	Both	Yes
Moderate	Low	Minimal	Planning	No
Minimal	Moderate	Minimal	Control	No
Minimal	Low	Minimal	Control	Yes
Minimal	Low	Minimal	Both	No
Moderate	High	Moderate to High	Both	No
Moderate	Moderate	Moderate	Planning	Yes
Moderate	Moderate	Minimal	Both	Yes

Management Accountants of Canada, 1996: 42.

The *capacity cost containment model* takes a different approach. Specifically, it extends capacity measurement to the activity and process levels by assessing current process activities and their effectiveness against customer-defined value attributes (see Figure 7.8). Its objective is to help an organization analyze and control future spending, not by enacting across-the-board cost reductions, but rather by isolating nonvalue-added and wasteful activities from those that the customer values. Spending guidelines are based on customer value rankings or benchmark data, which provides the basis for developing a gap analysis and action plan for increasing the effectiveness of non-physical asset deployment.[24]

Figure 7.8　Cost Containment Model

Step One:　Detail the Value Chain

Customer calls in order	Inventory and Credit Check done on-line	Order processed/ Packing slip printed	Items picked by Stockroom	Backorders noted with expected shipping dates	Ordered Packed	Box sealed and labeled	Box weighted and paperwork done	Moved to pick-up area	Ship to Customer	Invoice	Collect Cash

Step Two:　Attach resources to the activities and then evaluate their spending levels against customer-defined value.

	ACTIVITY	ANNUAL RESOURCES USED	% OF TOTAL	CUSTOMER –DEFINED VALUE
1	Answer Phone	$25,000	less than 1%	1 (priority activity)
2	Process order/send credit and inventory	500,000	11.6%	1 (priority activity)
3	Process order/send To storeroom	150,000	3.5%	3 (low value)
4	Pick items on order	750,000	17.4%	1 (priority activity)
5	Note backorders and expected ship dates	750,000	17.4%	2 (Low Value: should be done right)
6	Pack order	500,000	11.6%	1 (Priority activity)
7	Seal and lable box	125,000	2.9%	2 (Low value: should be done right)
8	Weigh and complete paperwork	125,000	2.9%	3 (Low value)
9	Move	75,000	1.7%	4 (No value)
10	Ship	500,000	11.6%	1 (Priority activity)
11	Invoice	350,000	8.1%	2 (Low value: should be done right)
12	Collect cash	450,000	10.5%	2 (Low value: should be done right)
		$4,300,000	100.0%	

Step Three:　Determine Spending Gap

Total Resources Used: $4,300.00

Percent spent on priority 1 activities: $2,275,000 / $4,300,000 = 57%

Desired spending on priority 1 activities 60%, or $2,580,000

Spending gap 7% or $305,000

Source: *Measuring the Cost of Capacity*, op.cit., pg. 29.

Capacity modeling and measurement can also be done within an Activity-Based Cost framework, or it can reflect the basic tenets of Goldratt's Theory of Constraints model (TOC), or even be an integration of these two approaches. Robert Kee's[25] integrated approach uses a mixed-integer mathematical model to identify a least-cost solution to the capacity utilization challenge. The resulting equations capture the interactions among the cost, physical resources, and capacity of production activities through opportunity cost and contribution margin assessments.

Whether a traditional, plant-focused system such as Gantt's 1915 idleness chart, or a modern, systems-oriented CAM-I model is employed, the role of capacity measurement efforts remains constant: to optimize utilization and profitability by identifying idle and nonproductive capacity. In reporting this information, a company recognizes that the various forms of idle capacity costs are controllable, or can be acted upon, at different management levels. A decision to maintain standby capacity is strategic in nature; changing these costs requires action by top management. Conversely, unplanned nonproductive capacity due to equipment breakdowns is an operational issue that is best addressed on the plant floor, at least in the short-term. In order to be relevant, Capacity Management data, including the cost of idle capacity, must be actionable and focused on identifying opportunities for improvement.

Capacity Management within the Extended Enterprise

No man is an island, entire of itself;
Every man is a piece of the Continent, a part of the main.

– John Dunne

All too often, Capacity Management is reduced to issues surrounding physical assets that can be seen, counted, weighed and measured. Yet, physical resources are of little use without the human and financial capital required to bring them to life. Effectively managing assets and their capacity calls for the ongoing involvement of individuals across the Extended Enterprise. It also depends on the development of Integrated Performance Management and human resource policies that knit diverse individuals into coordinated, focused teams working toward a common goal: optimizing value creation by meeting customer requirements better, faster and cheaper than the competition.

A second arena of concern in Capacity Management is the development and deployment of the Extended Enterprise or value chain. If Capacity Management is constrained within the four walls of a company's owned facilities, major opportunities for improvement can be overlooked. In a related way, if a company develops capacity that exceeds the ability of the value chain in total, it is creating waste that cannot be passed on to the final consumer. Finally, bottlenecks can often by found outside of the company, inside the plants or facilities of suppliers or distributors.

Leveraging assets across the Extended Enterprise can provide a company with the surge capacity needed to respond to cyclical production demands. In some companies, very few assets are really owned, yet Capacity Management remains an issue. Even in virtual corporations, the processes and competency center capabilities must be balanced against the demands of the final market. While "capacity" in a networked enterprise may be very flexible (because it is owned and managed by others and can be therefore quickly replaced by other types of 'capacity'), it is still the core value-creating ability of the organization. Managing capacity forward and backward in the value chain provides opportunities for improvement and asset optimization that might otherwise be overlooked. Gaining this control begins with a well-designed and managed information system, such as the CAM-I SMP Model.

CAPACITY MANAGEMENT AND INFORMATION TECHNOLOGY

In many ways, information technology is perhaps the primary constraint on the overall Capacity and Asset Management activities within a firm. Without sophisticated information technology, many of the models that have been developed in this and the preceding chapter would appear difficult to implement. In reality, these SMPs can be implemented within a PC environment. Achieving balanced production and continuously eliminating idle and nonproductive capacity depends on knowledge; this knowledge resides within the organization. Finding the most effective way to capture and manage the details and analysis of the Capacity Management SMP entails fitting it to the complexity, existing information systems, and needs of the firm.

Linking organizations across the Extended Enterprise depends on the use of electronic data interchange, intranet, and extranet solutions that all serve to support the development of integrated supply chain management. Receiving orders and balancing throughput is an information-dependent effort. To effectively monitor, utilize and improve Asset and Capacity Management practices, reasonable investments in some form of data warehouse technology or integrated information system will probably need to be made. Serving as the vital link between plants and operations within the global manufacturing and service network, information technology must be designed to allow management strategic and operational access to current capacity utilization. It should also support analysis of projected demand, idle and nonproductive global and network capacity, and options for investing in new asset structures that will improve performance. Good information is a necessary part of any Capacity or Asset Management system.

THE HUMAN ELEMENT

The human element impacts Capacity and Asset Management in two very distinct ways. First, it is important to gauge the capacity of the human system in designing processes and establishing capacity limits. Some systems are, in fact, human systems. Measuring and effectively deploying the capacity of people-based processes is much more complex than those faced in machine-based settings. Second, to ensure that the system in total reaches its optimal level of performance, role and responsibility issues need to be addressed. People must be motivated by the measures used to find ways to improve capacity utilization and eliminate waste.

In the first case, the use of capacity models such as the cost containment and activity-based costing models can improve the utilization of human systems. While it may be difficult if not impossible, to define theoretical capacity for a person or human system, it is possible to pinpoint the causes of waste in this area. Measuring human systems to identify activities and drivers that create waste, use excess time, or result in high levels of rework or failure provides the actionable information needed to improve performance. In a related way, benchmarking, or a similar data gathering approach, can be used to identify reasonable spending limits for different types of activities and service outputs. These limits can be used to drive improvement in the work methods and procedures used by individuals within the process. It may not be possible to identify "optimal" use, but measurements can be used to encourage continuous improvement efforts that can implicitly lead to improved capacity utilization in human systems.

On a second level, human issues are a significant concern in creating measurements that drive improvement in any capacity or asset management setting. As described earlier, the CAM-I Capacity Model explicitly identifies different types of capacity utilization, idleness and waste with specific management or operating teams or individuals. Making people accountable for improving asset utilization is an essential part of creating a viable, effective set of Asset Management policies. Holding individuals accountable over the long-term for the impact of their decisions on current and future asset acquisition and deployment can be done by a bonus approach that holds part of the potential improvement bonus in abeyance for an extended period of time. Only if the company enjoys improved performance over the long-term is the residual bonus released. Penalties can also be developed when it becomes clear that a manager has gamed prior performance reports. The key is to ensure that motivation is created to support ongoing improvement in asset and capacity utilization.

In designing and using Capacity Management, it is critical to assess the impact of various types of metrics and reports on the decisions and behavior of individual managers. For instance, labor efficiency-based measures of capacity can result in a company producing work-in-process even if no current or future demand for a product exists.[26] In this situation, it can be seen that the capacity metrics would be more likely to drive people to keep busy, not necessarily to create value for customers. Therefore, the key behavioral issues to consider whenever a firm is choosing a specific Capacity Management model should include the following issues:[27]

- If this measure were made available to me, or one of my key managers, what response would it be likely to create?
- Does the measure reinforce and reward continuous improvement and learning?
- What dysfunctional behaviors might the measurement create?
- Will the measure be used in the performance evaluation process? If yes, is it fair and objective?

- Is the measure actionable? If so, by whom?
- In the long-term, what would be the implication of always doing well against this measure?
- Will the measure support, or work against, other management programs and objectives?

In the race to gain a sustainable competitive advantage, companies need to find ways to better choose and use their resources. Value creation does not mean throwing all the resources the company can muster at the productive process; rather, it means achieving long-term improvements in products and services while reducing the long-term average cost of providing these products and services to the customer. Capacity Management is an issue that affects every organization and process, whether manufacturing or service based, as the final section suggests.

A SERVICE APPLICATION [28]

Assume a company has an accounts payable group that provides bill-paying services to several major corporations. The department works two shifts, five days per week, giving it the capacity to process 40,000 checks per week with existing resources and personnel. The overall process used to process the checks can be broken into a series of activities and events:

- 45% of all time is spent issuing 30,000 checks. This is productive time.
- Opening mail takes 5% of available time. This is set-up, or nonproductive, time.
- Resolving problems with key suppliers takes another 30% of total time.
- Errors on roughly 6,000 checks per month lead to rework (20% of total time used).

The last three activities are nonproductive. While they may be necessary at the current time, they do not add to the department's value-creating output. In order to support all of these activities, the department is allotted $372,000 of budget that is used as follows:

- $100,000 for space and computers (committed costs).
- $200,000 for personnel (managed costs).
- $72,000 is for direct resources consumed when processing a check (managed cost).

The processing team within the department has the ability to produce 40,000 checks in a week. Actual checks produced are averaging 30,000 per week plus 6,000 reworked items. Given this information, what type of measurements are possible for this process?

Available output capacity—40,000 checks	100%
Less actual output—30,000 + 6,000	90%
Idle capacity due to lack of demand	10%

We can then analyze how the department uses the 90% active time as follows:

Opening mail (5% x 90%)	4%
Supplier problems (30% x 90%)	27%
Rework (20% x 90%)	18%
Process good checks (45% x 90%)	41%
Active time	90%

A similar analysis can be done to compute the portion of available equipment time spent in various capacity states. The equipment is available 24 hours a day, but used only when the clerks are processing checks.

Available time (7 days x 24 hours = 168 hrs)	100%
Equipment use (5 days x 16 hours = 80 hrs)	48%
Idle equipment time (88 hrs)	52%

We can analyze the department's use of the equipment during the 48 percent schedule time. While the equipment was in use, it could process 40,000 checks but actually only processed 36,000 checks, or 90 percent of the capacity.

Process capacity-equipment available (40,000)	48%
Checks processed (36,000; 90% x 48%)	43%
Idle—No demand (10% x 48%)	5%

Next we analyze how the department uses the equipment during the 43 percent of the time that it was in active use:

Opening mail (5% x 43%)	2%
Supplier problems (30% x 43%)	13%
Rework (20% x 43%)	9%
Process good checks (45% x 43%)	19%
Active time	43%

We now have the data we need to prepare the time and quantity as well as economic template (Figure 7.9). In this example, the budget numbers provide the information needed to convert the time template to an economic template.

Figure 7.9   Time, Quantity and Economic Templates

Time and Quantity Template—Accounts Payable Example

	Equip/Space	People	Consumables
Idle—Off-limits Idle—Market Demand	52% 5%	10%	
Nonproductive—Setups Nonproductive—Supplier	2% 13%	4% 27%	
Nonproductive—Rework	9%	18%	6,000
Productive	19%	41%	30,000
Total	100%	100%	36,000

Economic Template—Accounts Payable Example

	Equip/Space	People	Consumables	Total
Idle—Off-limits Idle—Market Demand	A $52,000 $5,000	$20,000		$52,000 $25,000
Nonproductive—Setups Nonproductive—Supplier	$2,000 $13,000	$8,000 B $54,000		$10,000 $67,000
Nonproductive—Rework	$9,000	$36,000	$12,000	$57,000
Productive	$19,000	$82,000	C $60,000	$161,000
Total	$100,000	$200,000	$72,000	$372,000

A. 52% x $100,000 (Total cost of space and computers)
B. 27% x $200,000 (total cost of people)
C. 30,000 x $2 (Cost of each check)

Source: Klammer, op.cit., pp. 82-83.

Since management has determined that the accounts payable department should only work two shifts, five days a week, 52 percent, or $52,000 of the equipment cost was idle—off limits. The processing staff spent 27 percent of their time resolving supplier problems. This means that $54,000 of the $200,000 people costs are nonproductive—

supplier caused costs. Since each check, good or reworked, costs $2 in supplies, the productive cost of consumables was $60,000. Figure 7.10 completes the example, showing the economic template and a Pareto analysis of the accounts payable example presented here.

Figure 7.10 Economic Pareto Analysis

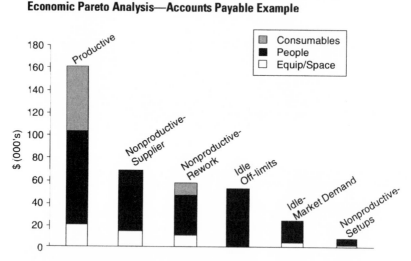

Economic Pareto Analysis—Accounts Payable Example

Source: Klammer, op.cit., pg. 83.

Summary

Let us not go over the old ground, let us rather prepare for what is to come.

– Marcus Tullius Cicero

Capacity Management begins before resources are acquired and continues on through deployment and eventual retirement of an asset. Effectively tracking the performance of resources, ensuring that they provide the required capacity flexibly and responsively, and constantly ensuring that purchased resources are used, not wasted, is an ongoing challenge involving everyone in the organization.

Capacity Management is a vital part of a company's arsenal of strategic and tactical tools and models. As part of the CAM-I SMP

Model, it serves to link together the total database by providing common definitions of the baseline value-creating capability of resources, as well as how much capacity they have available for use. Every time a cost, delivery, or quality estimate is made in any SMP, it requires data from Capacity Management.

Whenever Capacity Management is used to analyze current performance, it must pull its objectives, data, and metrics from all of the other SMPs. Capacity Management, due to its intense focus on creating communication networks within the firm and its Extended Enterprise, is a microcosm of the entire SMP Model.

Focused on improving asset deployment and reducing the need for new investments, effective Capacity Management practices enable the company to improve its use of resources to meet customer requirements. In the end the goal remains clear: all assets must earn more than their capital costs if firm value is to increase, and once purchased, must be effectively utilized to create value for customers and profits for the firm. Effective Capacity Management is a journey—a process of continuous improvement.

References

Cooper, R. and R. Kaplan, "Activity-based systems: Measuring the Cost of Resource Usage," *Accounting Horizons*, Spring, 1992: 1-12.

Coughlan, P. and J. Darlington, "As Fast as the Slowest Operation: The Theory of Constraints," *Management Accounting* (United Kingdom), June, 1993: 14-17.

Dilton-Hill, K.G. and E. Glad, "Managing Capacity," *Handbook of Cost Management*, New York: Warren, Gorham and Lamont, 1997: H3-1 to H3-8.

Gantt, H.L., "The Relation Between Production and Costs," reprinted in *Handbook of Cost Management*, New York: Warren, Gorham and Lamont, 1997: H4-1 to H4-8.

Institute of Management Accountants, *Accounting for the Costs of Capacity*, Research Report #39, Montvale, NJ, May, 1963.

Kee, R., "Integrating Activity-based Costing with the Theory of Constraints to Enhance Production-Related Decision-Making," *Accounting Horizons*, December, 1995: 48-61.

Klammer, T. and the CAM-I Capacity Interest Group, *Capacity Measurement and Improvement*, Chicago: Irwin Professional Publishing, 1997.

McNair, C.J., "The Costs of Capacity," *Journal of Cost Management*, Vol. 8, No. 1, Spring, 1994.

McNair, C.J. and R. Vangermeersch, *Total Capacity Management*, Boca Raton: St. Lucie Press, 1998.

Society of Management Accountants of Canada, *Measuring the Cost of Capacity*, Management Accounting Guideline #42, Hamilton, Ontario, 1996.

Endnotes

[1] Goldratt, in various of his Theory of Constraints publications, refers to the difference between activation and utilization. An asset can be utilized, but if this use does not result in throughput (revenues), the result is waste. Assets need to be used for value-creating purposes.

[2] McNair and Vangermeersch, *Total Capacity Management*, Boca Raton: St. Lucie Press, 1998.

[3] Womack and Jones, *Lean Thinking*, New York: The Free Press, 1997.

[4] The information in this background section is drawn from the book *Total Capacity Management*, C. McNair and R. Vangermeersch, Boca Raton: St. Lucie Press, 1998.

[5] If the reader wishes to get more information on these issues, they are referred to the McNair and Vangermeersch work cited here.

[6] These comments originally appear in *Measuring the Cost of Capacity*, Society of Management Accountants of Canada, Hamilton, Ontario, Management Accounting Guideline #42, 1996: 4-5.

[7] Ibid, pg. 6. Much of this section draws heavily from this document. Specifically, the definitions of capacity given here appear on pages 7-15. Pages will be noted here where appropriate.

[8] While appearing in MAG #42 (op.cit.), this term actually has its origins in work by A.H. Church, "Overhead—The Cost of Production Preparedness," *Factory and Industrial Management*, January, 1931: pp. 38-41.

[9] McNair and Vangermeersch, op.cit., pp. 35-36.

[10] It is important to note that these are traditional definitions of capacity that have undergone some change in the development of the CAM-I Capacity measurement model presented in *Capacity Measurement and Improvement*, T. Klammer, ed., and the CAM-I Capacity Interest Group, Chicago, IL Irwin Professional Publishing, 1996. This part of the discussion draws heavily from *Measuring the Cost of Capacity* (SMAC), op.cit., pp. 8-9 and related discussions on pages 16-17 of the CAM-I publication.

[11] There is significant thought that should go into any decision to step away from theoretical capacity in the measurement process. In setting the costing baseline, practical capacity measures permanently build idle capacity between theoretical and practical deployment levels into the costs of the goods and services that use the system. While this makes the cost estimate less accurate, the gap between theoretical and practical capacity is very difficult to bridge; practical capacity will provide the required stability and accuracy for the costing system under many conditions, and is easier to gain acceptance for within the firm.

[12] This entire section draws heavily from Klammer, op.cit., pp. 19-45. The source of these opening comments, which have been paraphrased, is pg. 19.

[13] Klammer, op.cit.

[14] Ibid, pg. 27.

[15] Ibid, pg. 27.

[16] Insights from Klammer, op.cit., pp. 47-40, are used in this section of the discussion.

[17] If a Theory of Constraints approach is used (E. Goldratt and J. Cox, *The Goal*, Hastings-on-Hudson, North River Press, 1986), then production time used to create inventory is also waste, as it represents utilization without activation (creation of throughput). This remains an ongoing point of contention between the TOC advocates and other management experts.

[18] Klammer, op.cit., pg. 56.

[19] This sentence is a direct quote from Klammer, op.cit., pg. 63. The entire paragraph is a paraphrase or distillation of pp. 60-66 of the cited work.

[20] Ibid, pp. 89-90.

[21] This example is a summary statement of a presentation made by A. Vercio.

[22] This section draws heavily from MAG #42, Society of Management Accountants, op.cit. If specific comments are more direct paraphrases than summaries, appropriate pages will be noted.

[23] Ibid, pg. 17-19.

[24] Ibid, pg. 28-30.kk

[25] R. Kee, "Integrating Activity-based Costing with the Theory of Constraints to Enhance Production-Related Decision-Making," *Accounting Horizons*, December, 1995: 48-61.

[26] *Measuring the Cost of Capacity*, op.cit., pg. 45.

[27] The source of this list and discussion are *Measuring the Cost of Capacity. pg. 45.*, ibid, pg. 45.

[28] This example originally appears in Klammer, op.cit., pp. 80-82 and is paraphrased for presentation here.

Chapter 8

Process Management

Whatever view of reality deepens our sense of the tremendous issues of life in the world wherein we move is for us nearer the truth than any view which diminishes that sense.

– Dean William R. Inge

Key Learnings:

- Creating explicit linkages of individuals and activities across the organization, a process approach to management, bridges communication gaps.

- Process Management emphasizes the flow of activities that are required to deliver desired products and services to customers when and where required.

- A process is a series of activities that are linked to achieve a specific objective.

- The primary elements of a process include: inputs, out-puts, transformation, process owners, process performers, control, repeatability and linkages.

- There are three main forms of processes within organizations: core, support and management.

Perspective is the key to seeing and solving problems. Shedding a unique light on modern business challenges, Process Management provides an organization with the ability to rapidly respond to changes in its customers' needs as well as to shifting market demands. Shaped by a clear understanding of the flow of activities that create value for a firm's customers, process management challenges the

Figure 8.1   The Process Management SMP Flow

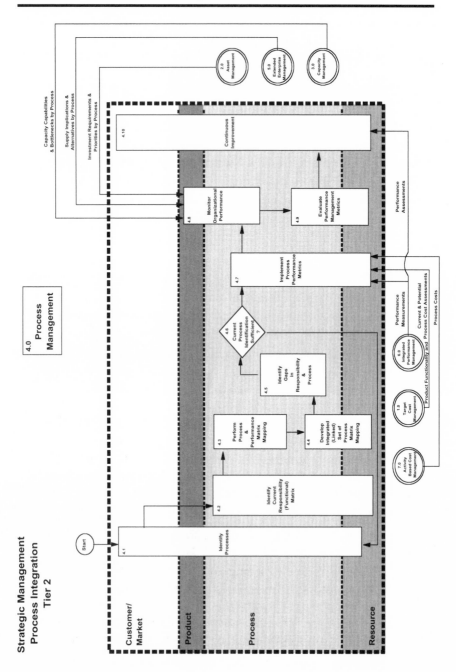

"business as usual" mindset that can blind a company to the issues and solutions that can create a competitive advantage.[1]

Effective Process Management builds from the vision, strategy and values of the enterprise. It serves as a vehicle to set strategy in motion by providing a better understanding of how, where, and why resources are consumed.[2] Creating explicit linkages of individuals and activities across the organization, a process approach to management bridges communication gaps—gaps that can result in fumbles, errors, and excess costs. The cross-functional perspective underlying process management provides a consistent framework for managing potentially diverse initiatives and activities, creating a common process mindset that helps the firm's management rapidly and effectively respond to stakeholder requirements. Process Management underlies the whole enterprise concept because it emphasizes the flow of activities that are required to deliver desired products and services to customers when and where required.

A process is a structured, measured set of activities designed to produce a specified output for a particular customer or market.[3] The primary elements of a process include: inputs, outputs, transformation, process owners, process performers, control, repeatability and linkages.[4] There are three main forms of processes within organizations: core, support and management. Core processes are the handful of processes central to the company's efforts to meet customer requirements—a customer is standing at the end of every core process.[5] Support processes represent much of the administrative work in a company, such as managing information and the firm's financial and physical resources. Finally, management processes refer to the activities that create the regulatory, legal and financial environment of an organization.[6]

Essential Elements of Process Management
We are confronted by a condition, not a theory.
– Grover Cleveland

Process Management is the "how" that makes the strategic objectives of the firm come to life. As suggested in Figure 8.1, the first step in the Process Management Strategic Management Process (SMP) is the identification of the core processes used to deliver products and services to customers. Spanning the entire set of decision domains, this first step creates the road map of linkages within the enterprise value chain. Process Management thus begins with creating a process mindset that emphasizes the horizontal flow of activities that define how work is done in the organization.[7] There are four elements in creating a process mindset: creating a process vision, achieving process clarity, imbuing process awareness throughout the organization, and implementing process ownership and control structures.[8]   A process vision involves a high-level consideration of customers and products. The vision must be responsive to the organization's strategic intent to address the needs of the customers.

The majority of the remaining activities that comprise the Process Management SMP fall naturally within the process decision domain. The migration from a functionally-oriented organization to a process-based one relies upon insight, policies and procedures occurring at the tactical level of activity. Steps two through seven of Figure 8.1 capture this migration. Specifically, having identified the primary flows of work within the firm, process management turns its attention to identifying the current responsibility/functional matrix and its primary points of intersection with the firm's core processes.

Widespread understanding of the concept of "processes" requires discussion and knowledge of how the activities performed by individuals and functions maps to process structures. Having created a process awareness, the organization can effectively migrate toward a process-centered organizational structure.[9] Achieving this objective begins with the performance of detailed process analysis to gain the requisite understanding of the way work is currently done in the company (the "as is" map). Processes are then revamped to eliminate nonvalue-added work and wasteful activities, resulting in a process vision (the "to be" map).[10] Movement toward the "to be" requires the development of process-based performance measurements that align the goals and efforts of individuals across processes and functions with the strategic objectives of the organization and the needs of its stakeholders.[11] The specific steps taken during this phase include:[12]

- Perform process/performance matrix mapping;
- Develop integrated (linked) set of process matrix maps;
- Identify gaps in responsibility or process flows;
- Analyze and assess sufficiency of current processes;
- Implement process performance metrics.

Implementing Process Management is not a one-shot effort.

Embedded in the dynamic logic of continuous improvement, Process Management is in itself a process. Ongoing Process Management builds from process design toward the development of monitoring, planning and improvement efforts that combine to reinforce the process perspective.[13] As seen in Figure 8.1, monitoring organizational performance and evaluating the performance management metrics are two critical steps completed on an ongoing basis to sustain the improvements from process management. Activities continue as before, but are now seen through "process-colored" glasses. The monitoring and measuring done within the firm has to reflect process performance, not traditional functional concerns. As with the migration to processes, the sustaining operation within processes is limited to a tactical mode at the Process and Resource levels of the CAM-I SMP Model. The continuous improvement efforts that comprise the final element, though, cut across all levels of the organization and have both strategic and tactical implications.

Overcoming resistance to change is a critical element of a successful Process Management implementation.[14] Understanding and effectively dealing with these barriers is not an option. A sound transition plan must constantly monitor the organization's comfort with the change process, its speed and focus. Achieving the final objective—the smooth, rapid, errorless flow of materials and transactions through the organization—is the key to creating a sustainable competitive advantage in the rapidly changing global market.

In the pages that follow, a process mindset will be explored as a concept. Having gained an understanding of how process approaches to management differ from traditional perspectives, attention will shift toward implementation of Process Management. Serving as a journey, the migration path from functional to process-based structures will then be examined as an ongoing initiative that strives to continuously improve performance against stakeholder expectations. In total, the discussion will provide the background needed to begin the journey toward a systemic, holistic enterprise.

Creating a Process Mindset
If we would have new knowledge, we must get a whole world of new questions.

– Susan K. Langer

Figure 8.2   Process Management

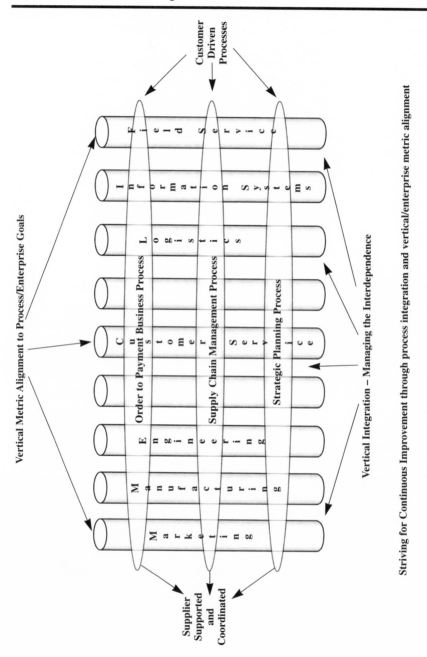

Source: *Implementing Process Management: A Framework for Process Thinking,*
CJ. McNair, Society of Management Accountants of Canada, 1998: 5.

A process is a series of activities that are linked to achieve a specific objective.[15] Business processes are the essential activities that span functional boundaries, linking together human resources, management proficiencies and technologies while drawing attention on meeting customer needs. A process is defined by the flow of resources that ultimately result in a satisfied customer. In a process-based manage-ment system, the drive for continuous improvement reflects the fact that organizational improvement is a cycle that is repeated in ongoing response to changing stakeholder needs.

The factors critical to a successful shift to a process-centered organization include:[16] (1) a mindset shift, (2) explicit process mapping, (3) process measurements, and (4) the use of process-based management methods. Of these, the mindset shift is a necessary prerequisite to successful process functioning. The desired mindset shift should allow managers to look beyond organizational and functional boundaries and support the development of a systemic, value chain-driven approach.[17] A correctly designed business process has the voice and perspective of the customer built in. Taking a process approach to management, then, means adopting the customer's point of view. This horizontal approach, with product inputs at the beginning and outputs and customers at the end, usually requires the de-emphasis of traditional vertical, functional structures.[18] Gaining a process mindset is enhanced by creating a vision of the "to be" organization.

CREATING A PROCESS VISION

An organization is only as effective as its processes.[19] Having noted this fact, it is interesting that the process level of an organization is normally the least understood and least well managed level of an organization. Given that between every input and every output there is a process, gaining control of this critical organizational dimension is an imperative.

A horizontal, value chain perspective is the defining element in creating a process vision for an organization. Focusing attention on the transformation of resources into value-adding products and services, a process mindset emphasizes the relationships between individuals, functions, activities and units, not their individual performance. As suggested in Figure 8.2, a Process Management vision seeks to integrate activities across the organization by effectively managing the interdependence between functions as well as by aligning vertical metrics to reflect both process and enterprise goals.

As suggested by Rummler and Brache, Process Management comes down to a simple goal: to manage the "white spaces," or gaps between functions and units on the organizational chart, more effectively. [20] The desire to improve business performance by coordinating the efforts of individuals across the organization is the driving force behind the migration from vertical/functional structures to process-based structures. This shift in focus increases the responsiveness of the company, improves the flow of products and services to customers, reduces cycle times, identifies and helps eliminate waste, and provides the basis for continuous improvement and learning. [21]

Figure 8.3 A Systems View of Business Processes

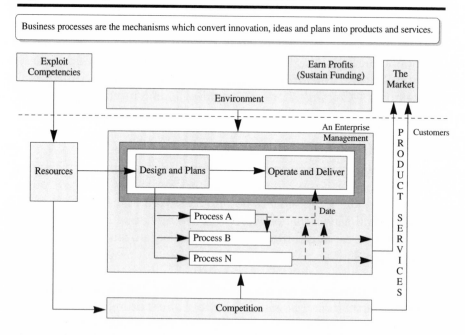

Business processes are the mechanisms which convert innovation, ideas and plans into products and services.

Source: The Rummler-Brache Group, 1995. This appears in McNair, op.cit.,pg. 12.

ACHIEVING PROCESS CLARITY

Once the organizational vision of a process-based management structure has been established and communicated throughout the organization, it is time to develop a "systems view" of the organization. The overall business system is composed of business processes that convert resources into products and services and provide feedback to enable the whole system to work more efficiently (see Figure 8.3). A holistic view of system interdependencies is key to optimizing the performance of the entire organization. The planning process must be integrated with customers and markets, as well as with the levels of demand that will be placed on each respective business process by market-driven strategies.

Shaped by the critical success factors defined by the firm's strategy, Process Management emphasizes cooperation and coordination rather than the meeting of functionally defined objectives and results. The first step an organization should take to implement process-based thinking and process-based management is to first understand, then define and document, key business processes. These core processes combine to create the skeleton of the process-based organization, one which visually links the entire value chain to the internal activities that create outputs customers value.

There is no common definition of a core process across organizations or settings.[22] The Corning Company is currently using two major "streams" to detail their core processes: an innovation stream and a delivery stream. The innovation stream is made up of four major processes: marketing, program definition, technology management, and product/process development. Conversely, the delivery stream includes demand capture, sourcing, manufacturing assembly and test, and distribution-aftermarket support. A third stream, management and control, serves to connect the innovation and delivery streams. The resulting coordinated stream of activities maximizes the value created today for Corning's customers.

Corning's process approach bears resemblance to other forms of process structures evolving in business. While uniquely reflecting its strategic objectives, the two core streams reflect activities and outputs common to many businesses. As suggested by Figure 8.4, the value creating processes within an organization often include both delivery and innovation streams.[23] What will differ markedly is the type and

Figure 8.4   Value Creation Processes

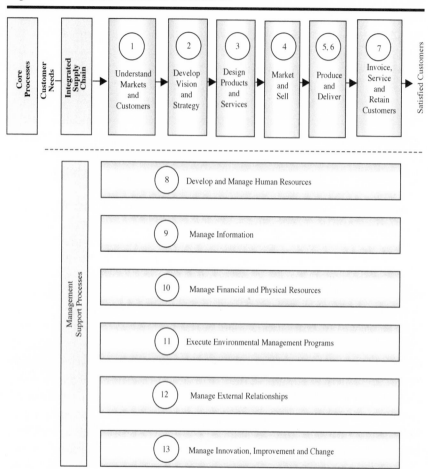

Source: Adapted from the Benchmarking Clearing House in Daly and Freeman, op.cit, pg. 29

sequence of activities bundled within a process as well as the type and nature of final output (goods or services) the stream provides.

Linking core, support and management processes to create an inte-grated view of the organization can be achieved through the development of a process hierarchy model. While it can be difficult to initially detail such a hierarchy for an organization, it is essential if a clear and uniform understanding of the relationships between functional areas and the processes they support is to be developed. Functions do not cease to exist in process organizations, but rather shift their attention from internal efficiencies and operations to external, process-based concerns. It is critical, therefore, that the linkages and accountabilities between functional and process managers be identified early in the implementation effort. Measurements are the basis for creating the necessary level of goal congruence between functions and the processes they support.

Processes should be given names that reflect the vertical and horizontal relationships they embody. They also should be carefully defined to ensure that they effectively focus the organization's efforts on meeting stakeholder requirements. The key in defining effective process structures is to avoid overlaps between processes, as these cloud accountability-controllability linkages and can lead to gaps or redundancy in work flows. Careful delineation of process boundaries facilitates the development of time, cost, and quality performance metrics for the process as it makes the boundaries between processes and the responsibility for specific activities and outcomes visible.[24]

Figure 8.5 details a structured process hierarchy for an automotive manufacturer, DaimlerChrysler Corporation. In contrast to Corning, there are three dominant streams at DaimlerChrysler: product creation, volume production and customer acceptance. The main driver of this difference is the after-market support that is a core part of an automotive "transaction" over the life cycle of ownership, an event missing from Corning's core business activities.

As the hierarchy suggests, there are three mega-processes within DaimlerChrysler: customer acceptance. A *mega-process* or core process *is an essential business process that is designed to meet customer needs.*[25] Incorporating a number of processes and sub-processes, a mega-process is a primary channel that is used by the company to create specific forms of value for its customers. Spanning functional boundaries, mega-processes allow management to see the company from the customer's perspective.

Processes, once defined, can be further broken down into sub-processes that capture the key activities, tasks and work steps that are used to support the firm's various product/service bundles. The documentation of the key process relationships should include:[26]

- detailed specification of process inputs (an event that causes an activity to be performed);
- suppliers of inputs;
- input/supplier relationships;

- output;
- customer per process or sub-process;
- the actual activities performed;
- the drivers of the activity;
- any and all cost objects of interest;
- resources required; and
- the drivers of resource consumption.

Similar to the type of information required to build an Activity-Based Costing Model, this documentation supports downstream analysis and improvement efforts.

Figure 8.5 A Structured Business Process Hierarchy

1 Product Creation

1.1 Perform Research
1.11 Perform Market Research
1.12 Analyze Competitive Data
1.13 Synthesize Market And Consumer Input

1.2 Develop Product Strategy
1.21 Estimate Volumes And Assess Impact
1.22 Assess Make Versus Buy
1.23 Establish Marketing Position/Strategy
1.24 Establish Long Range Product Plan

1.3 Develop Product Concept
1.31 Package The Vehicle System
1.32 Establish Concept Direction
1.33 Develop Workplan - $, Timing, Resources
1.34 Identify Components/Systems

1.4 Develop Major Product Elements
1.41 Develop Transmissions
1.42 Develop Engines
1.43 Develop Vehicle Body
1.44 Develop Vehicle Interior
1.45 Develop Vehicle Underbody
1.46 Develop Bill Of Materials
1.47 Source Components
1.48 Create Parts/Service Documentation

1.5 Validate Major Product Elements
1.51 Build Prototypes Vehicles
1.52 Test Vehicle System
1.53 Build Prototype Components
1.54 Test Components

1.6 Develop Production Methods
1.61 Define Manufacturing Process/Objectives
1.62 Develop Stamping Dies
1.63 Pilot Production Process
1.64 Develop Production Tooling
1.65 Develop Job (build) Assignments

2 Volume Production

2.1 Capacity Plan Production Resources

2.11 Capacity Plan Production Processes
2.12 Capacity Plan Tooling
2.13 Capacity Plan Facility
2.14 Capacity Plan Material
2.15 Capacity Plan H/R

2.2 Prepare Production And Support Resources

2.21 Design/Construct & Renovate Production Processes
2.22 Design/Construct & Renovate Production Tooling
2.23 Design/Construct & Renovate Production Facility And Grounds
2.24 Prepare H/R

2.3 Schedule Production Resources

2.31 Schedule Production Processes
2.32 Schedule Production Tooling
2.33 Schedule Production Facility
2.34 Schedule Material
2.35 Schedule H/R

2.4 Move Material/Products

2.41 Transport (external) Material/Products
2.42 Receive Material/Products
2.43 Handle WIP Material/Products
2.44 Ship Material/Products

2.5 Produce Products

2.51 Stamp, Manufacture And Assemble Components
2.52 Assemble Vehicles

2.6 Maintain Production Processes

2.61 Maintain Production Equipment
2.62 Maintain Production Tooling
2.63 Maintain Production Support Equipment
2.64 Maintain Production Facility and Grounds
2.65 Maintain H/R

2.7 Manage And Administer The Business

2.71 Keep Books
2.72 H/R Administration
2.73 Plan, Communicate And Coordinate

3 Customer Acceptance

3.1 Facilitate Purchase Experience

3.11 Sell Products
3.12 Define Terms And Conditions

3.2 Obtain Service Material

3.21 Process Warranty Claims
3.22 Obtain Service Parts
3.23 Obtain Service Tools
3.24 Obtain Service Documents/Training

3.3 Service Product/Customer

3.31 Service Products
3.32 Diagnose Problems
3.33 Service Customers

3.4 Stimulate Owner Loyalty

3.41 Analyze Field Data/Claims
3.42 Provide Input To Development
3.43 Respond To/Connect With Customers

3.5 Assess Customer Preferences

3.51 Survey Current Buyers
3.52 Survey Future Buyers
3.53 Market Products
3.54 Stimulate Interest

Source: *The Road to Excellence: Becoming a Process-Based Company,* CAM-I, 1997: 34-35.

As noted by Rummler and Brache, [27] *since the purpose of a function is to support processes, it should be measured on the degree to which it serves those processes. When we establish functional goals that bolster processes, we ensure that each department meets the needs of its internal and external customers.* Summarizing the process clarification initiative, three steps are completed: [28]

- business processes are viewed and analyzed as holistic systems of interdependencies;
- processes are identified and structured into a hierarchical model;
- processes are decomposed to the activity and task level necessary to drive improvement.

CREATING PROCESS AWARENESS

Ensuring the buy-in and support for Process Management requires the creation of process awareness within all levels and functions within the organization. The first step in creating this awareness is to define a clear, practical vision of the desired end-state and a description of what the organization will be like in the future. [29] The goal is to have every employee own a piece of the change initiative. This ownership leads naturally to the second major step in awareness building, namely to address employee concerns about the change process by establishing a two-way communication process. Effective, open communication will strengthen the change process by creating enhanced buy-in and enthusiasm for potential improvements.

Creating buy-in for the process initiation throughout the organization is a third critical step in creating a process awareness. Education and role modeling are two ways to spread process knowledge and understanding of the implicit and explicit changes entailed by a process-based structure. Other change initiatives should be integrated into the process effort to reduce confusion, avoid a "fad" culture, and to eliminate redundancies and rework in the process analysis, design, and implementation activities.

Finally, it is imperative that management actively and openly deals with the organizational and behavioral issues that normally accompany any major change. Five major factors need to be considered at this stage: [30]   employee involvement, incentives,

Figure 8.6   Barriers to Change

Barrier	Tactic
Individual barriers: • Comfort with status quo	• Create a desire for change that will override their discomfort with changing the status quo: ◊ Explain reasons for change ◊ Describe a clear view of the future ◊ Sell benefits of the change ◊ Commemorate milestones/successes
• Fear of the unknown	• Keep people informed; take the mystery out of change
• Lack of necessary skills	• Train employees on requisite skills
Organizational barriers: • No linkage between processes and strategic plan	• Help management to: ◊ Clarify the role of process-based management ◊ Link processes to strategic plan
• Inappropriate performance measures	• Make top management aware of the benefits of developing and installing appropriate performance measures • Jointly develop performance measures as a feedback loop to employees.
• Inappropriate organizational structures	• Determine a structure that promotes a horizontal as opposed to vertical flow of work
• Right people not involved in right way	• Select the best people to be process champions and in charge of individual processes
Cultural barriers: • History of change	• Admit that changes may have been handled poorly in the past; describe how this change will be handled differently • Involve people in the change process
Environmental barriers: • Union and other employee groups	• Involve union leaders in the decision-making process

Source: *The Road to Excellence: Becoming a Process-Based Company*, CAM-I, 1997: 52.

training, resistance to change, time, and organizational alignment. Gaining employee involvement is best accomplished by having individuals map their own work processes. Mapping encourages people to discuss current and potential problems, identify opportunities, and establish a common purpose and language. The result is commitment, not simply compliance, to the objectives of process management.

Aligning incentives to process goals helps create the necessary level of employee commitment. These incentives should support both short-term improvement needs and long-term advances defined at both a team and individual level. Non-financial as well as financial measurements should be used, with identified shortcomings addressed through skills development and training, not punishment. Training can be used to both teach and gain support for process concepts, helping individuals see their decisions and actions through a process perspective. Employee involvement, incentives, and education programs all help overcome the resistance to change (see Figure 8.6).

Creating process awareness takes time because it requires changes in the organization's culture, personal beliefs, and social structures. Initially, a pilot approach may ease the transition to a process structure. Relatedly, simply redefining the objectives of functions to meet process objectives can go a long way in building awareness and understanding of cross-functional issues. The final step, creating process ownership and control systems, provides the incentives and clarity needed to ensure long-term use of and benefit from process thinking.

PROCESS OWNERSHIP AND CONTROL

The establishment of a management infrastructure and chain of accountability to lock in Process Management is the final step in creating a process mindset.[31] Unless accountabilities are redefined and assigned to specific individuals, the process initiative will undoubtedly flounder. Process ownership is required to set policies for the process, to deploy the process, and to support process performers.[32] In some companies these three tasks fall to distinctly different individuals (process executive, process director and process coordinator). In others, the specifics of the jobs involved in the process management infrastructure are simplified into team-based and coordinator roles. The more complex an organization is the more elaborate will be the process structures needed to ensure that activities are performed and coordinated as required to meet process objectives (see for example, GTE's structure, Figure 8.7).

The basic elements of control remain unchanged by the type of management structure it serves. The type and frequency of one form of control (action, result or personal) versus another may change, but the need to set objectives, monitoring performance, analyze results, and make adjustments (Plan-Do-Check-Act) remain constant.[33] Specifically, goals have to be clearly established and aligned to organizational strategies. Second, individual and team accountability for achieving these goals need to be established. Third, the assigned responsibilities have to be complemented with the requisite resources and ability to control or have major influence on the process and its focus. Fourth, measurements have to be developed that support

Figure 8.7   GTE Telephone Operations Process Management Roles and Responsibilities

Process Executive
- Champion Process Management
- Formulate Process Vision
- Champion Process Across Enterprise
- Identify Critical Process Business Issues
- Balance Process Focus/Functional Focus
- Process Performance Measures/Targets
- Resource/Capital Allocation/Reallocation
- Appoint/Support Process Champions
- Approve Gap Closure Plans

Process Champion
- Identifies Critical Subprocess Business Issues
- Defines Scope of Project
- Creates Permanent Process Team
- Serves on Process Panel
- Champions Subprocess/Team
- Manage White Space of Process/Subprocess
- Provide Team Rewards/Recognition

Process Team Leader
- Coordinate Long-Term Vision and Migration Plan for Each Process
- Create Quantum Leaps for Processes
- Advocate/Maintain Enterprise Process Focus
- Link With Continuous Process Improvement Teams

Process Panel
- Provide Alignment Across Subprocesses
- Integrates Process Improvements Cross-Functionally
- Reallocates Resources to Fund Action Plans
- Provides Clear Line of Sight to Customer Needs
- Link Subprocess Performance to Process Performance

Permanent Process Team
- Bring Subject Matter Expertise to Team
- Conduct Root Cause Analysis
- Design Improvements and Measures
- Develop/Recommend Process Improvements/Gap Closure Ideas
- Maintain/Update Process Documentation
- Advocate/Maintain Process Focus Throughout the Enterprise

Facilitator
- Manage Team Logistics
- Facilitate Group Meetings
- Monitor Timelines & Project Schedules
- Mediate Interpersonal Conflicts

Scribe
- Document Team Meetings
- Distribute Minutes & Progress Reports
- Coordinate Formal Communications

Source: *The Road to Excellence: Becoming a Process-Based Company*, CAM-I, 1997: 68.

individual and team learning, allow for mid-stream adjustments of process activities or efforts to avoid undesirable or unplanned outcomes, and that create goal congruence. Fifth, incentive and reward systems need to reflect the process goals and the team or individual's success in attaining them. Finally, feedback and continuous improvement have to be built into the control process to encourage learning over the short- and long-term.

The matching of accountability and controllability to reflect the process structure is essential if a process awareness is to be effectively created. Process owners need to be identified, assigned responsibility and authority to achieve objectives, and have their performance evaluation reflect these roles and results. If measurements and accountabilities are not redefined, there will be little incentive to change. Even more important, the Process Management initiative will be seen as a fad or passing management fancy—people perceive that if it is ignored long enough, then it will probably go away.

It is critical to ensure that controls are constantly reviewed as new management change initiatives are developed and processes are adjusted to accommodate them. A comprehensive change strategy that reinforces process management and incorporates the major elements of related change initiatives (such as Total Quality Management, Quality Function Deployment, Target Costing, etc.) aids in ensuring consistency in the core processes and performance of the firm around a common philosophy. The simple maxim, "You get what you measure and reward" remains as true in Process Management as it is in any other organizational setting.[34]

Migrating to Process Management
All that is human must retrograde if it does not advance.
– Edward Gibbon

At Texas Instruments (TI), the implementation of Process Management is seen as a migration path.[35] The TI model develops a process description for each level of process maturity. It also defines the basic requirements needed to move from one level of process maturity to the next. The TI model provides a comprehensive framework for assessing current process management capabilities and ensuring that long-term improvements in these skills are achieved.[36]

Figure 8.8   Process Management Maturity Phases

Requirements for Process Maturity Level Advancement

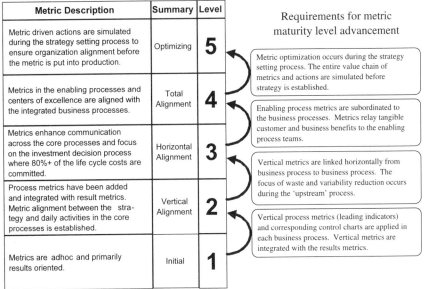

TI 'Metric & Process Maturity Model'

Metric Description	Summary	Level
Metric driven actions are simulated during the strategy setting process to ensure organization alignment before the metric is put into production.	Optimizing	5
Metrics in the enabling processes and centers of excellence are aligned with the integrated business processes.	Total Alignment	4
Metrics enhance communication across the core processes and focus on the investment decision process where 80%+ of the life cycle costs are committed.	Horizontal Alignment	3
Process metrics have been added and integrated with result metrics. Metric alignment between the strategy and daily activities in the core processes is established.	Vertical Alignment	2
Metrics are adhoc and primarily results oriented.	Initial	1

Requirements for metric maturity level advancement

Metric optimization occurs during the strategy setting process. The entire value chain of metrics and actions are simulated before strategy is established.

Enabling process metrics are subordinated to the business processes. Metrics relay tangible customer and business benefits to the enabling process teams.

Vertical metrics are linked horizontally from business process to business process. The focus of waste and variability reduction occurs during the 'upstream' process.

Vertical process metrics (leading indicators) and corresponding control charts are applied in each business process. Vertical metrics are integrated with the results metrics.

© 1996 Texas Instruments Inc.

Source: *The Road to Excellence: Becoming a Process-Based Company*, CAM-I, 1997: 75

The migration model consists of four primary phases: assessment, development, implementation, and embedding of the process management mindset and methods (see Figure 8.8). During assessment, the Process Management infrastructure is established and current process performance assessed. The specific efforts and initiatives to establish a process management infrastructure include:[37]

- Establish process executives, process panels, and permanent process teams;

- Develop a process management deployment proposal, including a "to be" process map;

- Assign members to the permanent process team, including job performers and key supervisors who participate in, and have detailed knowledge, of the process;

- Assess current level of process performance against a pre-defined critical process or business issue, such as reducing process-driven defects by 50% within one year;

- Assess impact of strategic direction and how the process team will address these both in the structuring of the processes and its downstream deployment;

- Prioritize major process deficiencies and incorporate the tools necessary to address them into the training of the permanent process team;

- Provide process team/individual training including process management change methodologies, process analysis and mapping techniques, team building, and project management.

Having completed the development of the infrastructure, Process Management efforts should be focused onto the assessment of current process performance.[38] The first step is to develop required process documentation, such as process maps, activity definitions, and key interdependencies and functional overlays in order to tightly define and identify the current work flow. The second step, gathering existing measurements, seeks to understand and begin integrating existing functional measurements with process-defined performance requirements. Finally, performance trends and issues should be identified and prioritized through root cause analysis, looking for disconnects and key performance gaps. The resulting list can be used to structure and plan performance improvement initiatives.

The second major phase in process management migration toward its ideal end-state is the development of improvement and deployment plans.[39] Identifying improvement opportunities begins with determining a specific improvement approach, such as emphasizing the development of long-term systems or information enablers prior to pursuing short-term improvements. Benchmarking can be used by the process team to identify alternative approaches to current process challenges and issues. Integration issues should then be resolved, emphasizing interdependencies and their active and effective management.

With basic issues addressed, the permanent process team can begin to define proposed Performance measures and establish process performance standards. Disconnects in the process should be addressed through improvement goals and related efforts (such as reengineering). The implementation plan can then be developed, which includes the evaluation and prioritization of disconnect solutions and the development of a high level business case to assess the costs and benefits of improvements targeted at removing or remediating process disconnects. The business case should include four basic steps:[40]

- Prioritize the short-term improvements to coincide with the future state vision;
- Conduct cost/benefit analysis;
- Analyze risks and returns; and,
- Review and approve the business case.

Having explored key details, a formal process improvement plan should be developed and accountabilities assigned to specific teams or team members. The improvement plan should be linked directly to an operational plan in order to secure funding and support the reallocation of scarce resources to approved initiatives. Plans to develop the required new skills and competencies to perform to the "to be" process design end should be a priority of the implementation team.

Implementation of process management includes the launching of process improvement projects, the pilot testing of process changes, development of specific performer accountabilities, and the deployment of recommended process improvements to transform the "to be" map from vision into reality. [41] Process performance can then be evaluated by conducting process certifications, identifying process performance variances from specifications, and evaluating customer survey results to monitor the effectiveness of process improvements.

In the end, the goal is to improve the performance of the organization and the processes that comprise it, creating an ongoing cycle of change (phase 4 of the migration). It is this ongoing effort to improve and learn that sets process management apart from more traditional, static management systems. A representative set of activities that can be used to improve performance of a process include:[42]

- estimate the relationships between financial objectives and overall satisfaction;
- set strategic satisfaction targets;

- estimate the relationship between satisfaction and attribute performance;
- select one or more value attributes for improvement and set targets to meet them;
- estimate the relationship between service-level and process-level attributes;
- select process-level improvement alternatives;
- evaluate the benefits and costs of different improvement alternatives;
- select and implement optimal process improvement initiatives;
- measure improvement on an ongoing basis against defined targets; and,
- continuously evaluate process performance tools for applicability, accuracy, and fit to current strategic and customer satisfaction objectives.

A core issue embedded in the fourth phase of the process management migration path is that learning never ends in a process-based organization—continuous learning is the essence of process management. There is no standing still, no acceptance of the status quo, and no opportunity to calcify existing structures, outputs, objectives or measures in successful process management efforts.

Corning is one firm that has applied the basic concepts of the four-stage migration model to create a process-driven organization. In the process of integrating its efforts along both cost and growth dimensions, Corning's management has discovered four elements critical to locking in process-based changes:[43]

- formalizing process steering committees that have responsibility for sharing best practices and driving continuous improvement on an enterprise-wide level increases overall learning;
- establishing a small reengineering "Center of Excellence" ensures that required process and teaming skills are retained and used to consistently deliver value to customers;

- deploying measurement systems to support the identification of best practices can bolster continuous improvement efforts; and,

- continuing communication by senior management can reinforce new behaviors.

Figure 8.9   Creating a Learning Culture

1. *Shared Mindset (Organizational culture)*
To what extent does our culture promote learning?

2. *Competence*	3. *Consequence*	4. *Governance*	5. *Capacity for Change*
To what extent do we have individual team and organizational competencies that facilitate learning?	To what extent does our performance management system encourage learning?	To what extent do our organizational structures and communication processes facilitate learning?	To what extent do our work processes and systems encourage learning?

6. *Leadership*
To what extent do leaders throughout our organization demonstrate a commitment to learning?

Source: Ashkenas, et.al., *The Boundaryless Organization*, San Francisco: Jossey-Bass, 1995: 183

Learning should be a visible part of the Process Management strategic and operational plan, playing a central role in its initial implementation and long-term deployment. Investments in learning, and their impact on the organization, should be tracked by ongoing comparison to benchmark data and other standards. It is also critical that top management clearly articulate what "learning" means within the context of the organization and its new process structures.

There is more than one way an organization can learn to learn (see Figure 8.9). Learning can take place through continuous improvement efforts, through competence acquisition, through experimentation, and through boundary spanning.[44] No one approach works well in all settings. For instance, GM's Saturn Division employs learning through experimentation, while Boeing participates in inter-industry consortia to gain new knowledge. The generation and institutionalization of innovative ideas and methods remains central to achieving long-term continuous improvement goals.[45]

In the end, the goal of Process Management is not to replace the traditional vertical, functional structure with a horizontal structure with its own unique set of gaps and "white spaces," but rather to create a collaborative environment where teams form and dissolve as customer requirements change. Process Management seeks to make impermanence permanent. It is an evolutionary change in mindset, methods, and activities. It emphasizes value creation and growth based on meeting or exceeding customer expectations. The effective deployment of Process Management requires a total rethinking of how work is managed in an organization.

PROCESS ANALYSIS

At several points in the above discussion, the terms "as is" and "to be" process maps have been used. Process maps serve as an important analytical tool in all phases of process management planning, deployment, and improvement. *Process analysis* is a formal data gathering approach that seeks to involve employees in the change process, determine how work is currently done, understand why work is done, begin to focus on management by process, and identify opportunities for improvement.[46] At the heart of this effort lies the identification of the activities, tasks and detailed work steps to develop a comprehensive understanding of how work is performed within the current environment by the specific process job performers.

Preliminary efforts to undertake process analysis should ensure that: the overall goals of the mapping process are well understood; the scope of the mapping project is clearly defined (what level and sub-processes are to be mapped); a detailed project plan has been developed; and the project kick-off results in clear understanding of priorities, objectives and responsibilities by affected individuals and teams.[47]

The first map prepared during process analysis is called the "as is" map. Its development entails the creation of detailed process descriptions and activity/sub-task identifications.[48] The detailed information, gathered from those who perform the work, is combined to create a visual picture of the flow of work through a process (see Figure 8.10). The "as is" map should also be measured and assessed for current effectiveness or shortfalls. Key performance attributes should be collected for each major activity (such as transaction volumes and timings). Specifically, the value-creating aspects of the process and activities should be identified along with a detailed narrative and analysis of technology enablers, people enablers (communication, education, training and leadership style), and current customer needs and requirements for change.

The current state analysis should be validated for accuracy with current process owners and participants to ensure its accuracy and increase overall buy-in to the process approach. Understanding what is done is only part of the Process Management equation; why the activity is performed is just as critical to understand if performance improvements are to be achieved without the creation of new problems. Finally, an intricate part of creating and analyzing the "as is" process map is to develop short-term improvement objectives to address readily apparent process performance shortfalls, process disconnects, and develop and prioritize plans to address the identified problems.

Correcting obvious problems is an intermediate step in the development of future state "to be" process maps. These maps should incorporate industry and best practice learnings to create a sequence of activities and outcomes consistent with company strategies and fine-tuned to optimize performance against customer requirements.[49] Several core tasks are performed in the development of a future state vision, including: analyze corporate objectives and assess the business environment, conduct best practices and benchmarking research, conduct future state visioning sessions, develop initial future state process design maps, and review and approve the future state vision.

The process team seeking to improve performance of the order-taking and payment process through the use of electronic data interchange (EDI) determines that reaching the 20% cycle time improvement goal will require routing any customer orders failing the credit check directly to the sales department (see Figure 8.11). These orders are currently cancelled if credit is refused, creating customer dissatisfaction and generating a complete rework cycle once required credit verifications or assurances are obtained. The team believes customer relationships will be improved and that the sales force will become more aware of credit issues by implementing these new procedures. A second change, namely instituting a perpetual inventory system, is recommended to improve the accuracy of the inventory checking and order release efforts. Moving from the current to the future state vision requires the effective implementation of these, and other, improvement efforts.

Creating a process mindset does not end with developing a new process flow or implementing process improvement projects. Without

Figure 8.10   An "As Is" Process Map

Process Name: <u>Order Fulfillment</u>

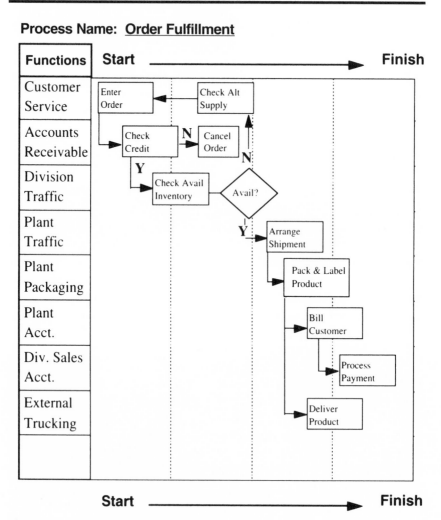

Source: *The Road to Excellence: Becoming a Process-Based Organization,* op.cit., pg. 97

a shift in the type, and use, of measurements, the mindset change that defines the process approach cannot take place.[50] Both financial and non-financial in nature, process-based measurements should be integrated into a system that balances organizational goals for efficiency and profitability with customer-driven concerns; such as quality and effectiveness of the process and the products and services

Figure 8.11 A "To Be" Process Map

Process Name: Order Fulfillment

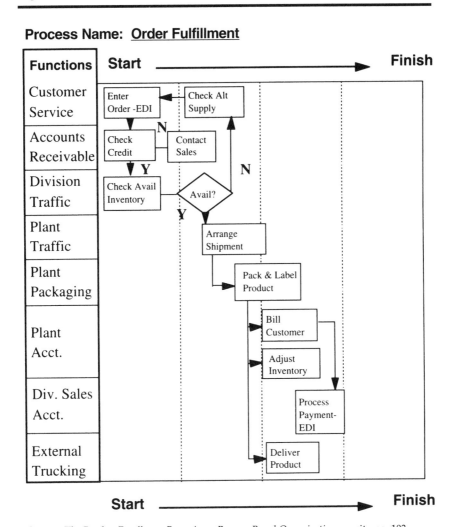

Source: *The Road to Excellence: Becoming a Process-Based Organization,* op.cit., pg. 103

they provide. The discussion now turns to the vital role played by measurement in Process Management.

MEASUREMENTS AND PROCESS MANAGEMENT

Developing a process-based performance measurement system begins with identifying the customers of the business process, determining their performance expectations, and understanding how customers use process outputs.[51] Three specific categories of measurements are developed based on the detailed understanding of customer and organizational requirements: efficiency metrics, effectiveness metrics, and capability metrics.[52] Reflecting the core customer value criteria for the process (see Figure 8.12), these metrics should emphasize the company's strategy, the relationship of strategy to company stakeholders, and the current and desired characteristics of key processes and their output. The failure to tie performance standards to the strategy of the organization can create problems not only in creating and implementing a process management approach, but in deploying and focusing resources downstream.

Efficiency measures include such traditional items as operating costs, resource utilization levels, and the productivity of an activity or process. Understanding the cost of performing process work or meeting customer requirements remains an essential part of any sound measurement system.   If a process is too costly, it can negatively impact the short-term profits and long-term viability of an organization.[53] The real issue to keep in mind is that the goal in designing a performance measurement system is alignment: first satisfy customer-driven performance needs and then satisfy the requirements of other stakeholders. Efficiency metrics should be counter-balanced by effectiveness and capability measures.

Effectiveness metrics compare the anticipated outputs of the process (specific products/services performed, delivery time, quantity produced/delivered) to the actual output, measuring what the organization has accomplished versus what it should have done.[54] The goal, to produce the right product or service, at the right time, delivered in the right place in the right amount and to the right specifications, drives effectiveness measurement efforts. In a process setting, effectiveness can also incorporate such critical dimensions as the flexibility and responsiveness of the process to current and changing customer requirements. Where efficiency measures focus on the input side of the process, effectiveness metrics emphasize the impact the short-term profits and long-term viability of an organization.[53] The real issue to keep in mind is that the goal in designing a performance measurement system is alignment: first satisfy customer-driven performance needs and then satisfy the requirements of other stakeholders. Efficiency metrics should be counter-balanced by effectiveness and capability measures.

Effectiveness metrics compare the anticipated outputs of the process (specific products/services performed, delivery time, quantity produced/delivered) to the actual output, measuring what the organization has accomplished versus what it should have done.[54] The goal, to produce the right product or service, at the right time, delivered in the right place in the right amount and to the right specifications, drives effectiveness measurement efforts. In a process setting, effectiveness can also incorporate such critical dimensions as the flexibility and responsiveness of the process to current and changing customer requirements. Where efficiency measures focus on

Figure 8.12 Customer Value Criteria

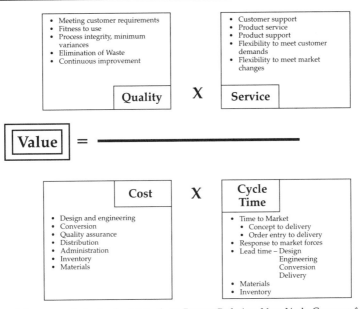

Source: Johansson, et.al., *Breakpoint Business Process Redesign,* New York: Coopers & Lybrand, 1992:30.

the input side of the process, effectiveness metrics emphasize the quality and overall performance of outputs against customer expectations.

The flexibility of a process is a relatively new effectiveness performance measurement. Examples of flexibility measures include: the ability to accommodate variation in the quality of purchased materials; ease of producing new products; ability to accommodate change in the current production and/or delivery schedule to accommodate unanticipated needs; the responsiveness to variances in aggregate production volumes from period to period; and the ability to adjust to modifications in the mix of resources (materials, labor and capital) used in the productive process. A flexible process has great value to both the customer and the organization, increasing the speed at which a company can respond to changing requirements. [55]

The final category of process measurements, capability metrics, are the average and standard deviations of process performance studied over time.[56] They are used to assess the current degree of variation in the process versus its defined standards and/or prior performance. Capability metrics provide early warning signals of future problems. Schonberger describes capability in terms of the "variation pile-up problem." Unique to interdependent processes, variation pile-up captures the cumulative effect of one activity, output or process interacting with the variation of something else. The two forms of variation do not cancel out. For instance, if an automobile door frame is within specifications, but falls close to the high end of this range in terms of overall size, while a door (also within specifications) comes close to the lower end of acceptance in terms of being almost too small, the "fit" between the door and frame becomes unacceptable. The door frame, which is a tad too large, and the door, being just a bit too small, combine to create a door/frame system that has a major gap and fails to meet quality requirements.[57] Clearly, the more elements there are interacting in the process, the worse this problem can become.

Regardless of the type of measure used, measurements can be used to lock the process management effort into place. The reason to measure process performance is to provide management with the basis for:[58]

- specifically communicating performance expectations to subordinates;

- knowing what is going on in the organization;
- identifying problems before customer satisfaction results reflect them;
- identifying performance gaps that should be analyzed and eliminated;
- providing feedback that compares performance to a standard;
- identifying performance that should be rewarded; and,
- effectively making and supporting decisions regarding resources, plans, policies, schedules and structure.

The benefits of measurement, though, do not stop with those experienced by the firm's management. Without measures, employees at all levels have no way of specifically: [59]

- knowing exactly what is expected of them;
- generating the level of motivation required to meet performance goals;
- aligning their performance with the overall strategy of the enterprise or to process objectives;
- monitoring their own performance and generating their own feedback;
- generating their own rewards and understanding what performance is required for rewards from others;
- communicating successes and shortfalls effectively; and,
- identifying performance improvement areas.

Measurements should be simple and easy to understand. They also need to be closely tied to operations to reflect current status as well as aligned with corporate strategies and continuous improvement efforts. As a process migrates through various levels of maturity, the metrics used to track it should also change, as suggested by an elaboration of Texas Instrument's process maturity model to include measurement requirements (see Figure 8.13).

The final element in creating process measurements that result in desired performance is to link individual and team rewards and incentives to process measurements and objectives. Variable compensation, recognition programs, and individual achievement awards based on actual versus planned performance are just a few of

Figure 8.13 TI Metric and Process Maturity Model

TI 'Metric & Process Maturity Model'

Metric Description	Summary	Level	Summary	Process Description
Metric driven actions are simulated during the strategy setting process to ensure organization alignment before the metric is put into production.	Optimizing	**5**	Holistic	Process management has enabled the enterprise to be a learning, agile, and forward looking organization.
Metrics in the enabling processes and centers of excellence are aligned with the integrated business processes.	Total Alignment	**4**	Enabling Processes Integrated	Enabling process management subordinated to business processes is implemented, in control, and in management's unconscious thinking.
Metrics enhance communication across the core processes and focus on the investment decision process where 80%+ of the life cycle costs are committed.	Horizontal Alignment	**3**	Core Processes Integrated	Business processes establish a common language or translator with each other business process. This enables inter-business process excellence (eg. DFM).
Process metrics have been added and integrated with result metrics. Metric alignment between the strategy and daily activities in the core processes is established.	Vertical Alignment	**2**	Customer Focus	Business process management which begins and ends with the customer, is established, in control, and in management's conscious thinking.
Metrics are adhoc and primarily results oriented.	Initial	**1**	Initial	Few processes are defined. Process management is not a strategic thrust.

Source: *The Road to Excellence: Becoming a Process-Based Organization,* op.cit., pg. 117.

the ways individual incentives can be brought into line with process objectives. Linking individual and team accountability, controllability and incentives to the core dimensions of process performance is the key to creating the mindset and culture change that is at the heart of a successful Process Management implementation.[60]

Continuous Process Management

*I don't care what becomes of me so long as it's
a change for the better.*
– William Feather

Continuous Process Management *is the embedding of a systematic, integrative, and cross-functional approach to perpetually managing processes to increase customer value.*[61] Managing the organization as an integrated set of processes that is undergoing continuous, evolutionary improvement requires the constant attention to, and pursuit of, improvement opportunities large and small, throughout the process team.[62] Everyone in the organization is responsible for identifying process deficiencies and developing process improvements. In order to continuously improve a business process, key information regard-ing process performance must be available to the individual with the responsibility and authority to modify processing. This concept is often defined as the co-location of knowledge and decision rights, the essence of effective responsibility accounting and control systems.

In order to fully integrate performance monitoring into the business process, several supporting management techniques should be used in combination: work flow tracking, activity-based manage-ment, benchmarking, statistical process control, target costing, asset management, and performance management. Integrating these tools will create the integrated perspective and database required to reach the ultimate level of process performance.

At its most basic level, though, process performance improvement involves only two basic components: learning and doing. Process improvement results from the combined learning derived from many failed experiments and the incremental advances in understanding that can turn failures into success. Monitoring and evaluation tools, applied consistently and continuously, provide the feedback and information required to gain incremental knowledge and create process innovations to increase performance against customer and organizational requirements. In the learning organization, process management is the pathway, not the destination. In the end, process management works because it:[63]

- establishes key objectives;
- builds on trust and openness;
- establishes a common focus across the organization;
- builds in early problem identification;
- uses the dynamics of teamwork;
- builds on partnerships and cooperation;
- results in self-fulfillment;
- supports and reinforces cultural change;
- challenges everyone to set stretch targets;
- enables continuous improvement;
- improves customer satisfaction; and,
- reduces process variability.

References

Ackerman, R.G., and G.L. Nielson, "Partnering for Results: A Case Study of Re-Engineering the Corning Way," *Strategy & Business*, Issue 3, 1996: 56-64.

Ashkenas, R., D. Ulrich, T. Jick and S. Kerr, *The Boundaryless Organization: Breaking the Chains of Organizational Structure*, San Francisco, Jossey-Bass Publishing, 1995.

Born, G., Process *Management to Quality Improvement*, New York: John Wiley & Sons,1995.

Bowman, E., and B. Kogut, *Redesigning the Firm*, New York: Oxford University Press,1995.

Daly, D.C., and T. Freeman, eds., *The Road to Excellence: Becoming a Process-Based Organization*, Bedford, TX: Consortium for Advanced Manufacturing—International, 1997.

Davenport, T., Process Innovation: *Reengineering Work through Information Technology*, Boston, MA: Harvard Business School Press, 1993.

Gouillart, F.S., and J.N. Kelly, *Transforming the Organization*, New York: McGraw-Hill Publishing, 1995.

Johansson, H.J., D.K. Carr, K.S. Dougherty, H.J. R.A. King, and D.F. Moran, *Breakpoint: Business Process Redesign*, New York: Coopers & Lybrand, 1992.

Keegan, D.P., and S.W. Pesci, "Why Not Reengineer the Management Process Itself?," *Journal of Cost Management*, Summer, 1994: 63-70.

Lee, C.R., "Process Reengineering at GTE: Milestones on a Journey Not Yet Completed," *Strategy & Business*, Issue 5, 1996: 58-67.

Majchrzak, A., and Q. Wang, "Breaking the Functional Mindset in Process Organizations," *Harvard Business Review*, Sept.-Oct., 1996: 93-99.

McHugh, P., G. Merli, and W. Wheeler, III, *Beyond Business Process Reengineering: Towards the Holonic Enterprise*, New York: John Wiley & Sons, 1995.

Melan, E., *Process Management: Methods for Improving Products and Service*, New York: McGraw-Hill Publishing, 1992.

Ramaswamy, R., *Design and Management of Service Processes: Keeping Customers for Life*, New York: Addison-Wesley, 1996.

Rummler, G.A., and A.P. Brache, *Improving Performance: How to Manage the White Space on the Organization Chart*, 2nd edition, San Franscisco: Jossey-Bass Publishing, 1995.

Shunk, D.L., *Integrated Process Design and Development*, Homewood, IL: Business One Irwin, 1992.

Society of Management Accountants of Canada, *Implementing Process Management: A Framework for Process Thinking*, Hamilton, Ontario, 1998.

Viscio, A.J. And B.A. Pasternack, "Toward a New Business Model," *Strategy & Business*, Issue 3, 1996: 8-14.

Womack, J.P., and D.T. Jones, *Lean Thinking*, New York: Simon and Schuster, 1996.

End Notes

1 This entire chapter heavily uses three primary sources for its insights, at times paraphrasing and others directly quoting from these works. The three works are: *The Road to Excellence: Becoming a Process-Based Company*, D. Daly and T. Freeman, ed., Bedford, TX: CAM-I, 1997; G. Rummler and R. Brache, *Improving Performance: How to Measure the White Space on the Organization Chart*, San Francisco, CA: Jossey-Bass, 1995; and, *Implementing Process Management: A Framework for Action* drafted by C.J. McNair for the Society of Management Accountants of Canada, Management Accounting Guideline #47, Hamilton, Ontario: 1998. Attempts have been made to ensure that these cites are given credit where used.

2 McNair, op.cit., pg. 1.

3 T. Davenport, *Process Innovation: Reengineering Work Through Information Technology*, Boston, MA: Harvard Business School Press, 1992: 5.

4 McNair, op.cit., pg. 7.

5 E. Melan, *Process Management: Methods for Improving Products and Services*, New York: McGraw-Hill Publishing, 1992.

6 Ibid, pg. 8-9.

7 McNair, op.cit., pg. 6.

8 Ibid, pg. 10.

9 Daly and Freeman, op.cit.

10 These insights and the discussion of "as is" and "to be" for the most part originate in the seminal Process Management work by G. Rummler and A. Brache, *Improving Performance: How to Manage the White Space on the Organization Chart*, 2nd edition, San Francisco, Jossey-Bass, 1995. It is well defined and illustrated in Daly and Freeman, op.cit., pp. 96-104.

11 Daly and Freeman, op.cit., pg. 101-104.

12 Melan, op.cit.

13 Daly and Freeman, op.cit.

14 Ibid, pg. 51.

15 Ibid, pg. 24.

16 Daly and Freeman, op.cit. This four phase approach originally appears in this work and is used in McNair, op.cit.

17 McNair, op.cit., pg. 10j.

18 Most of this discussion draws heavily from McNair, op.cit.

19 Ibid, pg 11.

20 Rummler and Brache, op.cit. This is the theme of their entire book, as suggested by the title noted earlier.

21 McNair, op.cit., pg. 4.

22 Much of this paragraph appears originally in McNair, op.cit. pg. 14.

23 R. Ackerman and G. Nielson, "Partnering for Results: A case study of reengineering the Corning way," *Strategy and Business*, 2nd quarter, 1996: 61.

24 Daly and Freeman, op.cit., pg 33.

25 Ibid, pg 36.

26 Ibid, pp. 39-40.

27 Rummler and Brache, op.cit., pg. 53.

28 Daly and Freeman, op.cit., pg. 41.

29 Ibid, pg 46-48 is the source for these steps and comments.

30 Ibid, pg. 48.

[31] McNair, op.cit., pg. 22.

[32] Daly and Freeman, op.cit., pg. 58-61.

[33] McNair, op.cit.

[34] Ibid, pg. 17.

[35] The migration path model presented here was originally conceived at GTE.

[36] Daly and Freeman, op.cit., pg. 74.

[37] Ibid, pp. 76-79.

[38] Ibid, pp. 79-80.

[39] This section draws from Daly and Freeman, op.cit., pp. 80-82.

[40] Ibid, pg. 83.

[41] Ibid, pp. 85-87.

[42] McNair, op.cit., pg. 37.

[43] Ibid, pg. 26.

[44] Ashkenas, et.al., *The Boundaryless Organization: Breaking the Chains of Organizational Structure*, San Francisco, Jossey-Bass Publishing, 1995.

[45] McNair, op.cit., pg. 21.

[46] Daly and Freeman, op.cit., pg. 93.

[47] Ibid, pp. 92-103.

[48] This section draws heavily from Daly and Freeman, op.cit., pp.96-99.

[49] This section reflects the discussion in Daly and Freeman, op.cit., pp. 99-103.

[50] McNair, op.cit., pg. 33.

[51] Daly and Freeman, op.cit., pg. 110.

[52] McNair, op.cit., pg. 33.

[53] This entire section, with minor paraphrasing, is drawn from McNair, op.cit., pp.33-36. These comments appear on pg. 33.

[54] Ibid, pp. 34-35.

[55] Ibid, pg. 35.

[56] Ibid, pp. 35-36. The Schonberger quotation appears originally in *Creating a Chain of Customers*, R. Schonberger, New York: The Free Press, 1988: pg. 87.

[57] Ibid, pg. 87.

[58] McNair, op.cit., pp. 36-37.

[59] Ibid, pg. 37. These two bullet lists pull directly from the cited work.

[60] Daly and Freeman, op.cit., pp. 115-117.

[61] Ibid, pg 128.

[62] This last section draws heavily from Daly and Freeman, op.cit., pp. 128-147.

[63] McNair, op.cit., pp. 42-43.

Chapter 9

The Extended Enterprise

Life cannot subsist in society but by reciprocal concessions.

– Samuel Johnson

Key Learnings:

- The Extended Enterprise is the network of firms that creates value for its customers by developing, producing, selling, servicing and recycling products and services as an integrated system.

- The objective of the Extended Enterprise model is to develop an environment where all value chain members function as a single entity.

- The benefits of the Extended Enterprise Strategic Management Process (SMP) extend from early product and process design and development through the delivery of after-purchase parts and service support. At every stage of the product and service delivery cycle, cycle time and responsiveness are improved through the open collaboration of trading partners.

- An integral support mechanism for the primary order-to-payment process that directly links current customer requests to the ongoing activities of the core value chain, the Extended Enterprise ensures that the right product can be made at the right time in the right place at required levels of quality and price.

There are few organizations that do not understand the importance of suppliers in developing and delivering the products and services required by customers. Yet many companies critically misunderstand and underestimate the untapped knowledge and resources of their supply chain. Developed within a traditional, adversarial environment where suppliers were pitted against each other to secure price and performance concessions, supplier relationships have represented a necessary evil of business life. From the supplier's perspective, the lack of loyalty, trust, and long-term commitment from buyers has discouraged them from investing in the assets and processes need to improve supply chain performance. Each firm, pursuing its own self-interest, has focused on its own performance improvement with apparently little or no regard for the quality of the total experience of customers with the supply chain.[1]

The cost of these adversarial customer-supplier relationships is becoming evident as organizational boundaries are bridged and supply chain collaboration emerges. Chicago-based A.T. Kearney estimates that traditional supply-chain costs represent more than 80 percent of a typical manufacturer's cost structure.[2] Attacking these costs through the development of inter-organizational process awareness and improvement efforts, facilitated by integrated software and communication systems, the Extended Enterprise (EE) empha-sizes improved performance throughout the value chain.

Radical reductions in cycle time and waste are the outcomes of improved EE. As the supplier-customer relationships migrate toward trust and open collaboration, transaction and inventory costs plummet. Organizations are recognizing that it is not as much the physical links in the supply chain that are causing inefficiencies, but rather the existing buying/selling patterns of behavior that are driving costs in the system. This is leading organizations to create EEs that are tailored to the unique characteristics of the chain's products and distribution channels.[3]

The Extended Enterprise is the formation process managing the flow of materials and finished product from supplier to customers, usually with a series of manufacturing facilities, warehouses, or distribution centers as intermediate stopover points.[4] It focuses on decision making throughout the supply chain, addressing key processes such as demand forecasting, demand management, production planning and scheduling, distribution planning, deployment and transportation. Interpreted within the organizational structure, this means creating organizational and process links and seamless information flows between marketing, sales, purchasing, finance, manufacturing, distribution and transportation as well as externally to customers, suppliers, carriers and retailers. It also means aligning corporate strategies, incentive functions and supply chain partners to achieve common goals, and physically redesigning the movement of goods to maximize channel value and lower net landed cost.

As the logic of integration of the supply chain expands, EEs result. The EE concept views the entire network of organizations that combine to deliver products and services as a collective team.[5] In most cases the team is led by a market maker (such as an OEM) who is the one who identifies and assembles other organizations into a trading alliance that provides specific value-added activities which result in delivered products and services. The trading partners work together to form a unique system of collective competencies and resources that have a strong focus on creating value for customers.

The objective of the Extended Enterprise model is to develop an environment where all value chain members function as a single entity. Aligning the purpose and strategies of diverse entities into a cooperative whole opens opportunities for cost reduction, investment leveraging, cycle time reductions, and knowledge sharing, all of which can contribute to increased customer satisfaction.[6] Eliminating many of the wasteful transaction costs and removing redundancies, delays, and inefficiencies from the supply chain, companies embracing the EE model are creating new forms of competitive advantages for themselves and their trading partners. It is an improvement in performance that shows up in the bottom line of every member of the Extended Enterprise.

The benefits of the Extended Enterprise SMP extend from early product and process design and development through the delivery of after-purchase parts and service support. At every stage of the product and service delivery cycle, cycle time and responsiveness are improved through the open collaboration of trading partners. Beginning with the identification and documentation of market requirements, the EE is involved early in the design and development process where product specifications are set. Recognizing that 90% of the downstream cost of making a product or providing a service is defined during product/process design, supply chain teams engage the support of potential suppliers to identify improvement areas. They also seek to eliminate unnecessary or costly design alternatives and establish a smooth mechanism for ongoing partnerships with key vendors.[7]

Electronic enablers, such as Enterprise Resource Planning systems (ERP) and Electronic Data Interchange (EDI), are used once the product is in production to help eliminate transaction costs and create a seamless flow of information and performance from the beginning to the end of the value chain. Costs caused by downstream companies are examined and optimized, as the entire value chain turns its attention to maximizing process performance against customer expectations. The development of mutually beneficial supply agreements serve a central role in defining expectations, establishing responsibility and feedback loops, and specify measures of performance. The result is an exponential improvement on all core dimensions of performance against customer expectations by the entire value chain.[8]

In the pages that follow, the basic elements of the Extended Enterprise will be presented. The opening discussion will be extended to include core issues and benefits of adopting an EE perspective. Finally, the challenges and opportunities entailed in the migration to and management of the EE will be explored. In total, the chapter will provide a basic understanding of the issues, challenges, and benefits of adopting a collaborative Extended Enterprise approach.

Essential Issues in the Extended Enterprise

If we devote our time disparaging the products of our business rivals, we hurt business generally, reduce confidence, and increase discontent.

– Edward N. Hurley

The Extended Enterprise can dramatically improve the bottom line performance of all participants. Discarding the adversarial relationships that have led to high transaction costs, delay, buffer inventories, and long cycle times, EE seeks to align the strategies and performance of a wide variety of firms into a seamless delivery system driven by customer requirements. Suppliers and customers, dealing with diverse departments in a traditional firm have often faced uncoordinated plans and conflicting demands. This, in turn, causes confusion, distrust, a highly reactive environment, and unintegrated planning systems. Trading partners do not cooperatively share projections about future needs, resulting in buffers of inventories and time required to allow each supply-chain function to perform with reasonable efficiency.[9]

Process inefficiency is the result of these disjointed, unco-ordinated, and at times conflictual supply chain relationships. Process inefficiencies have been found to account for 90 percent of the waste in organizations. Process waste is also created by the traditional belief that suppliers must be dealt with on a "negotiate-to-win" basis rather than with a win-win solution for both sides. There are several ways that these traditional supplier relationships are revealed through the following beliefs:[10]

- you need to keep three bids to keep suppliers honest; treat suppliers at arm's length so you can "keep them guessing;"
- have multiple suppliers so you can trade off one with the other;
- evaluate suppliers on the main basis of product pricing;
- focus on short term (one year) contracts; and,
- involve the supplier after the design is complete.

These practices result in waste. The supplier has little or no incentive to look at the overall cost of doing business with the immediate or value chain customer. Minimal investment is made in process and product improvement and performance because of the transitory, volatile nature of the underlying business relationship.

Faced with the need to improve customer service and decrease operating costs, firms are turning to EE to coordinate product flows and streamline process performance. But, if inventory and time are simply ripped out of the supply chain, massive disruptions will occur and customer service and satisfaction will be adversely affected. The key is not to remove the buffers, but rather to eliminate the problems that led to their need. Information about current and projected product flow must be substituted for inventory and time buffers. Effective planning processes need to be established to ensure that design, purchasing, manufacturing, distribution, transportation, marketing and sales work together to drive product flow. The result is reduced costs and cycle time, and improved customer service.

Figure 9.1 The Extended Enterprise SMP Flow

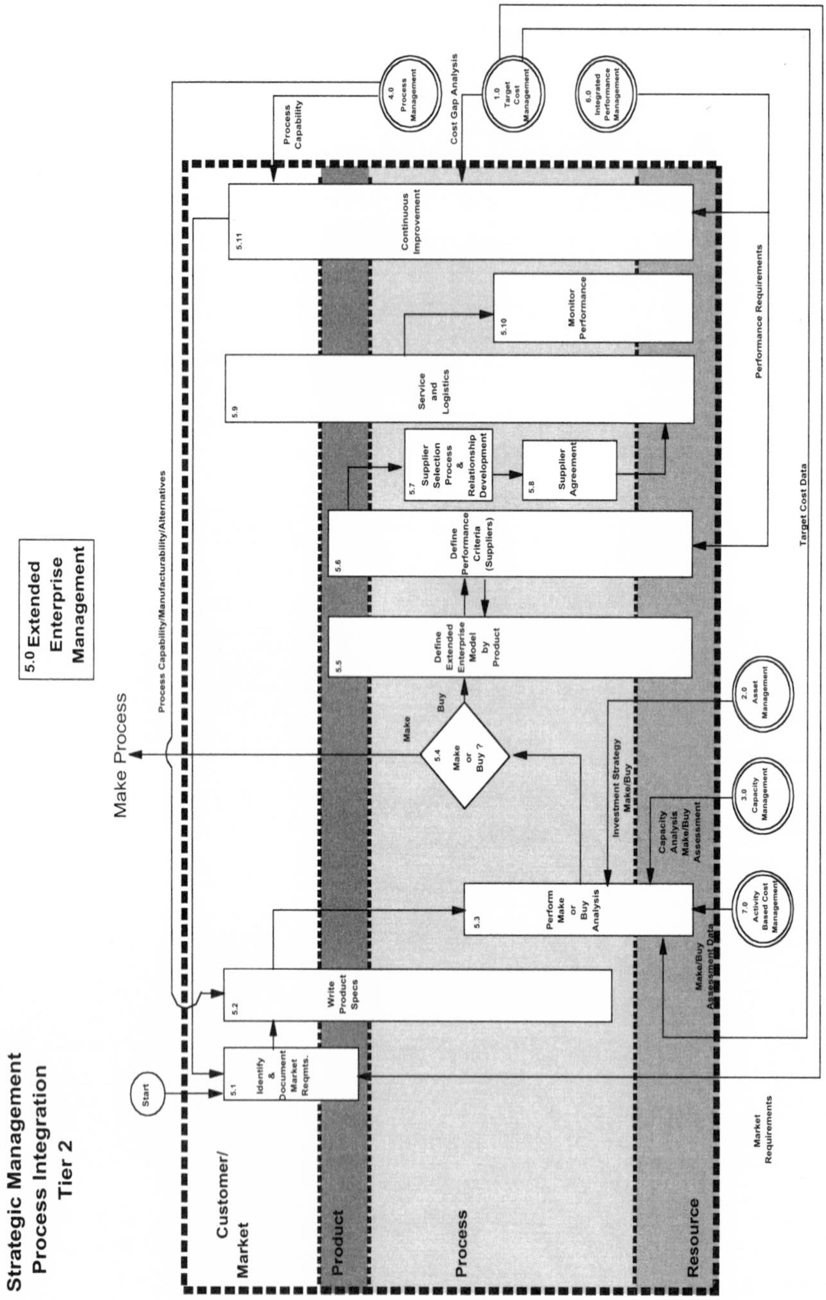

At DaimlerChrysler, the EE SMP is seen as the key to improving time-to-market and reducing the waste embedded in traditional supply chain structures. These changes are driven by a recognition that the final consumer of the EE's efforts is the one who pays for, and defines the price/value relationship, for a product. As noted by Jeffrey Trimmer in a recent interview,[11] "The final user of our automobiles is the only person who puts any money in the supply chain. We're all passing his tokens up and down the chain." EE helps a firm gain a better understanding of what the final consumer wants as well as helping it leverage the entire supply chain to meet these needs better, faster and cheaper than the competition.

BASIC ELEMENTS OF THE EXTENDED ENTERPRISE

The Extended Enterprise is an SMP that provides the major portion of its benefits, and places most of its attention, within the Process decision domain. An integral support mechanism for the primary order-to-payment process that directly links current customer requests to the ongoing activities of the core value chain, the EE ensures that the right product can be made at the right time in the right place at required levels of quality and price.

As suggested by Figure 9.1, EE begins with the identification and documentation of market requirements. These requirements flow from the Target Cost Management SMP as well as other core information and strategic management processes in the firm. Within EE, the expectations and needs of customers (internal and external) are identified and matched to internal and external capabilities. Some of the issues making up this first crucial step include:

- Define the marketplace;
- Define targeted customers and their needs;
- Identify core product characteristics, such as uniqueness, universality, ease of use, custom versus premium, low cost, commodity, quality, leverage, technology base, and related core value attributes for the item;
- Detail performance characteristics in customer view and language, then rate the firm's versus competitor's performance and product leadership capability;
- Build a business case for the market and product strategy,

including volumes, costs, margins, market share, capital requirements, R&D needs, promotion and distribution plans.

Having clearly identified what the market requirements are, attention turns to writing specific product specifications. These specifications include physical characteristics and appearance, performance requirements, manufacturability issues (e.g., does the new product, match existing manufacturing and process capabilities and capacities), and quality/reliability testing needs. Spanning the market, product, and process decision domains, this effort requires a cross-functional perspective and input from all levels of the organization. Designing a product or defining specifications without the input of the people who make the product, sell it, or use it can result in downstream process or product failures and/or excess costs.

The product specifications provide input to the decision on where and how to source a product, component or material. Make-buy analyses are performed, resulting in a decision to internally source an item or to turn to a supplier for the needed materials. Key elements of this analysis include the choice of technology (new or existing), capacity and capital requirements, fit within existing manufacturing strategy and core competencies, estimated and required time to market, and cash flow and cost analysis. While economics play a dominant role in this part of the sourcing initiative, an enterprise is constantly assessing key qualitative factors as well. Qualitative issues include control over the production and delivery process, quality of supplied items, timeliness and reliability of delivery, down-stream potential for price increases, and competitive concerns arising from sharing core technologies or designs with external firms.

While risks are inherent in outsourcing, there are also many benefits that accrue to partnering firms within the Extended Enterprise.[12] First, there are economies of skill and scale provided by suppliers, who are specialists in a specific technology or business area. In a rapidly changing technological environment, suppliers may be more well informed than buyers about recent advances. Such specialized knowledge can lead to improved quality and innovation. Outsourcing also frees up capital because the supplier will often assume responsibility for investments in fixed assets and labor, diversifying the risks of production and distribution over many firms rather than just one. When realized, everyone wins.

As suggested by Figure 9.2, the outsourcing decision can be broken into a series of steps.[13] The entire value chain is examined to identify activities that are potential outsourcing candidates and determine where this service is currently available. Questions used to guide the outsourcing analysis include the need to control the activity, the ability to achieve or benefit from best practice performance, cost consider-ations, and the relationship of the activity to the core strategy. Little will be gained in the long term if management seizes short-term cost savings at the cost of a broad strategic focus or the loss of control over a core competency. Outsourcing decisions are not easily, or quickly, reversed—they create long-term effects. The implications are that the criterion for acceptance shifts from an income perspective to one that emphasizes shareholder value.

Figure 9.2 Steps in the Outsourcing Decision Analysis

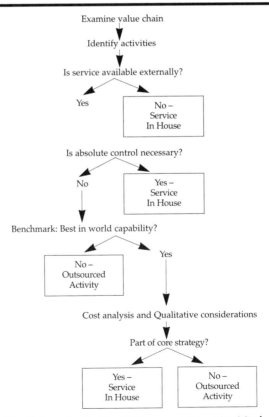

Source: R. Drtina, "The Outsourcing Decision," *Management Accounting*, March, 1994: 62.

Of course, there is also the potential for cost increases if the new relationships are poorly managed. In fact, the Boston Consulting Group study of over 100 manufacturing firms in Japan, the U.S., and Europe found that many companies are facing higher costs after oustourcing than they did before the relationship was established.[14] Both transaction costs and coordination costs, such as the development and maintenance of in-house teams, may lead to higher costs. In addition, new business risks, such as the breach of proprietary information, unexpected demand, and the unwillingness of the supplier to invest in new technologies can combine to make outsourcing less effective.

When outsourcing is chosen as the best alternative, it is possible to define the EE Model by product (see Figure 9.1). This activity ensures that the source of, and requirements for, the materials and services required to meet customer expectations are clearly identified and defined. Core issues in designing and managing the EE are discussed in more depth below.

DEFINING AND CREATING SUPPLY PARTNERSHIPS

Once the outsourcing decision has been made and the EE Model defined, the details of the supplier-enterprise relationship are defined. Performance criteria are established and negotiations undertaken that ultimately result in the selection of a specific vendor. Developing a solid relationship with a supplier begins with agreeing to the parameters of performance. Captured within the parameters of the Supply Agreement, the key expectations, terms of performance such as lead time, delivery, quality and payment are detailed at this point.

The supply agreement plays a pivotal role within EE. Within it the basic specifications of the product, component, material or service supplied are clearly detailed with supporting documentation. In addition, the basic supply relationship is defined, such as the method and timing of orders, the allowed lead time, delivery methods and timing, and the level of incoming quality/inspection expected. Other issues addressed by the supply agreement include size and shape of delivery containers, allowable defect levels, methods for adjudicating quality or service disagreements, credit requirements, penalty clauses for non-performance, key performance measures, and timing and means of payment for invoices. In addition, ownership and ongoing operations of product-specific assets (physical or intellectual) are detailed, along with any other physical or process-based investments that will be required to meet defined performance requirements. On the customer side, commitments to volume, schedules, lead time and magnitude of design changes, and capital commitments must be clearly defined. The more clearly the supply agreement is stated, the less likely there will be unmet expectations or major difficulties downstream. In the end, both parties must feel the agreement is fair and will provide them with required benefits.

The management of these new relationships is facilitated by several information technology enablers, such as Enterprise Resource Planning systems (ERP).[16] For instance, advanced planning software establishes production requirements over time horizons of months or years for the entire supply chain using constraint models that balance capacity, costs and responsiveness for the integrated network. Many of these models download data from an ERP to a dedicated server that does the planning analysis and evaluates various production scenarios. Other companies are turning to compliance labeling that uses bar coding to eliminate transaction and coordination costs. Warehouse management systems are also being used to increase coordination with minimal cost.

Electronic Data Interchange (EDI), Intranets, Internets, Electronic Funds Transfer (EFT) and dedicated EE software are being used in increasing intensity to reduce the hidden costs of outsourcing. In fact, one author suggests that EE:[17]

> ....can be defined as the use of information technology to endow automated intelligence to an ever-growing network of factories, distribution centers, warehouses, material suppliers, and delivery trucks. The aim for each player in the supply chain is to conduct business with the latest and best information from everyone else in the chain, the point-of-origin to that of consumption in the least amount of time and at the smallest cost.

The core elements of an information-enabled supply chain include an ERP transactional backbone, a forecasting module, advanced planning system, dynamic scheduling model, a demand/distribution management system, a transportation and logistics system, and a warehouse management system. Integrating these subsystems into a complete EE system provides the entire network with the information needed to drive effective decision making and balance demand and supply concerns.[18]

Figure 9.3 Cost Savings from Reengineering the Supply Chain

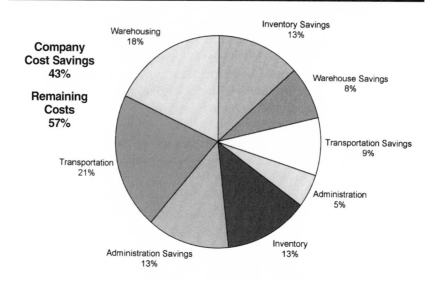

Source: G. Gagliardi, "Tightening the Flow," Manufacturing Systems, October, 1996: 108.

Data reengineering software is also supporting the integration of legacy data from disparate sources and network partners into a compatible, consolidated, decision support tool set. According to the Gartner Group, 75 percent of data entry consists of re-entering information from another computer. This human connection between systems is expensive and slows the supply chain. Every minute spent entering data is a nonvalue-added adminstrative cost.[19] Eliminating these delays and communication breakdowns is an essential element of effective EE.

The cost savings possible from reengineering the supply chain to incorporate enabling information technologies throughout the system is summarized in Figure 9.3. Filling information gaps, electronically connecting trading partners, eliminating redundant data entry, sharing real-time status information across the supply network, and finally integrating the supply chain into the larger electronic commerce community through Internet solutions can reduce costs significantly. For instance, the Gartner Group evidence suggests that an IT-enabled supply chain can reduce order processing costs from $50 per order to $4 per order.[20]

Monitoring the performance of the supply chain and finding ways to institute continuous improvement comprise the final stages of EE. As with all the SMPs, the ongoing efforts to find new and better ways to serve customers, to streamline relationships, and eliminate nonvalue-added costs is part of the required maintenance of the system. Market conditions, technologies, and requirements are constantly changing. The EE has to be a fluid organism, capable of responding to changing requirements with minimal variation, disruption and cost.

The development of an effective structure is the initial step in creating an effective EE system. Moving beyond outsourcing concepts to a structure that emphasizes and maximizes the value created through the core competencies of enterprise members, the Extended Enterprise elevates external resource acquisition to a strategic level.

The Extended Enterprise

Three helping one another will do as much as six men singly.
– Spanish Proverb

The realities of the ever changing, complex business environment faced by companies as they enter the 21st century is driving them to rethink the relationships and interdependencies that exist within a supply chain.[21] Limited resources, global competition, and a demanding customer base dictate the variability and complexity of the marketplace. To gain and maintain a competitive advantage, organizations will need to reconfigure themselves on an ongoing basis in order to optimize the value created by the total available resources within the value chain.

The impact of these competitive pressures on the supply chain is striking. Collaboration, not adversarial relations, is becoming a competitive necessity. DaimlerChrysler Corporation is one of the firms most noted for making early, and frequent, use of value chain leveraging to improve its responsiveness to customer needs and increase its overall effectiveness and profitability. As suggested by Figure 9.4, the supplier management practices used by DaimlerChrysler have undergone major changes since the late 1980s. Moving today toward an EE model, Daimler Chrysler is using supply chain leverage to create a competitive advantage.

Figure 9.4 DaimlerChrysler's Changing Supply Management Practices

Process Characteristics		Relational Characteristics	
1989	1994	1989	1994
Suppliers chosen by competitive bid • Low price wins • Selection after design	Suppliers presourced • Cost targeted to a set price • Selection before design based on capabilities	Little recognition or credit for past performance Transaction oriented	Recognition of past performance and track record Relationship orientation
Split accountability for design prototype and production parts	Single supplier accountable for design, prototype, and production parts	No responsibility for supplier's profit margin	Recognition of supplier's need to make a profit
Minimal supplier investment in coordination mechanisms and dedicated assets	Substantial investments in coordination mechanisms and dedicated assets	Little support for feedback from suppliers	Feedback from suppliers encouraged
Discrete activity focus No process for soliciting ideas or suggestions	Focus on total value chain improvement Formal process for soliciting supplier's suggestions	No guarantee of business relationships beyond the contract	Expectation of business relationships beyond the contract
Simple performance evolution	Complex performance evaluation	No performance expectations beyond the contract	Considerable performance expectations beyond the contract
Short-term contracts	Long-term contracts	Adversarial, zero-sum game	Cooperative and trusting positive-sum game

Source: R. Boykin, III, et.al., *Beyond the Moment: The Key to Renewable Competitive Advantage*, Bedford, TX: Consortium for Advanced Manufacturing, 1997: 16.

THE NEW ORGANIZATIONAL STYLE

The Extended Enterprise *is the network of firms that creates value for its customers by developing, producing, selling, servicing and recycling products and services as an integrated system* (see Figure 9.5).[22] This organizational approach is based on the belief that a significant amount of resources and value are added by each member of the trading alliance that participates in the industry value chain. Participating firms, acting as a value creating system rather than individual links, adopt a shared customer focus and pursue a synergy of resources, communications, cooperation and trust, knowledge sharing, and an understanding that all members mutually benefit from participation within the EE.[23]

The benefits that accrue to members of the EE include improving profit margins.[24] Pursuing the belief that companies can only deliver maximum value to their customers if they receive maximum value from their supply partners, a competitively aligned enterprise provides improvements in customer satisfaction and profit margins through reductions in total costs and cycle times. A second major benefit is the exponential improvements in responsiveness and resource allocation that result from the concurrent development of products and processes across the supply chain. Each member of the Enterprise must be not only the most efficient or low cost producer, but must also be able to contribute to the design and development of new products and markets.

As the EE matures, the ability to accept, commit, and deliver orders quickly increases markedly.   Being able to schedule manufacture-to-order production through the supply chain and to closely coordinate delivery schedules creates a competitive advantage for Extended Enterprises. In markets where customers are assuming more power, this enhanced competency is becoming part of the price of admission to major business opportunities. The benefits gained from improved coordination also include reduced costs of inventory throughout the supply chain. With enterprise-wide inventory

Figure 9.5 Extended Enterprise Model

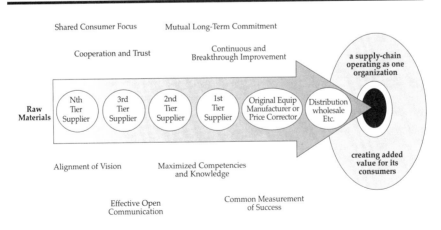

Source: R. Boykin, III, et.al., *Beyond the Moment: The Key to Renewable Competitive Advantage*, Bedford, TX: Consortium for Advanced Manufacturing, 1997: 12.

visibility, participating companies can rely on virtual inventories and handle remote inventory requirements from a central inventory. Material costs and other transaction costs plummet as unnecessary efforts are removed and waste eliminated at the Enterprise level as the benefits of EE are experienced by the trading alliance.

THE EXTENDED ENTERPRISE STRATEGIC PLAN

Gaining the benefits of the EE entails the framing of the entire business, strategic, and execution planning process to leverage supply chain resources effectively. This requires the acceptance and understanding from each enterprise member that substantial knowledge and ability exist beyond the organization's walls, and that those resources may be brought fully to bear with the appropriate alignment of vision, commitment and reward. [25]

It is very difficult for any single organization to migrate to the EE viewpoint without a leadership commitment to enterprise members as essential value contributors. [26] Similarly, individual organizations within the EE need to continuously improve their ability to contribute value, identify core competencies, and to build on the other capabilities within the trading alliance. Core elements in the migration to an EE perspective include leveraging joint contributions and core competencies, optimizing supplier relationships, creating multiple linkages, leveraging of resources and learning, and the development of extended business planning models and concepts.

Visionary companies are beginning to see their external suppliers as natural extensions of their own activities and processes. This perspective enables them to work with other trading partners to coordinate and optimize the set of interrelated value-added activities that tie the value chain to customer requirements. Each member of the trading alliance contributes unique knowledge, capacity, resources, and assets that serve to add value to the products and services being produced. The EE framework aligns these individual contributions to the core expertise of the entire value chain. While each organization remains free to pursue its own strategic goals and objectives, the ongoing, carefully managed collaboration of the entire supply chain allows the trading alliance to utilize individual member competencies and expertise to satisfy the requirements of EE customers.

The ability to leverage knowledge and capacity is a key advantage of the EE. This advantage can be utilized by the trading partners to create a competitive advantage. The collective resources and assets of an EE can distribute, and assume, a greater degree of risk than any individual organization would be willing or able to bear on its own. No one organization can realistically expect to be competitively competent in all of the major processes and activities that are necessary to meet existing, let alone emerging, customer requirements.[27] The leveraging of individual core competencies within the Extended Enterprise provides in total the comprehensive set of skills and capabilities needed to meet these ever-changing requirements with optimal efficiency and effectiveness.

The development of the EE requires a new mindset about the best way to structure and manage supplier-customer relationships. There have traditionally been strong linkages between market makers (OEM's) and their first-tier suppliers, but lower-tier vendors have often been treated as inconsequential, second class citizens. These "lower level" suppliers, though, often have core competencies that could be leveraged by one or more members of the trading alliance to drive value chain performance improvements. Extended Enterprise membership should not be based solely on a firm's impact on the total EE cost structure or its relative importance to the total cost or performance of the value chain. Rather, specific competencies, knowledge and resources, and the ability of a participating firm to improve the system's alignment with or attainment of customer requirements should dominate the decision whether to include a specific firm in the EE structure.

An Extended Enterprise infrastructure can include partnerships with other supply chain structures, which are linked to provide "pick and place" capabilities for needed resources and assets. It is quite possible for a first-tier supplier in one enterprise system to be a third-tier participant in another EE. Creating an interlocked, value optimizing, coordinated, and collaborative business structure leads to the willingness to challenge all boundaries and breach all gaps in value chain and enterprise performance.[28]

Resource leverage is a core component of an EE framework. With external suppliers becoming a natural extension of the core company, an increased respect for and utilization of the unique competitive advantages each enterprise member represents leads core firms to give suppliers responsibilities unthought of just a few years ago. The alignment and integration of resources affects how members

Figure 9.6 Extended Enterprise Framework

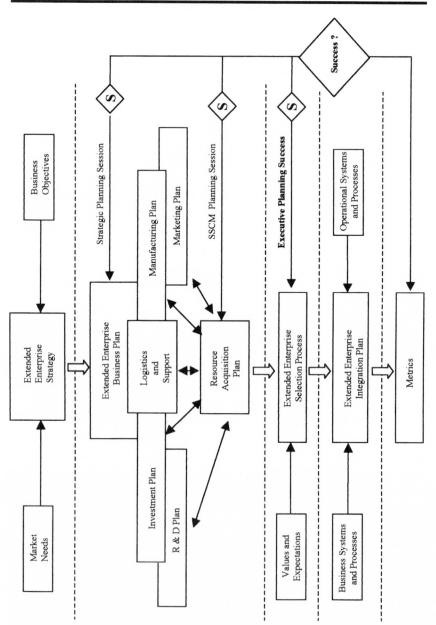

Source: R. Boykin, III, et.al., *Beyond the Moment: The Key to Renewable Competitive Advantage*, Bedford, TX: Consortium for Advanced Manufacturing, 1997: 21.

contribute to the product realization process. While the business planning process may provide the structure and discipline necessary to leverage external resources, it alone cannot guarantee success. Each member must, instead, think and act as part of the integrated system. Leveraging resources to attain seemingly unattainable goals is a driving force behind the development, management, and performance improvements embedded in the EE framework.

Learning is also a point of leverage in the extended organization structure. Since an organization's ability to improve existing skills and to learn new ones is one of the most defensible competitive advantages it can have, the natural leveraging of skills and learning with the EE becomes a competitive resource for all enterprise members.[29] Gaining the advantages offered by leveraging learning, though, requires a specific, committed strategy within the Extended Enterprise as well as the ongoing assessment of individual firm and total alliance competencies. The goal is to ensure that needed new competencies are acquired as market conditions change. Each enterprise member must use its individual strategies, competencies, and resources to drive its own choices of where and how to participate in current and future EE initiatives (see Figure 9.6).

Business planning plays a central role in implementing the EE framework.[30] Transforming vendors to partners, the Extended Enterprise SMP transforms traditional "make vs. buy" analyses to a higher-level strategic level resource and competency decision. The result of this change in focus is the movement of traditional business planning efforts away from a series of company-focused effort. Specifically, independent marketing, research and development, investment, manufacturing and logistics analyses give way to initiatives that are based upon the active collaboration of all enterprise members. This new planning structure helps to ensure that the activities, resources, and knowledge provided by the various members of the EE are coordinated and integrated in order to optimize the amount of value created while incurring minimum costs.

The Enterprise business plan begins with the integration of the individual firm's strategic plans, reviewing such issues as engineering-to-engineering coordination, manufacturing-to-manufacturing coordination, concurrent marketing activities, collaborative research investment planning, level of alignment, and future visions of core competencies.[31] Taking advantage of inter-enterprise integration helps the EE partners increase their return on assets, reduce overall costs, and reduce existing cycle time.

Nike is one of the best known examples of the leverage and benefits of the EE model.[32] During the physical fitness boom of the 1980s, Nike positioned itself through specific resource acquisition planning to become the market leader in sales of athletic shoes. This leadership position was secured without Nike owning any full-scale production facilities. Nike's strategy involved concentrating on its core competencies of research, design, and marketing. By developing and engaging supply chain members to manufacture and distribute its products, Nike has created an integrated supply network that compliments its own core competencies. Nike's resulting competitive structure reflected the core values that drive EE models.

EXTENDED ENTERPRISE VALUES AND EXPECTATIONS

Behavioral problems can serve as a major roadblock to gaining the full benefits of supply chain integration. As noted by Boykin, et.al., *without a common set of understandings and values, it is difficult to create a level playing field within the EE structure.*[33] Experiences by several leading EEs (Chrysler, Nike, Xerox and others) have led to the creation of a set of axioms to guide the expectations and values of enterprise members. These axioms are:[34]

- There is a shared, specific focus on satisfying the common end consumer.
- There is an alignment of vision.
- There is a fundamental level of cooperation and performance to commitment (trust).
- There is open and effective communication.
- Decisions are made by maximizing the use of the competencies and knowledge within the EE.
- All stakeholders are committed to generate long-term mutual benefits.
- There is a common view of how success is measured.
- All members are committed to continuous improvement and breakthrough advancements.

- Whatever competitive pressures exist in the environment are allowed to exist within the EE.

These axioms are applied across the various Extended Enterprise levels, including strategic members, tactical members and operational members.[35] Strategic members provide a critical, difficult-to-replace value-added component to the end product or service. Few in number, the highest level of alignment in values and expectations occurs among the strategic EE members; their ongoing efforts are tied directly to the success of the end product.

Tactical members, on the other hand, are the source of a needed component to the end product or service, and are also very committed to fulfilling the needs of the EE, but their values and expectations are not as closely aligned as those of the strategic members. Contingency plans may be developed by strategic EE members if there is a concern that the secondary, tactical members may have problems meeting their commitments. Finally, operational members are the source of predominantly low-cost, high volume parts or components. Value alignment of operational members is not essential, but ensuring that their individual performance meets the quality, availability and cost requirements of the EE is important.

Selecting suppliers or potential participants in the Extended Enterprise is based on the assessment of potential performance on three core dimensions; ability, compatibility and availability (see Figure 9.7).[36] *Ability* is the technical capability of a supplier, in terms of both design and manufacturing, to provide a product or service that will satisfy the needs of the EE's customers. *Availability* is concerned with capacity and flexibility of the supplier, specifically their potential for delivering goods and services when required. Availability also notes that supply partners need to be able to rapidly and effectively respond to changes in customer and EE demands. Finally, *compatibility* encapsulates the concept of "fit" between a firm and the technical and cultural features of the trading alliance. Technical compatibility can be bought; cultural compatibility must be learned. Compatibility is clearly more important for strategic and tactical enterprise members than for operational ones. More compatibility is always better than less, because the more closely members are aligned the easier it will be for process integration to occur.

Each member in the EE plays a different role and has unique support requirements. These differences can be broken into five core components: strategy, expectations, relationships, processes and measurements.[37] *Strategy* is used to denote the key abilities of the EE; it is defined for each member by the core organization that is initiating the integration effort. *Expectations* may vary by firm, but all members of the alliance face the same minimum requirement: to deliver the products, services and support the EE requires to meet its objectives. Current and future expectations shape the *relationships* that form within the trading alliance. The higher the expectations of performance, the stronger and more interdependent all alliance relationships need to be.

Three different types of *process* structures underlie the EE: business processes and systems (e.g., activity-based cost management and target cost management), product-related processes, and operational processes and systems that provide the basis for technological integration. Finally, *measurements* provide the feedback that helps the trading partners adjust and improve their performance as well as ensuring that each member organization knows, and accomplishes, its overall objectives.

Taken together, these principles shape the nature and effectiveness of the EE system. Knitting together diverse firms with

Figure 9.7 Extended Enterprise Selection Model

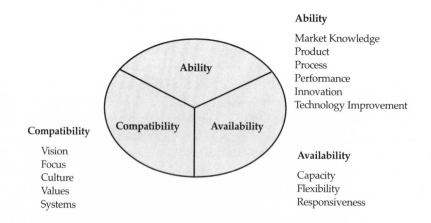

Source: R. Boykin, III, et.al., *Beyond the Moment: The Key to Renewable Competitive Advantage*, Bedford, TX: Consortium for Advanced Manufacturing, 1997: 27.

different, but compatible skills and competencies, EE supports the elimination of costs, waste, and delay that can arise when supply chain efforts are not integrated. Eliminating unnecessary transactions and leveraging the unique competencies of each member organization creates a competitive advantage for the EE. When everyone "wins," the group as a whole performs better. Recognizing and acting upon this fact is the key to creating high value enterprise structures. Integration of member firms is the basis upon which the Extended Enterprise rests—its reason for being.

Integration within the Extended Enterprise

There is no one subsists by himself alone.
– Owen Felltham

Enterprise integration is the discipline that connects and combines people, processes, systems, and technologies to ensure that the right people and processes have the right intellectual and physical resources at the right time.[38] To meet customer requirements seamlessly, the entire network of firms has to understand what is expected of them, be able to adjust their performance on an ongoing basis to respond to changing requirements, and constantly pursue improvement and learning in everything they do. When one member of the alliance learns or improves, the entire system should be better off. If this learning can be dispersed throughout the EE, quantum improvements can occur. Integrating efforts and objectives to create a holistic, coordinated supply system is the key to gaining these ends.

Three specific bundles of activities need to be completed during the integration process: alignment, systems couplings, and enabling practices and technologies.[39] Key points to be addressed, as noted by Boykin et.al., include:

- Use of the company's work force, technology and management practices should ensure that organization's business and product-related processes are aligned with Enterprise strategies, concepts and values.

- Systems that create well-managed physical, financial, people and information infrastructures should be used to bind the Enterprise together.

- Enabling technologies such as fully implemented,

seamless information networks and Enterprise-supporting performance metrics and tools need to be deployed wherever possible to increase Enterprise effectiveness and efficiency.

Achieving these integration objectives depends on the EE's overall performance on several factors:[40] leadership, process simplification through integration, integrated product and process design, overcoming the complications of systems diversity, achieving a balanced structure, and seeing the supply chain as an organizational entity.

The goals of EE integration include the elimination of nonvalue-added activities and processes, simplification of processes, practices and policies, and the optimization of Enterprise knowledge and capacity. Integrated information technologies, such as Enterprise Resource Planning (ERP) systems and supply chain planning software, support the achievement of these goals. Achieving integration objectives can create challenges, though, as the Enterprise extends beyond traditional organizational, geographic, and political boundaries.

The objective of the integration effort is to knit together free-standing systems and organizations into a coordinated whole that is capable of both effective concurrent design as well as the development of products and processes. Many Extended Enterprise efforts start as a potpourri of systems, data requirements, information and capabilities. Melding these diverse and potentially conflicting perspectives and cultures into one smoothly operating unit requires a clear strategy, strong leadership, behavioral changes, and supporting metrics for learning and control. Information technology remains the primary enabler of integration efforts.

In the end, all members of the EE need to organize their internal structures and processes to support the flow of information and knowledge across the entire supply chain. As alliance performance improves, each Enterprise member benefits; ensuring that everyone benefits from these gains has to be one of the primary goals of the core organization. Establishing and tracking performance is an essential element in transforming the EE from a vision to a reality.

CREATING AND MEASURING THE EXTENDED ENTERPRISE

The seamless integration of knowledge and improvement that defines the EE requires the development of new customer-supplier relationships. It also requires the creation and use of new metrics that evaluate performance on several core dimensions:[41] alignment of vision or purpose, compatibility of culture and values, trust, effective and efficient communications, shared risks and rewards, and constant improvement. The need to control and manage performance and costs becomes more important than ever as external suppliers account for higher and higher percentages of a finished product's value.

Several issues have to be addressed before an EE can be designed and developed. Chief among these are:

- The critical success factors (key processes as well as performance factors) that must be addressed and improved to gain a competitive advantage must be identified and agreed to by the strategic Enterprise partners.

- Current performance on each of these key dimensions needs to be assessed through process analysis and activity-based approaches in order to create improvement strategies.

- Acquisition of needed information or skills should take place as quickly as possible. This may require retraining staff, hiring new staff, or developing alliances with other organizations.

- Organizational learning and documentation of past experiences should be incorporated into a continuous improvement effort that will help enterprise members learn while avoiding prior mistakes.

The assessment process is the initial step in any performance improvement program. As suggested by the questionnaire presented in Figure 9.8, this assessment should begin with understanding where the organization ranks with respect to spanning inter-organizational boundaries. The resulting assessment requires judgment, calculation, appraisal and estimation, as well as significant dose of honesty and openness in the evaluative process. A well-designed assessment effort provides a foundation for an organization to examine the value of current business processes objectively.

Completion of the survey leads to a series of actions (see Figure 9.9) whose intensity will vary based on how well the EE is currently performing. *Getting started* actions are needed when an organization or EE is in the early stages of developing relationships across the value

Figure 9.8   Value Chain Linkage Assessment Questionnaire

Instructions: Diagnose your company's progress toward a boundaryless relationship with customers and/or suppliers in your value chain. Select a strategically important customer and/or supplier (or category of customer/supplier) in your value chain. Circle a number on each scale to reflect where your customer/supplier relationship now stands.

	Traditional							Boundaryless		
1. Strategies/operating plans	Developed independently			Shared		Coordinated		Developed jointly		
• Marketing plans	1	2	3	4	5	6	7	8	9	10
• Product development plans	1	2	3	4	5	6	7	8	9	10
• Production/inventory planning (including who owns inventory)	1	2	3	4	5	6	7	8	9	10
• Distribution/transportation planning	1	2	3	4	5	6	7	8	9	10
• Information systems planning	1	2	3	4	5	6	7	8	9	10

	Highly guarded	Selective sharing as needed	Joint sharing/ problem solving	Integrated data systems/processes on common issues						
2. Information sharing/problem solving										
• Cost structure	1	2	3	4	5	6	7	8	9	10
• Profit margins	1	2	3	4	5	6	7	8	9	10
• Quality/production problems	1	2	3	4	5	6	7	8	9	10
• Problem-solving methods	1	2	3	4	5	6	7	8	9	10
• Market information/feedback	1	2	3	4	5	6	7	8	9	10

	Related	Understood but unconnected	Consistent but separate	Interconnected						
3. Accounting, measurement, and reward systems										
• Accounting procedures	1	2	3	4	5	6	7	8	9	10
• Quality measures	1	2	3	4	5	6	7	8	9	10
• Costing systems	1	2	3	4	5	6	7	8	9	10
• Rewards and incentives	1	2	3	4	5	6	7	8	9	10
• Communication process	1	2	3	4	5	6	7	8	9	10

	Independent/ differing views	Selective collaboration	Two-way understanding	Consultive partnership						
4. Sales process										
• Establishing sales goals/quotas	1	2	3	4	5	6	7	8	9	10
• Assessing customer needs	1	2	3	4	5	6	7	8	9	10
• Determining optimal product usage	1	2	3	4	5	6	7	8	9	10
• Providing product feedback	1	2	3	4	5	6	7	8	9	10
• Setting terms of the deal	1	2	3	4	5	6	7	8	9	10

	Separate	Called upon in emergency	Transfer of knowledge	Shared resources/ colocated						
5. Resources/Skills										
• Technical expertise	1	2	3	4	5	6	7	8	9	10
• Financial expertise	1	2	3	4	5	6	7	8	9	10
• Organizational/management skills	1	2	3	4	5	6	7	8	9	10
• Information systems	1	2	3	4	5	6	7	8	9	10
• Training	1	2	3	4	5	6	7	8	9	10

Questionnaire Scoring

Add up the numbers from each boundary to find your score. (For example, total boundarylessness- which is probably not possible- would score 250, that is 10 points on each of the twenty scales.) Interpret the numbers as follows:

- 75 or less. You are probably just getting started on developing a boundaryless relationship with the customer or supplier. Your main challenge is to tune in to the needs of the other organization and find where the opportunities for further collaboration lie.
- 75 to 150. You have made good progress on the relationship and are probably poised to build momentum toward long-term collaboration. Your challenge is to create action experiments that can generate results and provide further experiences of success.
- More than 150. You have experienced a good deal of success in the relationship, and are probably ready to design mechanisms for sustaining progress in the long-term. Your challenge is to align and integrate systems and structures and to institutionalize a boundaryless relationship.

Source: Ashkenas, et.al., *The Boundaryless Organization*, San Fransisco: Jossey-Bass Publishers, 1995: 217-219.

Figure 9.9   Creating Boundaryless Enterprise Relations

Score on Value Chain Self-Assessment	Appropriate Actions
75 or less	*Getting started.* Tune in to customers and suppliers and figure out where the opportunities are. • Arrange customer/supplier … appearances. • Take customer/supplier field trips. • Hold open-agenda dialogues with management teams. • Map customer/supplier needs. • Collect customer/supplier data.
75-150	*Building momentum* Experiment with collaboration to experience success and learning. • Hold customer/supplier town meetings. • Organize cross-value chain task forces. • Share technical services. • Teach sales people to be consultants.
Above 150	*Sustaining progress* Align/integrate systems, structures, and processes to sustain gains in the long term. • Integrate information system. • Reconfigure roles and responsibilities.

Source: Ashkenas, et.al., *The Boundaryless Organization,* San Fransisco: Jossey-Bass Publishers, 1995: 223.

chain. Old patterns of behavior need to be broken and new behaviors, attitudes and competencies developed. Getting individuals both within an organization and across the trading alliance to see the business challenges facing the value chain from a variety of points is essential to creating a collaborative culture.

After the EE effort is underway, it is important to build momentum for the change. The key to achieving this goal is to design some short-term, relatively low-risk experiments that will serve to strengthen the value chain that can then be used to underscore the benefits of collaboration for all affected alliance partners. Finally, sustaining the progress made by the EE is critical if the new business model is to become permanent. Expanding the collaborative efforts, assessing the learnings, consolidating the gains, and moving the entire EE toward ever-greater levels of performance are the goals to be reached if improvement is to be sustained.

While the linkage assessment survey and the implementation of improvement efforts drives an organization to accept self-assessment, it is also important to get the trading partners involved in a collabor-

Figure 9.10   Assessing Member Requirements

There are hundreds of ways to describe an effective relationship between buyers and suppliers. The following list of characteristics or qualities has been compiled from a number of studies of salesmanship and vendor relations. All seem to be important. Your task -- first individually, then as a team --- is to rank the characteristics from 1 to 12, in the order you feel should be the most important to the customer-supplier relationship

		Your Ranking	Team Ranking
Part 1:	*Characteristics important to suppliers*		
1.	Reliability. Always keep commitments and delivers on promises		
2.	Candor. Provides us with all the information we need; willingly shares information		
3.	Authority. Has the authority to make final decisions.		
4.	Loyalty. Values a long-term relationship; sticks with us over the long haul.		
5.	Trust. Believes that we have the customer's best interests in mind; does not take advantage of the relationship.		
6.	Openness. Is open to new ideas and alternative ways of doing things		
7.	Fairness. Negotiates fair contracts; prices product fairly.		
8.	Clarity. Knows what he or she wants; clearly communicates performance requirements.		
9.	Organizational savvy. Gets things done effectively within the customer organization; works "the system" well.		
10.	Honestly. Gives us a straight answer; never misrepresents things.		
11.	Competence. Understands the product development process; knows what is required for us to produce a quality product.		
12.	Flexibility. Is always willing to compromise in order to create a win-win situation.		
Part 2. Characteristics important to customers			
1.	Reliability. Always keep commitments and delivers on promises		
2.	Candor. Provides us with all the information we need; willingly shares information		
3.	Quality. Meets our expectations in terms of product quality.		
4.	Consistency. Provides us with a consistent level of overall service over time		
5.	Trust. Has our best interests in mind; does not take advantage of the relationship.		
6.	Creativity. Offers us new ideas and product improvement; develops new products to meet our needs.		
7.	Fairness. Negotiates fair contracts; prices product fairly.		
8.	Responsiveness. Goes the extra mile for us.		
9.	Organizational savvy. Gets things done effectively within the supplier organization; works "the system" well.		
10.	Honestly. Gives us a straight answer; never misrepresents things.		
11.	Competence. Thoroughly understands the product features and how the product can meet our needs.		
12.	Flexibility. Is always willing to compromise in order to create a win-win situation.		

Source: Ashkenas, et.al., *The Boundaryless Organization,* San Fransisco: Jossey-Bass Publishers, 1995: 236-37.

ative, 360 degree analysis of the strengths, weaknesses, opportunities and relative performance of each member in the EE (see Figure 9.10). The goal is not only to evaluate individual members, but also to understand what aspects of the buyer-supplier relationship are most important to Enterprise partners. Effectively fine-tuning the expectations and efforts of trading partners depends on the open assessment of expectations as well as the bridging of expectation gaps.

To promote the integration and rapid response that are the hallmarks of successful Enterprise systems, measurements must be developed that are can be adapted to a wide variety of collaborative relationships and to changing competitive demands. Six questions help shape the choice and use of metrics within the EE:[43]

1. Are we developing and producing the right things?

2. Are we producing the right things well?

3. Are we delivering the right things quickly enough?

4. Are we creating the best operational climate?

5. Are we collectively anticipating and improving?

6. Are we all becoming more successful?

All measures and evaluation approaches adopted by the EE should be directed at improving the effectiveness of the supply base and the performance of internal functions in order to meet finished product and overall business goals.

The first three questions noted above address the traditional dimensions of cost, quality, and delivery time. Collaboration and responsiveness is also critical to the EE, though, leading to the use of the last three questions.   The first question, "Are we developing and producing the right things?" addresses the issues of product and service development and their match to known or anticipated customer requirements. Three major factors are embedded in this question: [44]

- Effective Product Development. The chain must demon-strate that it is developing products and services that meet, exceed, or anticipate customer requirements.

- Customer-Supplier Satisfaction. Mutual acceptance and satisfaction of each member's capabilities, interactions, and results as well as the belief that the relationships are mutually beneficial should be built into the EE early in implementation efforts and continually revisited as the chain matures.

- Joint Service and Support. Seamless, responsive, flexible customer-driven service and support systems must be developed to ensure that both internal and external needs are met.

In a similar way, question two addresses such issues as how a supply chain defines, achieves, and improves quality and safety throughout the organization. Measures that can be used to gauge performance at this level include total defects throughout the value chain and product life cycle, safety and environmental performance, and the development of ongoing quality improvement efforts. Finally, time-to-market, competitive response time, delivery-to-commitment, and total supply time are several of the measures that can be used to assess current and required capability for on-time delivery within an EE production system.

As the measurement emphasis shifts to qualitative and collaborative concerns, the measures and issues they address change. For instance, the question "Are we creating the best operational climate?" leads Enterprise members to assess the effectiveness of current communications, including whether technology enablers are being used effectively and appropriately to reduce transaction and coordination costs. Trust, although difficult to gauge, is also an important indicator of how well the integration effort is proceeding. Vision and value alignment measures complete the package for this performance dimension, emphasizing the extent to which a vision of collaborative strategy or integrated operations exists and is consistently implemented among members of the EE.

Four major concerns, reflecting the last two questions in the assessment set focus attention on learning and the economic success of the integrated value chain. Achieving innovation and improvement rates that are best-in-class or best-in-industry should be the goal of the EE system. Tracking technology and knowledge transfer across the value chain helps the Enterprise members identify areas where collaboration is working as well as those where more effort is needed. If learning and best-in-class performance is taking place, every member of the Enterprise should experience improved financial performance. These improvements should be fairly distributed throughout the chain to ensure that the behaviors of the key members remain aligned. Finally, all of the members of the Enterprise must be strategically compatible if competitive and continuous improvement goals are to be met.

A seven-step approach can be used to develop more effective measurement systems within the Extended Enterprise:[45]

> 1. *Decide what's needed.*
>
>> How will success be defined and measured given the level of participation of the organization in the EE system?

2. *Determine behavior.*

Knowing what kind of behavior is needed, by whom, and when is a crucial part of creating effective measurements. Metrics must provide incentives to achieve organizational and Enterprise goals and objectives.

3. *Draw up a measurement profile.*

A business profile should drive the choice of specific measures. Each profile will identify a specific behavior that needs to be emphasized and measures to help the firm, and Enterprise, compete. Many of the measures will relate to quality, technology, cost, total cost, total value, delivery, and flexibility; but the specific measures will vary based on the relative importance of these characteristics to Enterprise partners andthe customers who rely upon them.

4. *Review the current system.*

Assessing the current performance measurement system against the measurement profile is critical if strategic goals are to be met. Alignment of measures, incentives, and rewards is necessary if performance goals are to be met.

5. *Alignment.*

Once the review is complete, it's important to identify core performance metrics and to realign the rewards system so that the benefits in terms of salary, recognition, and short-term benefits of individual organizational members reflects entity and the EE objectives and needs.

6. *Analyze the process.*

Based on the effectiveness measures being used and behaviors required, it's important to analyze the strategies and process needed to achieve performance goals and fix any problems as they occur.

7. Review.

Once established, the metrics should be reviewed regularly to ensure that they remain consistent with dynamic performance requirements for the Extended Enterprise. Unless firms are willing to take this last step, they may end up using outdated measures that work against, instead of supporting Enterprise objectives and performance goals.

Creating and sustaining the levels of collaboration and performance improvements that are possible within the EE requires an ongoing dedication, and attention, to the performance capabilities and success of Enterprise members. Aligning strategies, objectives and performance as well as creating a coordinated, collaborative network requires the development of measurements that reinforce desired behaviors throughout the value chain while isolating undesirable outcomes and events for elimination. As with most of the advanced management processes, EE effectiveness hinges on the cooperation and efforts of the entire extended organization.

An example of how measurements are being used by organizations is the General Motors' "Targets for Excellence" program.[46] Each supplier within GM's extended network is evaluated against five key performance elements: cost, delivery performance, quality, technology, and leadership. Valued suppliers clearly cannot focus on quality alone; GM expects its Enterprise partners to significantly add value to the entire value chain's performance. Internal process improvement activities often require supplier participation. Using integrated supply concepts, the overall impact of supplier relations on the buying organization's operational effectiveness, and the value chain's ability to meet or exceed customer requirements is constantly assessed. Collaborative efforts include the co-development of hardware and software solutions to transaction, coordination and cost problems. Using ERP, EDI, and related integrated software solutions, the GM-based EE links core suppliers to the operational, tactical and strategic objectives of the firm.

Summary

The creation of collaborative supply chains offers a sponsoring firm many benefits, including reduced cost, improved responsiveness to the market, reduced cycle times, improved product quality and reliability, inventory reductions, transaction cost reductions, and heightened technological and business process capabilities. Gaining these benefits requires the development of trust, open communications, shared visions and a culture of cooperation.

Replacing a traditional adversarial buyer-supplier relationship with a collaborative one, the Extended Enterprise approach will help the entire value chain leverage its knowledge and capabilities to ensure improvement against customer requirements and the creation of an agile enterprise. The changes required by Enterprise members are behavioral in nature, leading to the need to fine-tune performance measures and unambiguously defined expectations and objectives. The payoffs received—increased flexibility, profitability, and effectiveness—make the effort worthwhile. In a constantly changing, increasingly demanding market, firms must turn to new models and constructs. Permeating organizational boundaries is the key to creating the corporate future.

References

Ashkenas, R., D. Ulrich, T. Jick, and S. Kerr, *The Boundaryless Organization,* San Francisco: Jossey-Bass Publishing, 1995.

Boykin, R.E., III, P. Zampino, R. Graham, A. Fraser and the CAM-I SEE Program, *Beyond the Moment: The Key to Renewable Competitive Advantage,* Bedford, TX: Consortium for Advanced Manufacturing—International, 1997.

Burch, G., "Clean Data," *Manufacturing Systems,* April, 1997: 104-106.

Chalos, P., "Costing, Control and Strategic Analysis in Outsourcing Decisions," *Handbook of Cost Management,* New York: Warren, Gorham and Lamont, 1997: P2-1-7.

Dilger, K.A.,"Change of Design," *Manufacturing Systems,* April, 1997: 69.86.

Drtina, R., "The Outsourcing Decision," Handbook of Cost Management, New York: Warren, Gorham and Lamont, 1997: P1-1 to 9.

Fox, M, "Integration for the Future," *Manufacturing Systems,* October, 1996: 99.104.

Fulcher, J., "Marching Orders," *Manufacturing Systems,* October, 1997: 44-50.

Gable, R., "The History of Consumer Goods," *Manufacturing Systems,* October, 1997: 70-84.

Gagliardi, G., "Tightening the Flow," *Manufacturing Systems,* October, 1996: 104-110.

Michel, R., "Whatever It Takes," *Manufacturing Systems,* July, 1997: 94-105.

"The Heart of the Matter," *Manufacturing Systems,* April, 1997: 26-33.

Monczka, R.M., "Today's Measurements Just Don't Make It," *Purchasing,* April 21, 1994: 47-50.

Shepherd, N., "Integrated Supply Management and Supplier Certification," *Handbook of Cost Management,* New York: Warren, Gorham and Lamont, 1997: P3-1 to 5.

Weil, M., "The Enterprise Extended," *Manufacturing Systems,* March, 1998: 1A -20A.

White, A., "Supply Chain Link-Up," *Manufacturing Systems,* October, 1996: 94-98.

Endnotes

1 This opening paragraph draws heavily upon (paraphrases) opening comments in R. Boykin, P. Zampino, R. Graham, A. Fraser and the CAM-I SSCM Program, *Beyond the Moment: The Key to Renewable Competitive Advantage,* Bedford, TX: CAM-I, 1997: 4.

2 G. Gagliardi, "Tightening the Flow" *Manufacturing Systems,* October, 1996: 106.

3 Boykin, et.al., op.cit.

4 IMA, *Implementing Integrated Supply Chain Management for Competitive Advantage,* working draft of a Statement on Management Accounting, February, 1999. This paragraph draws heavily from this work.

5 Boykin, et.al., pg. 4. This entire draft draws heavily from this source document.

6 Ibid, pg. 10.

7 Ibid.

8 This paragraph reflects arguments in *Implementing Integrated Supply Chain...* (IISC), op.cit.

9 This paragraph draws heavily from Boykin, op.cit., pp. 9-12.

10 This list of problems and many of the insights in this section are based on N. Shepherd's article, "Integrated Supply Management and Supplier Certification," *Handbook of Cost Management,* New York: Warren, Gorham and Lamont, 1997: P3-1 to P3-5. This list appears on page P3-2.

11 J. Couretas, "Chrysler exec seeks to trim waste in supply chain," *Automotive News,* Sept. 14, 1998.

12 IISC, op.cit.

13 This section draws heavily from R. Drtina, "The Outsourcing Decision," *Management Accounting,* March, 1994: 62.

14 I. Teresko, "Outsourcing: Tie it to the Right Objectives," *Industry Week,* June 1, 1992: 42-44.

15 This list and discussion draws heavily upon insights in W. Copacino, *Supply Chain Management: The Basics and Beyond,* Boca Raton, FL: St. Lucie Press, 1997.

16 This enabling technology discussions upon insights in The IMA Statement on Management Accounting, *Tools and Techniques for Implementing Supply Chain Management,* Working draft, Feb., 1999, pp.33-34.

17 M. Weil, "The Enterprise Extended," *Manufacturing Systems,* March, 1998: 2A.

18 Drawn from the IMA Statement on Mgt. Acctg, *Tools and Techniques for Implementing....* (TTI).

19 G. Gagliardi, "Tightening the Flow," *Manufacturing Systems,* October, 1996: 108.

20 Ibid, pg. 108.

21 This paragraph and related discussion draws heavily from Boykin, op.cit., pg. 16.

22 Ibid, pg. 12.

23 This paragraph draws heavily upon Boykin, et.al., op.cit., pp. 12-14.

24 This discussion of benefits draws heavily from Boykin, et.al., op.cit., pp. 10-12.

25 Ibid, pg. 19.

26 This entire section draws heavily upon Boykin, et.al., op.cit., pp. 19-21.

27 Ibid, pp. 12-14.

28 Ibid, pg. 15.

29 Ibid, pp. 20 is the underlying source for this part of the discussion.

30 Ibid, pp. 22-24 serves as the basis for the next set of issues and comments.

31 Ibid.

32 Ibid, pg. 24.

33 Ibid, pg. 24.

34 Ibid, pg. 24.

35 Ibid, pp. 26-27.

36 Ibid, pg. 27.

37 Ibid, pp. 26-27.

38 Ibid, pg.29.

39 Ibid, pg. 30.

40 Ibid, pp. 30-33. This entire section draws heavily from this original document, with most points paraphrased for presentation here.

41 N. Shepherd, "Integrated Supply Chain Management and Supplier Certification," *Handbook of Cost Management*, New York: Warren, Gorham and Lamont, 1997: P3-1 to P3-5. This article is drawn upon heavily in this section, specifically pages P3-3 to P3-4.

42 Ibid. This is a paraphrased list of original comments.

43 Boykin, et.al., op.cit., pp. 36-41. This last section draws heavily from this document.

44 This list appears, verbatim, on pg. 38., ibid.

45 R. Monzcka, "Today's Measurements Just Don't Make It," *Purchasing,* April 21, 1994: 49-50.

46 Ibid.

Chapter 10

Integrated Performance Management

*The only place where success comes before work
is in a dictionary.*

– Vidal Sassoon

Key Learnings:

- Integrated Performance Management (IPM) is a comprehensive management process that provides a systematic link between organizational strategy, resources, and processes and the attainment of customer- and stakeholder-defined objectives.

- Driven by customer requirements and stakeholder expectations, IPM serves as the primary means to:
  1) link functional areas to synchronize their efforts, 2) communicate strategies, 3) achieve goals, and 4) motivate individuals to meet or exceed performance expectations.

- The outcomes of a well-designed, effective IPM are:
  (1) effective, targeted deployment of organizational strategies; (2) well-defined measures to gauge the success of improvment initiatives; (3) coordination of efforts across all key management processes through the provision of well-defined objectives and measures that are cross-functional and process driven; (4) clearly linked between the efforts it measures and achievements it rewards; and,

(5) a competitive advantage developed by keeping everyone, at any level or in any job, focused on gaining and maintaining a core competence.

Measurement lies at the heart of the organization. What is measured becomes visible, what is rewarded gets done.[1] Defining the playing field for organizational action, signaling the score in the competitive arena, and linking past, present and future actions into a coordinated system, Integrated Performance Management (IPM) is the basis for optimizing current and future performance. Driven by customer requirements and stakeholder expectations, IPM serves as the primary means to: 1) link functional areas to synchronize their efforts, 2) communicate strategies, 3) achieve goals, and 4) motivate individuals to meet or exceed performance expectations.[2] In every conceivable way, measurements shape organizational actions and results. Only by linking performance measurements between organizational levels and across processes can an organization ensure that its resources are being used effectively.

The pivotal role played by measurement in the attainment of organizational goals has long been recognized. Today, though, as the pace of change has accelerated, effective measurement has become the key defining feature of top performing firms. The "command and control" orientation of traditional performance measurement is giving way to the onslaught of change, resulting in systems that "predict and prepare" the organization and its management team to meet the next challenge and create the next opportunity for improvement, profitability and growth. IPM aligns the goals of individual workers with process objectives that span functional and organizational boundaries in order to deliver goods and services that satisfy the needs of customers.

The changes taking place inside organizations are accelerating the demand for new and creative forms of measurement. Process Management initiatives emphasizing value and service to the customer, and the bridging of vertical and horizontal organizational boundaries, is driving the demand for cross-functional, customer-defined measurements. The proliferation of self-directed work teams and the ongoing flattening of management structures is creating the need for flexible, focused measurements that are matched to the decision requirements across all levels of the organization. Emerging virtual and network enterprise structures are triggering the development of performance measurements to support management across organizational boundaries and throughout the industry value chain. Each of these shifts has implications for the IPM Strategic Management Process (SMP) and its ability to effectively serve the organization and its stakeholders.

Relentlessly driven by its key stakeholder—the customer—to meet or exceed current and future performance requirements, today effective IPM structures reflect the customer perspective in their every element. As customer requirements filter through the organization, the performance measures chosen at the product, process, sub-process, team and individual level and related boundary interfaces need to be unambiguously linked to identified needs.   These requirements define the essential features of IPM.

ESSENTIAL FEATURES OF THE INTEGRATED PERFORMANCE MANAGEMENT SMP

IPM is a comprehensive management process that provides a systematic link between organizational strategy, resources, and processes and the attainment of customer- and stakeholder-defined objectives. Serving to frame the journey toward continuous improvement, IPM helps keep an organization "on track," ensuring that everyone understands where the organization is in terms of its performance objectives today, as well as what it needs to do to better meet customer requirements. The outcomes of a well-designed, effective IPM are:[3]

- Effective, targeted deployment of organizational strategies;

- Well-defined measures to gauge the success of reengine-ering or Total Quality Management (TQM) efforts;

- Coordination of efforts across all key management processes through the provision of well-defined objectives and measures that are cross-functional and process driven;

- Clear linkage between the efforts it measures and achievements it rewards; and,

- A competitive advantage developed by keeping everyone, at any level or in any job, focused on gaining and maintaining a core competence.

Figure 10.1   Integrated Performance Management SMP Structure

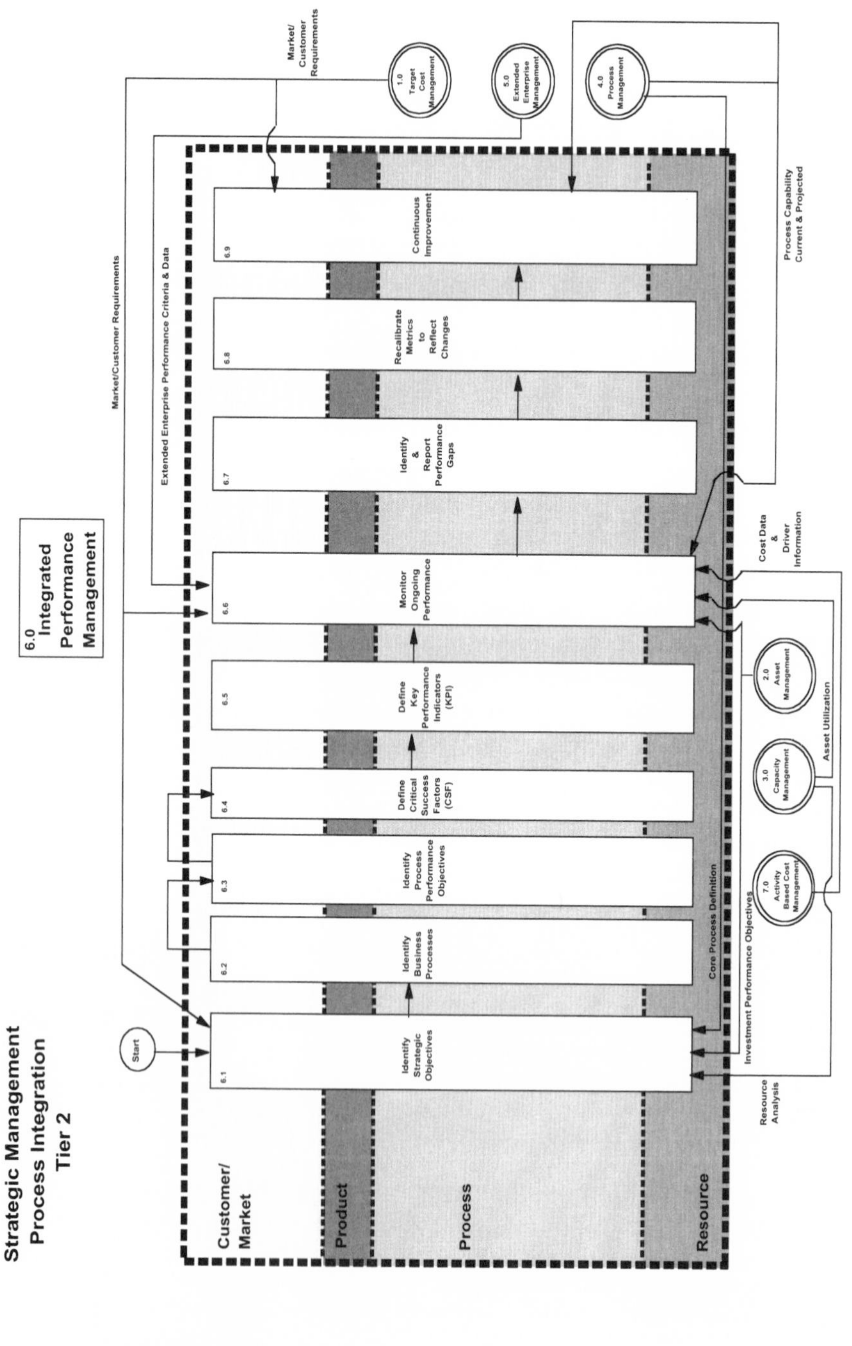

Achieving these outcomes require the development of a measurements framework and paradigm that supports learning, encourages experimentation, rewards achievement of customer-defined objectives, and aligns the entire organization with the goals and strategies that are deemed to offer optimal opportunities for growth and profitability.

As suggested by Figure 10.1, nine primary steps comprise the Integrated Performance Management Strategic Management Process:

1. Identify performance requirements;

2. Identify business processes that support these requirements;

3. Identify primary objectives for processes, activities and individuals;

4. Define critical success factors;

5. Define key performance indicators;

6. Monitor ongoing performance;

7. Identify and report performance gaps;

8. Recalibrate measures to reflect changes; and,

9. Continuous improvement.

Of these steps, the identification of performance requirements (1) and primary objectives (3), ongoing monitoring (6) and continuous improvements efforts (9) span two or more decision domains. While measurements need to capture the essence of the work performed by individuals within processes, activities or units, they are driven by the need to communicate entity objectives and monitor progress toward them. The strategic nature of Performance Measurement is reflected in the intersection of the Market/Customer Decision domain and key IPM elements.

Breaking the Integrated Performance Management SMP into finer steps, Figure 10.2 provides a basic framework for implementing and sustaining new measurement strategies in terms of its four core activities: (1) develop strategy, (2) set measures and targets, (3) plan and execute, and (4) monitor and evaluate.

In the pages that follow, the essential elements of an IPM will be developed, focusing on the linkage between strategies, critical success factors, key performance indicators, and a balanced set of measures that create goal congruence at all levels of the organization. These points will then be expanded to include key linkages that need to be leveraged to create optimal performance, as well as the primary behavioral issues that must be addressed in IPM design. Finally, the relationships between IPM and the continuous improvement journey will be explored, providing a comprehensive framework for understanding and utilizing measurement systems to gain and maintain performance excellence.

Figure 10.2   Essential Elements of Performance Management Implementation

Develop Strategy	Plan and Execute
Identify stakeholder needs	Develop communications plan
Identify critical business issues	Implement pilot
Identify performance requirements	Link incentives to performance
Identify business processes	Create responsibility structures
Identify activities	Training
Identify primary objectives	Assess success of pilot
	Establish underlying technology
Set Measures and Targets	**Monitor and Evaluate**
Define critical success factors	Monitor on-going performance
Define key performance indicators	Identify & report performance gaps
Link CSF's to departments	Recalibrate metrics to reflect changes
Link CSF's to major processes	Continuous improvement
Develop process output measures	

Core Elements of IPM Design

*One of the greatest pieces of economic wisdom
is to know what you do not know.*

–John Kenneth Galbraith

Integrated Performance Management (IPM) is *an enterprise-wide management system that links strategic objectives, core business strategies, critical success factors, and key performance indicators.*[4] It is an ongoing process of improvement that focuses priorities on learning and results, integrates measures, facilitates analysis and action, encourages continuous improvement, and defines and reinforces accountability/controllability structures. An intricate part of the management control system of the firm, IPM is the critical link between individual, team, and organizational objectives and efforts. The more accurate and unequivocal a set of measurements is, the more likely desired results will be achieved. Clarity in purpose and measure, as defined by the strategic vision and mission, drives the design, structure and functioning of effective IPM.

STRATEGY AND THE SHAPING OF IPM

At the heart of the IPM is a strategic vision and mission. A vision statement *describes the basic goals, characteristics and philosophies that shape the strategic direction of the firm*.[5] The vision guides future actions aimed at improving performance and aids the firm in isolating opportunities to enhance the firm's strategic position; it also aligns actions across the vertical and horizontal boundaries of the organization by providing a clear signal of desired outcomes and preferred actions. The clear delineation of a vision improves the coordination and communication within the organization as well as with the firm's suppliers and customers.

A well-defined vision statement has three primary components:[6] (1) a focused concept or value creation promise that people can visualize; (2) a sense of noble purpose, something that is worth doing; and, (3) a plausible chance of success. Starbucks' vision statement, namely to be a premier purveyor of the finest coffee in the world, leaves little or no doubt regarding the nature of this firm's objectives and strategies.

A mission statement creates a framework for bringing the vision to life, providing a clear statement regarding the efforts a firm is making to meet specific customer requirements. It is a cultural statement, reflecting the values, beliefs and philosophy of the firm—what the firm is, not what it does.[7] At Southwest Airlines, the mission of the firm is stated as: *"Southwest Airline Company is the nation's low-fare, high customer satisfaction airline. We primarily serve short-haul city pairs, providing single-class air transportation which targets the business commuter as well as leisure travelers."* This mission statement leaves no doubt as to what industry Southwest is in, or what its focus and defined markets are. Reflecting the distinctive core competencies of the firm, the mission statement provides the framework for creating effective IPM as well as the definition of clear strategic objectives.

Strategic objectives shape an organization's current and future actions and results.[8] Defining a firm's critical success factors along the primary dimensions of the competitive challenge facing the company, strategic objectives direct employee attention to different elements of the business and define unique ways for enhancing performance. When strategic objectives are combined in a logical and yet creative way, they provide the basis for integrating the diverse activities of the firm into a powerful, focused, competitive whole.

Corporate strategy is a plan that specifies two areas of overall interest to the firm:[9] (1) definition of the businesses of the entity; and, (2) the acquisition and allocation of corporate resources to support each of these businesses. Business strategy, similarly, is a plan specifying the scope of a given business and its link to the corporation's strategy. Business strategy specifies how the business unit will achieve and maintain a competitive advantage. Process strategy links business and corporate strategy to the underlying flow of work and activities that provide the products and services that fulfill customer needs within the chosen strategy. Finally, functional strategies are plans created for marketing, manufacturing, research and development, finance, distribution, field services, and other areas that reinforce the business and process strategies.

As suggested by the work of Prof. Robert Eccles of Harvard University (see Figure 10.3), companies create shareholder value through the development of products and services that meet customer requirements and draw upon the primary people and process skills and competencies the firm has at its command. Balancing the diverse elements of performance into a smoothly functioning, integrated whole begins with understanding what the firm is about, what its customers expect, and how best to leverage the firm's multitude of resources and skills to create a unique competitive profile.

Figure 10.3   A Generic Business Model

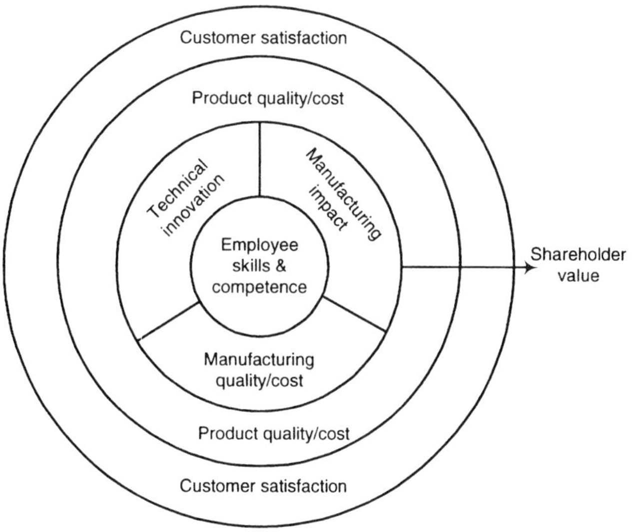

Source: Arthur Andersen and the Institute of Management Accountants Statements on Management Accounting, *Tools and Techniques for Implementing Performance Management Systems*, 1998: 24.

SETTING MEASURES AND TARGETS

Measures and targets are set primarily:

- To help an individual manager determine his or her information needs;
- To aid an organization in its general planning process—for strategic, long range and annual planning purposes; and
- To aid an organization in its information systems planning process.

Visually linking the measurements to their strategic element, superior IPM is not only best practice, it represents a logical, implementable, and easily comprehensible measurement strategy. It relates actions and measures to strategic objectives, focusing attention from "managing by the numbers" at the top of the organization to the pursuit of continuous improvements in activities at the business system, team and individual level that provide competitive advantage.

Figure 10.4   Performance Management—An Integrated View

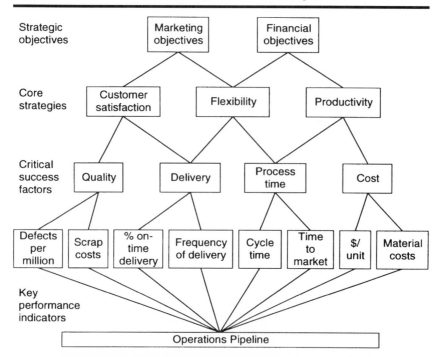

Source: Arthur Andersen and the Institute of Management Accountants Statements on Management Accounting, *Tools and Techniques for Implementing Performance Management Systems*, 1998: 3. Adapted from Lynch and Cross, 1991.

IPM relies on a comprehensive, complementary set of key performance indicators (KPIs) that help direct performance at all levels and all areas of the firm. (see Figure 10.4) Serving to bring together financial and nonfinancial measures of performance, IPM provides management with early warning of potential problem. It also furnishes the timely feedback required to identify emerging opportunities as well as to take corrective action when problems arise. Key performance indicators should be directly linked to a specific strategic objective and direct attention and action to those elements of performance that are crucial to the firm's short- and long-term success. [10]

A series of characteristics and related questions can be used to help identify and choose a set of key performance indicators for a firm (see Figure 10.5). To be effective in coordinating or directing

Figure 10.5   Identifying Relevant KPIs

Characteristics	Related Questions
They are linked to strategic objectives	Can the measure be aligned with an objective or specific customer value?
The measured results are controllable.	Can results be controlled or significantly influenced under a specific span of control?
The measures can be acted upon.	Can action be taken to improve performance on the measured dimension?
The KPI can be accurately measured.	Can the desired performance measures be quantified in a meaningful, realistic way?
They are simple and few in number.	Can the measures be explained easily and clearly by employees? Do the measures focus employee attention on key areas?
The measures are credible.	Are the measures resistant to manipulation?
The measures are integrated.	Can the measures be cascaded or linked down through the organization? Are they compatible with related processes/functions?

action within the firm, KPIs must reflect a balance between time, quality, cost, or other key strategic categories. Balanced measures provide insurance against dysfunctional behavior by visibly tracking relationships that could be manipulated to achieve desired ends. For example, achieving a cost objective can result in impaired quality or delivery unless cost improvements can be reviewed for their impact on other strategic imperatives.

Balance is not the only issue that needs to be addressed in the development of IPM measurements. To achieve its objectives, the organization must focus on identifying the right KPIs—those that will guide actions and decisions toward strategic and operational goals—as well as placing the right amount of emphasis on each specific measure. Areas to focus on when defining critical success factors and their corresponding KPIs include:[11]

- *What are the cost drivers in today's business and how are they controlled?* If a company does a poor job identifying actual cost drivers, then it will be very difficult to develop effective KPIs.

- *Which factors have the biggest impact on cost?* It is imperative that the KPIs target those areas where improvement is needed the most and the resulting impact will be greatest. Some areas that might be explored would be scrap, raw materials, and labor.

- *What are the major problems in the process or organization that act as barriers to meeting performance objectives?* Problems such as excessive or unplanned machine downtime, absenteeism, and production or process bottlenecks can inhibit or prevent the attainment of strategic objectives.

- *What things do we have to do correctly to retain our current customers?* Specifically, the organization needs to understand what factors are critical if desired growth objectives are to be met and what factors are really not very important in this regard.

General Electric (GE) provides an example of how these concepts can be operationalized. At GE, six primary strategic goals are linked directly to performance measures that capture the essence of the strategic intent. Specifically, profitability goals are captured by residual income measures, while market position goals are measured through market share. Relatedly, productivity is captured through targeted output measures, while product leadership is defined as the unit's competitive standing in the industry. The final two goals, focused on building the firm's human capital, are personnel development (captured through a metric called "inventory of promotable people") and employee attitudes (measured as percent of satisfied employees). Combined, these six goals and key performance indicators provide a balanced view of firm performance that can be easily tracked and reported across the levels of management.[12]

Every organization needs to develop its own unique blend of KPIs in order to ensure that a balanced perspective is taken that reflects the firm's strategy, structure and needs. While no one right way to measure, or to choose what to measure, exists, there are common measurement dimensions.[13] Some of these would include: environmental indicators, Market/Customer indicators, competitor indicators, internal business process performance indicators, human resource indicators, and financial indicators.[14] Choosing a small, targeted set of KPIs is a critical part of reaching strategic goals. The final number of indicators chosen should be small enough to ensure that they will be paid attention to, and yet large enough to create a balanced view of organizational performance.

Summarizing the points to this stage, a strategically focused IPM system brings with it a unique perspective and set of performance criteria.[15] Specifically, IPM that is strategically focused is a customer-driven (future focus), flexible and dedicated system for operational control. It tracks current strategies and serves as a catalyst for process improvements. Systematically optimized, strategic IPM improves performance by focusing attention on critical success factors through the use of KPIs as well as through the use of horizontal reporting formats that serve to link individual and team efforts to business process and strategic goals. Integration is achieved by measuring and reporting KPIs simultaneously, along such dimensions as quality, delivery, time and cost, actively addressing key trade-offs. Well-designed IPM supports organizational learning through the use of group incentives tied to strategic and business unit goals. Cast in real-time operational terms that capture strategic intent, IPM should link all levels of management and all functions with common goals and compatible measures.

TOP-DOWN, BOTTOM-UP AND HORIZONTAL IPM PERSPECTIVES

To this point, many of the top-down issues entailed in designing, implementing and using Integrated Performance Management have been emphasized. Driven by the customer through strategic goals down to key performance indicators, a top-down perspective of IPM creates the learning loop (plan-do-check-act) that is the essence of top management-based management control approaches. The top-down view is not only where the critical success factors and key performance indicators are defined, it is where specific measures are given their relative weight—a signal of how important performance on the different KPIs is to overall performance goals.[16]

In 1985, a study was completed that compared the corporate objectives in 291 Japanese companies versus 227 firms in the U.S. The resulting measures and rankings are presented in Figure 10.6.[17] As can be seen, Japanese managers give far more emphasis to market measures, such as market share and ratio of new products (future market share) than do American managers, taking a more balanced perspective overall on financial and market-based KPIs. The weights attached to these measures suggest a heavier short-term, financial emphasis in American firms. In 1985, these comparisons were undoubtedly accurate. Over the last twenty years, though, American firms in both domestic and global settings are shifting attention to more operational, less financial measurements.

Figure 10.6   US versus Japanese Measurement Emphasis

OBJECTIVE	US	JAPAN
Return on investment	8.1	4.1
Share-price increase	3.8	0.1
Market share	2.4	4.8
Improve product portfolio	1.7	2.3
Rationalization of production and distribution	1.5	2.4
Increase equity ratio	1.3	2.0
Ratio of new products	0.7	3.5
Improve company's image	0.2	0.7
Improve working conditions	0.1	0.3

J.C. Abeglen and G. Stalk, Jr., *Kaisha: The Japanese Corporation,* New York: Basic Books, 1985: 177.

Emphasizing the core activities and the drivers that define operational performance, a bottom-up perspective is process-based. It seeks to understand what factors impact cost and what major problems in the process or organization may act as barriers to meeting performance objectives.[18] One useful technique to facilitate the development of the bottom-up perspective and identification of KPIs is Pareto analysis (see Figure 10.7). Using a bar chart structure to graphically capture the frequency with which problems occur, Pareto analysis helps focus measurement and improvement efforts on the most frequent problems. The basic principle of Pareto analysis is that 80 percent of the problems can be traced back to only 20 percent of the variables.[19] By evaluating the process using this principle as a guideline, areas on which to focus KPIs should be apparent.

Another approach that can be used to identify critical success factors is to review existing measurements to better understand what information management uses today to run the organization. When considering existing measures, it is important to recall that one of the objectives of Performance Management is to focus on the few

Figure 10.7   Pareto Analysis

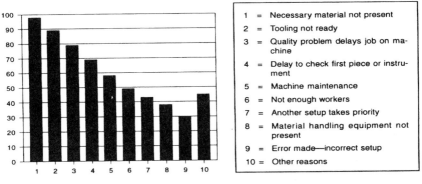

1 =	Necessary material not present
2 =	Tooling not ready
3 =	Quality problem delays job on machine
4 =	Delay to check first piece or instrument
5 =	Machine maintenance
6 =	Not enough workers
7 =	Another setup takes priority
8 =	Material handling equipment not present
9 =	Error made—incorrect setup
10 =	Other reasons

Source: Arthur Andersen and the Institute of Management Accountants Statements on Management Accounting, *Tools and Techniques for Implementing Performance Management Systems,* 1998: 21.5

significant factors. The following questions can help in this assessment. Measurements that do not meet these criteria or are ambiguous in terms of what they measure or what information they convey should be modified or removed from the IPM system:

- What do the current measures measure?
- What do they tell management?
- Do they encourage constructive activity?
- Who uses them?
- Are they controllable within the operating unit?
- Do they support management strategy?
- Are they easily understood?
- Are they fully labeled?
- Are they measured at the appropriate frequency?
- Are they presented at the appropriate level of detail?

Existing performance measurements often collect information from a bottom-up perspective that does not tie to strategic objectives. Some of the measures may be of limited value in a Performance Management system and may even be detrimental if they focus attention and limited resources on unproductive activities. Measures should only be retained if they supply vital information that cannot be incorporated into the proposed set of new operational measures.

The most important role that the various measures play in Integrated Performance Management is to provide the information necessary to help align diverse activities and resources to work together to achieve shared objectives. IPM needs to communicate strategically defined performance objectives and expectations throughout the organization via horizontally and vertically integrated KPIs. KPIs are designed to encourage a horizontal, process view of the business by treating downstream operations as internal customers. The resulting "chain of customers" seeks to optimize the entire business process, not individual functions.

Effective IPM reinforces the alignment of the overall business and its core and support processes, helping to identify activities that are out of alignment and reinforcing the efforts and results that contribute to achieving the shared vision. By monitoring actual performance against quantified goals, KPIs are used to identify areas that are not meeting expectations and that require additional attention and resources. Conversely, they also identify performers who are exceeding expectations and provide the opportunity for positive reinforcement through the recognition and reward of outstanding achievement. By placing measurements at key organizational boundaries, and creating a measurement architecture that balances current and future performance objectives at all levels and areas of the firm, IPM creates an integrated, reinforcing process of continuous improvement.

BALANCED MEASUREMENTS

The concept of a "balanced scorecard" has recently received a tremendous amount of attention in the popular business press. While originally coined by Lynch and Cross in their seminal measurements work, Measure Up!, published in 1991, the term has been brought to the forefront by recent works published by Norton and Kaplan of the Harvard Business School. Balanced scorecard models are based on the belief that a set of measures needs to be developed that balances the competing demands and drivers of company performance and that emphasizes the interdependencies in key performance areas. Therefore, a balanced scorecard needs to be anchored to strategic goals, reflect best practices, include a predictive/results mix that will prevent excessive focus on short-term results, and must truly contain a broad set of measures evenly populating the domain of core business drivers.

At AT&T, the development of a balanced scorecard led to the recognition that there are six key factors that define a successful system. These criteria are:[20]

- *Link every measure to strategy implementation.* Following the credo that "you measure what you manage," this is the most critical test that any scorecard must pass to be not only a barometer of strategy success, but also a diagnostic tool. In other words, a measure should not be included on the scorecard unless it can directly be aligned with an initiative contained in the strategic plan—otherwise the "critical" measure will soon find its way to the "useless measure junkyard."

- *Maximize use of "externally benchmarkable"* measures and leading indicators, so that internal, lagging measures do not "blind" you. A scorecard can enable strategy success only if historical measures are complemented by predictive, leading success indicators (e.g., daily trans- actions) and comparisons of internal performance to "best in class " competitive benchmarks.

- *A balanced scorecard is more than developing a bunch of measures.* It requires a process to build and implement successfully across the organization. This is the most overlooked, but arguably the most critical, key to success. Before embarking on implementation of a balanced scorecard, make a substantial investment in process management, including processes to determine the few and critical measures for the scorecard, processes to develop a set of best practices, processes to conduct internal interviews across the organization, processes to engage executive management at critical junctures (feedback loops), processes to manage the acquisition of data to populate the scorecard, and processes to determine and manage the delivery vehicle selected for the scorecard (e.g., Executive Information System, or EIS).

- *Do not go overboard on the number of measures; too many could distract management focus from the critical measures* and drivers of strategy success. The process of condensing what likely will start out as a large number of proposed measures to a critical few is often long and arduous, but important to the successful implementation of the scorecard because it helps to better understand the company's strategy. Also, maximize the use of exception reporting techniques to determine the subset of critical measures that warrant attention, analysis and action by upper management at a specific point in time.

- *Managers must insist on more than support from upper management.* To be successful, upper management must be actively and directly involved from the beginning in formulating and communicating the strategy, in providing input on the critical measures for the scorecard, in frequently reviewing project status at critical junctures, and in actually using the scorecard to enable strategic success.

- *Make the measure compensation-impacting.* Making a balanced set of measures that will affect compensation helps not only to provide a performance incentive, but also demonstrates the seriousness of the nonfinancial measures of success (e.g., customer and people value-added measures).

At AT&T, these principles were used to create a "dashboard" model of a balanced scorecard (see Figure 10.8). Conceived in early 1995 by the Communications Services Group Leadership Team, the fully functioning dashboard was deployed in August of 1995. It serves as the primary delivery vehicle in the monthly review of key performance results. It is also seen by AT&T management throughout the organization as an excellent vehicle to communicate the company's overall performance and operating unit outcomes in both financial and non-financial terms. Emphasizing the linkage across the various entities and functions of the firm, the balanced scorecard/dashboard at AT&T is serving as the basis for reengineering and improving process and organizational performance.

A "three tier" set of measures should be used to evaluate and round out the balanced scorecard structure. Specifically, measures that are static need to be combined with motivational and dynamic measures to create a fluid, prevent-and-predict enabled IPM.[21] *Static*

Figure 10.8   AT&T's Performance Dashboard

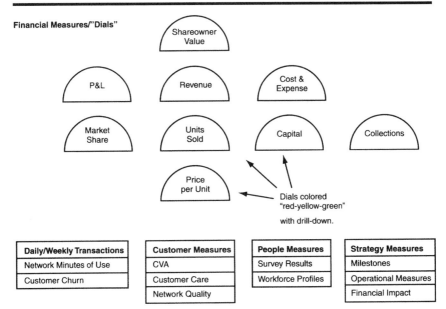

Source: J. Thomson and S. Varley, "Developing a Balanced Scorecard at AT&T," *Journal of Strategic Performance Measurement,* Aug/Sept, 1997: 16.

measures emphasize results such as profitability and market share, items that have a long lag time between an action and a measured result, making it difficult to take corrective action until it is too late. *Motivational measures,* on the other hand, provide a clear line of sight on the scale of improvement needed—from the customer's perspective—to remain competitive over a five- to ten-year horizon. Finally, *dynamic measures,* such as control charts, generate real-time data that allow immediate judgments to be made about whether an activity is in or out of control. This allows corrective action to be taken based on an analysis of root causes of the problem.

The three-tier measurement concept emphasizes performance interdependencies by transforming the top-level business objectives (the scorecard) into *motivational half-life performance gaps* at the core process level and then into targeted actions executed within short time frames by those closest to the work. The "half-life" concept, developed by Art Schneiderman at Analog Devices in the late 1980s, reflects the fact that although what needs to be improved varies by organization, the rate at which required improvements can be gained follows a uniform pattern. Specifically, it takes almost the same amount of time to achieve an initial 50 percent reduction in a process weakness, such as late deliveries, as it does to make the next 50 percent reduction, and so on. Schneiderman determined that only three of four ingredients were necessary to build a half-life improvement curve:[22]

- A valid data starting point;
- An anticipated data point showing 50 percent improvement;
- An estimated half-life time span reflecting the process complexity; or
- A theoretical capability for the process in question.

A major corporation used this logic to create a set of motivational goals for the product development process.[23] Starting with the assumption that the CEO's initial three-year goal for reduction of quality costs by half to 1.25 percent of cost of sales was possible, it was determined that it would take another three years to reach 0.625 percent. It was also estimated that it would take three years more to reach 0.31 percent of sales quality cost targets, and so on. Determining an outer limit for these improvements was set aside, as the firm concentrated on reaching the first three year goal and learning about the interdependencies in the process that would lead to quality enhancements and quality cost reductions. Pareto analysis was then used to identify the specific cost target, reflecting the highest impact, or core, processes (i.e., product development) as well as the goals that would be pursued to reduce costs in the phase one (first 50 percent drive) improvement effort. The resulting model combines process and strategic information to create an integrated set of measures that reflect the impact of core processes on achievement of performance goals (see Figure 10.9).

Creating a linked set of measurements is the key to unlocking the profit and performance potential of the firm. Unambiguously defined measures, though, are not enough to create the drive toward continuous improvement so essential to surviving and thriving in today's global market. It is crucial that measures be tied to incentives and reflect the accountability-controllability realities of the firm's structure and functioning.

Figure 10.9   Business Objectives Conversion Matrix

	Business Objectives	Product Dvlp.	Order Acqu.	Order Fulfill.	After Sales/ Support
OEBIT$$	a. 11-15% annually for COMML b. 6-10% annually for RESIDENTIAL	△	●	△	△
OEBIT & RONA%	3 times better over next business cycle	○	●	△	△
MARKET SHARE	#1 or #2 position in every product line for COMML and RESIDENTIAL	●	●	○	△
CUSTOMER SERVICE LEVEL	On-Time Delivery	△	○	●	○
INVENTORY TURNS	15 (50 Stretch Goal)	△	△	●	△
QUALITY	50% reduction in cost of quality in 3 years	●	△	●	△

IMPACT: High ●   Medium ○   Low △

Source: D. Dimancescu, "Enterprise-focused Metrics in Three-Tier Management Systems," *Journal of Strategic Performance Measurement,* Feb/March, 1998: 27.

Incentives and IPM

Between saying and doing many a pair of shoes is worn out.

– Proverb

Gaining the competitive benefits of well-designed, effective IPM demands that the goals and behaviors of individuals across the organization be congruent with strategic and operational objectives, and that ongoing emphasis and reward is given for reaching performance targets. These elements, plus the development of strong communication plans, training, and technology enablers, comprise the key elements of the plan and execution phase of IPM development and implementation.

In creating performance incentives, it is important to recognize that there are three primary types of measures that can be used: results, action and personnel.[24] *Results measures* involve rewarding, or otherwise holding accountable, individuals, teams, or units for accomplishing particular results or outcomes. While it is common to define desired outcomes in financial terms (net income, earnings per share, or return on investment), non-financial measures are also quite common (market share, growth, or the timely accomplishment of tasks). The implementation of results controls requires three specific steps: (1) defining the dimension(s) on which results are desired (or not desired), (2) measuring performance on these dimensions, and (3) providing rewards (or punishments) to encourage (or discourage) the behaviors that will lead to these results.

Action measures are used to ensure that individuals perform (or do not perform) certain actions that are known to be beneficial (or harmful) to the organization. Serving as the most direct form of control, action measures involve taking steps to ensure that individuals act in the firm's best interest—actions themselves are the focus of the control and measurement process. Action-based measures emphasize influencing effort before or during the execution of the activity. Implementing action controls requires: (1) defining what actions are acceptable or unacceptable; (2) tracking what happens; and (3) rewarding or punishing deviations from the defined limits.

Personnel controls are the least measurable of the various controls available to the firm, but remain the most powerful in terms of influencing behavior. Personnel controls, or the tapping of either self-control or social control (culture or group norms), require little or no monitoring of actions and results. Performance objectives are gained because goals and incentives are aligned at a behavioral level—the desired results are seen as the "right thing to do". Creating a culture that encourages learning, that rewards innovation, and that supports the development of individuals and self-directed work teams is the most important leverage point a firm can utilize in its performance system. The development of group-based rewards is one way that firms are using personnel controls to create the integrated, coordinated focus and effort required to support the emerging process structures. Having many advantages over other forms of control (feasibility, cost, and avoidance of dysfunctional behaviors), personnel controls can be created and implemented through effective personnel selection and placement, training, cultural control, group-based rewards, and the provision of necessary resources.

Figure 10.10 Quantum Performance Measurement Matrix

QUANTUM PERFORMANCE			
	Value		**Service**
	Cost	Quality	Time
Organization	Financial Operational Strategic	Empathy Productivity Credibility Competence	Velocity Flexibility Responsiveness Resilience
Process	Inputs Activities	Empathy Productivity Credibility Competence	Velocity Flexibility Responsiveness Resilience
People	Compensation Development Motivation	Reliability Credibility Competence	Responsiveness Resilience

Source: *Developing Comprehensive Performance Indicators,* Society of Management Accountants of Canada, Management Accounting Guideline #31, 1994: 30.

At the process level, quantum performance approaches emphasize inputs and activities in the determination of current and potential cost, conformance and productivity as quality indicators, and velocity and flexibility as the key measures of the time dimension of process performance. In a related way, the organization level measures look at cost from three dimensions: financial, operational, and strategic. Quality, defined at the organizational level as empathy, productivity, credibility and competence provides the basis for de-livering quality service and products to customers. Finally, time at the organizational level includes velocity of materials through core processes, the flexibility of the organization in the face of changing demands, its responsiveness to customer needs, and its resilience in the market (see Figure 10.10).

Each of these control and measurement classifications has a dif-ferent behavioral implication and provides a unique form of control over individual and group actions and results that occur from them. Results controls can quite easily result in goal displacement due to poor understanding of desired results or over-quantification of measurements. Not every result or desired outcome needs to be quantified in financial terms or be concrete—meeting or exceeding customer requirements is results-focused, but difficult to quantify. Similarly, if a results measure focuses on the wrong thing (sales quotas set on volume, not profitability), it can generate undesirable outcomes.

Gamesmanship (e.g., mis-reporting performance to meet goals), the creation of slack resources, and data manipulation are three other concerns that need to be addressed in a well-designed IPM system. While the development of a balanced scorecard can help alleviate some of these problems, still it is difficult for a manager to change one element of an integrated system without causing impacts in other areas. Since the resulting impact may not be very favorable when looked at holistically, the incentive to try to game the measurements to achieve a favorable evaluation is reduced. In a continuous improvement setting, it is also quite difficult to increase slack resources. The relentless pressure to improve gradually squeezes waste and slack out of the process.

The advantage of using multiple forms of control (i.e., personnel, action and results), and a balanced set of measures, is that many of the undesirable consequences of control can be avoided or minimized. IPM should attempt to include all three forms of control, including a mix of static, motivational and dynamic measures, and incorporate all primary performance dimensions in its design, development and utilization of the chosen measurements. Quantum performance improvements come from creating an IPM framework that supports key strategic initiatives, links business processes, people and organizational goals, and rewards desired behaviors.

CREATING RESPONSIBILITY STRUCTURES AND TARGETED INCENTIVES

The underlying goal in implementing IPM is to develop a shared vision and coordinated actions that will move the organization ever closer to its strategic objectives. The two critical elements in bringing this desired end state into being are the creation of a responsibility structure and the use of targeted incentives to motivate and reinforce desired behavior.[25] A responsibility structure is the matching of specific goals to individuals and/or groups that have the ability and control necessary to bring them about. Matching the accountability for the result or metric attainment with the requisite level of control is what transforms the static measurements into an action-generating and supporting tool.

Many different tools can be used to create the required match between accountability and controllability. For instance, an individual action plan can be developed (see Figure 10.11) that provides a detailed work plan and set of results measures to guide a specific individual or group toward half-life or annual goals. Key completion dates and deliverables are identified, core measures are detailed, and improvement goals are defined so that the individual or team has a clear understanding of what is to be done, when, where, and why.

Figure 10.11   Individual Action Plan and Accountabilities

Objective: improvement of the reliability of the welding installations in the car welding management center

Person responsible: maintenance supervisor

Description of the Action	Person Responsible	Action Plan Indication	J	F	M	A	M	J	D
Training of the welders. After training, welders will be able to do basic maintenance operations.	Welding management center	Number of trained welders	10	20	30	40	50		100
Installation of catchers to detect failures	Welding management center	% of equipped machines	20	50	70	100			100
Hiring of workers for the maintenance department	Maintenance	Number of workers hired	1	1	1	1	4		4
Use of preassembled spare parts	Maintenance	% of spare parts	5	10	20	30	40	50	50
Total benefits on the indicator (expressed in number of cars/month with unreliable welds)			500	400	300				50

Source: Arthur Andersen and the Institute of Management Accountants Statements on Management Accounting, *Tools and Techniques for Implementing Performance Management Systems*, 1998: 31.

The nature and focus of measurement changes as the various levels and processes of the organization are traversed. At the top of the hierarchy, most of the measures used and information required deal with financial information or other forms of results measures. More static in nature, these top level measures assign responsibility to specific business unit managers to achieve strategic and operational goals. At the bottom of the organization, the data required is real-time, operationally focused measures that identify and track performance on key process characteristics such as number of defects or performance against daily output targets. Finally, in the middle of the organization, a "hinge" manager serves to help translate strategic objectives into operational goals that can be pursued on the line.

In a well-designed IPM system, there should be little overlap in the measures at each level. The measures should link together, providing a smooth pathway from strategic intent through performance and back up to encourage assessment and learning. Each level, team, or individual should be given the measures and information required to manage their activities and to increase their ability to meet preset objectives. Complementary measures, designed to the decision requirements of each specific job or process, should be used to communicate and coordinate efforts to meet customer requirements and achieve organizational objectives.

INCENTIVES AND IPM

Aligning accountability and controllability within the IPM is critical if the most severe dysfunctional consequences are to be avoided. Gaining major improvements in performance, though, requires more than avoiding problems, it entails motivating efforts beyond current levels of performance. *Performance incentives*, whether monetary or nonmonetary, are the final key to creating a sustainable learning environment through the deployment of IPM.

Incentives are taking many forms today. For instance, top performing organizations like Caterpillar and Motorola are using individual incentive systems that are made up of three primary components: (1) individual performance, (2) team or process results, and (3) organizational outcomes. Every individual, from the boardroom to the shop floor, has all three of these elements in their incentive package. While the percentages vary as one moves from the top to the bottom of the organization, everyone has pay at risk tied to the performance of the entity.

Individual performance incentives and their related goals are best tied to growth targets, such as "pay for learning" or incentives tied to learning new skills and competencies. Since building the human capital of the firm is critical to both its short- and long-term success, ensuring that individuals engage in ongoing training and development is crucial. In some firms, a required number of training hours is established for individuals at each level of the organization. In others, a set of competencies is assessed annually (or more often) resulting in a new set of individual improvement objectives as defined by the individual's supervisor. Whether defined in terms of classroom hours, new skills acquired, or progress against defined competencies required for future promotion, the act of tieing individual raises to learning creates a productive, reinforcing cycle of change.

Team or process results are the basis for another major segment of a balanced incentive package. Since most of the operational and strategic outcomes are based on the coordinated, integrated efforts of multiple firm members, it is important to build a team orientation into the core compensation package. In some firms, this is taking place through the use of *360 degree* evaluations where an individual's supplier, customer, supervisor, and subordinates all provide feedback on the individual's performance. In others, the team itself is the focus of attention and measurement; the choice of internal actions used to generate desired outcomes are left to the discretion of team members and managers. If the process meets its goals, then the entire team wins; if it doesn't, the entire team loses.

At Motorola, core process measures such as defects, on time delivery, and cost are tracked for improvement. Team bonuses are earned when improvement takes place on at least one measured dimension *without any reduction in performance on other dimensions*. A form of gain-sharing, team incentives can range from financial bonuses to dinners, rewards, and other forms of compensation.

Putting everyone's pay at risk for organizational performance provides the cross-functional, cross-process integration that is essential if major improvements in overall performance are to be gained. While not everyone can directly affect the core value chain, everyone should be looking for ways to improve firm performance, whether that means as simple a thing as not wasting cleaning fluids to a more elaborate set of decisions to change distribution strategies. Individuals with greater control at the entity level should clearly have a greater percentage of their pay at risk, but everyone needs to be linked to organizational performance if an entity perspective is to become part of the organization's culture. Performance Management, then, plays many roles in addition to simply measuring the outcome of efforts to meet objectives and individual goals. IPM systems also:[26]

- Communicate critical success factors and performance expectations throughout an organization;
- Enable all personnel to better understand how their jobs contribute to achieving strategic objectives;
- Encourage teamwork through team-oriented goals and by encouraging a process view of the organization;
- Provide each individual with the shared vision and decision support information necessary to make informed, decentralized decisions;
- Encourage continuous improvement by highlighting goals and recognizing outstanding achievements;
- Serve as diagnostic tools to help identify problems and opportunities for improvement; and
- Serve as assessment tools to evaluate the effectiveness of implemented solutions and improvement initiatives.

The most important role that performance measures play is to provide the information necessary to help align diverse activities and resources to work together to achieve shared objectives. IPM communicates strategically defined performance objectives and expectations throughout the organization via horizontally and vertically integrated KPIs. Linking individual and team incentives to the results generated creates the motivation required to achieve goals and build continuous improvement into the heart of the organization.

TRAINING, ASSESSING AND SUPPORTING INTEGRATED PERFORMANCE MANAGEMENT

Planning and executing the development and implementation of an effective IPM system that supports strategic and tactical objectives and shapes behavior in desirable ways does not end with developing new responsibility and incentive structures.[27] Training plays a critical role in ensuring that individuals can perform desired work and reach targeted objectives. Education serves to communicate the reasons for the measurements, define clearly what the measures and expectations mean, and provide a medium for gaining feedback on the impact of proposed measures on behavior. Keeping the measurements open to question can help prevent unforeseen side effects, such as measurements that drive people to actually decrease the level and completeness of service provided to customers in order to decrease the wait time for customers in the queue.

Technology can serve as a major enabler in designing and sustaining IPM.[28] Magnetic personnel identification cards, for instance, can be used to capture information about the type of work done, length of time required, and related core facts that would otherwise require significant time and effort to maintain. Electronic reporting formats can be used that allow individuals to peel away detail until the measurement and resulting feedback information is fully understood. Similarly, relational database structures can be used to support balanced scorecard initiatives by linking operational and financial data into a seamless, integrated, readily accessed storehouse of measurements. Technology can enable the data collection, analysis, reporting, and evaluative elements of IPM.

Finally, to ensure that IPM is meeting its objectives, it should be subject to periodic assessment. This is especially important after the pilot project has been fully completed, as the review can reveal both strengths and weaknesses in the implementation methodology or the underlying set of measurements currently being developed or used. Gathering information on the behavioral and motivational impact of measurements, the degree of perceived control (and hence acceptance) felt by individuals held responsible for specific objectives, and the adequacy of existing reporting formats and frequencies, are just a few of the areas that a post-implementation review can emphasize. As with every other SMP, continuous improvement and learning have to be embodied in the design and use of IPM.

Continuous Improvement: An IPM Perspective

All experience is an arch, to build upon.

– Henry Adams

After the IPM system has been designed and implemented, all members of the organization must strive to use the performance data to promote continuous improvement. Several steps are involved in ensuring that the IPM system itself is constantly undergoing improvement: (1) consider human factor issues related to performance management; (2) periodically evaluate, review and revise KPIs; and, (3) implement "hit squad" KPIs to address specific problems.

At the human level, three specific questions need to be dealt with. First, are the incentive and personnel evaluation programs being used consistent with the performance management system or do they encourage counterproductive activity? Second, are people being adequately trained to realize the full benefits of the new system as well as being able to meet the newly defined performance requirements? Finally, are the production and other core process teams being provided with the resources and opportunity to implement improvements identified by the KPIs?

Once the KPIs are being regularly tracked and the interactive support tools are in place, the implementation and maintenance of IPM turns its attention to finding potential improvements in the system and its information. Some key questions that can be used to drive the first phase of system evaluation include.[29]

- Is the system measuring what it was intended to measure?
- Is what is being measured also being managed?
- Do the KPIs address factors that present the opportunity for improvement?
- Are the production and other core process teams utilizing the KPIs?
- Do the KPIs support performance objectives?
- Are there critical objectives that are not being addressed by the IPM?
- Have the problems or cost drivers that the current KPIs were designed to address been resolved or decreased in significance?
- Have new problems, cost drivers, or key success factors surfaced that are not being addressed?
- Can other KPIs more effectively promote continued improvement?

In doing early and ongoing evaluations, it is quite possible that some KPIs will prove to be less valuable than expected, while some other critical factors may have been overlooked. There may be too many or too few measures in the system. Finally, it may be determined that how the measures are being presented makes them less informative than they could be.

The IPM system and its KPIs need to change with the environment. They have to focus on new problems as old ones get resolved, reflecting new objectives and organizational changes. New techniques and technologies may alter the key success factors for a business unit. Wherever or whatever the source of change may be, it is important to constantly monitor and update the IPM system to reflect their impact. Effective IPM is a living system, modified to meet new needs to ensure that the information needed by decision makers remains current and relevant.

A third consideration in building continuous improvement into IPM is to consider the implementation of "hit squad" or targeted performance measures to address specific performance problems. Short-term in nature, hit squad KPIs should be removed from the system once the underlying concerns have been addressed. If this isn't done, measures will proliferate leading to a loss of clarity in the system as well as ongoing visibility to an old, already resolved problem.

A new performance indicator system is just that—new—and will probably need to be adjusted after it has been put in place. New indicators may need to be added and others dropped. The frequency with which information is provided may have to be adjusted to ensure that everyone's decision support requirements are met. Just as yesterday's approaches to performance measurement are inadequate and have changed, the future will quite likely require new perspectives and measures. As the external environment changes, what's important and unimportant within the firm also changes, leading to the need to develop new measures and eliminate old ones.

The IPM is a dynamic system; KPIs must be changed as the firm evolves. The implications of these unavoidable facts are that the data collection, analysis, and presentation systems that underlie IPM should be made as flexible as possible. Flexibility will ensure that building new measures and eliminating old ones is done with minimal impact on ongoing activities and on the effectiveness of the firm and its management. Achieving this success starts with avoiding as many implementation and design pitfalls as possible.

Figure 10.12   IPM Critical Success Factors

Critical Success Factors ("Do's")	Pitfalls ("Don'ts")
Recruit a dedicated, senior executive to ensure top management participation.	Don't begin a project without senior management commitment.
Throw out old measures that are not necessary to the overall functioning of the business.	Don't retain old measures that confuse or don't add value.
Include KPIs as part of the new evaluation and compensation systems.	Don't continue to evaluate and compensate personnel based on obsolete performance goals.
Invite front-line employees to help define KPIs, and encourage use of KPIs as self-measurement and self-education tools, so there are no surprises at evaluation time.	Don't use KPIs as a weapon against personnel.
Develop concise, intuitively obvious KPIs focused on strategic goals.	Don't design too many, or too complex, KPIs – this may confuse employees.
Keep the big picture in mind when defining KPIs – all KPIs should work together to achieve strategic goals.	Don't define KPIs too narrowly – this may encourage suboptimization of specific segments.
Make sure that all KPIs can be influenced by the actions of the person or group whose performance they are measuring.	Don't design KPIs for areas that are not controllable by employees.
Pay attention to the cultural change caused by the new system. Keep communication open and train/educate employees to make best use of the system.	Don't implement a new performance management system without addressing change management issues.

Source: Arthur Andersen and the Institute of Management Accountants Statements on Management Accounting, *Tools and Techniques for Implementing Performance Management Systems*, 1998: 49.

As suggested in Figure 10.12, the do's and don'ts of IPM implementation and ongoing utilization reflect many of the points that have been made throughout this chapter. KPIs have to be built into the evaluation and compensation system, be influenceable by the people being given responsibility for them, and keep the big picture in mind at all times. IPM design and use should reflect elegance in structure and use. Only critical KPIs should be included, and these should be measured in straightforward ways. Old measures that do not fit the new performance paradigm should be eliminated. Finally, the cultural changes that fall on the heel of any measurement or control system change must be attended to through open and ongoing communication and training to smooth the transition to the new model.

The essential message embedded in the "don'ts" list is that the IPM system must reflect a solid, effective management control strategy—defined and supported by top management. Measures have to be designed to support action, identify problems, highlight opportunities, and communicate performance against customer expectations. Measures that don't add value are worse than no measures at all. Measurement done well and integrated across processes and units can support attainment of strategic and operational goals. Measurement done poorly, in fragmented ways, can destroy the momentum of improvement and damage the culture of an organization. In the end, keeping strategic goals clearly in front of everyone, with a keen recognition of operational realities, provides the basis for creating the future through effective management and action today.

References

Atkinson, A., "Linking Performance Measurement to Strategy: The Roles of Financial and Non-financial Information, " *Journal of Strategic Performance Measurement,* Aug/Sept, 1997: 5-13.

J.H. Waterhouse, and R.B. Wells, "A Stakeholder Approach to Strategic Performance Measurement, " *Sloan Management Review,* Spring, 1997: 25-37.

Bruns, William J., ed., *Performance Measurement, Evaluation, and Incentives,* Boston: Harvard Business School Press, 1992.

Forsan, A., "Performance Measurement 2000: The Growth of Real-Time Reporting, " *Journal of Strategic Performance Measurement,* Dec, 1997: 22-29.

Gale, B.T., *Managing Customer Value,* New York: The Free Press, 1994.

Hoffecker, J., and C. Goldenberg, "Using the Balanced Scorecard to Develop Companywide Performance Measures, " *Journal of Cost Management,* Fall, 1994: 5-17.

Imai, M., *Kaizen: The Key to Japan's Competitive Success,* New York: Random House, 1986.

Kaplan, R.S., and D.P. Norton, *The Balanced Scorecard,* Boston: Harvard Business School Press, 1996.

Lynch, R.L., and K.F. Cross, *Measure Up! Yardsticks for Continuous Improvement,* Cambridge, MA: Basil Blackwell, Inc., 1991.

Maskell, Brian H., "Implementing Performance Measurements, " *Journal of Strategic Performance Measurement,* Aug./Sept., 1997: 42-47.

Performance Measurement for World-Class Manufacturing, Cambridge, MA: Productivity Press, 1991.

McNair, C.J., *The Profit Potential,* New York: Wiley & Sons, 1995.

Nagashima, S., *100 Management Charts,* White Plains, NY: Quality Resources, 1990.

Rummler, G.A., and A. Brache, *Improving Performance: How to Manage the White Space on the Organization Chart,* San Francisco: Jossey-Bass, 1995.

Sharmon, P., and J. Gurowka, "Implementing Integrated Performance Measurement Systems, " *Journal of Strategic Performance Measurement",* Aug/Sept., 1997: 32-41.

Thomson, J., and S. Varley, "Developing a Balanced Scorecard at AT&T, " *Journal of Strategic Performance Measurement,* Aug./Sept., 1997: 14-21.

Wayland, R.E., and P.M. Cole, *Customer Connections: New Strategies for Growth,* Boston: Harvard Business School Press, 1997

Endnotes

[1] This entire section draws heavily upon the Institute of Management Accountants, Statement on Management Accounting, *Tools and Techniques for Implementing Integrated Performance Management Systems*, 1998. The draft was drafted by Dr. C.J. McNair under the direction of Randolf Holst of Arthur Andersen, and is considered to be a statement of best practice in Performance Management. It will be noted as IMA in the following notes.

[1] Ibid, pg. 1.

[2] Ibid, pp.2-3.

[3] Ibid, pg. 3.

[4] Ibid, pg. 11.

[5] This list and the Starbuck's example are from IMA, op.cit., pg. 11.

[6] Ibid, pg. 12.

[7] Ibid, pg. 12-13.

[8] Ibid, pp. 13-14.

[9] These comments are based on IMA, op.cit., pp. 17-19.

[10] Ibid, pg. 19.

[11] Ibid, pg. 4.

[12] IMA, op.cit.

[13] Ibid, pg 4.

[14] Lynch and Cross, op.cit., pg. 37.

[15] IMA, op.cit., pg. 7.

[16] This information appears in Lynch and Cross, op.cit., pg. 72. It is based on original work by J.C. Abegglen and G. Stalk, Jr., *Kaisha: The Japanese Corporation*, New York: Basic Books, 1985: 177.

[17] IMA, op.cit., pg. 7.

[18] Ibid, pg. 21.

[19] J. Thomson and S. Varley, "Developing a Balanced Scorecard at AT&T", *Journal of Strategic Performance Measurement*, Aug/Sept, 1997: 20. This entire list of critical issues is taken verbatim from the argument developed by these two authors.

[20] The source for this part of the discussion is D. Dimancescu, "Enterprise-Focused Metrics in a Three-Tier Management System, " *Journal of Strategic Performance Measurement*, Feb/March, 1998: 34.

[21] Ibid., pg. 29.

[22] This example originally appears in Dimancescu, op.cit.

[23] These insights were originally developed within the book *Control in Business Organizations*, by K. Merchant, Boston: Pitman Publishing, 1985. This entire section draws heavily from various pages within this original text as well as the author's own experience and work.

[24] This part of the discussion draws upon IMA, op.cit., pp. 29-31.

[25] Ibid. Various points in document serve as basis for creating this list of goals and objectives for IPM efforts.

[26] This section draws from the discussion in the IMA document, op.cit., which appears on pages 29-31.

[27] Ibid, pp. 33-34.

[28] This section is a compilation of various paraphrased comments and points made in the IMA document, op.cit.

[29] Ibid, pp. 35-36.

Activity-Based Cost Management

It is a capital mistake to theorize before one has data.
Insensibly one begins to twist facts to suit theories,
instead of theories to suit facts.

– Sir Arthur Conan Doyle

Key Learnings:

■ Activity-Based Cost Management is a methodology that measures the cost and performance of activities, resources and cost objects.

■ ABCM is a discipline that focuses on the management of activities as the route to improving the value received by the customer and the profit achieved by providing this value.

■ ABCM is based on the belief that accurate and relevant information is critical to any organization that hopes to maintain or improve its competitive position.

■ ABCM develops a multi-dimensional view of cost.

ABCM is one of the oldest of the "new" cost management techniques. ABCM's historical roots can be traced back to the turn of the century. ABCM gained its present prominence in the mid-1980s with the publication of Relevance Lost by Johnson and Kaplan, subsequent ABCM development efforts spearheaded by Robert Kaplan and Robin Cooper, and the efforts of the CAM-I organization and member firms. Serving as the foundation for a range of new models and management concepts, ABCM provides a new way to see the facts and a new basis for creating theories about the firm and optimizing its performance.

ABCM is based on the belief that accurate and relevant information is critical to any organization that hopes to maintain or improve its competitive position. As described by the Institute of Management Accountants' (IMA) Statement on Management Accounting (No. 4T: 1):[1]

> ....*For years, organizations operated under the assumption that their cost information actually reflected the costs of their products and services when, in reality, it did nothing of the kind. While hiding their shortcomings behind a cloak of precision, over-generalized cost systems were actually misleading decision makers, causing them to make decisions inconsistent with their organizations' needs and goals.*

Providing a cross-functional, integrated view of the firm, its activities and its business processes, ABCM has been credited with triggering a revolution in management reporting and decision support.

Activity-Based Cost Management is defined as a *methodology that measures the cost and performance of activities, resources and cost objects.*[2] This relationship between cost and performance is emphasized in ABCM through the causal relationships of cost drivers to activities. ABCM ensures that resources are assigned to the appropriate activities, and then activities are assigned to specific cost objects based on their use.

ABCM is an outgrowth of early activity-based costing models that were predominantly focused on product costing. Activity-Based Cost Management is a discipline that focuses on the management of activities as the route to improving the value received by the customer and the profit achieved by providing this value.[3] ABCM includes such initiatives as cost driver analysis, activity analysis, and performance management. It utilizes activity-based costing as its major source of data.

The basic difference between traditional forms of costing and ABCM is that ABCM develops a multi-dimensional view of cost and the causes underlying resource usage versus the one-dimensional, one cost attribute-driven view of the organization that dominated earlier work. Final products and services are depicted as the only drivers of cost; support activities, processes and complexity are just a few of the potential consumers of resources. Some of the key differences between ABCM and ABC are:[4]

- ABC focuses on understanding costs and their drivers; ABCM seeks to change them.

- ABC can provide information on process, product, and market performance; ABCM finds ways to improve them.

- ABC is cost centered; ABCM lies at the heart of the management process.

- ABC is the result of a static analysis of the organization. ABCM is embedded in the dynamics of change.

- ABC is predominantly historical and focused on controlling existing costs; ABCM is forward-looking, seeking ways to avoid unnecessary costs and putting existing resources to maximum use.

- ABC reports on internal operational and tactical results; ABCM is strategic, focused on understanding the key elements of value from the customer's perspective.

- ABC is a source of explanatory data; ABCM provides actionable information.

ABC and ABCM are complementary systems of costing, providing the basis for developing economic assessments of product, process, and activity performance and targeting opportunities that increase the value creating potential of the firm. In this discussion, ABCM will be used to encapsulate the combined methodology, recognizing these stated differences at all times.

Within an ABCM system, *resource cost drivers* are used to replace the step-down allocations of traditional costing with cause-and-effect driven assignments of costs to the activity, not the departmental level. Resource drivers, often captured by estimates of the time, effort or cost of doing certain work, can be obtained through interviews or a number of other data collection techniques. Demonstrating a logical and quantifiable relationship between the utilization of resources, the performance of activities, and the final cost objects, resource cost drivers are a crucial part of the overall system design.[5]

Cost drivers are depicted in the CAM-I Cross (Figure 11.1) at both the resource and activity level. This dual usage of driver concepts has given rise to a pseudonym for ABCM cost assignment: two-stage allocation.[6] During the first stage, the economic resources are driven

Figure 11.1 The CAM-I ABCM Cross

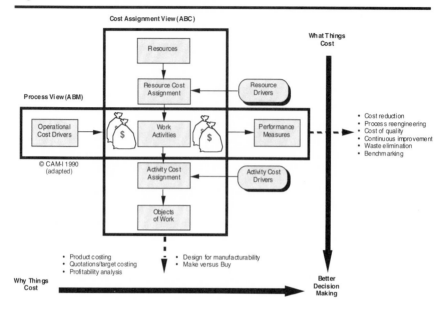

Source: T. White, *The 60 Minute ABC Book*, Bedford, TX: Consortium for Advanced Manufacturing—International, 1997: 19.

into activities or activity centers using "resource" cost drivers. Some examples of resource cost drivers include manpower hours, material moves, floor space, travel time, machine set-up time, parts count, order numbers, etc. Regardless of which variable is chosen, the objective remains the same: to link the performance of a specific activity with the specific economic resources consumed by it.

In traditional systems, controllers usually create elaborate allocations that distribute service or department costs to production work centers based on some allocation scheme using percentages and degree of interdependence. The resulting allocations are often misleading because they are based on arbitrary relationships, such as square feet of space used by an area or its current head count. These allocations do accomplish one goal: all the costs get charged somewhere. The downside is that they hide information, eliminate the responsibility-controllability doctrine, and greatly reduce the information value of the cost system. Having detailed the basic structure of ABCM, how does it fit within the CAM-I Strategic Management Process Model structure?

ACTIVITY-BASED COST MANAGEMENT PROCESS INTEGRATION

ABCM is built from the bottom up, but is shaped by strategic objectives. This fact is reflected in the placement of key ABCM process steps on the CAM-I SMP template (see Figure 11.2). In the initial definition of the requirements of an ABCM system, the information requirements of managers within the Market/Customer, Product and Process Decision domains need to be recognized. Without a clear understanding of the strategic, tactical and operational information the ABCM system is to provide, it is difficult to focus the data collection and analysis initiatives.[6]

Having identified the data and information requirements for ABCM, attention turns to planning the ABCM system in detail and training individuals within the firm on its core elements, proper use, and overall capabilities. While training early in the development of the system may seem counter-intuitive, it is important to remember that the value of activity-based data depends on how well it meets the needs of its internal customers. Educating the customer is a key first step in ensuring that individuals can conceptualize and verbalize their ABCM information needs. Knowing what is capable, the down-stream users can aid in the design, development and implementation of the ABCM system. This increases user commitment while improving the value delivered by the new information system.

The definition of system requirements leads naturally to an important step in the ABCM process—assessing existing financial structure and data. ABCM builds from traditional financial data contained in the general ledger and budgeting system. In the first phase of ABCM implementation, the ability to tie the data back to the total costs in the general ledger is one way to validate the accuracy of the new costing system. Anchored in the financial history of the firm, an effective ABCM system does not stop with the general ledger but rather turns its attention to estimating future costs.

Once the existing financial structure and data is assessed, the majority of the detail design and development work for the ABCM system takes place. Specifically, activities are identified and analyzed, activity cost pools are developed, and cost drivers are developed for each activity cost pool. Spanning the Resource, Process/Activity and Product Decision domains, these core steps in ABCM design and development seek to match resource usage with specific activities and

Figure 11.2   ABCM Process Integration

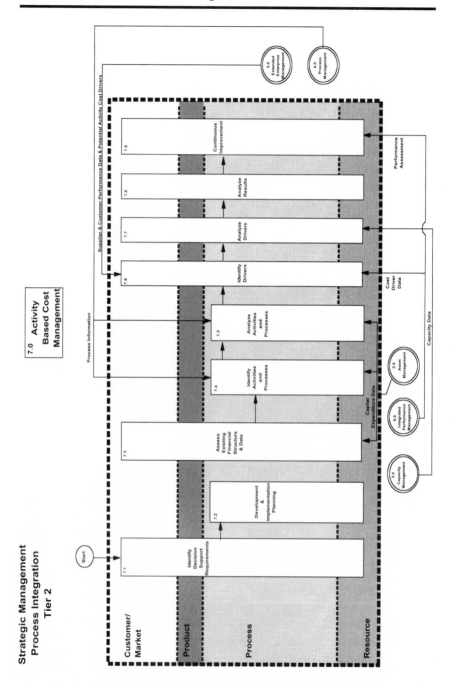

outcomes. The resulting cost estimates are the core of the CAM-I SMP Model, serving as a means to understand how various potential products, processes, activities and strategic foci will impact current and future costs and profits. ABCM estimates are the basic building blocks for the information that is developed and shared among the other SMPs making up the CAM-I SMP Model.

The analysis of drivers and results is part of the sustaining activities for an ABCM system. Reports are developed, and information provided, to support decisions across all key domains. Serving as the feedback loop in the quest to continuously improve performance, ABCM reports and analysis help managers understand the reasons for current outcomes and the potential risks and opportunities on the horizon. New products can be analyzed for their cost impact using ABCM estimates; process redesign initiatives can be evaluated and tracked using ABCM data. Continuous improvement is both facilitated by, and serves as an intricate part of, the ABCM process.

Organizations adopt ABCM for different reasons. They believe that ABCM will help them make better decisions, improve performance, and earn more money on assets deployed. As suggested by Figure 11.3, companies in many situations can find value in ABCM information.

Figure 11.3 General Uses of ABCM Information

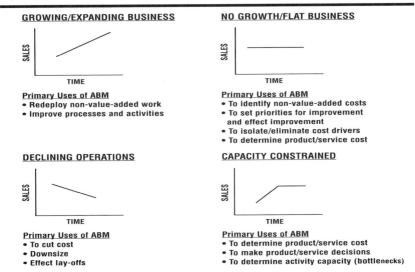

Source: J. Miller, *Implementing Activity-Based Management in Daily Operations,* New York: John Wiley & Sons, 1996: 26.

In the pages that follow, the essential elements of activity-based approaches will be presented, followed by the ways ABCM supports the wide variety of decision contexts in an organization. The final section will explore the ABCM implementation process, including the common pitfalls and how to avoid them. In total, this chapter provides the core information and concepts that drive the development and effective utilization of cost information within the organization.

Essential Elements of Activity-Based Costing

Get your facts first, and then you can distort them
as much as you please.

– Mark Twain

Activity-Based Cost Management is, in essence, only data—data developed using time-tested costing principles applied to a new set of cost objects and organizational structures.[7] ABCM becomes more than a simple data set when it is effectively and creatively used by individuals or organizations to enable continuous improvement or to support operational and strategic decisions. Replacing a traditional costing system overwhelmed by mix, complexity and variety in the business environment, ABCM supports cross-functional management and strategic initiatives. With ABCM data, organizations, teams and individuals are empowered to reengineer business processes, identify waste, reduce cycle times, and to accomplish these tasks profitably. Developing this capability is the objective of the ABCM framework.

THE ABCM FRAMEWORK

ABCM system design focuses first on understanding the activities performed in the firm. *Activities* are what people and equipment do to satisfy customer need—they are the efforts and outcomes that consume business resources. By focusing on business activities as the essential organizing feature of cost-based reporting and analysis, ABCM makes visible actions, results, responsibilities and opportunities that are hidden from view by traditional costing models.

Activity analysis is the first step in the development of an ABCM system. Costs, conventionally reported organizationally by department, are first traced to activities to better understand how work is done. The people who do the work, and those that manage them, can relate to costs described in this manner because they know they can affect or change an activity that is performed by a person or a machine. Activities are therefore best defined using an active verb and object convention, such as "create labor routings." Within this process perspective, functions and organizational boundaries become less important, as focus turns toward cross-functional processes and performance.[8]

After defining activities and assigning costs to them based on estimated amount of people and non-people resource used by each activity, attention turns to distributing activity costs to the cost object that uses the activity. Cost objects are *usually parts, services, ingredients, products, customers or distribution channels,* but can be any decision, outcome or event that has economic impact. Measuring how much of the resources in an activity pool are consumed by a specific cost object leads to the need to identify and define activity cost drivers. *Activity cost drivers* help management understand the relative amount of the activity pool's resources and capacity used by specific cost objects.

Effective ABCM systems remove distortions from cost distributions by minimizing overhead averaging so prevalent in traditional allocation-based cost approaches. As described by Cokins, et.al.:[9]

> *Advanced ABCM implementers recognize that multiple steps can make up the first-stage cost assignment, the resource drivers (the second-stage cost assignment uses activity drivers). After general ledger resource costs are unbundled and accumulated into activities, additional optional steps are to redistribute the activity costs into macro activities or processes. For example, the activity "unscheduled machine repair" may draw resources from multiple departments. This activity cost might be an intermediate step to be combined with similar activities to feed the macro activity of the machine, such as "drill holes." This process is the "step-down allocation," but with ABCM it is accomplished at the activity level, not percent-of-department, a critical distinction.*

ABCM attaches indirect costs to their logical consumers, using cause-and-effect reasoning to ensure that costs are charged to the events or drivers that cause them. First, ABCM links resource costs to activities based on effort expended or material consumed. Activity drivers are then used to attach indirect activity costs to cost objects in proportion to their consumption by the cost objects using a device such as a "bill of activities" (see Figure 11.4). The resulting cost hierarchy reflects the primary and secondary causes of cost within the organization.

Figure 11.4 ABCM Cost Flow Diagram

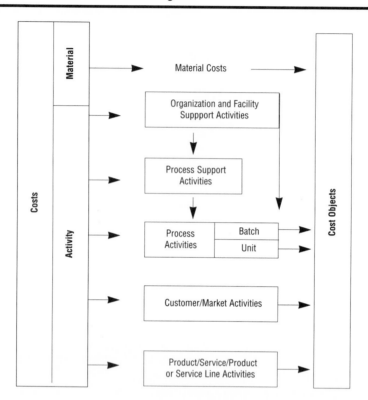

Source: IMA, Statement on Management Accounting 4T, *Implementing Activity-Based Costing*, 1993: 24.

THE ABCM HIERARCHY

An activity and cost hierarchy underlies the primary ABCM resource flows. Activities performed to produce outputs can be grouped into several classifications based on the nature of the underlying work and where it occurs in the organization. Some of the more common ABCM groupings include: (1) Process activities, which include unit- and batch-level activities; (2) Process support activities; (3) Organizational/facility support activities; (4) Customer/market-related activities; and (5) Product/product line-related activities.[10]

Process activities are ones that relate directly to the products or services produced by an organization. Most easily identified through process mapping, these activities are part of the core value chain of the firm. There are three primary forms that process activities can take: unit-, batch- and direct process-based. Unit level activities are performed in the same manner for every unit or service performed and the total number of them completed varies proportionately with changes in volume or sales. Not to be confused with variable cost concepts, which relate to changes in how resources are consumed by activities (cost flows and cost behavior), a typical unit level activity might include the basic series of procedures used with each complete physical examination given by a physician.

Batch level activities, which include such efforts as the setting up of a machine to run a specific order or the completion of the procedures required to mail a group of invoices, are performed for each batch or cluster of work performed. They are independent of the number of units in any specific batch. The more production runs or invoice runs completed by a firm, the greater the number of batches and therefore batch-driven activities that will be done.

Process-support activities are ones that facilitate efforts in other parts of the organization, but do not directly relate to the products and services produced. These activities are not part of the core value chain, but rather ensure that productive capability is available when needed. In a manufacturing setting, process-support activities include equipment maintenance, quality assurance, production control, and scheduling. Organization and facility-support activities are those used in the general management of the firm or to provide the facilities the rest of the organization uses. Activities included under this designation include planning, general supervision, building and grounds maintenance, heating, and so forth.

Customer or market-related activities are those efforts that are undertaken in support sub-sets of the organization's customer base or markets. One customer or group of customers might require activities and services that are not requested by other customers, or one customer group may place heavier demands on one form of activity or service than others. For instance, some customers may use a design already provided by the firm, while others may provide sketches of desired products, and yet a third customer group might work with the firm to develop jointly a custom product with tight specifications and requirements. Completing work for these three customer groups would place quite different demands on the organization. Customer-related activities can occur at the customer, distribution channel, market, or enterprise-wide level.

Product or product line-related activities are ones that exist to support sub-sets of the company's product base. It is possible that certain products, services, or product/service lines may require support activities that are not required by others, or some may demand much greater levels of certain activities than others. For example, some services provided by professional firms or products produced by manufacturing firms have a great deal more liability exposure connected with them than others. There may be a much higher level of engineering support required for some products than for others.

In designing and developing the ABCM system, then, input from individuals across all of the decision domains is clearly important, as suggested earlier in this chapter. Part of the organization's business, product-driven activities, can occur anywhere inside or outside of the core value chain, and have significant impact on product line and segment profitability. The difference between an activity-based and traditional accounting general ledger view of the organization is presented in Figure 11.5.

Collecting the information to identify and classify the activities of the firm (activity analysis) can be done in a number of different ways. The specific technique chosen should be based on the available information, time constraints, philosophy, and planned use of the system within each company. The more common forms of activity analysis include:[11] (1) *Story boarding,* where file cards are used to pictorially depict activities and tasks in an interactive setting; (2) *Observation,* where visual observation and recording techniques are utilized to identify and classify activities and tasks; (3) *Time keeping,* where individuals are asked to report how time is spent using existing or new forms of time reporting mechanisms; (4) *Questionnaires,* or written surveys that ask individuals to define what they do and how much of their overall effort this activity or task represents; and (5) *Interviews,* or personal one-on-one discussions with managers and employees. The data collection method used to perform the activity analysis will have impact on the amount of effort required to create and sustain the ABCM system.

While preliminary examination of a process and organization is often quite detailed, it is possible to employ activity centers as a means to simplify the ABCM system. *Activity centers* are groups of activities that make up a business process.[12] They are particularly useful when

Figure 11.5 ABCM Transformation of Costing Data

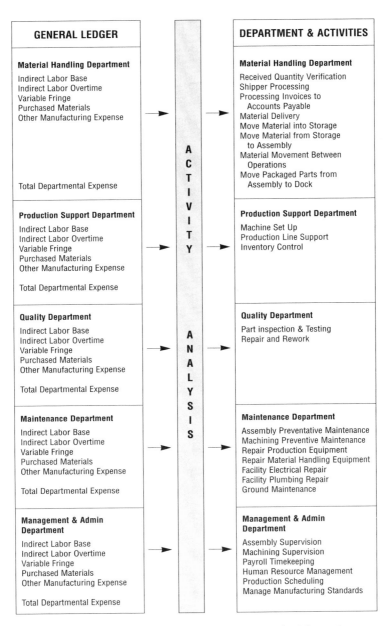

Source: T. White, *The 60 Minute ABC Book*, Bedford, TX: Consortium for Advanced Manufacturing—International, 1997: 29.

functional areas have been decomposed into large numbers of activities and a major objective of the system is to understand the cost of business processes. The activities from each functional area can be combined into activity centers for each business process to arrive at the desired cost information. Activity centers can simplify an ABCM system by taking activities with similar cost behaviors and drivers and combining them into macro-activities. This must be done with care, though, as the object of a well designed ABCM system is to provide relevant performance measurement information as well as more accurate cost assignments.

Creating an effective system requires a series of trade-offs in terms of implementation and maintenance costs, time, and the types of information that will be automatically provided to support decision-making. One rule of thumb is to keep data at one level deeper in the organization than 80-90 percent of the decisions made require. This will reduce the number of ad hoc studies performed while minimizing the total data collected and maintained. As with most situations, the 80-20 rule (80 percent of the decisions will require 20 percent of the detailed cost information that could be collected) provides a realistic way to limit an ABCM system's scope.

ASSIGNING COSTS—ACTIVITY/RESOURCE DRIVERS

Having accumulated the economic resource costs into activity centers, attention in the development of the ABCM system now turns to driving activity costs to the final cost object (e.g., final goods and services).[13] As with the resource cost driver, the key is to identify a variable that is quantifiable and logically relates the activity(ies) within the activity center to the end product or service. Examples of activity cost drivers include production volume, machine hours, labor hours, batches made, set-up times or number, and number of purchase orders or invoices completed.

An activity driver measures how much of an activity is used by a cost object. It is a measure of output, and as such is integral to ABCM product costing. An activity driver provides a bridge linking ABCM's informational elements—a bridge that distributes activity dollars into cost objects. It is important that major differences in how cost objects consume activity capability be captured in the system, through the use of "intensity" factors (difficulty weightings) or a similar costing technique.

Activity drivers may not be the "true" drivers of cost in the sense of triggering or being the root cause of an activity. Root cause drivers are operational drivers; they reveal what is making an activity happen. Activity drivers are, then, the consequences of what has happened. Since costs tend to be incurred at the process, not activity, level, one use of activity cost drivers should be limited to understanding the frequency and intensity of the demands placed on activities by output-oriented cost objects. To serve these roles, activity cost drivers must be measurable in terms that reflect a core cost object characteristic (such as number of setups). Where an operational cost driver mirrors how efficiently an activity or group of activities is performed (such as cost of each purchase order issued), an activity driver captures the consumption of an activity and its resources by its supported cost objects (such as number of parts on the product's bill of materials).

The set of specifications that lead to the assignment of activity costs to activity drivers is the single most important decision made when creating an ABCM system. If the activities are defined at an extremely detailed level, the ABCM calculations become too complex—particularly when taken to the object level. On the other hand, if activities are defined too broadly, the resulting system will fail to reveal important information that can direct management's attention to the most important problems and opportunities. Several guidelines can be used to specify activity cost pools, as suggested by Ostrenga, et.al.:[14]

- *Do not view the activity cost pools merely as intermediate vehicles for attaching costs to product.* The cost pools should provide operational information of a relevant nature. The cost that is collected in the cost pool should answer specific operational questions, such as "What does it cost to generate purchase orders? What does it cost to produce engineering changes? "

- *The types of activities within a pool should be as homogeneous as possible* without creating "cost pool proliferation".

- *Consider the relationship between the activity cost pools and important dimensions of performance you want to measure.* For example, if your company has high utility costs, and if you want visibility into the utility cost by process, then isolating utilities as a cost pool within each department can provide that information. If, however, the cost of utilities is grouped into one pool with all the other machine-related costs, then the visibility you want will be lost.

- *Use the findings from the business process analysis to help you distinguish the* "significant few" *from the* "trivial many" possible activity groups. Select the combination that best captures the essence of your business operations.

- *Distinguish between the level of detail needed for better management of the process and that needed for more accurate costing of objects.* If the difference in detail is significant, do both. If there is a difference, the extra detail almost certainly will be needed at the process level. After you have calculated the activity costs at the process level, combine similar activities into summary activity pools before taking them to cost objects.

- *You must be able to specify an "activity driver" for every activity pool you want to take to the object level.* You must also have available, or be able to collect, statistics for each activity driver you specify. If, for instance, you specify "number of calls received" as an activity driver to be used for costing customers, then you must be able to gather the data that shows the number of calls received from each customer.

- *You should sketch out the definitions for all the activity cost pools* before you perform consolidation of the general ledger data.

One of the important things to keep in mind in choosing resource or activity drivers is that they are part of the performance measurement system, creating a "visibility" or unit of cost awareness that is directly tied to the defined driver. What is measured gets done, especially when it is tied to the performance evaluation process. That means that driver choices can have significant behavioral effects. For instance, if "number of sales calls" is the driver for a sales activity center, it can lead to a decision to not make a sales call at the end of the month if doing so will cause the salesperson to exceed "budget" for this activity. People respond in unusual, but predictable ways to performance measurements. When choosing cost drivers, the lessons learned in Performance Management about influencing behavior for the better or worse should be used to ensure that resource or activity drivers work with, not against, the other measurement systems used in the firm.

USING ABCM TO UNDERSTAND CUSTOMER DEMANDS AND PROFITABILITY

Products do not cause all of the resource consumption in a firm; their impact is most felt on the manufacturing floor. As attention shifts from the plant to the back office, a greater proportion of total costs begins to be traceable to customers and channels of distribution (see Figure 11.6). As the resource-cost continuum moves from production to administrative functions, the cost-object continuum moves from parts to customers and markets served.

Figure 11.6   Understanding Customer Profitability

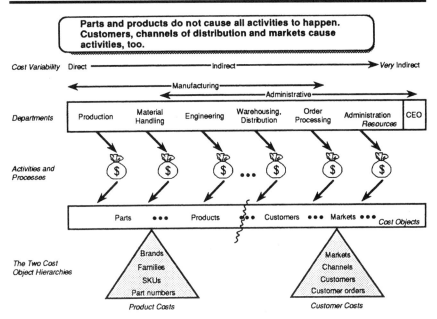

Source: G. Cokins, et.al., *The ABC Manager's Primer*, Chicago: Irwin Professional Publishing, 1993: 51.

The two main cost object families, products and customers, can be expressed as pyramidal hierarchies. This representation reflects the fact that some resources, such as a product engineer, cannot be attached at a part number level but rather should be charged out higher in the hierarchy.

Companies are beginning to recognize that customers with the highest sales volume do not necessarily generate high profits. When sales and marketing costs are combined with ABCM manufacturing stock-to-dock estimates, a very different profit profile may emerge. It is a customer's total demand for support on the system, not the number of units purchased, that ultimately defines profitability. As consumer feature and function preferences become increasingly segmented, it will become ever more challenging to ensure that optimal satisfaction is provided within reasonable cost boundaries. ABCM supports the analysis that will help keep these conflicting demands in balance.

Activity-Based Cost Management serves as both product costing and performance improvement tools, depending on the direction of resource flows that are emphasized (see Figure 11.7).

Figure 11.7 The Cost Assignment and Process Axes

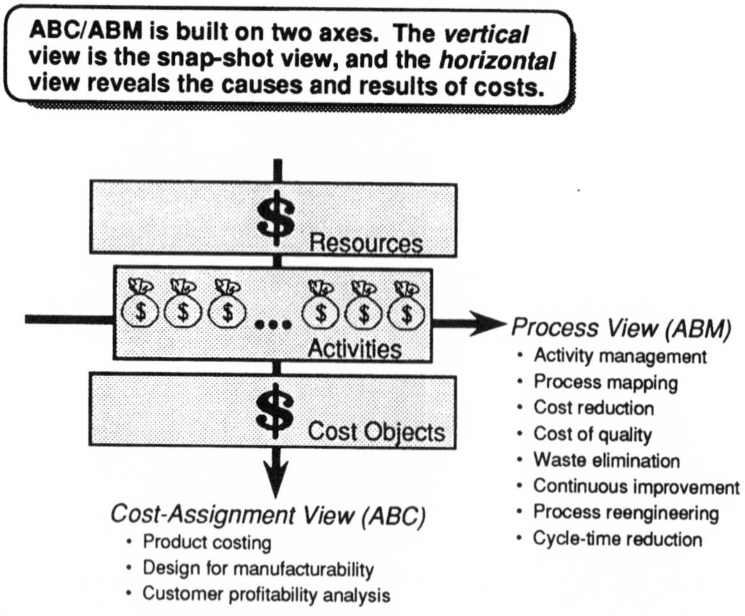
ABC/ABM is built on two axes. The *vertical* view is the snap-shot view, and the *horizontal* view reveals the causes and results of costs.
Resources
Activities
Cost Objects
Process View (ABM)
• Activity management
• Process mapping
• Cost reduction
• Cost of quality
• Waste elimination
• Continuous improvement
• Process reengineering
• Cycle-time reduction
Cost-Assignment View (ABC)
• Product costing
• Design for manufacturability
• Customer profitability analysis

Source: G. Cokins, et.al., *An ABC Manager's Primer*, Chicago: Irwin Professional Publishing, 1993: 25.

For instance, the cost assignment view of ABCM assigns resource costs to activities and activity costs to cost objects, such as products and customers. Concentrating on the cost-assignment view increases product cost accuracy, which in turn leads to improvements in strategic analysis and decision-making, pricing decisions, product mix assessments, sourcing decision, and product design.

On the other hand, the process, or horizontal view of ABCM concentrates attention on managing processes and their constituent activities as well as evaluating activity performance. Activity-Based Cost Management provides activity-based information to focus employee efforts on continuously improving quality, time, service, cost, flexibility and profitability within processes. This operational view provides an operational and tactical tool to improve performance.

Regardless of what focus is taken in the early stages of ABCM design and development, the ultimate goal is to help managers manage better by providing economic information in useful formats that reflects the way work is done in the organization. Activity-Based Cost Management focuses on priorities and drives employee behavior, shaping the way the organization sees itself and responds to changing customer requirements. One of the primary tools for achieving these behavioral impacts is through the use of data attributes.

THE POWER OF ATTRIBUTES

Attributes are descriptive labels given to activities. Two of the more popular attributes are nonvalue-added versus value-added activities and cost-of-quality attributes. In many ways, attributes make activity data robust, adding a third dimension to the Activity-Based Cost Management system that provides an orderly way to accumulate data for supporting decision analysis. Attributes quantify different aspects of business processes as well as provide multiple concurrent views of the issues and events to be emphasized, prioritized, analyzed and measured.

Activity analysis promotes creative ways to associate activities with attributes. By using attributes, ABCM supports emerging management improvement programs such as business process reengineering and benchmarking. Matching cost information, through data attributes, to the various management initiatives underway or planned, allows for planning of performance

improvements, tracking progress toward them, and initiating efforts
to get and keep these initiatives on track. Caterpillar's "Factory with
a Future" program was constantly tracked for progress against pre-
launch goals using the firm's cost management system data tagged
and sorted by this defined attribute.[15]

Attributes support the use of ABCM as a change management
tool, providing answers to the following common questions:[16]

- Why are there so many nonvalue-added costs?
- Why do costs of nonconformance exceed costs of
  conformance?
- What portion of costs actually can be controlled locally
  with well-defined responsibility accounting assignments
  and reporting?
- What portion of overhead costs vary with unit-volume or
  with batches, or are specifically product-sustaining,
  technology-sustaining, or customer-sustaining costs?

The success of installing an ABCM model depends greatly on the
level of acceptance by potential users. The effective use of data
attributes can help overcome initial resistance to ABCM use,
providing insights into ongoing operations or the impact of planned
changes that can create a strong interest in and acceptance of ABCM
data, analysis and reports.

Relational database technology facilitates the drill-down
capability that underlies the use of attributes. Providing a third
dimension to the costing analysis, the initial use of attributes is to rank
activities by dollar amounts and show them to employees and
managers. This feedback brings awareness to managers about where
and how resources are being consumed. It is for the purpose of
understanding what people and machines do, though, not to pressure
or penalize individuals or groups for prior outcomes. Attributes can
help managers identify where, and why, value-added is such a low
percentage of total costs and efforts, or to understand the dimensions
of current cost of quality performance (see Figure 11.8).

Figure 11.8   Value-added and Quality Cost Data Attributes

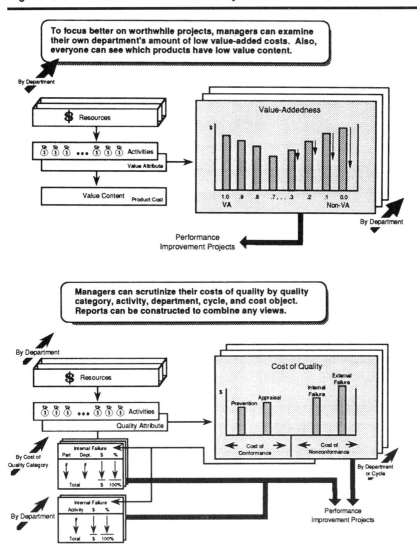

Source: G. Cokins, et.al., *The ABC Manager's Primer,* Chicago: Irwin Professional Publishing, 1993: 34, 37.

Process Value Analysis is another management technique that can be supported by the data attribute approach. For instance, the evaluation of processes such as engineering change notices can be done by combining two or more activities bearing the "Engineering Change Notice" (ECN) data attribute. Process Value Analysis can also be facilitated by prioritization of nonvalue-added costs and causes using data attributes that can compare these activities by both their size and value content. Supported by ABCM data, Process Value Analysis can provide managers with a framework and systematic approach for planning, predicting, and influencing cost by emphasizing departmental and functional interdependencies. It helps managers identify and act on the causes of cost, not their symptoms.

In summary, activity attributes add more to activity analysis than just the costs of activities. Attributes make activities more understandable, usable, and meaningful. They can also provide leverage for decision making, supporting the prioritization of efforts based on economic consequences and potential benefits of improvements as well as understanding the profitability of unique customer segments.

ABCM AND CHANGE

Activity-Based Cost Management models can serve as a catalyst for change, providing a way to summarize the natural laws surrounding resource consumption into a system that can be utilized by managers to query current and potential future performance. What are these basic laws? Specifically, the total cost consumption, or profile, of a firm is affected by: [17]

- The mix of products, services, customers and channels of distribution;
- The physical design features of and the specifications for products;
- The effects of processes, which often are influenced by formal or informal policies; and
- The presence of waste due to neglect or errors of nonconformance.

These components cause costs to occur. Insight gained from ABCM analysis can have a favorable impact on resource consumption by reducing or eliminating nonvalue-added activities or by substituting a more economical alternative for an inefficient activity or unnecessary process.

The range of initiatives directly supported by ABCM today is listed in Figure 11.9. The magnitude and pace of ABCM implementations is likely to continue gaining speed because it links costs to causes and directly supports a broad array of management initiatives. Illuminating interdependencies and opportunities, rather than masking the relationship between all forms of work and their economic consequences, ABCM can help management understand the relationship between processes, products and profits in order to take corrective action to address performance shortfalls. Strategic applications for ABCM are even more obvious than operational and tactical ones, as controversies over the use of costing as a control tool are avoided when ABCM information is used in conjunction with other improvement philosophies in a balanced manner.

Figure 11.9 Activity Accounting as Catalyst for Change

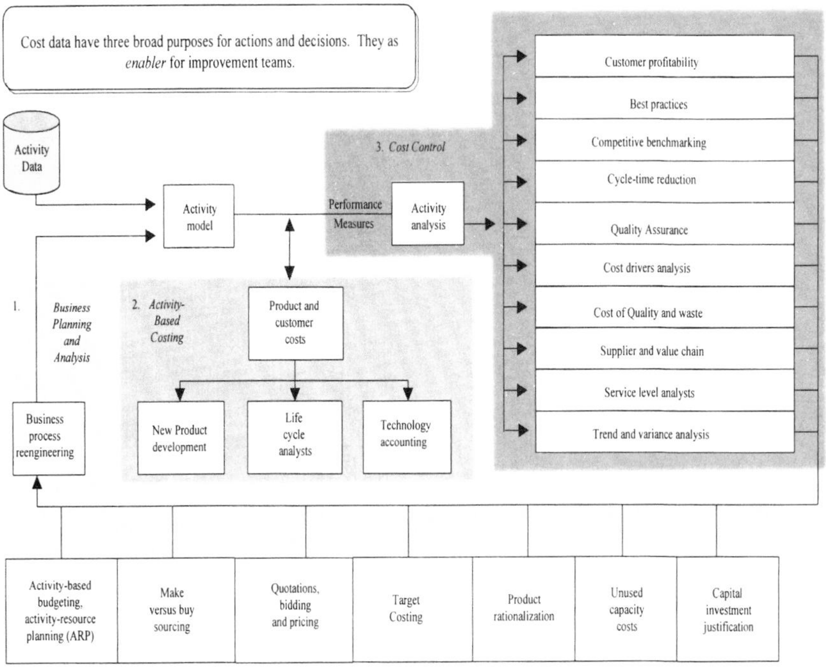

Source: G. Cokins, et.al., *The ABC Manager's Primer,* Chicago: Irwin Professional Publishing, 1993: 60.

The moral of the story is that, to effectively drive change, the various performance and management techniques used by a firm must be integrated. ABCM provides a valuable integrating logic that ties together the diverse initiatives and outcomes through activity, process, and driver definitions to align organizational efforts and performance. ABCM's strategic value (the ability to correct product-cost distortions) and ABCM's operational value (linking fresh financial metrics with resource-cost consumption to improvement programs) combine to create a solid basis for analyzing and improving performance of the integrated and extended enterprise. Usable in all organizations, whether manufacturing or service-based, ABCM is the basis for creating and sustaining change in organizational performance and profitability.

Lessons from the Field: A Service Case Study
A fact in itself is nothing.
It is valuable only for the idea attached to it,
or for the proof which it furnishes.
– Claude Bernard

An example of how ABCM works in a service setting will provide a useful way to frame and consolidate the above discussion.[18] Beginning with the B&W seaplane in 1916, The Boeing Company has built on its presence in the aerospace industry to become the premier firm in its industry. Two main operating divisions (Commercial Airplane Group and Space & Defense Systems) are the primary basis for structuring the firm.

The Information and Support Services (ISS) function was formed to support the shared services needs of the two operating divisions. It provides computing, administrative, safety, environmental, security and other support services, partnering with the operating divisions to provide quality, cost-effective services to meet the company's needs. The largest portion of ISS support is in the computing area, where it performs services for distributed and large-scale computing as well as voice and video support for the Puget Sound area. Its 3,700 Puget Sound employees support over 170,000 distributed computing devices, 60,000 voice mail boxes, and 150,000 phone lines in the Puget Sound area alone (other ISS sites include Philadelphia, Wichita, and Huntsville).

In response to an increasing dependency on its distributed computing services, and rising costs of these services, in 1995 ISS began to look for ways to improve its performance using activity-based management. Several major processes were defined for this segment of the ISS, including: acquisition, computing administration, restoration, relocation, disposition, technical integration and design, and large scale (mainframe) voice and video support. A dedicated manager was established for each of these services, with cross-functional participants added to form service analysis teams. One element of this initiative, the Boeing ISS restoration service, will be the focus of the remaining discussion.

The ISS restoration service responds to distributed computing hardware and software problems. The process spans the boundaries from the initial request for service due to a functionality failure through to the restoration of full functionality of the equipment or network. It includes processes and tools that were used to provide restoration support services to the Puget Sound locations, and entails the ongoing management of cost, cycle time, defects and work force issues. Day-to-day management of any site organization, large scale computing needs, or voice and video support, are excluded from the boundaries of the ISS restoration group.

Three different components define the core activities performed by restoration services: data network restoration, server system restoration, and work-station restoration. There are eight underlying activities used to support the three component processes. The first two activities involve receiving a call for restoration and determining any first level problem resolutions and computing infrastructure faults. The second set of bundled activities involves assigning a vendor, ISS in-house, or additional technical sources to the problem. Finally, managing the vendor-maintenance contracts, providing spare parts to solve the restoration problem, and managing the systems that track and collect restoration service information and assist in overcoming the problems complete the set of basic activities.

In analyzing the service's classification dimensions, restoration was found to have the characteristics of a service shop, namely a people, front-office, process focus with considerable contact time made available by front office staff. Once the service was identified as being similar to a service shop, the question, "What measures a successful restoration?" had to be answered. The team determined that five measures were key for managing restoration: defects, cycle time, cost per unit, volume and efficiency.

A labor survey was implemented to collect labor costs of the participants in the CNO services. The individuals in the ISS organizations that contributed resources to restoration recorded the percentage of their time spent on this service. Next, the total hours charged to the accounting system were applied to the survey percentages to estimate hours spent on each service. The survey helped identify the ISS organizations that contributed resources to restoration, and a process flow audit determined how non-people costs were consumed by this service. These other cross-functional resources included external vendor maintenance contracts, inventory management groups, technical services, and site computing operations.

Figure 11.10   Tracing Resource Costs to Activities

Resources

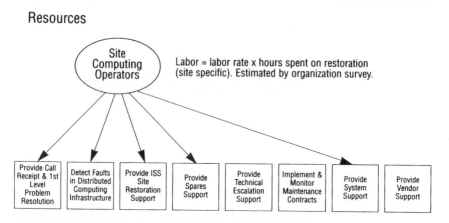

Source: K. Euske, et.al., *The Service Process Management: Breaking the Code, Applying Activity-Based Performance Measures to Service Processes*, Bedford, TX: CAM-I, 1997: 53.

Having identified the affected areas, the next step was to trace the cross-functional resource costs to the activities and to the component processes (see Figure 11.10). To trace some activity costs to the component processes, the percentage of the total volume that each component incurred was used. For example, in analyzing the "provide technical escalation support" activity, if server problems were 10 percent of the total problem volume, then 10 percent of this activity's costs were traced to the server system component process. Other methods involved analyzing accounts payable records to trace resource and activity costs through the process.

After tracing and attributing all of the cross-functional costs to the process, the team worked through its data collection method to create credible, useful information. Cost by resource, cost by activity, and efficiencies were reported monthly for each component process. Furthermore, the measures established in the measurement plan were reported using a "four-up chart" format that jointly depicts the volume, defects, labor efficiency, cost, cost per unit, and cycle time measures on the same page. The chart helps the user more readily understand the interaction between the various measures and their impacts on each other, leading to a higher level of process knowledge that allows for process improvement optimization, resource planning, and better decision making.

The result of the process and activity-based analysis performed on the ISS restoration service is enhanced visibility for improvement activities centered around software maintenance and contract management. By providing cost and non-cost data by site, the process team has been able to identify best practices among the sites as well as to develop improvement plans specific to each site. The transition to an activity-based management approach has strengthened line management ownership of site specific data and targets.

In addition, the service owner can now monitor service performance, forecast resource levels based on volume fluctuations, and respond to specific customer requests. For example, the customer may be unsatisfied with current cycle time to solve a restoration problem. ISS can use the process analysis information to determine the amount of resources needed to reduce cycle time and calculate the expected cost increases or defect fluctuations due to the change. The customer can then decide if the additional cost is affordable in relation to the improvement in cycle time performance. The ABCM model, and its integration with other management initiatives, has provided the basis for improvement of this service support process in ways meaningful to its internal customer.

References

Cokins, G., A. Stratton, and J. Helbling, *An ABC Manager's Primer,* Chicago: Irwin
   Professional Publishing, 1993.

Cooper, R., R. Kaplan, L. Maisel, E. Morrissey, and R. Oehm, *Implementing Activity-Based
   Cost Management: Moving from Analysis to Action,* Chicago: Irwin Professional
   Publishing, 1992.

Eiler, R., and C. Ball, "Implementing Activity-Based Costing", *Handbook of Cost Management,*
   New York: Warren, Gorham and Lamont, 1997: B2-1 to 2-32.

Forrest, E., *Activity-Based Management: A Comprehensive Implementation Guide,*
   New York: McGraw-Hill, 1996.

Institute of Management Accountants, Statements on Management Accounting, *Implementing
   Activity-Based Management: Avoiding the Pitfalls,* Montvale, NJ: 1998.

Statements on Management Accounting #4T, *Implementing Activity-Based Costing,*
   Montvale, NJ: 1993.

Ness, J., and T. Cucuzza, "Tapping the Full Potential of ABCM", *Harvard Business Review,*
   January, 1995: 22-26.

Miller, J., *Implementing Activity-Based Management in Daily Operations,* New York: John Wiley
   & Sons, 1996.

Ostrenga, M., T. Ozan, R. McIlhattan, and M. Harwood, Ernst & Young's *Guide to Total Cost
   Management,* New York: John Wiley & Sons, 1992.

Player, S., and D. Keys, *Activity-Based Management: Arthur Andersen's Lessons from the
   ABC Battlefield,* NewYork: Master-Media, Ltd., 1995.

Romano, P., *Activity-Based Management in Action,* Montvale, NJ: Institute of Management
   Accountants, 1994.

Sharmon, P., "Activity-Based Costing Implementation Issues", *Handbook of Cost Management,*
   New York: Warren, Gorham and Lamont, 1997: B6-1 to 6-32.

"Activity-Based Costing Implementation Applications," *Handbook of Cost Management,*
   New York: Warren, Gorham and Lamont, 1997: B7-1 to 7-36.

Turney, P., "Common Cents: The ABCM Performance Breakthrough", Hillsboro, OR:
   Cost Technology, 1992.

White, T., *The 60 Minute ABCM Book: Activity-Based Costing for Operations Management,*
   Bedford,TX: CAM-I, 1997.

Endnotes

[1] Institute of Management Accountants, Statement on Management Accounting Number 4T, *Implementing Activity-Based Costing*, Montvale, NJ: 1993: 1.

[2] Institute of Management Accountants, *Statement on Management Accounting, Implementing Activity-Based Management: Avoiding the Pitfalls*, Montvale, NJ, 1998: 5. This entire section draws heavily from this document, specifically pages 5-6.

[3] While this definition and that of ABC appear in IMA "Pitfalls, " ibid, pg. 5, they are based on CAM-I definitions that can be found in the CAM-I Gossary of Terms.

[4] Ibid, pp.5–6.

[5] T. White, *The 60 Minute ABC Book*, Bedford, TX: CAM-I, 1997: 21-23.

[6] There are several core CAM-I and related publications that were used to develop the majority of this summary chapter on ABCM. While only direct quotes will be referenced in these notes, the insights and information in the following sources are recognized: T. White, ibid; G. Cokins, ed., An ABC Manager's Primer, Chicago: Irwin Professional Publishing, 1992; APICS, *Activity-Based Management II: Best Practices for Dramatic Improvement*, 1997; S. Player and D. Keys, *Activity-Based Management: Arthur Andersen's Lessons from the ABCM Battlefield*, New York: Master Media, Ltd., 1995; and the IMA statements *Tools and Techniques for Implementing ABC/ABCM (1998), Implementing Activity-Based Costing* (4T; 1993); and, *Implementing Activity-Based Management: Avoiding the Pitfalls*. Most of the steps in the development of ABC data and related comments on such things as resource drivers, activity analysis, etc. appear in Cokins, et.al., op.cit. In fact, summary sentences from key graphics in this text are used verbatim when appropriate. While specific page cites are not made in the draft for each of these occurrences, the heavy reliance on the arguments and flow of the Cokins, et.al., book is duly noted.

[7] This basic thought first appears in G. Cokins, op.cit.

[8] Cokins, op.cit., pp. 7-8.

[9] Ibid, pg. 10.

[10] This part of the discussion is based on the IMA Statement #4T, op.cit., pp. 20-22.

[11] J. Miller, Implementing Activity-Based Management in Daily Operations, New York: John Wiley and Sons, 1996.

[12] Cokins, et.al., op.cit.

[13] As with the previous section, this part of the discussion draws heavily from Cokins, op.cit.

[14] These guidelines are originally found in M. Ostrenga, T. Ozan, R. McIlhattan, and M. Harwood, Ernst and Young Guide to Total Cost Management, New York: Wiley and Sons, 1992: 228-29.

[15] As with several points made and examples given, the author's experience is the basis for this point.

[16] Cokins, et.al., op.cit., pp. 31-40 are the basis for the details and comments on data attributes.

[17] Cokins, et.al., op.cit., pg. 60. As can be seen by these endnotes, one of the first texts a company that is just beginning to implement ABCM should reference is the Cokins, et.al., document.

[18] This final section draws very heavily from Service Process Measurement: Breaking the Code, CAM-I publication R-97-CMS-01.1 authored by K. Euske, et.al. Note that at times comments are taken from this document verbatim or with minimal paraphrasing. The authors of this book and the related case studies are duly noted for their efforts and insights.

Chapter 12

Optimizing the Value Position

Decision in The Customer/Market Domain

It is a piece of great good luck to deal with someone who values you at your true worth.

– Baltasar Gracian

Key Learnings:

- Decisions made about what customers and markets to serve lie at the heart of the strategic process, defining the structure, required capacity, and desired operational capabilities of the firm.

- Customer/Market decisions draw upon information about the range of customer values and preferences, core competencies of the firm and its supply partners, available or potential capacity, flexibility and responsiveness of the supply pipeline, as well as current performance.

- The decisions and analysis facilitated by the CAM-I SMP Model at the Customer/Market level include: definition of customer value segments, choice of key segments based on the firm's existing core competencies, competitive positioning within chosen segments, and the development and maintenance of reporting and control tools to keep initiatives on track.

- The linkage of the SMPs ensures that communication, analysis, and action are guided by the same set of facts, figures, and objectives—eliminating the gaps and "white spaces" that can undermine strategies and inhibit performance.

Understanding what customers value, and delivering the optimal product/service bundle to meet these preferences, is the key to creating a profitable competitive position. This fact holds true no matter what industry an organization participates in, or what segment of the market is the chosen competitive battleground.

Decisions made about what customers and markets to serve lie at the heart of the strategic process, defining the structure, required capacity, and desired operational capabilities of the firm. Strategy directs action, shapes tactical and operational decisions, creates a vision of the future to guide behavior, and defines and constrains potential outcomes. It also sets the framework for subsequent Customer/Market decisions.

Among the most critical choices made by a firm, Customer/Market decisions draw upon information about the range of customer values and preferences, core competencies of the firm and its supply partners, available or potential capacity, flexibility and responsiveness of the supply pipeline, as well as current performance. This information is combined to define the firm's market and competitive position—what customer segments and markets are to be served.

Supporting these Customer/Market decisions is the goal of the CAM-I Strategic Management Process (SMP) integration within the Customer/Market decision domain. Specifically, the SMPs are combined to create a powerful storehouse of facts, estimates, capabilities, and expectations about key issues and implications of the available alternatives for profitability and competitive position.

The decisions and analysis facilitated by the CAM-I SMP Model at the Customer/Market level include: definition of customer value segments, choice of key segments based on the firm's existing core competencies, competitive positioning within chosen segments, and the development and maintenance of reporting and control tools to keep initiatives on track. Each of these decisions depends upon information provided by one or more SMP, as management explores the potential costs and benefits, core competency matches and mismatches, of potential segmentation strategies. Taken in total, decisions in this domain set the stage for downstream development of tactical and operational plans at the product, process and resource levels. (See Figure 12.1)

This chapter explores the integration of the various SMPs within each of the four major decision classes within the Customer/Market domain: (1) Value Creation, (2) Segment Strategy, (3) Positioning, and (4) Evaluation. Integration, defined around information, will emphasize the contribution of the core tools to the decision-making process. Using the CAM-I SMP Model helps direct the linkage of the SMPs to ensure that communication, analysis, and action are guided by the same set of facts, figures, and objectives—eliminating the gaps and "white spaces" that can undermine strategies and inhibit performance.

Figure 12.1   Customer/Market Decision Groupings

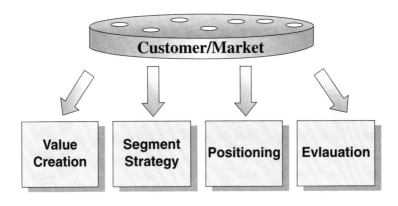

Value Creation

Knowledge is power.
– Proverb

The key to business success is providing customers with the precise set of goods and services they require, at a price they are willing to pay. This is a commonly known fact, but one that a company can sometimes lose sight of. Over the past several years, a great number of trade books and articles have been written about the need to focus a firm's strategy and efforts to ensure that customer requirements are met. Emphasizing the *value attributes,* or the set of characteristics of the product/service bundle that a customer is willing to pay for, these new strategic models are redefining business practice.

VALUE AND STRATEGY

Wayland and Cole, in their recent book *Customer Connections*,[1] suggest that a value-driven Customer/Market strategy provides unique insights, and suggests markedly different market approaches, than more traditional strategic models. Specifically, when customer preferences are queried, new segments that span geographic and product/service bundles emerge. One group of customers might place the greatest emphasis on service, product quality, and features, while another might be most concerned with price and delivery. A company that fails to recognize these differences in value preferences would likely miss the target for both segments—neither would receive the product/service bundle they require.

An example from a small public relations firm may help in highlighting what a value-based strategy entails. The firm has traditionally organized itself around the client industry, creating teams that service a specific industry segment. While customers within these segments often requested different types of support, the firm always conducted extensive research and development for the client as the starting point. Costly in nature, the research often led to budget overruns that could not be passed on to the customer.

Figure 12.2   Value-based Segmentation

ATTRIBUTES	PUBLIC RELATIONS	RESEARCH	MARKETING SUPPORT
Research	5	70	25
Placements	60	-0-	15
Acct. Management	10	5	5
Marketing Support	5	-0-	15
Crisis Management	-0-	10	-0-
3rd Party Endorsements	15	-0-	5
Develop Plans	5	15	35
	100	100	100

When asked to think about their clients from the perspective of the types of services they required, and the value they placed on basic activities within the firm, a very different segmentation emerged (see Figure 12.2). Clients were sorted into three basic clusters: Publicity clients, Full Service Marketing Research clients, and Strategy clients. The management team then estimated the percentage of total value each segment placed on the basic activities of the firm. Publicity clients were perceived as placing minimal value on research, while Research clients placed almost all of their value assessments on this activity. An activity was only value-adding if the client within the segment was willing to pay for it.

The matching of activities to actual value segment preferences was an eye-opening exercise for this firm. It became clear that having an unfocused value strategy was resulting in dissatisfaction and reduced profits. The decision was made to develop a client budgeting system that would embed value preferences, queried during the initial discussions with a new client, as the basis for planning and controlling an engagement. Activities would be focused on those areas where value was perceived by customers (value added), but would be tracked in total to also identify nonvalue-added and waste costs. A value-based client model will provide this firm with a unique product/service profile that will help clients define and assess how well the firm meets their needs.

Understanding how to create optimal value for each customer is the key to creating a unique Customer/Market segmentation strategy. A value-based strategy ensures that the firm is doing what customers want, and only what they want. It also serves to define *value-added* activities more precisely than ever before. Gaining these insights is the basis for initial integration of the SMPs in the Customer/Market domain.

THE VALUE PROPOSITION

The core SMP for creating a value-based segmentation strategy is Target Cost Management (TCM). Emphasizing the development of product/service bundles that meet customer needs and wants, TCM creates a framework for identifying and analyzing the value preferences of existing or potential customers. Serving as a planning tool, TCM looks to the market for guidance on specific product/service attributes, price and value ratings.

The activities that are undertaken at the Customer/Market level of TCM are: perform market analysis, understand customer requirements, define market/customer niche, determine price, and develop required profit. Organizational analysis is an activity that influences the Customer/Market domain in TCM, drawing from all the various levels of the organization to support analysis and choice of a segmentation strategy. Of these, performing market analysis and understanding customer requirements are essential to the segmentation decision. Five basic steps, or activities, are undertaken during this decision process:

1. Identify value preferences.
2. Determine relative value rankings, or importance of value attributes to different customers.
3. Benchmark firm's current performance against expectations for the customer population versus that of key competitors.
4. Conduct price and value tradeoff analyses for the various segments.
5. Develop cost and profit projections for each viable segmentation strategy.

Figure 12.3   SMPs and Segmentation Analysis

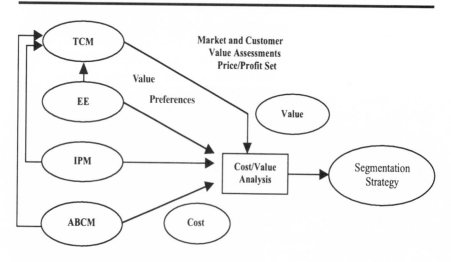

Completing these activities requires information on customers, value preferences, current performance, price and profitability. The sources of this information include the SMPs of Target Cost Management, the Extended Enterprise, Integrated Performance Management, and Activity-Based Cost Management (see Figure 12.3).

As can be seen from this figure, the Extended Enterprise (EE) provides insights into value preferences of customers, rankings and the price/value tradeoffs that seem optimal given market requirements. Linking the firm across the supply pipeline to the final customer, EE management provides a reliable, effective way to get close to the customer. Integrated Performance Management, on the other hand, comes into play during the benchmarking phase of the segmentation strategy decision analysis. Serving to scan the environment and compare firm performance against internal goals, customer needs, and competitive performance, Integrated Performance Management creates the basis for evaluating and identifying those areas where improvement is needed or most likely to create competitive advantage.

The third supporting SMP during the initial analysis of customer requirements is Activity-Based Cost Management (ABCM). Providing basic economic data on the costs and potential profits for various product/service bundles and customer segments, ABCM helps management create a segment map that reflects not only value preferences and prices, but also current performance and projected profitability. The supporting SMPs provide critical input to the Target Cost Management-based analysis of customer requirements.

TCM uses the information from Extended Enterprise, Integrated Performance Management, and Activity-Based Cost Management to complete the overall analysis of customer value preferences and identify potential segmentation strategies. The outcome of this analysis is an array of segments with unique value profiles. Focusing on understanding what customers require, and how these requirements differ for different clusters, this early phase of TCM serves as an input to the next major decision: the choice of optimal segments to compete in given the firm's core competencies.

Segment Strategy

We know what happens to people who stay in the middle of the road. They get run over.

— Aneurin Bevan

Gaining an understanding of customer preferences, and how these value profiles vary across different segments and product/service bundles, is essential to crafting an effective Customer/Market strategy. Once the knowledge is gained, though, it must be acted upon. For what other reason would the company expend the resources necessary to better understand customers except as the basis to choose a strategic approach that will optimize the match between the firm's competencies and the chosen Customer/Market segments?

The answer to this question is simple. The only justification for spending resources to better understand customers is to create a competitive advantage. Serving as the means to differentiate the firm from its competitors, the choice of a Customer/Market segmentation strategy begins when the analysis of customer requirements is completed.

Figure 12.4   Segment Analysis and Choice

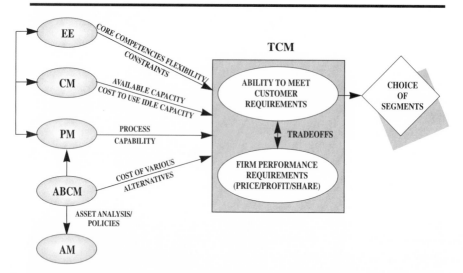

Choosing the optimal set of Customer/Market segments requires three unique forms of information: The firm/Extended Enterprise's core competencies, the array of value-based segments with preferences, and an analysis of the firm/Extended Enterprise's capability to meet requirements within given resource and capacity constraints. The breadth of these information requirements encompasses all seven of the core SMPs.

TCM once again provides the framework for combining the information and shaping the decision process (see Figure 12.4) during the choice of Customer/Market segments. Specifically, this decision emphasizes two initiatives: understanding customer requirements and performing organizational analysis. Segment choice requires not only the completion of these two efforts, but also the integration of the output of these two efforts. The outcome of the decision analysis, a segment strategy that reflects the firm/Extended Enterprise's core competencies and constraints, drives management to seek information from all sources and all levels of the organization.

Decision analysis leading to segment choice moves through a series of activities, including the following:

1. Document and post the complete value segment array.
2. Analyze organizational requirements for each value segment.
3. Assess organizational abilities, competencies, and constraints for each value segment.
4. Evaluate compatibility of segments and organizational capabilities.
5. Assess investment and operational implications of various segments.
6. Choose a segmentation strategy.

As suggested by Figure 12.4, the various SMPs provide information to facilitate different parts of this analysis. Beginning with the use of Target Cost Management as the framework for analysis and choice, the first key issue that must be addressed is the organization's ability to meet customer requirements in each potential segment.

The Extended Enterprise is one of the first sources of this information, providing detailed analysis of the current core competencies, flexibility, and constraints of the firm and its trading alliance. Looking beyond the boundaries of the organization, the EE ensures that each strategic option is evaluated for its impact, and viability, for the entire supply chain. It would do little good to develop a segment strategy that requires a high degree of responsiveness and the use of ongoing *point-of-sale* data input if the existing EE does not have this capability. Unless the trading alliance perceives that the investment required to gain the required level of responsiveness will provide mutual benefit, any customer segment requiring this ability will not be in the firm's feasible set.

While the Extended Enterprise supports the analysis of value chain competencies, the firm must also conduct internal assessments. Capacity Management, Process Management, and Activity-Based Cost Management are the three SMPs that are used to gather data about current or potential internal competencies, capabilities, and constraints. Capacity Management details the amount of available capacity, the cost of activating idle resources, and the impact of new demand on the current facilities. Process Management provides similar data, emphasizing the capabilities of the various core and support processes and their ability to absorb new demand. Where Capacity Management details physical asset characteristics, Process Management captures the complete socio-technical system that brings people and machines together.

Activity-Based Cost Management (ABCM) supports the process and capacity analysis, providing cost and performance information. It also provides its own unique set of data for the overall segment analysis. Specifically, ABCM details the impact of various strategies on the activity structure of the firm, identifying areas where constraints may be triggered or incremental resources required.

Asset Management plays a pivotal role in fleshing out the analysis of the feasibility of different segment strategies. Where gaps exist between current capabilities and required levels of responsiveness or throughput, attention turns to identifying the costs and conditions under which the performance shortfalls could be addressed. Asset Management provides this analysis, drawing upon data from Activity-Based Cost Management, The Extended Enterprise, Process Management, and Capacity Management to identify costs and understand the implications of various investments on overall performance. Underlying the segment analysis is Integrated Performance Management. Containing non-cost data on current performance capabilities and the ability to meet new segment demands, Performance Management ensures that quality, delivery and productivity concerns are factored into the organizational assessment.

Having analyzed the segments and their organizational impact, attention turns to identifying the optimal set of segments. These segments are either an ideal match between customer requirements and firm/Extended Enterprise competencies or represent areas where the investment required to meet defined needs can be made profitably. The chosen segments should provide the firm with a competitive position that enables it to maximize its profits and performance because it naturally meets customer requirements in that segment or has the ability to meet them with minimal new cost or investment.

Positioning

Production only fills a void that it has itself created.
– John Kenneth Galbraith

The third major decision analysis conducted at the Customer/Market level deals with the choice of competitive position within the chosen customer segments. In TCM, this decision is embodied in the activity, "Define product and customer niche." Emphasizing the "how" in the strategic equation, this form of decision analysis bridges the gap between planning and execution, creating a focused framework for action and for making tactical and operational decisions.

The choice of a specific set of segments serves as input to the third major decision made within the Customer/Market domain: choosing a competitive position within each segment. Is the firm to emphasize differentiation? If so, will quality, responsiveness, flexibility, and/or variety be the key differentiating dimension? Is cost/price more important to the chosen customers? If so, how can the firm/Extended Enterprise be leveraged to achieve optimal productivity and efficiency? Positioning leads to a defined market strategy, one that serves to shape product, process and resource decisions at all levels of the firm.

As with all of the decisions made at the Customer/Market level, TCM provides the decision analysis framework for choosing a competitive position. Bringing together historical information about the costs and benefits of various segments, assessing the profitability of different approaches to the market, and ensuring that the firm/Extended Enterprise can deliver on promised performance to customers, Target Cost Management ensures that information is consistently applied to this entire class of strategic decisions. Common frameworks, common language, and common data are implicit elements of TCM.

The information needed to determine an effective market position includes assessments of the firm/Extended Enterprise's flexibility, responsiveness, and capacity; defined market trends and competitors'

Figure 12.5   Strategic Positioning and the SMPs

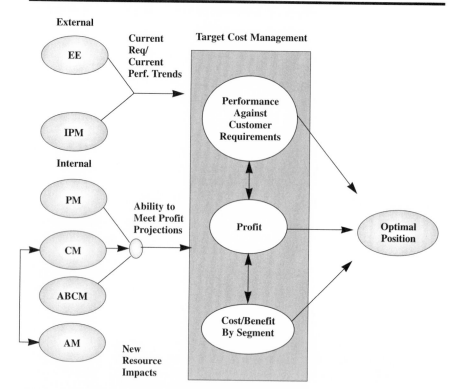

actions; technology developments and constraints; and costs to serve. All of the SMPs are drawn upon to meet these information demands (see Figure 12.5).

One of the first pieces of information needed to choose an optimal strategic position within specific Customer/Market segments is the existing expectations of customers. The Extended Enterprise and Integrated Performance Management are the two SMPs that provide this information to the organization. Specifically, current customer requirements, the responsiveness of the firm and its competitors to these needs, and trends in customer expectations are obtained from supply partners closest to the customer and from firm- or supply-chain driven measurements of customer satisfaction and loyalty.

The EE is the source of a tremendous amount of information about trends in the market and the potential of the value chain to differentiate itself from competitors on a core performance dimension. Synchronizing the flow of information from the beginning to the end of the supply pipeline, data is constantly gathered through the EE on what customers are buying, when, where, and trends in their consumption patterns. Market research efforts by the firm and its trading partners can add to this database, identifying emerging needs and areas where the "bar" has been raised in terms of required products, services and features.

While the emphasis in positioning is on choosing an approach to the market, it remains vitally important to constantly assess the ability of the firm to meet the demands each unique segment strategy will place on it. Process Management, Activity-Based Cost Management and Capacity Management provide information about internal constraints and capabilities to deliver on specific performance promises. If the plant is running at close to maximum capacity, a strategic position requiring rapid delivery of products on demand may not be viable. If the segment strategy calls for extensive electronic data interchange to be successful, and the firm does not currently have this capability, management may need to alter its approach or choose another segment.

Activity-Based Cost Management and Asset Management are used to do ongoing assessments of the relative costs, profitability, and investment requirements of each of the potential segment positions. Understanding the underlying cost to serve a specific segment in a specific way (e.g., just-in-time delivery) is a critical piece of information in the analysis to choose an optimal blend of segments and positions to maximize the value created for customers and the profits earned by the firm.

Having chosen a segment, position, and overall Customer/Market strategy, management turns its attention to ensuring that defined objectives are achieved by creating a tracking and control system at the Customer/Market domain level.

Evaluation

It looks impossible until you do it, and then you find it possible.
– Evelyn Underhill

Continuous improvement is part and parcel of every decision made within the firm, no matter what Decision domain is involved or what aspect of the firm is examined. Ensuring that once a decision is made, resources deployed, and that desired outcomes are attained, is one part of organizational learning. Where performance meets expectations, expectations can be raised. Where performance fails to hit desired targets, attention can turn to improving processes or eliminating waste to get the organization back on track.

Management reporting is a key part of the evaluation cycle, providing information and assessment on key performance dimensions such as cost, quality, profitability, delivery, and customer satisfaction. Embedded within the core database of the firm, evaluation draws upon four primary SMPs: Activity-Based Cost Management, Integrated Performance Management, Capacity Management and Asset Management.

Integrated Performance Management is the pivotal SMP for conducting evaluation and supporting improvement efforts. Whether focused on Extended Enterprise, firm, process or individual efforts and accomplishments, Integrated Performance Management provides a framework for comparing current outcomes to those needed to hit strategic objectives. The basis of integration of the evaluation process at the customer/market level is some form of executive information system, whether it be a sophisticated Enterprise Resource Planning (ERP) system or a simple set of graphs and tables maintained by hand or on spreadsheets. Creating management reports that summarize current performance and trends on key competitive dimensions within the chosen markets and segments, performance management ensures that consistent information and analysis are completed.

ABCM feeds performance management systems with detailed cost and resource data, supporting the development of customer/market profitability analysis. AM assesses the progress of various strategic investments. CM reports on actual utilization of resources, planned versus unplanned idle time, and areas where bottlenecks are emerging that may inhibit the attainment of strategic goals. Providing feedback on the efficiency and effectiveness of activities, investments, and operational assets, these three SMPs feed the integrated set of management reports (see Figure 12.6).

The evaluation process brings the organization full circle, providing input to downstream decisions about potential segments, markets, customers, and products. Understanding what is working, where goals are being met, and where performance is missing the

Figure 12.6   Evaluation and Control at the Customer/Market Domain

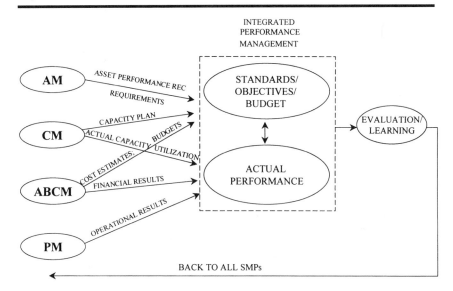

mark, are all essential if the organization is to learn from experience and continually improve its performance against customer requirements. Serving to link the organization from top-to-bottom, and side-to-side, evaluation and control not only keep the organization on track, they support attainment of superior performance.

Integration Summary — Customer/Market Domain

Now who is to decide between
"Let it be" and "Force it"?

– Katherine Mansfield

The Customer/Market domain is the arena of planning, of setting the stage for action, and of choosing among available options those alternatives promising optimum returns. Focused on understanding customer requirements and assessing whether, and how, the firm/Extended Enterprise can best meet these needs, effective Customer/Market domain decisions are the key to competitive success.

While all of the SMPs play a role within this domain, TCM dominates the analysis and structuring of key decisions at the Customer/Market level. It provides the decision framework for three of the four major decision analyses at this level: value segmentation, development of a segment strategy, and competitive positioning. Integrating the information from supporting SMPs into a consistent structure, TCM ensures that a firm analyzes all of the potential costs, benefits, opportunities and constraints it faces consistently and completely.

While Target Cost Management provides the decision "shell" for the Customer/Market domain, it cannot operate in isolation. Pulling information from all of the Decision domains through the Integrated Performance Management, Activity-Based Cost Management, Process Management, the Extended Enterprise, Capacity Management, and Asset Management conduits, TCM relies upon these supporting SMPs to fill in the analysis and complete the required evaluations. It is the integration of the critical information these SMPs provide that facilitate the firm's decisions in the Customer/Market domain. Having this "umbrella" of information, the TC SMP will help the firm create its competitive position.

Endnote

1 Wayland and Cole, *Customer Connections,* Boston, MA: Harvard Business School Press, 1998.

Chapter 13

Transforming Plans to Reality

Designing and Delivering the Product/Service Bundle

The question is not whether to adjust or to rebel against reality,
but, rather, how to discriminate between those realities that must
be recognized as unalterable and those that we should continue to
try to change however unyielding they may appear.

– Helen Merrell Lynd

Key Learnings:

- The Product Decision domain spans the planning, provision, and management of the various product/ service bundles offered by the firm to its customers over their entire life cycle.

- The goal of these decisions is to identify the optimal blend of features and functions to maximize the value delivered to customers while ensuring that company profit and performance goals are achieved.

- While all Strategic Management Processes (SMPs) are required to support the decisions made within this domain, not all are equally important in all situations. As the objective of the decision(s) changes, so do information requirements.

Plans become reality when they become concrete—when they can be defined in physical terms that support action. Target Cost

Management plays a dominant role in defining the overall objectives and focus of the Customer/Market strategy, but unless these goals are tied to specific product/service bundles, their attainment is questionable. The need to transform Customer/Market strategies into organizational reality drives the decisions and actions comprising the Product Decision domain.

At the heart of the Product Decision domain is the need to define a specific product/service bundle and the precise attributes and features it will provide to customers. While the competitive position is defined within the Customer/Market domain, the decisions made at the Product level provide the detailed specifications and requirements that will shape day-to-day decision-making (see Figure 13.1).

Figure 13.1   Product Decision Groupings

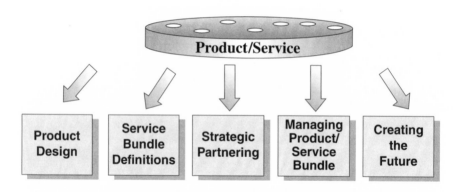

For instance, the Customer/Market strategy may be to achieve 40 percent market share within the farm implement market by providing a high quality product line with overnight delivery of spare parts. The customer value attributes being addressed by this strategy would include reliability, durability, and responsiveness.

At the Product level, this strategic vision for the product line is transformed into concrete models or service packages. Supported by a wide range of design tools that link the company to its customers (quality function deployment, or QFD) and the design effort to the plant floor (e.g.,design for manufacturability and assembly, or DFMA), product and service designers explore a wide variety of products, services, and features. The goal is to identify the optimal blend of features and functions to maximize the value delivered to customers while ensuring that company profit and performance goals are achieved.

Achieving key product/service design and development goals requires a tremendous amount of information and analysis. First, the company has to understand what specific product/service attributes are valued by the customer, and to what extent these features are valued. This information is obtained through Target Cost Management and translated into actionable terms through quality function deployment. The assessment of the cost/performance tradeoffs inherent in each design or service alternative requires the combination of data from a multitude of sources, including Activity-Based Cost Management, the Extended Enterprise, and Integrated Performance Management.

As the product/service bundle moves from initial design to operational reality, a multitude of decisions needs to be made. These include what forms of warranty to provide, how best to leverage the competencies of strategic trading partners, how to optimize production and the provision of services, and when to abandon a product/service bundle. Reflecting the key issues faced during the life cycle of the product/service bundle, these decisions rely heavily upon the information provided by the various SMPs.

The rest of this chapter explores the role of the various SMPs for making core decisions within the Product Decision domain. While all SMPs are required to support the decisions made within this domain, not all SMPs are equally important in all situations. As the objective of the decision(s) changes, so do information requirements. It is this shift in perspectives and demands that this chapter will explore.

Product Design

Thinking always ahead, thinking always of trying to do more, brings a state of mind in which nothing seems impossible.
– Henry Ford

It is a well known fact that between 80 and 90 percent of the costs for making a product or providing a service are locked in during the design phase (see Figure 13.2). Detailing the features of the product, quantities, required technologies, and the type and quantity of process and machine capacity needed, product design defines the performance limits and organizational implications of a specific product/service bundle.

Figure 13.2 Comparison of Committed and Incurred Costs

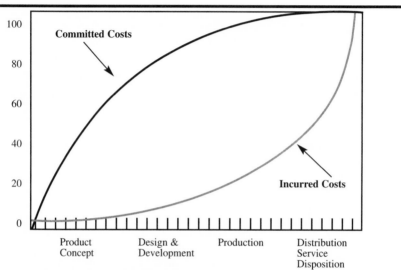

Source: Adapted from depiction in *Cost Management for Today's Advanced Manufacturing Systems,* Arlington, TX: CAM-I, 1988: p. 140

There are many issues and questions that shape the decisions made during the design of a product or service bundle, including the following:

- What are the current customer requirements for this type of product or service?
- How well are the firm and its Extended Enterprise partners currently meeting these needs?
- What changes are taking place in technologies, the competitive arena, or distribution channels that might influence customer expectations or required product/ service capabilities?
- What are the firm/Extended Enterprise's current core competencies and how can they best be leveraged to create optimal value?

- What are the firm/Extended Enterprise's performance requirements (e.g., return on investment or return on sales) for the product/service bundle?
- When will the product/service bundle be launched, and what is the expected duration of its life cycle?

Each of these decisions serves to narrow the range of alternatives and product/service features finally offered by the firm. Reflecting an iterative process guided by estimates of profit, performance, and value delivered by the set of feasible product/service alternatives, the effectiveness of the design process is the litmus test for organizational performance in the intermediate- to long-term.

At the heart of the design process lies Target Cost Management. (See Figure 13.3). Providing the framework for the analysis and evaluation of various design alternatives, TCM serves to tightly link the decisions made at the Customer/Market level to those made within the Product Decision domain. For instance, during its high level strategic analysis, a decision was made by a major office equipment manufacturer to target customers desiring a full-service product line

Figure 13.3   Product Design and Life Cycle Costs

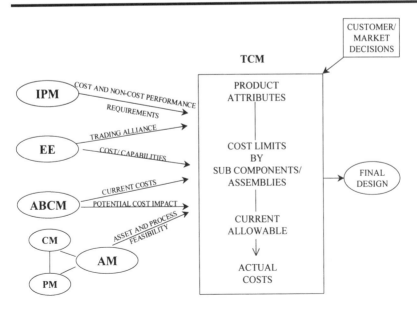

with a 24-hour hotline for service and performance information and support. This Customer/Market segment was felt to be most likely to reward the value chain for its ability to mass customize its product as well as to provide effective repair service and support. These are the core competencies top management felt define the competitive advantage of the firm and its network of trading partners, and that could be leveraged to provide desired returns.

TCM at the Customer/Market level was used to identify the volume, price points, allowable costs, and range of product and services that will be bundled to meet firm and customer requirements and provide desired profit and market share levels. The resulting decisions require that the products designed for the market use an optimal number of common, easily replaced parts, be easily repaired on site by the customer or a service technician, and that support services be available at all hours with minimal wait times. Full product line requirements have been defined to mean that five different products will be offered within the line, covering the full range of needs from copying to fax/modem and computer printing capabilities for small to medium organizations.

Price points and models have been defined across the range from simple, inexpensive single-function machines to complex, multi-function units. The ability to use one universal toner/ink cartridge will be a key design criteria for the product line, as will be the ability to upgrade simpler models to the more complex functions with minimal cost and complexity.

Reaching these goals requires a heavy reliance on simple, easy-to-assemble components that can provide increasingly complex functioning within commonly-defined size and shape constraints. The components must provide error-free functioning and over 99 percent reliability to customers, who often have only one machine to perform a task for the entire firm. Replacement parts and repairs must be easily obtained and installation completed with minimal down-time. If possible, customers should be able to identify the problem, obtain service advice, order replacement parts, and service the machine themselves, all with less than 24-hours of total downtime. This competitive position drives the design decisions made as specific models and features are defined. Using the TC SMP, the office equipment manufacturer had a logical framework to develop a product line and service support for the market segment they had identified.

TCM serves to transform general requirements into specific product and service features, setting limits on the costs of each component and process required to make the product or provide the service. Defined over the entire life cycle of the product/service bundle, performance requirements serve as input into the Quality Function Deployment (QFD) and Design for Manufacturability and Assembly (DFMA) analysis. Target Cost Management also serves to discipline the design process, constantly returning attention to the necessary relationship between the features, costs, and profits of each design alternative.

While TCM sets the limits and mediates the potential conflict between customer requirements, design constraints and preferences, and overall firm profit and performance goals, it does not do so in isolation. In order to provide the information needed to assess the feasibility of various designs, whether in terms of cost, performance, or impact on the firm and its trading partners, Target Cost Management depends on other SMPs to provide critical inputs to the product/service design stage.

Direct support of the design effort within the Product domain requires information on current and projected costs and performance of materials, conversion and service activities as well as of the product/service bundle itself. The cost and impact of new technologies, as well as the capabilities of the Extended Enterprise, play heavily into this aspect of the design decision process.

Three SMPs provide information to directly support Target Cost Management during the product design phase. First, Activity-Based Cost Management (ABCM) provides current and projected cost information on various activities and materials. This information reflects prior experience with related processes and products. In a well-designed ABCM system, information is richer than historical cost data and estimates of the potential, or projected cost, for a broad range of alternative product and service features should be accessible by the design team.

While ABCM details the economics of various activities and materials, Integrated Performance Management provides non-financial information on the quality, reliability, and flexibility of the core processes as well as the performance capabilities of trading partners. Emphasizing the effectiveness of the total value chain, Integrated Performance Management provides insight into the impact of design features on the various parts of the organization.

A key element to consider when assessing the feasibility of the new product/service bundle is its impact on the entire value chain. Looking beyond traditional organizational boundaries, the Extended Enterprise provides input on the ability of the value chain to meet customer requirements. Returning to our office equipment example, providing a 24-hour guarantee of repair part and service support requires the cooperation of final distributors who are closest to the customer. The firm cannot include this element of serviceability at a reasonable cost without extending its reach beyond company boundaries and partnering with its distributors in the effort to provide parts quickly and cost effectively. The optimal decision may be to have parts distributed directly from the supplier's stocks rather than from the equipment manufacturer. Only the Extended Enterprise SMP can provide this information to the design team.

While direct input is required from these SMPs, Process Management, Capacity Management and Asset Management also play a role during product design. Process Management provides information on the capability of the processes to provide the level of quality and functionality required by the new product, while Capacity Management details the physical system's ability to absorb the new demand the product represents. Where shortfalls are found in either processes or physical asset capacities, Asset Management is called upon to analyze the feasibility of new equipment purchases to meet required performance levels. In combination, these three supporting SMPs can help answer specific queries about the existing and potential capability of the firm's processes and assets.

Using the CAM-I SMP Model to support the design phase will help the organization optimize design decisions to increase customer satisfaction without unknowingly reducing margins.

Defining the Service Bundle

Good will, like a good name,
is got by many actions, and lost by one.

– Lord Jeffrey

A product can have tremendous value embedded in it, yet fail to meet customer requirements because of the service bundle attached to it. In the global market, it is the combination of products and services that define a firm's competitive position. They need to be designed in tandem, ensuring that the service and support provided combine with the product itself to create "delight" for the customer.

Several different issues have to be considered when a firm develops its service/support strategy. Specifically:

- What warranty should be provided with the product, if any?
- What support services should be provided?
- How should these support services be provided? Should distributors be relied upon for after-sale service, or should a service/support group be created within the firm?
- How should spare parts requirements be met? Should they be shipped directly from the vendor or should inventories be maintained at the plant or in the field?
- What customer services will be provided, during what hours, and using what technology?
- How extensive should owner manuals be, and how should additional information be made available?

These are just a few of the many questions that have to be addressed as the service/support bundle of activities is designed. Framed once again within the Target Cost Management SMP, these questions direct attention to the activities, costs, and value creating aspects of the service bundle. Specifically, TCM allows the firm to look at the product/ service bundle in terms of its total life cycle cost for both the company and its customers. Minimizing the total cost of ownership for the customer is the primary objective of these efforts.

While TCM provides a framework for this analysis, other SMPs also play a key role during these activities (see Figure 13.4). For instance, ABCM is the source of information on the estimated impact and costs of the new support activities on the existing processes. Combined with Process Management and Capacity Management, ABCM serves to support economic and activity analysis of the system and its ability to meet the new demands.

Figure 13.4   SMPs and the Definition of the Service Bundle

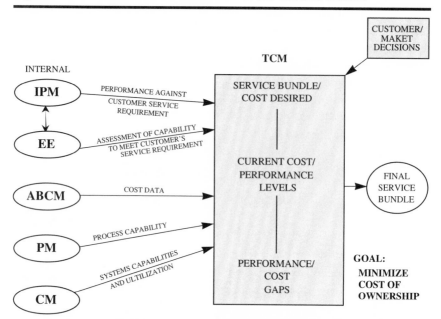

Cost is not the only concern in planning a service strategy. The total set of value attributes for the product/service bundle need to be addressed. Integrated Performance Management focuses attention on the non-financial performance issues, including the projected quality, reliability, and serviceability of the service bundle and its internal physical and process assets. It also provides information on the Extended Enterprise and its ability to support the service demands placed on it. Where shortfalls are discovered, Asset Management helps the firm explore investment options and requirements if new service/support capability is needed, such as new telephone or computer systems.

The same issues and concerns frame the development of the service/support strategy as drive the initial product design. It is crucial that a service/support strategy is chosen that optimizes the value delivered and leverages the resources of the value chain effectively. The firm must know what a customer values in a service bundle, then must link the information flow from the point-of-sale back through the entire trading alliance and identify the optimal process for handling the entire range of customer needs and inquiries before and after the initial purchase event.

During the design phase, customer service performance requirements and costs information are proxied by the various SMPs. Once the product/service bundle has been launched, though, the Extended Enterprise must provide ongoing feedback and analysis of the value chain's performance against customer expectations. As the opening quote to this section suggests, it only takes one error during the entire life cycle of the product to negatively color the customer's perception of the value embedded in the product/service bundle.

Developing, implementing, and executing an effective service strategy is critical to the long-term success of the firm. The support of trading partners in this effort cannot be understated, leading to the third set of decisions that need to be made within the Product Decision domain.

Strategic Partnering

The improvement of understanding is for two ends: first,
our own increase of knowledge; secondly, to enable us
to deliver that knowledge to others.

– John Locke

Within the Product Decision domain, the hand-off between Target Cost Management and the Extended Enterprise takes place as the product/service bundle is moved off the design board and into implementation and execution. Illustrating the importance of effective integration of the Strategic Management Processes, the smooth transition from planning to action requires that all key processes and partners are brought on-line synchronously. Avoiding fumbles, miscommunications, lack of shared vision, and conflict as implementation begins requires that core SMPs (e.g., Target Cost Management and the Extended Enterprise) be linked from the outset.

Developing a sourcing strategy does not begin when the product is launched. Key trading partners need to be included in the decision process from the beginning of the design of the product/service bundle if value chain resources are to be effectively leveraged. For instance, a vendor may help the design team optimize the materials used in a product by providing insights into how components are made and what forms of technology are available to improve the development process. This information can include materials, production or assembly details, or serviceability/functionality data.

Including key trading partners ensures that the maximum amount of expertise is brought to bear on the design process. It also helps guarantee that the design of the product/service bundle captures the key value attributes desired by customers and the Extended Enterprise is aligned to reduce time and costs.

In the same way that the Extended Enterprise links directly with TCM to ensure the smooth flow of information and decisions from design to implementation of the product/service strategy, Process Management serves to link these SMPs to the Process and Resource Decision domains. Ensuring that information flows smoothly up and down the decision hierarchy, as well as across the entire value chain, is the ultimate goal of the CAM-I SMP.

What types of information are required during the transition from design to execution? Specific concerns include:

- What is the best sourcing strategy for key components and services?

- Which trading partners can best provide key competencies and support?

- Which elements of the total product/service bundle should be controlled by the firm?

- If core technologies are outsourced, what form of relationship should be developed?

- What are the required performance levels for the value chain?

- If bottlenecks or constraints exist, what is the optimal way to manage them?

- How many strategic partnerships should be developed? Why?

- If a strategic partner fails to meet the needs of the trading alliance, what should be done to address this problem in the short- and long-term?

- Which enabling technologies should be explored?

Each of these questions about the nature, structure, function, and responsibilities of the various trading partners requires unique forms of information (see Figure 13.5). Specifically, if Capacity Management reports that there is significant internal idle capacity, it would affect the

Figure 13.5   SMP Information Flows and Strategic Partnering

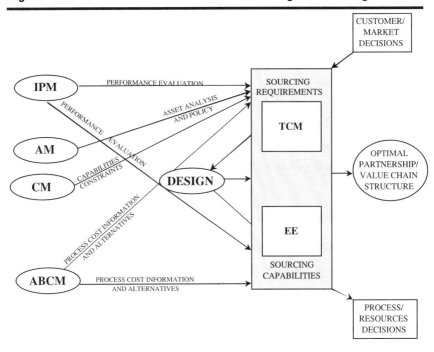

decision about the degree and type of partnering needed. In a related way, as various strategic alliance structures are explored, Activity-Based Cost Management and Integrated Performance Management can provide detailed cost and performance information to guide the choice of partners and performance expectations.

In the development of strategic alliances, there is increasing tendency to participate in joint investment efforts. For instance, the trading partners may identify a need for a high speed, flexible production capability at one of the primary raw material suppliers. The supplier may not have the ability to make the investment needed, leading the alliance to consider several alternatives. Another supplier could be sought out, but if the quality and performance of the current vendor is on target, the decision to change sources may add significant risk of failure to the total product/service effort. An alternative decision might be to join forces to obtain the necessary investment funds. In this case, the Asset Management SMP would be called upon to analyze this decision to co-invest in the value chain's capacity.

The very nature of strategic partnering brings with it new information, decision, and management challenges for the various firms in the trading alliance. An effective, integrated information system that spans organizational boundaries and provides detail about the core issues and performance capabilities of the trading alliance can help eliminate the noise and complexity from the trading channel. Strategic partners share more than their relationship within the value chain. They share physical and intangible assets, including knowledge, technology, machines, and capital. The greater the degree of integration achieved, the higher the likelihood that the goals established by Target Cost Management will be reached.

Having established the design of the product/service bundle, defined the service strategy, and developed the cross-organizational linkages necessary to transform these plans into reality, attention turns to ongoing management of products and processes.

Managing the Product/Service Bundle

Men are wise in proportion, not to their experience,
but to their capacity for experience.
    – George Bernard Shaw

The Product Decision domain spans the planning, provision, and management of the various product/service bundles offered by the firm to its customers over their entire life cycle. As the product/service bundle begins to be offered to the market, the nature of decision-making shifts from analysis to monitoring, management and adjustment. If continuous improvement targets have been set during the design phase, management needs to ensure that these objectives are met. Similarly, it is critical that ongoing monitoring of performance against customer expectations takes place. While a well designed product/service bundle should meet the needs of all stakeholders, it remains important to monitor progress and make adjustments as conditions change.

Issues and concerns to monitor include:

- Are there changes in the competitive market that would require adjustments to the product/service bundle?
- Are continuous improvement goals being met in the production/distribution of the product?
- What issues are arising in the field with respect to service and warranty concerns?

- Do we have adequate capacity to meet the actual demand? If not, should more capacity be added or an outsource vendor be found?

- Do we have too much capacity in place? If so, how can it be filled profitably?

- Are quality and performance goals being met? If not, what changes need to be made?

- Are new technologies becoming available that could compete with, or cause adjustments in, the product/ service bundle?

The Strategic Management Processes combine to provide the information needed to address these issues. Integrated Performance Management plays the pivotal role, though, serving to set the initial performance parameters and tracking outcomes against these goals (see Figure 13.6).

Figure 13.6   Integrated Performance Management

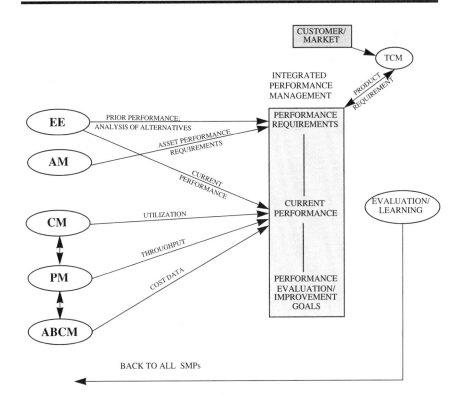

For instance, capacity questions are answered with information provided by the Capacity Management SMP, but the Integrated Performance Management SMP serves as the primary contact point for the reports and analysis of all performance, including capacity utilization. The Extended Enterprise SMP, on the other hand, ties directly to the database that feeds the Integrated Performance Management, providing real time data on market trends, customer demand, and other core issues.

ABCM combines with Process Management to provide information on the cost and performance levels of internal processes and activities. Process Management ensures that the processes are operating effectively and that continuous improvement goals are met, but it is Integrated Performance Management that provides the data to create the reports and analysis used by management to gauge progress.

While farther removed from ongoing operational issues, Target Cost Management and Asset Management should be linked to this class of decisions. TCM should be the source of many of the standards and performance goals developed for internal processes, trading partners, and the product/service bundle itself. It relies upon the new data collected by Integrated Performance Management and related SMPs to develop future product and service objectives. Asset Management provides performance targets for new assets, systems, or products.

Ensuring that profit and performance goals are met in the face of changing conditions, management relies upon the information embedded in the SMPs. In the day-to-day world of management, this integrated information system can help a firm develop and sustain a competitive advantage. Information is power. Applied within the CAM-I Strategic Management Process Model, it is a power that can be accessed and turned to benefit all stakeholders. As the CAM-I SMP Model provides information for the product/service bundle design, it also provides crucial data to support next generation product/service redesigns or even product abandonment decisions.

The abandonment of a product/service bundle is as natural a part of business life as death is to human life. As resources are freed up from existing demands, new opportunities form for creating value for customers in new forms. Abandonment is one step in creating a new future for the organization and its trading partners.

Placing abandonment with a circular continuum is important because it is not an end, but rather a new beginning. As such, it is critical to ensure that trading partners' needs are addressed, that downstream customer requirements for spare parts and service are factored into the analysis, and that optimal uses for the newly freed resources be found.

Seamlessly managing these transitions is the goal of the decisions made at this stage of the life cycle of the product/service bundle. These decisions might address the following:

- What level of spare part inventory should be kept? Where should these inventories be kept, and how should replenishment take place?

- What forms of service are customers likely to need? What is the optimal way to provide these services to ensure that customers remain loyal and open to downstream products and services provided by the firm?

- In what ways can the skills and competencies of the trading alliance be redirected to seize new opportunities?

- What is the best downstream use of existing capacity?

- In evaluating the entire product/service bundle's performance, what targets were attained, which ones missed, and what learning can be gathered from this information for future projects?

Being transitional in nature, the decisions made at this point of the product/service life cycle require that the Integrated Performance Management and Target Cost Management SMPs be effectively linked, for this is where the major hand-offs between the old bundle and the new take place (see Figure 13.7).

As suggested by this diagram, the abandonment phase decisions make use of information provided by the entire set of SMPs. Decisions to abandon build from the Integrated Performance Management SMP, which signals that the effective life of the product/service bundle has come to a close. As this information becomes available, resources are redirected by TCM to new opportunities. Integration of these two core SMPs provides transition of process, alliance, and asset capabilities and efforts from existing tasks to those required to meet future objectives.

Figure 13.7   Creating the Future

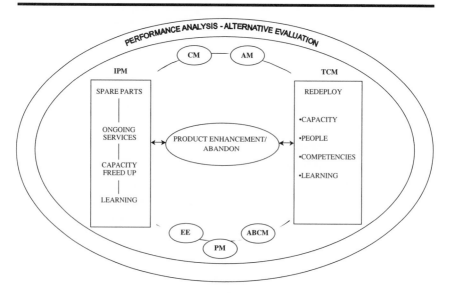

While TCM is redirecting resources, Integrated Performance Management efforts remain focused on ensuring that ongoing customer requirements associated with the abandoned product/service bundle are being met. The end of the life cycle is not a good place to begin disappointing customers. Since long-term success comes from loyal customers who repeatedly purchase from the trading alliance, it is crucial that the customer remains comfortable with the support provided. After the physical product is discontinued, the service component of the bundle becomes more important than ever.

While these two primary SMPs coordinate the information requirements and analysis surrounding the transition of the product/service bundle, they rely heavily upon the input of the other five SMPs to gather data, perform analysis, and prioritize alternatives. For instance, the Extended Enterprise details the impact of the change on the supply chain and manages the transition process to ensure alliance integrity. The downstream and upstream trading partners will play an active role in meeting ongoing service needs for customers who have, and continue to use, the existing product/

service bundle. Coordinating these efforts is a critical part of an effective transition plan.

In a similar way, Process Management provides detail on the progress made in phasing out unnecessary activities and processes and redirecting those that remain to new uses. It also ensures that internal processes remain intact for dealing with service and support needs, including the development of an effective spare parts inventory management process. If there is an inventory of existing product left, decisions have to be made on how to optimally discard them. Should existing customers be offered remaining units at reduced prices? Should the units be retained for downstream parts and replacement purposes? Process Management plays a primary role in creating an effective post-abandonment process for the service component of the bundle.

Asset Management provides guidance on the physical asset issues, such as the sale of existing machinery, identification of new uses for this equipment, mothballing of items for later use, and so on. Part of the original justification process, these decisions reflect an overall asset strategy that can have significant impact on the profitability of the firm during the transition from one product/service bundle to the next. Capacity Management goes hand-in-glove with Asset Management to provide information to guide these post-abandonment resource decisions.

ABCM provides the final set of inputs, monitoring the cost and impact of abandonment effort and the cost to transition resources, processes, and activities to new uses. Feeding economic information to the other SMPs, ABCM ensures that the transition is kept on track and that planned profit targets for the total life cycle are tracked.

Taken in total, the SMPs each provide unique insights into the impact of abandonment, serve to link the past to the future through information, and improve the effectiveness of this transition by coordinating the data and analysis used by management to make this set of decisions. Without integration, both across time within one SMP, and across the entire Product Decision domain of all SMPs, management is unlikely to anticipate and adjust to needed changes efficiently or effectively. Integration is the key to creating a continuous process of growth and rebirth, profits and performance.

Summary

History may be viewed as a process of pushing back walls of inevitability, of turning what have been thought to be inescapable limitations into...possibilities.

– Helen Merrell Lynd

The Product Decision domain is the center of organizational action, transforming abstract strategies and objectives into concrete realities. Spanning the entire range of issues and decisions that begin with the inception of a new product/service bundle and continue on past downstream abandonment, the effectiveness and efficiency of the decisions made within this domain set the limits for the profitability and performance of the value chain.

The Strategic Management Processes used to structure decisions across the Product domain shift as the focus of the analysis changes. Early efforts to translate the Customer/Market requirements into specific product/service bundles with defined value attributes are shaped by TCM. Once key design and development decisions have been made, emphasis turns to creating the trading alliance (the Extended Enterprise) and optimizing ongoing management of the processes and product/service bundle (Integrated Performance Management).

Abandonment, the final stage in the product life cycle, links the past to the future. Integrated Performance Management bridges this gap, handing off information and resources to Target Cost Management for redeployment to new opportunities. Each SMP is involved in this final transition, ensuring that each affected resource, relationship, process or activity is moved smoothly from old to new uses. The service component of the bundle continues on past abandonment, providing the customer with needed support and ensuring that loyalty is gained and retained. In the end, it is a loyal customer, not simply a satisfied one, that defines the long-term success of the value chain.

Integration of the SMPs within this Decision domain improves the ability of the firm and its trading partners to leverage their core competencies, reap the benefits of prior investments in resources and capabilities, and optimize their delivery of valued products and services to customers. Creating a comprehensive, consistent information warehouse, the CAM-I Strategic Management Process Model can help identify, attain, and sustain a competitive advantage.

In the end, it is the level of coordination and synchronization of efforts that sets a top performing company apart from its peers. Creating a holistic system, where the actions of the many combine to create abilities and strengths not attainable by individuals, requires communication. It is communication that the SMP integration facilitates, turning the organizational "Tower of Babel" into the common language and common vision required to optimize the value created for all stakeholders. Integration is a goal to be pursued and the CAM-I SMP Model provides the framework to facilitate this integration. It is the process of the SMP integration that allows management to create competitive knowledge from the plethora of availible information.

Optimizing the Flow

Integration of the Process Decision Domain

The chains of habit are too weak to be felt until they are too strong to be broken.

– Samuel Johnson

Key Learnings:

■ Decisions in the Process Decision domain emphasize the flow, or linkage of activities into seamless delivery channels that provide products and services to the defined customer segments.

■ The decision bundles that comprise this platter of the SMP framework include: designing processes, sourcing strategies, ongoing process management, and the management of performance gaps.

■ The Process Decision domain is the arena of action, where plans become reality. As such, it is the focus of the majority of management's time and effort.

One of the major changes in the way that companies structure and manage themselves has been the shift from a vertical to horizontal focus. Faced with the need to increase their responsiveness, eliminate excess costs and redundancy, and reduce errors due to miscommunication, more and more leading edge firms are embracing the concepts of *Process Management* as the key to improving performance.

The Process Decision domain deals with issues arising from the shift to a process orientation. Concerned with helping firms optimize the amount of value created within its core processes, decisions at the Process level focus on ensuring that the customer-defined performance requirements are met consistently. The decision bundles that comprise this platter of the SMP framework include the planning and designing of enterprise-wide processes as well as the daily challenges of managing their performance.

Emphasizing the flow, or linkage of activities into seamless delivery channels that provide products and services to the defined customer segments, this Decision domain is dominated by the Process Management and Capacity Management Strategic Management Processes (SMPs). These SMPs are integrated with other key tools used within the Process Domain, including Total Quality Management (TQM), ISO 9000 certification programs, the Theory of Constraints (TOC), Just-In-Time manufacturing and inventory (JIT), Flexible Manufacturing Systems (FMS), benchmarking, and operational performance measurement systems, just to name a few. The Process Domain is the arena of action where plans become reality. As such, it is normally the focus of the majority of management's time and effort. The plethora of tools and techniques to aid decision-making reflects the volume and complexity of decisions that characterize operational and tactical Process Management.

While any number of decisions need to be made at the Process level, four specific bundles are most directly tied to the SMP framework: designing processes, sourcing strategies, ongoing process management, and the management of performance gaps. (See Figure 14.1). The first of these decision bundles directly links the Process domain to the strategic decisions made at the Customer/Market and Product levels. Processes are designed to meet the demands identified during strategic planning.

The second bundle, or sourcing decisions, begins when the product is designed as part of the Target Cost Management initiative, but continues on an ongoing basis in the form of "make versus buy" analysis. As the company embraces the Extended Enterprise, the number and focus of sourcing decisions changes, moving forward in the planning horizon as an integral part of the "design" of the product/service bundle.

Figure 14.1 Process Decision Groupings

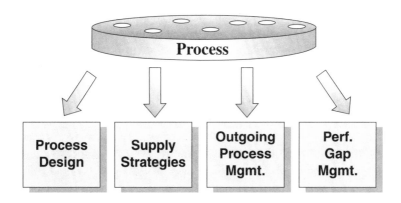

Daily management of processes requires a broad range of financial and non-financial information. Synchronizing the flow of materials and effort through core value-creating processes, managers are called upon to make numerous real-time decisions about what to produce, when, where, and how to alleviate constraints that emerge as the process is deployed. As products are managed over time, performance gaps appear that need to be addressed. Part of the natural life cycle of an organization, decisions within the Process Domain move to the rhythm of the product life cycle.

In the following pages, each of these decision bundles will be discussed, focusing on the key issues raised and the role of the CAM-I Strategic Management Process Model in answering these questions and providing guidance. The goal is to help management leverage core competencies and process capabilities to profitably optimize the value created for customers.

Creating a Process Orientation

Thought is the blossom; language the bud;
action the fruit behind it.

– Ralph Waldo Emerson

Creating a process orientation, and designing the workflow to optimize its ability to flexibly respond to customer requirements—to optimize the value created by the organization—begins with a change of mindset. *Process Management* is more than a set of tools and techniques to increase the throughput,[1] it is a way of thinking about an organization and its logical structure. Even if a firm does not formally use Process Management techniques, it will need to face and manage the decisions within the Process Domain.

Linked with TCM at the Customer/Market and Product levels, and the Extended Enterprise framework, process design decisions emphasize the development of workflows that meet the needs of the entire range of products and services they will be called upon to support. A process is a shared resource. Designing a process begins, then, with understanding what demands it is expected to meet, the degree of flexibility and responsiveness it will need to have, and the resource and performance constraints that will limit what is possible. This design effort requires the active exploration of man/machine tradeoffs in terms of flexibility, responsiveness, capacity, quality, and cost, given the performance required, and valued, by customers.

A large number of questions need to be answered during the process design phase, including the following:

- What is the maximum demand the system needs to be able to handle on a daily/weekly basis?
- What level of quality needs to be maintained?
- Where are quality problems likely to occur, and how can they be avoided or detected?
- What resources are currently available?
- What is the capacity of the process given planned demand?
- Where is the bottleneck? What can be done to reduce its impact or improve its capability?
- How can gaps in the flow be best managed? Should time, space, or inventory buffers be used to ensure that the bottleneck is never idle?
- What variety of products and activities will need to be accomodated by the process? What is the optimal way to manage this variety?
- Does the process represent a core competency? If not, should the activities and output it embodies be outsourced?

- Do needed skills and competencies exist to make the process work smoothly?

- Are there any major functional, political, or structural impediments to creating the process?

- What performance measures should be used to ensure that process objectives are attained?

Understanding what activities will make up the optimal process, what performance and cost constraints must be factored into the design, and ensuring that the process can meet downstream needs requires information from the various SMPs (see Figure 14.2).

Figure 14.2   SMPs and Process Design

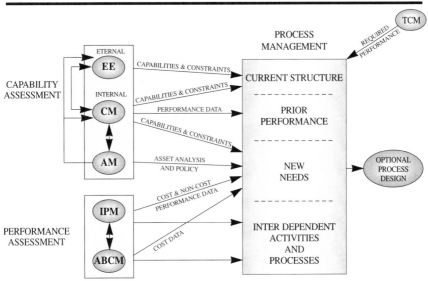

The dominant SMP during process design is Process Management. It provides the framework for all decisions on the process "layer", as well as supplying the underlying theory of integration that serves to link the customer directly to the ongoing management of the firm. Process Management ensures that integration, coordination, and synchronization of activities, functions, departments, and value chain entities takes place.

Process Management frames these design decisions within the context of current competencies, competing process demands, established relationships, and inviolate constraints. Emphasizing the bridging of gaps between activities and departments, Process Management ensures that the design process eliminates as many potential miscues and errors due to poor communication as possible. Process Management also helps identify optimal pathways through the existing organization, as well as noting when a new process needs to be developed due to unduly restrictive constraints or limits within existing areas.

Information provided by Process Management includes the current activity structure, existing linkages between areas and activities, and prior performance capabilities of the key process steps. It also draws heavily from supporting SMPs to provide a database of information to query and identify optimal structures. For instance, Capacity Management is called upon to identify available capacity of key activities or resources, idle capacity in affected areas, and the cost to create new capacity if inadequate throughput capabilities exist. Capacity Management feeds data to Process Management on each of the key dimensions, defining the constraints and costs of meeting projected throughput and quality requirements.

In a related manner, the Extended Enterprise provides insight into outsourcing/alliance capabilities to ensure that the process is optimally designed to meet everyone's needs, both within and outside the core firm. Wherever a capacity constraint is identified, management can turn to the Extended Enterprise for potential solutions. In addition, the ongoing input of trading partners sets the key parameters to the process and its required output. Quality, timeliness, responsiveness, and variety are just a few of the issues that must be coordinated throughout the supply chain if the process is to provide optimal value for invested dollar.

As noted in the opening discussion, Target Cost Management details the performance requirements for the various product/service bundles the process will be expected to support. It also provides Customer/Market and Product level information, such as key attributes of the product, design constraints, performance requirements, and cost parameters, all of which factor into the process design effort. Target Cost Management serves to link the process to the strategy of the firm, providing a basis for downstream performance evaluation and improvement. The benefit of the CAM-I SMP model is that it provides the means to link data across Decision domains, time periods, and markets to ensure the availability of consistent, fluid, and coordinated information, analysis, and action. Information is used to bridge the gaps that occur as the organization grows and fragments.

Continuing on with the relationships of SMPs to the process design effort, Asset Management helps designers query and assess any new asset or capability requirements needed for the process to perform as required. Working in tandem with Capacity Management, the Asset Management SMP provides the basis for determining what resources need to be acquired. It defines what returns and benefits these resources must provide, and how best to meet process requirements while minimizing the amount and type of fixed, inflexible assets added to the resource base. Asset Management also sets the baseline performance for the process itself, as the dollars spent to design and implement the process are assessed against the profits and returns it will provide.

The two final SMPs, Integrated Performance Management and Activity-Based Cost Management, provide essential details about the underlying activities and capabilities of the firm. This information includes the cost to perform various activities, the prior performance of affected areas (quality, schedule attainment, reliability), the projected increments in cost that will occur as throughput thresholds are crossed, and the impact of the new process on support areas. Wherever the process affects people-intensive areas, Activity-Based Cost Management provides vital information on the ability and cost to meet the new demand. Activity-Based Cost Management does for the people side of process design what Capacity Management and Asset Management do for the machine/physical asset elements.

Integrated Performance Management does more than feed Process Management data on prior performance of affected activities and areas. It creates the measuring system that will be used to make initial design decisions, inform downstream users of demands and expectations, and to provide the basis for ongoing improvements of process performance. Integrated Performance Management sets in place the measures used to coordinate the flow, identify problems as they occur, and track process performance against its objectives. Linking the past to the present, and the present to the future, the Integrated Performance Management SMP provides continuity in information, performance, and analysis to the process and the organization.

As the process design decisions are taking place, sourcing issues are being addressed. Sourcing of inputs, buffer capacity, and support activities are issues that are constantly revisited over the life of a product or process. Sourcing plays a central role in the Process Decision domain, as the following discussion suggests.

Sourcing Decisions

Planning and competition can be combined only by planning for competition, but not by planning against competition.

– Friedrich August Von Hayek

One of the greatest lessons learned over the past decade is that suppliers and customers are partners in the creation of value. Moving out of the arena of competition, pressure, power and conflict, the creation of long-term alliances with trading partners has become the key to leveraging the resources and capabilities of the firm to provide maximum performance. It is the trading alliance, the Extended Enterprise, which comes together to plan for competition, not the individual firm.

Having said this, it is clear that sourcing decisions are dominated by the Extended Enterprise SMP, regardless of what Decision domain is under consideration. The Extended Enterprise provides the framework to ensure continuity, long-term analysis across the supply chain, and the achievement of performance impossible without the coordinated efforts of multiple firms. The Extended Enterprise keeps the Process domain tightly linked to the customer, market, and future of the firm.

Of course, not every activity or element of the designed and implemented process has strategic import. Some elements are clearly part of the core competencies of the firm or alliance, and need to be tightly controlled and exploited. Other areas are less critical to the long-term viability of the Extended Enterprise. These can be freely outsourced as the economics of the moment dictate. To understand the use of the CAM-I SMP model in the sourcing activity, these two very different situations need to be explored.

As suggested in Figure 14.3, sourcing of activities and resources that are part of the defined core competencies of the process or organization lies at the heart of the Extended Enterprise SMP. Where it would be inadvisable to outsource core areas in a traditional,

Figure 14.3   Outsourcing and the SMP Model

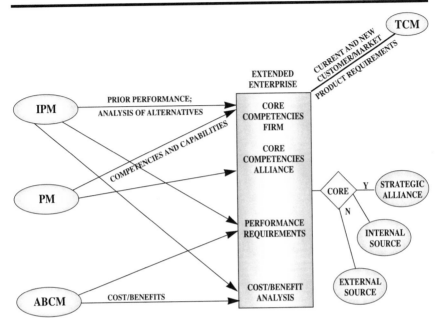

conflictual supply setting, within the Extended Enterprise trading partners become extensions of the firm. Replacing conflict with cooperation, firms are able to turn to, and rely upon, their trading alliances to protect and extend the benefits of their core competencies and competitive strengths.

A firm looking to set up an alliance to outsource a key component, service, process or activity needs to gather a tremendous amount of information. First, it must turn to the Integrated Performance Management system to understand prior delivery, responsiveness, quality, and related attributes of potential alliance partners. Target Cost Management, on the other hand, provides guidance for the decision by setting performance parameters for these efforts. Target Cost Management also serves to drive key customer requirements into the supplier assessment and choice effort. Finally, Target Cost Management helps the firm understand how critical the potential outsourced process, material, or activity is to the overall Customer/Market or product strategy.

It is imperative that Capacity Management and Asset Management be queried prior to the outsourcing decision to determine if there are current idle or available resources that could be used. A failure to deploy existing capabilities can increase the cost, not only of the process, but of the business as a whole as waste is embedded in its structure. Since waste can never be expected to result in value or revenue, its avoidance has to remain a high priority for the firm.

Looking further at Figure 14.3, it is apparent that Activity-Based Cost Management joins forces with Process Management to ensure that the impact of the outsourcing is understood in both operational and financial performance terms. The outsourcing effort has to improve the performance of the process, its responsiveness to customers, and the economics of doing business. The Process Management and Activity-Based Cost Management SMPs provide the basis for this analysis both before the outsourcing decision is made, and after it has been executed.

POST-DESIGN OUTSOURCING ISSUES

Outsourcing decisions do not cease once the process is designed. Ongoing shifts in customer requirements, changes in internal capabilities and tactical choices, and technological advances are just a few of the events that may lead to downstream outsourcing decisions at the Process level.

While early outsourcing decisions can include defined core competencies, non-core areas are the only ones that should be open to ad hoc or opportunistic sourcing. Non-core processes, such as payroll, should be periodically reviewed to determine if outsourcing is preferable to continued completion of the activity by the firm. Whenever customers are indifferent to the activities or outcomes of a process, outsourcing becomes a pure economic business decision. If outsourcing can lower costs, with little impact on core processes or the value creating potential they embody, then outsourcing should be undertaken.

Operational and tactical outsourcing is framed by the Activity-Based Cost Management and Integrated Performance Management SMPs. Activity analysis is used to determine which activities are affected, which processes, products, and services may be impacted, and what the firm's current costs are. IPM sets the expectations for outsourcing vendor delivery, quality, and costs given the overall objectives for the process and organization. Using both to make the initial decision and to perform ongoing monitoring, these two SMPs combine to provide information and analysis to the managers charged with exploring options for, choosing, and monitoring the outsourced process.

Sourcing strategies are driven by the importance of the process or activity being considered for outsourcing, the long-term alliances the firm participates in, and the dynamics of the markets and customers being served. Outsourcing processes, activities, or components can free up scarce investment and operating dollars for the firm. Done well, outsourcing can create superior performance. Done poorly, it can spell disaster for both the short- and long-term.

The CAM-I SMP model helps management assess alternative sources for its products, services, processes, and activities in light of current and future Customer/Market and Product objectives. Moving beyond simple economics into the realm of strategic analysis and value creation, outsourcing can be used at the Process level to enhance a firm's core competencies. It can help create a responsive, flexible, competitive, lean structure built on cooperation, not conflict, within the value chain. Gaining these benefits begins with having the ability to pinpoint key issues, obtain needed information, and complete a cross-functional, cross-process analysis. It is this capability that the CAM-I SMP Model provides.

Managing Processes for Optimal Performance
Trend is not destiny.
– Lewis Mumford

The majority of the effort and analysis conducted within an organization takes place within the Process Decision domain, and is executed, implicitly or explicitly, through Process Management. Determining what needs to be done, when, and why, how to respond to changes, how to eliminate unwanted variances in performance, and how to optimize the value created for customers, are events that take place in the domain of action.

Information is the lifeblood of this everyday world. If the right decisions are to be made in "real time," this information must integrate operational and financial data accurately and succinctly. Choosing a few key measures to support analysis, then ensuring that these measures provide consistent signals and insights, is one of the primary roles played by financial managers in today's organizations.

The CAM-I SMP model is the backbone of the data warehouse that is used to drive decisions in the Process domain. Using Process Management as the framework for defining the integration, the goal is to place key metrics at points where process breakdowns and can lead to missed deadlines and shipments. The Extended Enterprise is a key contributor to Process Management for this bundle of decisions (see Figure 14.4). Providing ongoing point-of-sale information back through the entire supply chain on current demand, customer satisfaction, current performance and needs of trading partners, and an external evaluation of process effectiveness, the EE ensures that the customer remains the driving force of operations. If adjustments are needed, it is the EE that is most likely to provide the first signal that schedules or shipments need to change. The EE also provides early warning that market dynamics are shifting, information which is critical to ensure that the entire trading alliance can refocus its efforts to meet shifting demands.

Figure 14.4   Ongoing Process Management

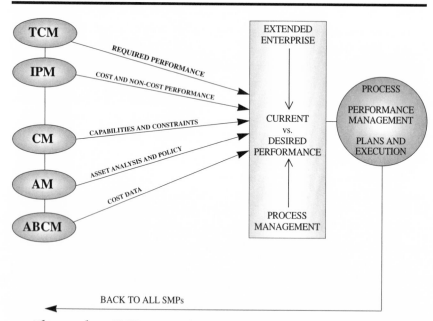

Three other SMPs provide ongoing information about internal dimensions of performance: Activity-Based Cost Management, Capacity Management and Integrated Performance Management. ABCM emphasizes the cost and capability of the underlying activity grid, assessing whether budgets and improvement targets are being met. ABCM also provides ongoing reads on the "people" side of the process—its ability to meet goals and respond to changing requirements.

Capacity Management summarizes data on the efficiency and effectiveness of the physical asset systems Current schedule attainment, planned versus unplanned idle time, and related information is used to adjust schedules and establish new production plans. Capacity Management is a comprehensive reporting system that links daily activities to the long-term Asset Management concerns.

Integrated Performance Management, the third leg of the operational database "stool", measures current performance levels for the process, provides benchmarks and other standards to assess this performance and establish improvement targets, and supports ongoing evaluation and goal setting efforts. Each of the SMPs provides a different type of information about the current status of the underlying processes. Combined with the EE, Process Management is provided with an end-to-end snapshot of the performance of the value chain.

An example of how this information comes together might be useful. The "order-to-payment" process (OTP) is the primary value-creating flow in most manufacturing or distribution companies. The OTP process physically links the activities performed by the various functional groups of the company into a seamless delivery channel that responds to customer orders rapidly and accurately, if it is operating effectively (see Figure 14.5).

Figure 14.5   Ongoing Process Management—An Example

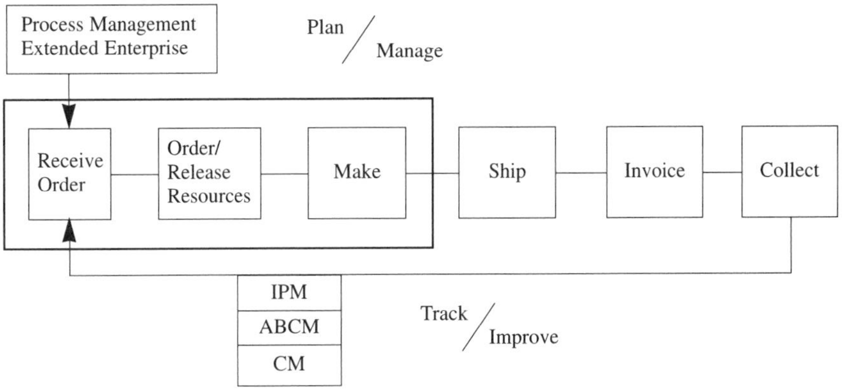

Based on prior performance and strategic targets, assume in this example that management has decided that it can offer 48 hour delivery of product any where in North America. To keep costs under control, though, this performance is not to be achieved by carrying excessive inventories. Instead, a trading alliance has been established that provides replenishment of minimal inventories on a "demand-pull" basis. The distributor, upon receiving an order, releases the information back through the supply channel (the Extended Enterprise), which responds by providing another unit of the demanded item.

The result of the application of Process Management to this setting is that the internal operations of the distributor are seamlessly linked, with data entry of the original order serving as a signal to the entire supply chain. This signal triggers the picking of the item from stock, packing it, preparation of shipping documents and invoices, shipment of the item, and stock replenishment, all with "one touch" of the button.

When working correctly, the OTP process provides a high level of service and value to the end customer. There are times, though, due to raw material shortages, weather delays, missed shipments, excessive order quantities, unexpected damage, or any number of other events, that promised deliveries aren't met. OTP managers need to be made aware of the problem as soon as it occurs, so remedial action can be taken. The signal comes from the shop floor through Capacity Management that a key machine is down, and that all orders for vacuum cleaner bags will be affected.

Having determined that the problem will take two to three days to address, attention turns to finding alternative solutions. The first option is to see if there is any way to make the product with available machines. A query of the Capacity Management SMP suggests that there is enough available capacity on an older machine to handle one half of the current need. The ABCM SMP is then used to provide a cost estimate for the activities that rerouting and additional set-ups will create. Integrated Performance Management history suggests that the defect rate on this older machine has been quite high on one of the three types of vacuum cleaner bags needed, but that the other two have been made quite well on the equipment.

Armed with this information, two of the three items are scheduled onto the back-up machine. Adjustments are made to the schedule for the machine, using Capacity and Process Management, to rebalance the line and minimize the disruption to other orders. The third item remains a problem. The Extended Enterprise database notes that one of the firm's trading partners makes a similar vacuum bag for another customer. While this firm normally buys only raw material from this supplier, the database notes that the company has received several offers from the vendor in question in the past to provide this product. When contacted, the supplier notes that the item can be made, but there won't be enough time to ship it through normal channels if the shipping deadlines are to be honored. The decision is made to drop ship this item directly from the supplier. Adjustments to costs, profit on each order, shipping instructions, invoices and inventories are all made within the firm through the CAM-I SMP Model. The Extended Enterprise system sends information back through the supply chain to ensure that its partners are notified of the problem, are informed of the remedial action taken, and are aware of the impact this may have on short-term performance.

After the crisis is averted, management returns to the issue of the vacuum bag machine. Should it be replaced? Repairs have been estimated to be quite costly, and the machine is extremely worn. This doesn't necessarily mean, though, that the machine should be replaced—maybe the process needs to be amended, shifting the production of the two bags that can be easily made using existing idle capacity to the older machine and permanently outsourcing the production of the third to the supplier. Activity-Based Cost Management and Capacity Management are used to assess the financial and operational implications of this alternative. It would appear that changing the sourcing and OTP process is the optimal decision. Changes are made to the process maps, modifications in the integrated database are made to incorporate the changes, and new performance metrics are established both internally (for the two rerouted bags and the inventory management of the newly outsourced one) and externally for the affected trading partners. A "crisis" in the Process Domain has resulted in an unforeseen opportunity for performance improvement for the entire supply chain.

> This example simply illustrates the role integrated information plays in supporting ongoing decision-making. No one set of data or one SMP can answer the questions raised—four separate SMPs were required to complete the analysis and make downstream improvements in the affected process.

Before leaving the ongoing management of processes, one further comment needs to be made. While Asset Management and Target Cost Management play only a limited role in this bundle of decisions, they are constantly collecting and using the information generated by the other SMPs. This information is used to guide future decisions about what asset investments should be made and what process and performance constraints will shape future production. In addition, with the aid of Integrated Performance Management, data needed to evaluate the attainment of improvement goals for the firm's assets, products and processes is obtained. This feedback is the starting point in a new round of strategic, tactical and operational decisions driven by the incessant need to provide ever greater levels of value to customers.

Performance gap analysis, the final set of decisions examined in the Process Decision domain, emphasizes ongoing improvement efforts that are made outside the realm of daily operations. It is to this decision bundle that the discussion now turns.

Performance Gap Analysis

In formal logic, a contradiction is a signal of a defeat;
but in the evolution of real knowledge it marks
the first step in progress toward a victory.

– Alfred North Whitehead

If a process is meeting all of its defined performance requirements, including its continuous improvement goals, it seems a contradiction to suggest that it should be changed or abandoned. Yet, gaining a deeper knowledge of a process comes from constantly questioning it, from revisiting process design and sourcing issues when no problem exists. This ongoing decision analysis is a critical part of ensuring that quantum performance improvements continue to be made. It is, in the end, these quantum improvements that distance the firm from its competitors.

Process Management once again plays a dominant role in this free-standing, objective, ongoing examination of processes, products, activities and resources. It provides the integrating framework for improving existing processes (reengineering), implementing identified improvements, and providing transition plans and purposes for processes, people and physical assets potentially idled if outsourcing or abandonment is deemed necessary.

The use of Process Management, and the process thinking approach that underlies it, ensures that the entire system is the beneficiary of improvements, not individual areas or managers. Only through a process-based thinking approach can these decisions be logically linked to prior decisions and actions, current process realities, long-term strategic concerns, trading alliance performance, and the ongoing effort to meet customer requirements. Process Management is supported in the initiative to find and close performance gaps by the other SMPs (see Figure 14.6).

Figure 14.6   Performance Gap Management

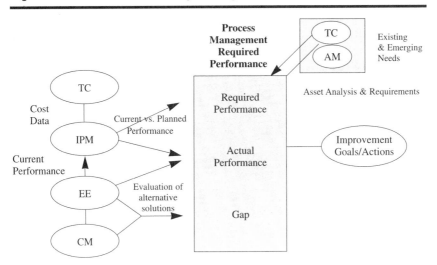

One of the key supporting SMPs in managing performance gaps within the Process Decision domain is Integrated Performance Management. This SMP provides information about current performance of the process and its key sub-process components. This data includes current demand levels, quality and reliability levels, throughput and cycle time, and delivery against requirements. It also identifies key constraints within the process and their impact on overall performance. This is the data needed by managers to prioritize their efforts, helping them choose among likely candidates for non-product driven improvement efforts.

Once an area has been chosen for gap management, Integrated

Performance Management aids in the creation of new metrics to evaluate and track planned improvements. Without a change in measurements, it is unlikely that required behavioral changes will occur. Measurement creates visibility for key performance requirements and reduces the ambiguity inherent in change management. Whether the change ends up impacting an internal process, or whether outsource vendors or alliance partners are affected, it is critical that clear, objective measurements be created to guide the change effort and downstream performance.

While IPM supports the identification of key opportunities for improvement, ABCM plays a strong supporting role. Detailing current and potential costs of the various processes, including the "hidden costs" of outsourcing, reengineering, or other gap management approaches, ABCM provides the economic perspective required to ensure that the organization gains improvements on financial metrics.

The concept "managing performance gaps" suggests an active search to reduce waste within the organization. While it should be a foregone conclusion that less waste will mean improved performance, the unfortunate fact of economic life is that many of a firm's costs are fixed, semi-fixed, or stepped-fixed in nature. Improvements in a process can lead to little or no economic improvement if idle capacity is the outcome of the effort. Fixed resources, once freed from a current use, must be redeployed if the firm is to increase its potential to create value for customers and profits for stakeholders. Without the insights coming from ABCM, improvements in operational performance could result in no real benefit for customers or the company.

ABCM also helps identify the potential impact of a proposed change on other areas of the process or firm. If a proposed re-engineering solution would actually increase the demand for support work in the logistics work area, and there is little or no available capacity in this area, it may not make sense to pursue it. ABCM helps management retain an entity perspective during improvement efforts, ensuring that costs are truly eliminated, not merely shifted from one area to another.

Both the Extended Enterprise and Capacity Management SMPs provide detailed inputs into Process Management as solutions to performance gaps are identified and explored for feasibility. The Extended Enterprise places its emphasis on current and potential outsource capabilities, trading alliance/customer requirements, and overall satisfaction with the quality, reliability, productivity, and outcomes of existing process solutions. Capacity Management, on the other hand, details the capability, current utilization, and availability of physical assets to meet redesigned process requirements as well as the impact/cost of asset abandonment decisions.

These primary SMPs do, at times, turn to Target Cost Management and Asset Management SMPs for information. TCM may be queried to identify emerging demand, as well as the key performance requirements for the process, given the entire range of product/service bundles it serves. It also links the process decisions back to earlier strategic analysis and Customer/Market decisions. TCM serves to link ongoing decision-making in the Process Domain to the past and future of the firm.

Asset Management, on the other hand, provides the basis for analyzing any new asset requirements for the redesigned process, or to shape the abandonment strategy for processes or sub-processes which are candidates for abandonment. Setting the requirements, or internal baseline improvement levels required to justify incremental spending on an existing process, Asset Management ensures that these issues are not lost in the journey to find operational improvements.

Taken in total, the decisions made within the Process Domain encompass the daily activities of the firm and its partners. Within the Process Domain, opportunities are seized, fires (problems) extinguished, incremental improvements identified and implemented, and ongoing management conducted. It is the primary arena of action, the domain of daily efforts, where the future is shaped by the successes, failures, and learnings of today.

Summary

The man who gets the most satisfactory results is not always the man with the most brilliant single mind, but rather the man who can best coordinate the brains and talents of his associates.

– W. Alton Jones

Without effective Customer/Market and Product strategies, the future is an accident of fate. Effective strategies, though, require effective execution to gain promised benefits. The Process Domain is where execution occurs, objectives are attained, and profits are earned or lost. If the Process Domain, and its key SMP, Process Management, were "humanized," they would meet Jones' description of the individual who achieves superior results through coordination, not competition.

In the preceding pages, the Process Decision domain, and its key decision bundles, have been explored. In each case, the SMPs have worked together to provide the information needed to identify and act upon strategic, tactical or operational opportunities. It is through integration that a balanced perspective is gained, and it is through integrated information, in the form of the CAM-I SMP model, that this perspective can be queried and transformed from insights into actions.

Four primary decision bundles were examined in this chapter: designing processes, sourcing strategies, ongoing Process Management, and the management of performance gaps. In all but the sourcing analysis, where the Extended Enterprise is emphasized, Process Management played the role of the dominant SMP. IPM and ABCM play critical rolls as the source of information on current financial and non-financial issues, the impact of new or redesigned process flows on the entity's performance, and the assessment of performance gains. They keep everyone's eyes focused on entity solutions by what they measure, report, and emphasize.

Capacity Management provides significant information to guide ongoing decisions within the Process Domain, helping to identify bottlenecks as they appear, tracking throughput, assessing potential solutions to throughput shortfalls, and tracking utilization of the asset base. The Extended Enterprise provides similar tracking information to Process Management, emphasizing external capabilities and issues. The requirements of trading partners can serve as Process constraints; the trading alliance can also be the source of performance solutions. Having information at hand to address internal and external capacity issues is highly desirable if the entity is to win.

TCM diminishes in importance in the Process Decision domain, serving primarily to set limits of performance and to ensure that operational decisions do not work at cross purposes with current and planned Customer/Market and Product strategies. In a related vein, Asset Management plays only a minimal role, providing baseline performance levels for any incremental Process asset purchase.

The CAM-I SMP Model provides the basis for the integration and coordination of information and perspectives necessary to knit the organization together horizontally and vertically—to eliminate performance gaps. As the decisions within the Process Domain suggest, this integration becomes ever more important as the time frame available for response and analysis shrinks. While a strategic analysis of a Customer / Market opportunity might have the luxury of creating reasonable cost and performance "proxies" for the actual costs and impact of the decision, there is little or no time at the Process level to fill information gaps. If information isn't available in the amount and type needed, intuition, experience, bias, and fate take over. It is difficult to believe that long-term performance goals can be reached if short-term decisions are made in a vacuum.

At the Process level, the answer to the burning question, "Why integrate the various SMPs and related tools?" is evident. It is here that managers have to be able to query strategic intent, explore system impacts, identify available resources, and estimate performance outcomes of daily decisions, made on the fly, with minimal preparation and until today, little guidance. The CAM-I SMP Model cannot make a good manager out of a poor one, or ensure good decisions, but it can assure that everyone is "singing from the same hymnal" by linking individuals and decisions through information. Only then can Jones' ideal manager be empowered to achieve superior performance through coordinated action. System solutions begin with a system perspective. It is this perspective the CAM-I SMP Model provides.

Endnotes

[1] Throughput is used in the sense of output that generates revenue. Reflecting the basic concepts in the Theory of Constraints (TOC) developed by Eli Goldratt, throughput is a concise way to capture the fact that processes are designed and built to create optimal value for customers, which should result in revenues and profits for the firm and its trading partners.

Chapter 5

Meeting Requirements

Issues and Integration of the Resource Decision Domain

People talk about the middle of the road as though it were unacceptable. Actually, all human problems, excepting morals, come into the gray areas. Things are not all black and white. There have to be compromises. The middle of the road is all of the usable surface. The extremes, right and left, are in the gutters.

– Dwight D. Eisenhower

Key Learnings:

■ The Resource Decision domain is where limits are placed on current actions, and where potential requirements of current and future Customer/Market/Management demands are addressed.

■ Decisions made within the Resource domain include: resource choice, sourcing policies/constraints, resource flexibility, and resource costs/performance vs. targets.

■ The Resource Decision domain is shaped by one driving concern: continuous improvement.

■ Information on current costs and performance, utilization and waste, opportunities for improvement and constraints are required to optimize performance within the Resource Decision domain.

The final Decision domain, where resources are procured and used to create value for customers, is intricately tied to every decision made in the organization. The Resource Decision domain is where limits are placed on current actions, and where potential requirements of current and future Customer/Market demands are addressed. Plans can be made, but without requisite resources they cannot be transformed into reality. Having the materials, people, machines, support services, and process capabilities needed to meet current throughput demands is not in question—these are required. At the Resource level, though, the wide variety of ways in which these needs can be met are explored, debated, and resolved. The Resource domain is the world of trade-off and compromise—the usable surface of organizational life.

Emphasizing the matching of resources (internal and external) to the demands of the organization and its stakeholders, the Resource Decision domain is dominated by ABCM and IPM. Both of these Strategic Management Processes (SMPs) provide detailed information on the impact of operations on the resources of the firm, the cost for changing this capability, and other core ongoing performance concerns. Value creation is maximized when the firm is able to ensure the optimal match between resources and the requirements of customers. Are materials of optimal quality? Are minimal amounts of resources consumed in nonvalue-added work? How can the firm best leverage its resources to meet customer needs? Are new sources of required goods and services needed? If so, what are the performance requirements for the new relationships? Can information be used as a substitute for inventory? These and related questions are addressed within the Resource Decision domain.

The decision bundles that comprise the Resource domain revolve around ongoing management concerns and the development of resource procurement/management policies that ensure that only those resources needed are obtained, and only when they are needed. At the Resource level, a company also becomes concerned with issues such as the storability, capacity, purchase package, shelf life, and other "resource life" issues that can affect the delivery of optimal value within desired profitability and performance parameters. Should the firm hold any inventory at all, or should it be held in "virtual space" within the Extended Enterprise? Key decision bundles within this domain include: (See Figure 15.1)

Figure 15.1   Resource Decision Groupings

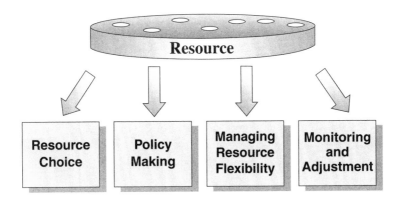

- *Resource choice:* What resources are needed? When? In what mix?

- *Sourcing policies/constraints:* What inventory policies are preferable for the Extended Enterprise? For less essential components and resources, how can inventories be minimized? What are the key investment policies for assets? R&D? Project planning? Should we outsource the activity and resource requirements, share them with trading partners, or should we own them?

- *Resource flexibility:* Which resources can be shared to minimize waste? Which must be dedicated? How well can we match requirements to the purchase/resource features (e.g., can we buy what we need when we need to, or do we have to obtain a large, fixed resource "chunk" regardless of need?).

- *Resource costs/performance vs. targets:* What is the cost of resources utilized? What are our core resources? Which resources serve as bottlenecks or process capability constraints? What are the costs to ease these problems?

Constantly examined, resource policies and choices are made during the entire life cycle of a product and the organization in which it is carried out.

Poor decisions at the Resource level negatively impact both short- and long-term performance. If a fixed asset is purchased that ends up not being fully deployed, the waste the permanently idle capacity represents will reduce profits and performance for as long as the asset is owned. Capacity Management and Activity-Based Cost Management help a company avoid building permanent layers of waste into their cost structures by providing information to analyze, and question, long-term systemic impacts of resource purchases before the money is spent.

As the following pages will detail, at no level in the organization is the need for the information embedded in the CAM-I SMP model so pervasive. Information on current costs and performance, utilization and waste, opportunities for improvement and constraints are just a few of the details needed to optimize performance within the Resource Decision domain. Examination of each unique decision bundle is the best way to illustrate these information needs.

Resource Choice
An old error is always more popular than a new truth.
– German Proverb

In the Resource domain, the choice of resources has been traditionally guided by concerns for the cost and productivity of *individual* materials, machines, or people. Following the "old error" or belief that the entire system would be optimized if each of its parts were pushed to their limits, resources were not examined in light of their impact on other resources or overall system performance. The result was that the system as a whole performed sub-optimally. It would seem that old errors were limiting the future of the organization.

The problems with this "old" approach to management have been detailed in such seminal works as *The Goal* by Eli Goldratt, *Lean Thinking* by Womack and Jones, and Senge's *Fifth Discipline*, to name just a few. Process Management is a completely new management model built from this recognition that "old errors" were creating miscommunication, fumbles, and error in organizations. In fact, the adoption of systemic, Extended Enterprise solutions by an increasing number of top organizations suggests that the old errors may finally stop shaping the actions of tomorrow.

In the Resource domain, the shift from traditional, reductionist approaches in management to systemic, flow-driven models has changed the nature of resource choice and the criterion used to guide it. Assessed as part of an overall system of value creation, a resource that is not the "cheapest" or "most efficient" may be the best choice for a company. Unless the resource is a process bottleneck, its efficiency takes a back seat to its effectiveness. A cheap resource may be no choice at all, especially if it has a negative impact on the value embedded in the product/service bundle.

Given this setting, what are the issues guiding resource choice in modern organizations? First and foremost, earlier decisions regarding what products, market/customer segments, and processes will be used to execute the firm's overall strategy and set the boundaries around the resource options that can be considered. The acquired resources must be able to meet the quality, reliability, availability, capability and cost requirements established by Target Cost Management, and by extension, the customer.

Resource choice provides a visible linkage of SMPs through the various Decision domains (see Figure 15.2). For instance, TCM defines the performance features of the resources, information which is passed from the Customer/Market domain down through to the Resource

Figure 15.2   Resource Choice and SMP Influence

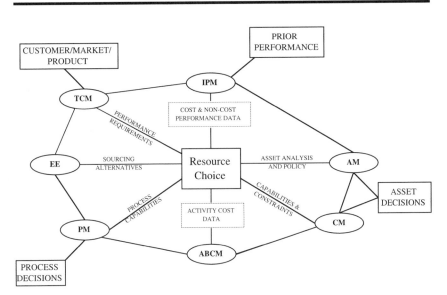

Decision domain directly as well as through its linkages with the Extended Enterprise and Process Management. These two pivotal policy-forming SMPs transform the resource requirements identified by TCM into detailed specifications.

Resource choice, once made, becomes a potential "old error." For this reason, if for no other, this decision must be constantly reviewed in the light of new opportunities, new processes, new technologies, and shifts in customer expectations. Iterative in nature, resource choice is a decision that is seldom set in stone. Even within the Extended Enterprise, there are situations that arise which lead to a need to change the source of a material or service. Sourcing decisions, once made, become the benchmark solution for down-stream opportunities to improve performance, value creation, or profits.

Resource choice is a process of continuous improvement that keeps the organization poised to respond to new demands and optimize the ability to meet existing requirements. It is a collaborative effort, spanning functions and Decision domains. Requiring pooled, integrated, consistent information to achieve its goals, resource choice within the Resource Decision domain is one of the best illustrations of the power, and need for, the integrated CAM-I SMP model. Resource choice defines the constraints and sets the boundaries on policies for the foreseeable future. It is to these decisions that the discussion now turns.

Developing Sourcing Policies and Constraints

To understand a matter properly, a man must dominate it,
instead of allowing it to dominate him.

– Ernest Hello

Sourcing policies provide a way to guide ongoing decisions by managers residing in diverse, and often distant, parts of the organization to ensure that company performance objectives are met. A policy helps stabilize the system, as common rules, decision criteria, and assessment methods are created and applied. A policy can also serve as a constraint on the options considered during resource choice. There are, in fact, some management experts who argue that the majority of the constraints on an organization's performance come, not from physical resources, but from the policies that embed assumptions about the "one best way" to manage.

Many of the policies developed with regard to resources do not have their origin in any of the SMPs. They are, instead, the result of inventory management methods, such as Economic Order Quantity (EOQ), Materials Resource Planning (MPR), or Just-In-Time approaches (JIT). Material resource policies are dominated by these, or similar, operational decision models. On the human side of the equation, policies often emanate from either general management or human resources. Of course, the government also has a hand in setting the constraints on labor as a resource. The majority of the other physical and intangible assets policies are influenced by management, financial accounting, or operations-based decisions and models.

In other words, the constraints that the SMPs are dealing with in the Resource domain are often set by outside forces. Once set, the defined policies shape the reality of individual managers, making certain events and outcomes obvious and actionable, and others invisible and/or unquestioned. Policies serve as assumptions, which while necessary to stabilize organizational action and ongoing decision-making, can also serve to blind an organization to obvious problems or solutions. One of the primary roles of the CAM-I SMP Model is to support the analysis that leads to policies, but also to provide ongoing signals and information about the impact of policies (good and bad) and the potential for improvements in this area.

The utilization of the Process Management SMP in combination with IPM and ABCM, forms the basis for analyzing the impact of existing policies on the value chain (see Figure 15.3). When problems

Figure 15.3   SMPs and Organizational Policy-making

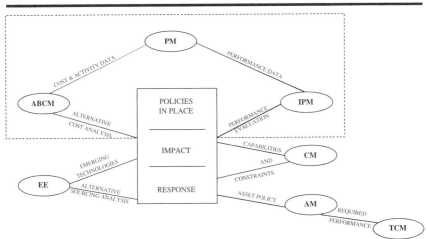

arise, these three SMPs also combine to provide management with the information needed to find solutions or develop new methods and policies. Linked most closely to current events within core value creating activities and processes, these three SMPs link information on financial, non-financial, and value chain performance into a real-time tracking and warning system for the firm.

Process Management plays a pivotal role in the SMP "triumvirate" in the policy arena. It organizes the information on policies and constraints in keeping with the structure of activities and the outcomes they affect. Since Process Management is in essence the embodiment of the value-creation process, it provides the means to place policies in context. The benefits obtained by taking a process view of policies is that the potential interdependencies and unforeseen consequences of policies in one area of the organization or process can be spotted when the systemic view integral to Process Management is deployed. Process Management provides key information about the range of options and issues that define, and result from, resource management policies.

Policies are clearly not only established and deployed at the Resource domain level, but spread across the entire spectrum of activities, decisions, and product service bundles the firm engages in. At the Resource Decision domain level, though, these policies are less questioned and more likely to create undesirable consequences because the individuals who know the policies best may have little knowledge of why they exist at all. Anyone who has heard the comment "we've always done it this way," has come in personal contact with the core problems presented by policies set within the Resource domain—they are seen as less actionable and more or less in stone.

The linkage of the SMPs into an integrated information model can help overcome some of the inherent risks of policies at the Resource level. Specifically, the Extended Enterprise can be relied upon to identify new opportunities and track emerging models and technologies that can pinpoint the impact of resource level constraints or ways to alleviate these performance inhibitors. Integrated Performance Management, tied to benchmarking and the gathering of external trend information, can identify problems before they create dissatisfactions among customers and identify key changes in the market place. It can also provide the stimulus to look for ways to improve resource utilization by providing objective, comparative standards for resources used per unit of work completed.

Ongoing ABCM, linked with Process Management, constantly examines the flow of resources through the firm and can help find ways to better leverage these short- and long-term investments of the firm's value-creating ability. The primary source of non-machine cost and capacity data, ABCM can help find areas where small reductions in volume or demand can have a significant reduction in costs due to the presence of high cost, low utilization, stepped-fixed costs. Process Management puts these potential improvements into perspective as a systemic occurrence.

As the time frame of analysis expands, Asset Management and Target Cost Management enter the Resource policy arena. Asset Management is a primary policy-setting source, defining required returns per dollar of invested funds, required improvements and documentation, the time frame over which returns must be earned, and related issues. Affecting policies regarding capital asset acquisition and management, Asset Management separates resources into those to be owned, those to be shared, those to be leased, and those to be "borrowed" (outsourced). Given the number of long-term constraints created by the acquisition of capital assets, it is important that these decisions be made within the boundaries of the strategic plan. Asset Management, taking its signals from Target Cost Management, ensures this is the case.

Having established the constraints, attention turns to incorporating key policies and process concerns, including Extended Enterprise initiatives and inventory policies. Perhaps the decision has been made that minimal inventories will be maintained (a Just-In-Time inventory system, for instance) and that preferred vendors will be relied upon to ensure incoming quality and reliability. These policies further constrain resource choice, but in so doing increase the potential for optimal performance of the entire supply chain. Whenever the Extended Enterprise is brought into the sourcing arena, information replaces inventory as the dominant resource linking together the firms in the trading alliance.

As specifications become more and more detailed, these pivotal "resource choice" SMPs draw more and more heavily on the information provided by Capacity Management, Integrated Performance Management and Activity-Based Cost Management to identify cost and performance issues and opportunities. Using an example, there may be a resource requirement such as a generic fastener, that the firm has decided to outsource as a noncore material based on analysis within the Process Management and the Extended Enterprise SMPs. Capacity Management is used to pinpoint what elements of the process were not capable of handling the new demand, while Asset Management gives early signals that gaining the required level of performance for this noncore activity would be too costly, negating any potential for internal sourcing of the production.

With outsourcing being the only realistic way to meet the performance requirements identified by Target Cost Management for this material, Resource domain managers turn to cost and performance information contained in Integrated Performance Management and Activity-Based Cost Management to find an acceptable list of suppliers. The choice of supplier is not a direct concern of the Extended Enterprise because of the noncore nature of the affected resource. Process impacts are also indirect, suggesting that the vendor will be chosen based on price and ability to meet defined delivery, quality, and reliability metrics.

Target Cost Management provides the basis for organizing and prioritizing resource choices into those that require the coordinated attention of the Extended Enterprise and Process Management as well as the detailed input of Capacity Management, Integrated Performance Management and Activity-based Cost Management SMPs. Asset Management serves as a delimiter on investment as an option to resource choice efforts. If internal capacity does not exist, or it is incapable of meeting defined performance requirements, then the source/outsource decision becomes an investment issue. The number and amount of resources that a firm can, or should, take on as a fixed part of its cost structure is limited. This fact has never been truer, as product life cycles shrink, technology changes accelerate obsolescence curves, and customer and competitive trends shift at ever faster speeds. Flexibility and responsiveness are the key to success in this fast-paced environment of constant change. Fixed assets limit an organization's performance on these two key dimensions. Asset Management, then, increasingly serves as the "stop-go" light on resource choice, not because of economic concerns, but strategic ones.

For core competencies or critical resources, the decisions made within the Extended Enterprise and Process Management SMPs have a much more direct impact on resource choice. Price takes a back seat to responsiveness, reliability, and effectiveness in the choice to produce or choose an alliance partner. ABCM provides information on the activities within the process and the current projected overall cost, which is constrained by Target Cost Management, but a low cost solution is not the only goal. Cost and inventory is taken out of the system by better managing relationships, reducing unnecessary efforts, and streamlining the flow of materials and services through the value chain—by improving performance through the effective leveraging of information.

The message being conveyed here is quite straightforward. Every policy set within an organization will stabilize and standardize decisions and actions. This is both the benefit, and challenge, of setting policies. Integrated information systems, such as the CAM-I SMP Model, can help build in early warning signals of emerging policy-driven problems because it provides a full view of the system and the multiple areas where these policies can impact current and future performance. If information is fragmented, policies can be set and followed that reduce effectiveness and rob the firm of needed profits and performance improvements.

Putting the "Flex" in Resources

The art of progress is to preserve order amid change
and to preserve change amid order.
– Alfred North Whitehead

Understanding resource flexibility, current performance and utilization levels, and assessing the organization's ability to meet changing needs with existing resources are just a few of the issues that define a "nimble" and responsive entity. Ongoing adjustments to processes and the resources they consume is the essence of the continuous improvement philosophy, a theory that has been credited with many of the turnarounds in performance by Western companies in the last fifteen years. Identifying, then either eliminating or redeploying wasted time and resources, is the heart of continuous improvement. These changes are all part of the effort to put "flex" in the resources at the firm's command.

One of the major challenges faced by managers making decisions within the Resource domain is the high level of interdependent, or shared, resources that make up the cost structure of the firm. Balancing competing demands for these shared resources makes it clear that the more flexibility and responsiveness that can be built into, or acquired, in the resource base, the better. When resources must be purchased in major "chunks" of fairly inflexible capacity, yet are integral to one or more core competencies, then it becomes imperative to ensure that whatever capacity is purchased is actively managed. Full disclosure of idle capacity and its cost is part of the information, and visibility, provided by the CAM-I SMP Model. Resource utilization must be optimized, and can only be accomplished by creating "flexibility" in the resource base.

ABCM plays the major role in supporting decisions that assess and manage resource flexibility (see Figure 15.4). Integrated Performance Management and Capacity Management link directly to ABCM, creating a database of current resource utilization and the potential for, and benefits of, improvements in this area. Feeding directly into Process Management, this database supports the constant search for new uses for idle resources, improved flexibility in existing processes and resource requirements, and enhanced understanding of the interplay between resource trade-offs and process performance. The opportunities for improvement are identified through the three "feeder" SMPs (ABCM, IPM and CM), but they are assessed, chosen, and executed through Process Management.

Figure 15.4   Using SMPs in Managing Resource Flexibility

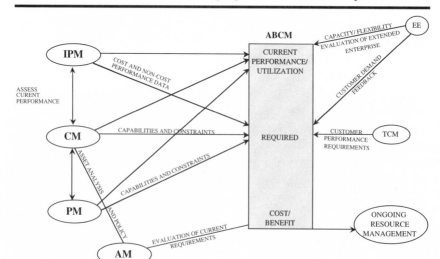

Unexpected shifts in demand, signaled by the Extended Enterprise and Target Cost Management, impact the Process Management SMP, where they are once again addressed through the integrated data warehouse of the three core Resource domain SMPs. As the search for flexible, available capacity in both human and physical resources is undertaken, Integrated Performance Management provides estimates of process performance impacts of potential solutions. The feasibility of proposed solutions to shifts in demand and their resource implications are also queried as the combined force of ABCM, Integrated Performance Management and Capacity Management are brought to bear.

The Extended Enterprise SMP is called upon to do more than monitor and report changes in the environment that may require enhanced flexibility or utilization of resources. It also provides detailed information on available capacity and services within the trading alliance. As surge capacity becomes necessary, the Extended Enterprise identifies areas outside the firm where these needs can be met. Since the entire trading alliance benefits as overall responsiveness is increased, with minimal incremental resource requirements, it is logical to turn to trading partners when resource constraints put incremental or new business in peril.

Putting the "flex" in resources is a key objective of the Resource Decision domain. Guided by the customer and market, these decisions are made every day, in every corner of the organization, with or without integrated information. What the CAM-I SMP Model brings to this class of common decisions is a consistent, systemic framework for making choices that ensures that performance truly is improved by these efforts. Keeping everyone's eyes on improving the amount of value created by the Extended Enterprise per dollar of consumed or invested resource is a benefit of SMP integration that is not available to a firm with a fragmented decision support system. Improvement of a balanced system of shared resources, attained by increasing their utilization and flexibility, cannot move forward without a comprehensive, coordinated, consistent, and responsive information system.

Monitoring and Adjusting Performance

Innovation is the new conservatism.

– Peter Drucker

Meeting the needs of customers and trading partners is one of the driving concerns regarding decisions made within the organization. Without reducing the importance of the external perspective, it is imperative that the demands of internal stakeholders (owners and employees) be addressed by any integrated information system used in decision support. The final bundle of decisions examined with the Resource domain emphasizes the tracking of performance against target cost, profitability, and asset management objectives established during the planning process. When most individuals think about management reporting and its supporting database, it is this bundle of decisions that come to mind.

ABCM and Integrated Performance Management are the two SMPs central to ongoing reporting and analysis of results. Fed objectives by Target Cost Management, Asset Management, and Process Management, and facilitated by ongoing reports and data provided by the Extended Enterprise and Capacity Management, ABCM and IPM combine forces to structure the available data into usable, actionable management reports (see Figure 15.5).

Figure 15.5   Management Reporting: A SMP Perspective

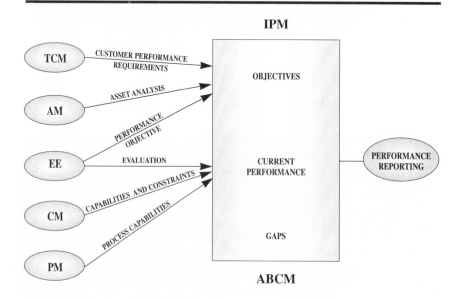

In constant risk of falling victim to the adage that "reports can make management happy or sad, but not smarter," the reporting process supported by the CAM-I SMP Model has to be constantly seeking out and detailing improvement trends and opportunities to enhance them. Current performance against goals is interesting, and vital information, but unless it enables improvement, this information is little more than a scorecard that, by definition, will be too late to change current results. Only in supporting learning does management reporting move from the realm of "bureaucracy feeding" to a "value-added activity" essential to increasing the amount of value created for customers and other key stakeholders.

To effectively guide future decisions made across the various domains (Customer/Market, Product, and Process), the Resource-based management reporting system must meet the following requirements:

- Incorporate all defined goals and targets in a meaningful way;
- Integrate the wide variety of available information using consistent definitions and treatment of key terms, metrics, and results;
- Support real time, on demand reporting and analysis capabilities;
- Provide "query" capability that will allow further analysis of key details and results;
- Support sensitivity analysis and simulation to project the impact of current trends;
- Use common language understandable by all areas of the business;
- Provide a balanced set of metrics to ensure that interdependence and systemic issues remain visible to users;
- Present information in ways that highlight improvement initiatives and their results, as well as identifying areas where trends suggest that new advances are needed or possible; and

- Use a maximum amount of graphics to portray information to ease in comparing results against objectives.

Informative, consistent, accurate, stable reports and estimates are basic requirements for any management reporting system. The CAM-I SMP Model can deliver on these requirements much more easily and effectively than other approaches. Integration is built into the development of the objectives, downstream metrics, management philosophy, and decision criteria from the initial design and development of a Customer/Market strategy through its execution and abandonment. The CAM-I SMP model does not force integration after the fact; it is the essence of the system, its reason for existence.

Looking further into Figure 15.5, the role played by each of the supporting SMPs to the ABCM and Integrated Performance Management reporting infrastructure is seen. The interrelationships begin with Target Cost Management, which sets the overall profit and performance limits for the product/service bundle that drives the rest of the assessment and adjustment process. Reflected in the Extended Enterprise and Process Management SMPs, the driving concern for optimizing the creation of value for customers is woven into the structure and functioning of the SMP model, from the very beginning in the development of performance objectives and the ongoing efforts to reach them.

The Extended Enterprise within this framework provides inputs to ABCM and Integrated Performance Management on vendor/partner agreements, issues raised by nonconformance to agreements or changes in requirements, and current performance levels. Process Management is the source for this information for internally-sourced products, services, activities and components. What objectives have been set for internal processes, and how well they are being met, are just two of the data elements provided by Process Management.

Asset Management is more of a recipient of the ABCM and Integrated Performance Management information flow than a direct contributor to it. The performance limits for invested funds are clearly part of the management reporting package, as is current performance against these expectations, but the heart of the analysis and management control process that comprise an effective asset management system flow out directly from Asset Management.

Clearly, the logical integration of the ABCM, Integrated Performance Management and Asset Management SMPs can ensure that consistent signals are given by these two systems, and that top management reports provide the same insights and information as those used by individuals in other parts of the organization. A firm that maximizes Economic Value-Added (an investment management metric), for instance, without paying close attention to the requirements of customers, markets, trading partners, and company employees, may show strong short-term performance, but at the peril of the long-term health of the enterprise. Balanced perspectives and measurements, such as that emerging from the CAM-I SMP Model, ensure that all stakeholders' needs are met within the constraints of the business and economic environment faced by the organization.

The reporting provided by the ABCM and Integrated Performance Management infrastructure must be available in real-time, on an "on demand" basis. This final requirement is perhaps the driving force behind the movement to integrate the information systems within an organization. Consistent, reliable information, available when needed, is the key to improving the quality and effectiveness of decision making in an organization. Managers can't afford to wait for some distant individual to find time to gather requested data, nor can they comfortably assume that the provided data really addresses the issue under consideration.

This is not a new insight. In fact, good managers have developed and maintained their own databases and information sources for as long as researchers have thought to ask them about the activity—perhaps even before they knew enough to ask. What is different when an integrated information system, such as the CAM-I SMP Model, is deployed is that private sources of information are no longer needed. Managers help define what is measured and why, and can then access information on current results and potential problems, as needed.

The benefits obtained from integration, though, go far beyond making it easier for managers to do their jobs well—it ensures they keep the entire organization's performance in mind as they make decisions and take actions. Linking the organization together from top-to-bottom and side-to-side, the SMP model bridges the gaps that lead to miscommunication, performance shortfalls, and competitive problems. Serving to put the "we" back in organizational life, integration helps undo much of the damage caused by the organizational growth, increasing market pressures, and time. Achieving integration is a journey worth the effort, providing the basis for sustainable, controlled, innovation and performance.

Summary

*It is a lucky means to an end which
gets within hailing distance of the end.*
– Henry S. Haskins

The Resource Decision domain is shaped by one driving concern: continuous improvement. While all Decision domains and SMPs emphasize this philosophy, it is at the resource level that the changes are identified and carried out. Whether focused on the original choice of resources, establishing sourcing policies and constraints, improving resource flexibility, or feeding ongoing management reporting and analysis needs, the Resource domain is where change is translated from concept to concrete fact.

As the preceding discussion has suggested, the Resource domain is dominated by the Activity-Based Cost Management and Integrated Performance Management SMPs. Process Management serves as a primary linkage between Customer/Market and Product decisions and resource sourcing and policy-setting, but with the ongoing support of the ABCM and Integrated Performance Management infrastructure. The Resource domain, it seems, is the natural home for the detailed data and integration logic embedded in the CAM-I SMP Model that enables strategic and tactical decision-making and ensures the attainment of goals through effective process- and resource-level execution.

The Resource Decision domain is also the source of the key constraints that must be incorporated in any decision made within the organization. A good plan that is not backed by the resources needed to make it happen is, in reality, no plan at all. It is this simple fact that underscores that integration of information is not an option for a firm—it is the first essential step in increasing the effectiveness of its decisions, and by extension, its ability to create value for customers. In the end, it is the effective deployment of resources that creates value for all stakeholders. Ensuring that decisions made in this last, but hardly least, domain reflect the strategy, vision, and objectives of the organization is the key to creating its future.

Chapter 16

CASE CORPORATION

*Target Cost Management — Spanning
the Market/Product Domain*

Case Study

On November 12, 1999, Case Corporation merged with New Holland N.V. to form CNH Global N.V. CNH is a leading worldwide designer, manufacturer and distributor of agricultural and construction equipment and offers a broad array of financial products and services. This case study addresses actions taken by Case Corporation in the mid 1990's to deliver maximum customer value by transforming its product development and delivery processes.

Following a significant restructuring program that began in 1993, Case management recognized the need to create innovative new products and revitalize its product line in order to achieve its mission statement of "leading the industry by providing their agricultural and construction equipment customers around the world with superior products and services that maximized their productivity and success".

The effort to regain its position in the market led Case to a new product development process, Case Integrated Product Development, or CIPD.[1] The new CIPD process changed product development to:

1. A more structured and disciplined approach that introduced cross-functional teams with well-defined roles for each member. The cross-functional platform team had complete responsibility for the product and profitability.

2. Involve Marketing throughout the development process, not just in the review process. Marketing played a greater role in defining the product. For the first time, the voice of the customer, through Quality Functional Deployment or QFD, was employed in the development process.

3. Involve Manufacturing throughout the development process. A new role, Advanced Manufacturing and Quality Engineering, was created to integrate manufacturing engineering with the platform teams and create a simultaneous decision-making environment. Prototypes were developed on production tooling, and the learning process was extended to the shop floor.

By emphasizing new products that create maximum value for customers, Case has effectively deployed its CIPD system to bridge the gap between markets and customers. One result of this process is the MX Magnum[2] tractor line, an agricultural tractor that is superior to competitive offerings on almost every feature. These results were achieved within product cost, investment and timing objectives— setting new company standards for developing and launching new products.

QFD – DESIGN AND DEVELOPMENT

The company initiative to create a new tractor product line began in 1993. Employees relied on customer focus groups to gather information on what features and attributes the new tractor should have, and made direct contact with over 1200 participants from 9 countries and 5 continents. This focus group effort resulted in the definition of over 20 product requirements that customers felt strongly should be part of the redesigned tractor line.

The groups further identified over 100 ways in which these needs could be met. Some of the requirements customers asked for included:

- Enhanced visibility;
- Enhanced comfort;
- Enhanced controls;
- Improved efficiency/performance;
- More dealer installed options;
- Improved serviceability and repairability; and
- Reduced complexity.

The result of the design and development effort was a state-of-the-art tractor design that provides far greater value to Case's customers than any competitive offering. Creating a vehicle to replace the traditional units, the MX Magnum series represents a major breakthrough in both the approach to product design and the criteria used to evaluate the success of a product launch. Driven by customer requirements, the MX Magnum Development Team did not look to competitors for learning. Instead, the design process was built around defined customer needs translated into specific product features through QFD.

Recognizing that the definition of quality for a farming system was now based on the customer's experience with other products (e.g. trucks, automobiles), Case designed its new MX Magnum tractor product line with the characteristics of on-highway vehicles. Sound systems, controls, air-conditioning, and ergonomically designed seating compartments were just a few of the ways that Case developers built the new "voice of the customer" into their products. Management expressed its drive to find the best design in the following way:

> The key is to have the best design possible. Iterate the design process as long as you can, because once you lock it in, you pay dearly to correct or change the design. When the design is still electronic, that's when 90% of the cost is committed. Once you commit to the hardware, your costs escalate exponentially.

QFD provided the basis for creating the new product line to ensure that customer requirements were met, but it was clear that cost and profit constraints needed to become an integral part of the design effort if all stakeholders were to be served.

TARGET COST MANAGEMENT

As the new CIPD program was being rolled out, management also looked for ways to ensure that the products would meet required return-on-investment targets. To ensure that the lessons learned from the customers during QFD were not lost, management looked for ways to measure value delivered as well as costs consumed. The common denominator became Target Cost Management.

Customer value was measured in terms of savings per day from reduced maintenance time, increased efficiency, and improved run times. A benchmark of $20 per hour for farm workers was used to place a value on the enhanced capability of the MX Magnum tractor line.

On the cost side, it was clear that traditional techniques wouldn't work because they emphasized cost-plus approaches rather than value-driven design and cost control. The design process had to be managed to ensure maximum value per dollar spent by the customer. Target Cost Management, which was integrated into the CIPD process, became the key to bridging the gap between customer requirements and product design.

A cross-functional management team led by Ross Thomson, Manager of Strategic Cost Development, began to work with the MX Magnum Platform Team early in 1997 to identify the gap between the CIPD process and the CAM-I Target Cost Management process. This work was the outgrowth of a white paper that explained the principles of Target Cost Management, identified some core tools available to Case and included charts and graphs crucial to understanding the process. The gap analysis was initiated by developing a MX Magnum Interactive Flow Diagram and comparing it to Arthur Andersen's global best practices provided by CAM-I. It became obvious how late Case was in the process of developing DFM, DFA, cost estimations and cost roll-ups, and that an effective VE/VA process was also lacking.

Using the enhanced CIPD system, Case designed the MX Magnum tractor line in 33 months at a delivered cost at launch within one-half of one percent of the original target. Representing a milestone in company history, CIPD provided a system for design and development that aligned the program (Customer/Market Decision domain with the Product/Services Decision domain), and reduced the initial 6 percent cost overrun to the one-half percent.

The structure of the CIPD program began with the customer-based QFD initiative. Once this basic information was collected, cross-functional design teams were created. Following a recommended project planning and scheduling format detailed by the master plan, teams were empowered to complete their assigned tasks. Performance against goals was reviewed weekly so that any setbacks could be quickly detected and addressed. Some of the development tools used to support the design teams in reaching their goals included:

- Task orientation;
- Ergonomics analysis;

- Robustness;
- Repair index;
- Benchmarking;
- Customer evaluations;
- Reliability;
- DFM/DFA software applications;
- Early costing capabilities; and
- Direct platform team communications.

For instance, the interior of the MX Magnum tractor cab was designed using the results of several extensive ergonomic studies. In total, thirty operators were studied for their ease and comfort with regard to fourteen key cab attributes, including: seat adjustment, seat controls, cushion shape, throttle location, gear shift function, and the pillar display unit's visibility, content, color and organization. Customer evaluations were used to ensure that the results met their expectations.

Within the CIPD system, the concept of a customer was expanded to include intermediate customers of the design effort, including manufacturing, management, suppliers, and support engineering. This served to integrate the process from design to production, to gather information and insight from across the supply chain, and to provide progress and controls to management. The resulting overall CIPD process ensures that all stakeholders, whether final customers or the supply partners that support the manufacturing plant, are informed of and considered in major design decisions.

Throughout the CIPD initiative for the MX Magnum tractor line, the teams relentlessly attacked mistakes and omissions that had resulted in development and execution problems in the past. Where the firm had designed for cost before, it was now seeking to deliver optimal value. That translated into minimizing errors, rework, non-value-added activities, and any other form of cost that did not directly benefit the customer. As noted by Ken Moehle, the MX Magnum Project Manager, *"I was told four years ago that I would know when I had successfully made the journey... it was when all my surprises came at the beginning of a project rather than at the end."* The goal was to find errors before they reached production, to design out unneeded complexity, and to design in every possible ounce of value. Ken also noted, *"You don't want to be below your target cost any more than you want to be above it. You should constantly be bumping up against it so that you drive as much value into the product as you can."*

The list of industry leading attributes of the MX Magnum tractor line include the following:

- Industry leading transmission reliability;

- Leading fuel economy of engine, with up to 7% improvement over earlier products;

- Leading total glass area for improved visibility, with over 68.7 square feet of glass;

- Leading cab interior volume;

- Leading power shuttle shift, controlled from a conveniently located lever on the left of the steering wheel;

- Leading seat comfort;

- Leading hitch lift capacity, with up to 16,000 pounds lift capacity due to improved power distribution over the load;

- "Best in class" maintainability;

- 30% reduction in total parts;

- Assembly labor hours reduced 15%;

- Program investment at 97.5% of target and product cost at 100.5% of target; and

- Rankings of "best in class" for 57 of 65 total attributes studied.

The Target Cost Management process has led to an impressive set of gains for Case, all achieved within the cost parameters of the original product proposal.

THE ROLE OF COST

The CIPD system represented a major innovation in Case's design process. By listening to customers, product designers focused on maximizing the value created with the new product line. Yet, it was not enough to design for customer delight—the company needed to make a profit by serving customers better. To gain financial insights, management turned to Target Cost Management for several reasons. In fact, all firms benchmarked for excellence in product design and development used Target Cost Management as one of their core tools. For Case, Target Cost Management became a process for managing the tension between quality, functionality and cost—to drive optimal value into the MX Magnum tractor given customer-defined price constraints. It helped employees put design decisions into context and prioritize improvements. It kept the project on track and ensured that resources were directed where needed so that all of the teams working on various elements of the tractor "came up to the water line together."

Ross Thomson described the use of Target Cost Management as follows: *"Product costs are derivatives of the design, the material and the manufacturing process. I don't believe you can manage costs: you have to manage the drivers of cost. The companies that can roll cost up the earliest in the development process, will maximize the performance of their product development teams."* The key is to use Target Cost Management to identify, and then manage the drivers of cost. One senior manager summed up the lessons learned this way:

> You are not going to stop the engineer from trying to design every widget into the product… that's how a design engineer thinks. But you can never lose sight of the cost objective here…that's to provide maximum value to the customer based on what the customer wants, not what technology is available. A simple solution may be best. Balancing value with the creative processes is our ongoing challenge.

To increase the speed at which the Target Cost Management-based data became available to the platform design teams, Case purchased off-the-shelf cost table capability. The SEER-DFM module provided software that included cost knowledge where no such detail existed. Decisions regarding outsourcing relied heavily on the cost tables, which provided the design team with information that could be used to assess the validity of a supplier's quote. Value Engineering concepts were expanded within the platform teams through cooperative, hands-on design engineering and supplier based workshops. These workshops effectively used information from the SEER-DFM software to focus on the cost of the product's subsystems with the aim of achieving the required functional purpose without any deterioration in quality and/or reliability.

Another important insight was the discovery that maintaining a part number cost the company over $20,000. Adding this cost "penalty" to the cost tables used by the design engineers motivated them to reduce the number of unique parts, substituting common parts or integrated modular components to reduce complexity and cost of the product's materials. The development teams were also aided by the Boothroyd-Dewhurst DFA/DFM software system, along with robust design techniques to drive down part count and reduce process complexity.

SEER is also seen as a means to improve the coordination and communication of management efforts, providing a common cost definition. A third use of the cost tables is to complete ongoing make-versus-buy decisions. As noted by Ross Thomson, *"We're creating knowledge to support supplier assessments. It's the next major frontier as we implement the Target Cost Management model. When it gets down to determining costs, we must know the capacity and capability of potential suppliers to understand and evaluate their bids."*

PROJECTIONS FOR THE FUTURE

As with all SMP implementations, Case is undertaking a journey that makes a quantum leap in ensuring its financial success, but will likely have no final destination. As noted by the management team, there are many future challenges:

- Reinforcing within the management team that the CIPD/Target Cost Management process will be used;
- Making the organization aware of the core tools and ensuring that they are used consistently;
- Developing Target Cost Management diagnostics to expand proficiency across all Target Cost Management activities;
- Keeping the teams moving forward in sync.;
- Standardizing the design and development processes;
- Integrating all internal systems, whether manufacturing or design, to ensure that everyone has the same data and tools available;
- Communicating constantly to reduce communication barriers and to improve the reliability and consistency in databases and reports;
- Building an artificial intelligence database and maintaining/loading it to get cost standards;

- Developing "projective costing" to support products that are not due to launch for several years out, so that design teams have accurate estimates of future actual costs in their decision analysis; and

- Transforming CIPD into more of a control process, working with suppliers and the design team over the entire life of the product.

Case management has made major strides in linking Customer/Market strategies and Product design efforts through the use of Target Cost Management. By understanding and managing the drivers of cost, Target Cost Management is supporting efforts to the value delivered to customers by Case products. Noting that "prevention is far better than reaction," the Case Management Team knows that its CIPD/Target Cost Management effort is the key to creating a sustainable competitive position based on customer-driven innovation and product design.

Endnotes

[1] Many of the details regarding the QFD and CIPD processes during the MX Magnum development are drawn from the article, "MX Magnum Tractor: A Customer Driven Process," by K. Moehle of Case Corporation, Society of Automotive Engineers, 1997.

[2] Magnum is a trademark of Case Corporation.

17

CITY OF INDIANAPOLIS

Case Study

I'm most proud of the fact that we're doing more with less.
We have our taxpayers' money invested in the most vital services,
and we're creating a competitive city that's booming
even in the face of declining federal support.

– Mike Carter [1]
Div. Asst. Admin. for Finance

There are any number of case studies and success stories from Activity-Based Cost Management (ABCM) implementation in manufacturing and service industries, but the aggressive use of this tool in government is still a novelty. As the opening quotation suggests, though, the City of Indianapolis is directly benefiting from the implementation of ABCM and its related core Strategic Management Processes (SMPs). These efforts are focused on improving resource utilization and improving the quality of services provided to taxpayers. The results to date are impressive, as the following discussion suggests. This case study, then, details the experiences of the City to date, as well as lessons learned and benefits gained from the SMP-driven improvement initiatives.

THE CHALLENGE

The City of Indianapolis has a population of over 800,000. Most famous for the Indy 500 races, this medium-size city has been faced with the same challenges as all cities in the United States—declining city services in the face of rising costs. While the total number of employees of the City is relative small at roughly 300-400 people, the diversity of work they perform for the citizens of Indianapolis is significant. In all there are 27 unique departments or functions that are performed by the City and its employees, including street maintenance and traffic, solid waste removal, sewer maintenance, zoning and building permits, tax collection, fire, police and emergency services, just to name a few.

Driven by pressure to decrease cost and improve productivity, the City of Indianapolis moved to Activity-Based Cost Management in the hopes of creating greater customer value. Given the constraints of limited revenues , The City of Indianapolis chose to utilize ABCM to better leverage the decision made at the Resource Decision domain. The Mayor, Stephen Goldsmith is using ABCM as the basis for cost management, budgeting, performance management, and process improvement efforts all directed toward one end—to give taxpayers a dollar's worth of services for every dollar collected in taxes. The proof is in the results: by putting more than 70 city services up for bid, the city government has saved nearly $100 million in its first four years of this SMP-based effort—a 29 percent reduction. At the same time the quality of service has gone up—customer complaints are down by over 90 percent.

The path taken by Goldsmith and his government to gain these improvements is both innovative and aggressive. Representing one of the first known applications of business tools in a government setting, the City of Indianapolis now serves as a model city that demonstrates the benefits that measurement and competition can bring to city government. Putting the customer first, and ensuring that only those activities that create value for customers are funded, the City has proven that good management methods traverse organizational boundaries. How were these benefits and improvements gained? They were achieved through the effective integration of the Activity-Based Cost Management, Integrated Performance Management and Process Management Strategic Management Processes.

THE APPROACH

Having gained office on the promise of improved performance and reduced costs, Mayor Goldsmith wasted little time after taking office before moving on his campaign promises. Recruiting nine local executives and entrepreneurs to form a project management team, the resulting group (SELTIC, or Service, Efficiency and Lower Taxes for Indianapolis Commission) began the arduous task of understanding the City's finances.

The underlying premise of these efforts was simple—if the City could not directly provide a service cheaper or better than an outside firm, the service would be outsourced to a private sector firm. To fairly make the comparison of outside bids to internal costs, SELTIC had to know what existing services were and what resources they used. This information was not readily available. As has been the case in many organizations, historically the City had allocated indirect costs based on the direct costs of a service with little or no proof that these costs were actually caused by the service or department. The result was that little or no knowledge of the cost of individual activities existed. To achieve its stated goals, SELTIC had to have a firm knowledge of existing activity costs. The only solution was to implement ABCM.

An initial assessment of every service performed by the city government resulted in a list of over 100 activities. While redundancies were easy to spot, and eliminate, the real question was how to gain the needed support to understand and improve the remaining activities once the initial pruning was completed. With employee resistance serving as the single biggest obstacle to the initiative, Mayor Goldsmith and SELTIC turned to outside help to train its employees in the basics of ABCM and Integrated Performance Management. With economic necessity on his side—job survival was the common thread uniting the diverse interest groups—Goldsmith worked to establish trust and communication through ABCM training and education.

The training and education effort was driven by the City's new vision: to become a more competitive city with safe streets, strong neighborhoods, and a thriving economy. The ABCM training helped staff members learn how to critically review their efforts using measures of quantity, efficiency, productivity and quality. The motivation to embrace these changes was increased by the decision to attach a new incentive payment structure to the performance management goals. Serving as a form of public sector "profit sharing," one-fourth to one-third of the savings achieved were placed in a bonus pool. To keep the effort balanced, the potential for lost bonuses if defined goals were not achieved was also established.

With everyone's incentives aligned toward the same goal—cost and performance improvements—the true effort began. Initially, the ABCM efforts led to internally-driven improvement projects. For instance, the Department of Transportation (DOT) was able to determine from the activity and cost analysis that the mix of its equipment and labor was grossly inefficient. With full labor support, the DOT determined that it could fill potholes with four workers instead of eight and one truck instead of two. It was an early win, one that illustrated that the City's managers could think like entrepreneurs if their information and incentives were aligned with this goal.

A key revelation of this early effort was that the prior methods used to prepare budgets and analyze performance were flawed. An activity perspective suggested that the budget should be structured around observable activities and outcomes. This would make the budget easy to understand and evaluate by both managers and taxpayers. In addition, the outcome of the activity had to include measures of its efficiency, quantity and quality—mere total cost per activity was insufficient to support improvement. For instance, the Division of Solid Waste switched its focus from the number of tons of trash picked up in a year to the number of complaints received per household served (see Figure 17.1). As described by Mike Carter, the Division Assistant Administrator for Finance, "We're not tracking people and vehicles any more, but rather what we accomplish with those people and vehicles...Our goal is to promote this measurement mentality so well it will come naturally to our staff."[2]

Figure 17.1   Examples of DOT Measurements

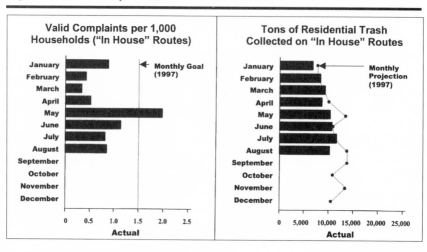

The results of early economic waste detection came as a surprise to the participants, leading to the creation of the Inaugural Waste Awards. One of the first winners of the "prize" was described as the "Golden Garbage" truck. It had been purchased for $90,000, but had subsequently required over $242,000 in repairs, resulting in a cost per mile of operation of $39. The decision to sell the truck was an easy one for city management to make.

Having taken the time and opportunity to gain internal improvements and ensure that its managers had gained essential new skills, the over 100 city services were then put out to competitive bid. By early 1996, the City had held 64 public-private competitions on more than $500 million of work in 29 separate service areas. Public workers won 16 of these bids and split 13 with private contractors. To avoid any problems with low-ball quotes from either outside or inside service bidders, an independent auditor was retained to ensure that the bids were based on realistic cost and performance estimates.

In one case, the sanitation department employees and union outbid 12 private haulers for their routes, resulting in a savings of $13.9 million in two years, while collections per crew went from about 700 per day to 1200 per day. The 75 jobs that were saved were won by the employees themselves. Drivers, participating in a study of route scheduling, determined that changes would result in significant efficiencies and increased tonnage collected per hour of operation.

In another early effort, the Fleet Services Division re-engineered its brake repair and other processes to increase mechanics' productivity by 21 percent. These improvements led to an increase in the percentage of vehicles serviced within eight hours of over 9 percent in five years. These gains were motivated by, and implemented by, the employees. The knowledge of what their activities were costing the taxpayers, combined with new tools and techniques, armed them to attack waste and improve services. Increased employee pride was the natural outcome of this empowered improvement process.

BENEFITS AND CHALLENGES

The benefits that have been achieved through the application of ABCM, Integrated Performance Management, and Process Management in the City of Indianapolis include:

- $100 million reduction in total costs of services;
- Significant increase in taxpayers satisfaction;

- Reduction in the number of complaints received;
- Increase in the services provided, including the addition of 27 more policemen and 12 more firemen;
- Improved relationships between city management and city employees and unions;
- Increase in employee morale and pride in their jobs;
- Improved communication with taxpayers regarding the services provided, the costs of these efforts, and options for redirection of resources;
- Improved relationships between the City government and the taxpayers;
- Avoidance of tax increases, which has served to make the City more competitive in the search for business relocation and growth;
- Increases in the City's fund balances, improving its top-tier credit rating and costs to finance major projects;
- Increases in the public safety budget;
- Freeing up of funds to support a capital improvement project entitled, "Building Better Neighborhoods"; and
- Provision of a funding source for bonds used in part to build a maintenance base at the airport.

The core SMP driving these changes and improvements is Activity-Based Cost Management. Activity-based logic and management techniques have provided a broad-based set of tools and knowledge to the City and its managers in their quest to make constant improvements in the efficiency and effectiveness of their services. As described by Canik, some of the benefits attributed directly to ABCM by the City's managers include:[3]

- Providing a technique for cost control;
- Resulting in improved management information leading to more informed decisions;
- Helping the city deliver a dollar's worth of service for each dollar of investment;
- Giving city planners the ability to benchmark against other cities and other departments and make adjustments toward greater efficiency;

- When the true costs are known, the City's permitting fees can be adjusted appropriately;

- Promoting a more in-depth understanding of the relationships among unit costs, subactivities, and phases; and

- Promoting innovation as it empowers employees to control and lower their own costs of operation.

One of the areas where these improvements have been observed is in the street maintenance process of crack sealing (see Figure 17.2). When the first pass ABCM analysis was completed, it was determined that it currently cost the City $1,200 per lane mile of roadway sealed. This cost was significantly above competitive costs derived from benchmark analysis.

Figure 17.2   Process Improvement in the City of Indianapolis

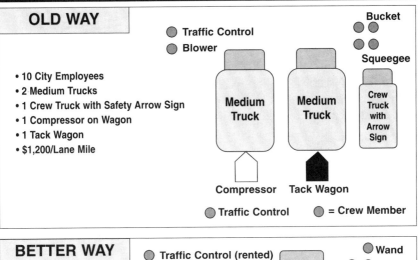

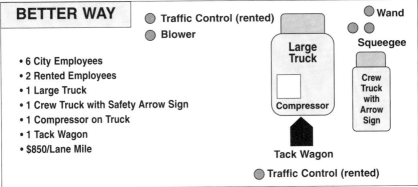

Source: Canik, op.cit., pg. 5

The improvements in this area required the employees to reach above the Resource Decision domain to gather knowledge about its processes. Using the mapping techniques integral to Process Management, employees were able to make major changes to the way that the road sealing process was performed. The new process reduced costs to $850 per lane mile, a cost below that of the closest private sector bid. This represented an 11 percent decrease in the Fleet Services budget despite the addition of 61 vehicles.

Measuring and Communicating Results

The changes around Indianapolis are very visible...from roads resurfaced to clean and safer neighborhoods. We have increased economic development, a revitalized inner city, and a new athletic facility—all without a tax increase.

– Chris Carter
Finance Administrator

Measuring and communicating both the successes and failures of the City of Indianapolis initiative is an ongoing effort. Employees want to know more about the strategy, goals, and performance of the City, and how their performance is impacting these areas. Citizens continue to want proof that the City and its employees are making the best use of their tax funds. Without a commitment to improvement, and communicating these changes effectively, the initiative would have become just another project, not a new way of life.

One of the key areas where the City of Indianapolis has stepped beyond the boundaries of normal government procedures is in the solicitation of feedback from both customers (the taxpayers) and employees. Human Resources often audits the log sheet at the Mayor's Action Center and then randomly selects and contacts individuals to determine their satisfaction with the City's response to their request. In addition, the City hires an outside consulting firm to coordinate the mailing and tabulation of written Citizen Satisfaction Surveys every two years. Sampling over 4,000 homeowners, with a response rate over 25%, this bi-annual survey seeks to obtain a quantitative measurement of the City's performance and image from the citizen's perspective.

Recent results suggest the citizens approve of the privatization of services effort. For instance, the maintenance of the municipal golf course was turned over to an outside firm, with a marked improvement in the condition of the course and a reduction in the costs to operate the facility. Results such as these are trended over time, providing a visible signal to city management on the perceived effectiveness of their efforts.

On the employee side, an "upward feedback" survey is used to find out how employees feel about the changes, the role of management, and their overall relationship with the city government. Survey questions are focused on identifying ways that the working relationship between the supervisor and subordinate can be improved. The results of the survey are distributed to directors and supervisors at the department level. The expectation is that an action plan to address concerns will be generated where necessary. While these efforts are not currently linked to supervisors' performance evaluations, they play an increasing role in assessing where changes need to be made.

These efforts, along with changes in incentive structures, union relationships, budgeting and management practices, and measurements in general, reflect a series of critical success factors for the City which include:

- The Mayor and city management had a clear vision of the objectives of the ABCM initiative;
- There was a clear understanding of the type of information that would be required to achieve the vision;
- There were many opportunities for improvement. The Mayor rallied support for the changes and the changes were made;
- City workers were motivated—they wanted to keep their jobs;
- ABCM was linked to performance measurement;
- Incentive pay was based on ABCM-measured productivity improvements. These incentives payments were in lieu of pay increases;
- There was non-financial ownership of the ABCM system;
- Extensive education and training ensured that every

employee understood and could apply ABCM terminology and concepts;

- Ensured that partnerships, whether with unions or outside contractors, were based on trust and well-defined expectations and measurements;

- Participation in the bid process ensured that employees and the union would buy into and commit to the process and the changes required to become competitive; and

- Resources were invested to ensure that the ABCM system could be maintained and effectively utilized throughout the city government.

Even with all of these benefits and successes, the City continues to face implementation challenges. First, the success has actually reduced the drive for change in the City. In some areas, all services have been outsourced, while others consistently remain internally sourced. There appears to be a less active push for improvement once competitive pressures have been incorporated in the culture.

A second issue is that ongoing technological problems with the City's Information Management System (IMS) impair the ABCM system. Specifically, reports are not received in a timely manner and the IMS remains cumbersome to use. The IMS has not been modified to make it possible to effectively and efficiently process the new forms of data, such as employee reporting of time against activities. Currently this information, when gathered, is entered manually, and the hours in the IMS do not always balance with the hours reported in the payroll system. Also, the ABCM reports are fairly detailed, with over 100 activities and cost objects maintained in the core database. These system problems need to be addressed if the system is to continue to provide benefits.

Finally, there are ongoing changes in leadership that have resulted in the departure of many of the senior managers who had learned about, and learned to use, ABCM data during the change initiative. New managers have not been as fully trained in the system or its benefits, reducing the management usage of, and commitment to, the ABCM system. Ongoing education and commitment to the ABCM program requires ongoing training and education—it is not a one-shot effort.

Despite these challenges, the City of Indianapolis experience remains a vivid example of how the use of the SMPs, integrated into a tool set that provides consistent information and support for decision-making and analysis, can lead to quantum performance improvements. Keeping the effort alive is not an option—taxpayers have come to expect that their government will provide more services at lower cost on an ongoing basis. Integrating departments, and the government as a whole, through a unified, consistent body of information and knowledge, the SMPs are the key to unlocking the potential of the City's resources.

> *Measuring our activities helps us be more competitive.*
> *I've seen it work, and I'm a believer now. And, although*
> *the news reporters used to criticize us regularly, now they*
> *actually brag about how efficient the City is becoming.*
> *The City of Indianapolis has proven it can be competitive,*
> *and we have the facts and numbers to back up our claims.*
> *The community as a whole has a new respect for the*
> *City of Indianapolis and its local government.*

> – Phil Irish
> Labor Union Representative

Endnotes

[1] The information in this chapter is drawn from a combination of the article "Aggressive Performance Management and Measurement Pays Off: City of Indianapolis Pioneers Privatization," by April Canik in *Measurement in Practice,* Houston, TX: American Productivity and Quality Center, Issue 10, Oct/Nov, 1997. Secondary source material is drawn from the Arthur Andersen Benchmarking Clearing House files.

[2] American Productivity and Quality Center, op.cit., pg. 4.

[3] Ibid, pg. 4

Chapter 18

DAIMLERCHRYSLER

Case Study

We're very interested in technology sharing with our suppliers, but we haven't had a good way to focus on it... We're hopeful that Tandem will give that to us.

– Gary Valade[1]
Manager, Global Purchasing

In one of the biggest mergers ever in the automotive industry, Daimler-Benz and Chrysler Corporation combined to become DaimlerChrysler on November 17, 1998. While the reasons for this historic marriage of two automotive giants are many, the ability to leverage global alliances with suppliers to gain a competitive advantage in both its new product design and ongoing production processes, ranks high in the list of benefits obtained. DaimlerChrysler is the embodiment of the Extended Enterprise.

Tandem, a Daimler-Benz program developed with its European suppliers, is focused on technology-sharing. It is one of a new set of tools being used by DaimlerChrysler in its ongoing search for ways to improve the product development process, smooth the transition from the drawing board to the plant floor, and ensure that technology is leveraged in all aspects of operations and management. Driven by the voice of the customer, product design and development seeks to provide the expected—and unexpected—to those who buy its products. From an entry level vehicle such as the Neon, to the high end Jeep or Mercedes Benz lines, the focus is the same—to continually deliver more value per dollar of purchase price than any of its competitors.

The following discussion traces the path of product development at DaimlerChrysler. It emphasizes the role of the Strategic Management Processes (SMPs) in providing information to both inform decisions and coordinate and communicate actions and objectives between the Decision domains. Achieving life cycle performance improvements requires an integrated information system that provides data for design decisions, for guiding operations, for adjusting performance, and assessing the success or failure of a product and process. The CAM-I SMP Model provides a bridge between product initiatives, projects, and the decisions made at various levels of the firm. It is this bridge which this final example illustrates.

BACKGROUND

If one were to compare the Chrysler Corporation of the 1970s, (with Lee Iacocca in front of Congress asking for government aid), to its modern counterpart DaimlerChrysler, the differences would far outstrip the similarities. Instead of a struggling domestic firm with antiquated systems and management processes, one finds a lean global competitor who exhibits an uncanny ability to create superior value for its customers and its other stakeholders. The results of this successful strategy are evident in the $132 billion in revenues in the merged firm, 4 million units sold, and $7 billion in before-tax income. The goal for 1999 was to add $1.4 billion to the bottom line through revenue enhancements and cost efficiencies. It was a reasonable goal because the processes and people necessary to make such quantum performance improvements possible were in place.

Chrysler Corporation was one of the first American companies to aggressively develop the Extended Enterprise as the key to achieving product and process improvement goals. With the merger, this core competence in supply chain management has achieved a global scale. Both companies bring unique capabilities in the Extended Enterprise to the table. Where Chrysler has mastered the processes needed to manage the supply chain effectively and efficiently on an ongoing basis, Daimler-Benz has created the technology and knowledge sharing platforms that ensure that the merged firm is always on the leading edge in applying technology to its products and processes. In combination they have gained a formidable global competitive advantage that will undoubtedly extend beyond the Extended Enterprise to encompass every aspect of operation.

One area where the benefits of the Extended Enterprise are evident is during the design and downstream production of a new product. Known for its mastery of the platform approach to product line design and production, DaimlerChrysler has learned the lessons of how commonality of parts, features, manufacturing characteristics, and structures can radically reduce costs while improving performance. Reducing unnecessary variety—variety that does not directly affect the customer—increases quality while reducing cost as scale economies are gained in new ways. Scale no longer solely means buildings and equipment—it is evident in the leverage a firm has on its value chain. The Extended Enterprise is the means to gain scale economies without direct investment. It is the best of both worlds.

DaimlerChrysler doesn't trade off product features for cost, though they attain the desired features at the target cost (or lower). Working with suppliers from the very onset of a product design effort, the firm is constantly in search of new technologies, materials, and methods that can simplify the production process, increase reliability, and improve performance.

MAKING THE NEON "FUN TO DRIVE"[2]

One of the prime examples of the capability to meet customer expectations profitably was the 1995 effort to develop the "Fun to Drive" steering and suspension characteristics in the 1995 Neon. (This was also a prime objective in developing the current-generation Neon for 2000.) Early in the pre-planning stage, a Customer Quality Function Deployment (QFD) effort determined that customers expected their small car to be reliable and fuel efficient, to have good value, to be well equipped, and have thoughtful features. As noted by several design team members, though:

"Beyond this they did not expect their vehicle to be "Fun to Drive," to have style, personality, comfort, versatility, and to be safe…The challenge…was to provide both the expected and unexpected attributes."

While the company had extensive knowledge in the key product attributes that customers expected, it had never before attempted to define what "Fun to Drive" would mean in terms of functionality and design. In response, a QFD "Fun to Drive" team was established, comprised of individuals from Chassis Engineering, Vehicle Dynamics, Vehicle Development, Planning, and Quality Synthesis.

The first objective was to identify the key drivers of the "Fun to Drive" attribute. Customer research clinics were conducted, resulting in the identification of six key "Fun to Drive" characteristics:

- Feeling of control
- Good ride
- Responsive powertrain
- Good outward visibility
- Controls/display easy to use/see
- Audio system sounds good.

Teams were set up to focus on responsive powertrain requirements, good outward visibility, good ride, and feeling of control—handling. It is this latter attribute that the rest of this example emphasizes.

Suspension performance was felt to be a key ingredient in the "Fun to Drive" recipe, resulting in the formation of a suspension team that was charged with digging deeper into what customers really meant in describing a car that was "Fun to Drive" in relationship to its suspension. The team turned to tapes from the customer research clinics to get untainted information—the true "voice of the customer". The resulting set of characteristics included:

STEERING
Precise
Responsive
Sense of Control
Smoothly goes into turns
Good Maneuverability
Light effort but with feeling of control

HANDLING
Handling ease
Good road holding
Solid handling – handles like a go-cart
Nimble, agile feel – tires quiet in turns

RIDE
Comfortable
Smooth
Good control
Quiet
Feels solid

Working with this data, it was soon recognized that structural integrity and steering capabilities were two primary factors in defining the "Fun to Drive" feature. Once again product design teams were established, this time to explore the specific product attributes and set measurable goals around these features. Benchmarking of existing vehicles, adjusted for the market position held by the Neon in the small car market, provided guidance on what physical and functional characteristics would need to be incorporated in the design (see Figure 18.1)

Figure 18.1   Neon's Phase I Planning Matrix for the "Fun to Drive" Attibute

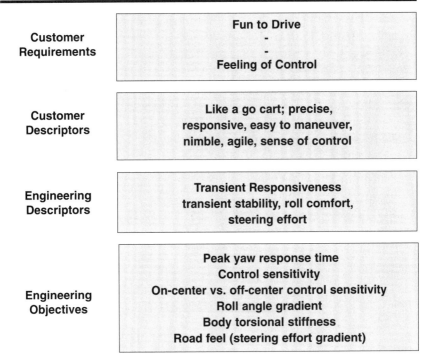

Customer Requirements	**Fun to Drive** - - **Feeling of Control**
Customer Descriptors	Like a go cart; precise, responsive, easy to maneuver, nimble, agile, sense of control
Engineering Descriptors	Transient Responsiveness transient stability, roll comfort, steering effort
Engineering Objectives	Peak yaw response time Control sensitivity On-center vs. off-center control sensitivity Roll angle gradient Body torsional stiffness Road feel (steering effort gradient)

Source: "Making the Neon Fun to Drive," J.E. Fernandez, et.al., 1994: 6.

Next, the team began developing functional measures and targets for the defined customer requirements and descriptors. Each system of the car deemed to impact these requirements was then broken down into components to determine what the critical design features were to attain customer requirements. The result was a series of defined requirements for the steering and suspension systems which were then validated through compliance testing to better understand the impact of each component on overall system performance. Having determined functional requirements for components within the system, attention turned to defining the key physical dimensions, such as material strength requirements, to ensure that a safe, reliable solution would be found. The basic objectives of Target Cost Management had been reached in terms of building the voice of the customer into the product.

Having reached a point where the performance expectations for components were now understood, the design team turned to the Extended Enterprise. Teaming with suppliers, the components were simultaneously engineered. Balancing the joint demands of reliability and manufacturability, the DaimlerChrysler supplier teams developed complete sets of component drawings that clearly specified critical dimensions and performance characteristics with jointly agreed upon quality and inspection requirements. The resulting component designs reduced component complexity by over 15 percent while producing a system that was easier to assemble. Both of these achievements would drive downstream production cost reductions.

Attention then turned to defining manufacturing requirements for internal suppliers. As described by the product team:[3]

This stage of a total QFD process involves moving the "critical" or "important" dimensional information to the factory floor. This stage is frequently neglected, but is vitally important to achieving the end vehicle functional objective. Reasons for this neglect are many, but perhaps the most basic is the lack of participation from Manufacturing in these early processes. Early involvement enables learning the importance of critical characteristics and the developing of a "what if" mentality that could result in possible re-design of the product or process.

Two key areas of early involvement of manufacturing in the design process were identified: suspension and final assembly. Since the suspension played such a dominant role in defining the "Fun to Drive" product attribute, it was crucial that the mounting points for the attachment of the front suspension had to be made correctly. The suspension crossmember team took this fact seriously, including the pursuit of a "Poka-Yoke" (mistake foolproofing) philosophy in the design and equipment. With representatives from the stamping plant, equipment suppliers, their designers, and process suppliers in addition to DaimlerChrysler design engineers, the suspension team ensured that customer expectations (and beyond) would be built into the product. The findings were translated into Process control checklists and Operation checkoff lists, both of which would guide production workers in the future.

The same logic and set of objectives drove the final assembly effort. Mistake-proofing the product and process was built into every aspect of the assembly process, ensuring that the product would meet its requirements on a reliable, consistent basis. In the assembly situation, the work team was comprised of process and design engineers, assembly supervisory personnel and assembly line workers. As noted by the authors, *"the line workers brought a unique "real world" experience that helped numerous issues surface that had not been previously addressed."* It was truly a cross-functional, cross-life cycle effort that yielded a car with superior performance features.

Overall, the drive to build a "Fun to Drive" Neon was a success. For the key subjective targets, 5 of 6 Best in Class objectives were met, and 11 of 12 competitive objectives were met. All other efforts came in close to target and were identified as key improvement projects for post-launch initiatives. The real proof of the success of this effort lies, once again, in the voice of the customer:

> *More than anything else, the Neon is a real kick to drive. Let's be stronger: It's more fun to drive than anything in its class…The Neon's handling is better than good. It's quick. It's lively.*
> — Detroit Free Press, January, 1994

> *Shifting, cornering grip and handling collaborate to make the Neon a tossable, lively piece. It's loaded and a blast to drive.…The Neon is tops in its class. It's a winner because it goes fast and looks good, things economy cars almost never do.*
> — Car and Driver, June, 1994

THE LEARNINGS

The DaimlerChrysler experience with the 1st generation Neon has duplicated itself in multiple product launches since 1994. Having learned the power of building the customer's voice into the design and development of its products, the company has moved beyond simply meeting these expectations to exceeding them on a regular basis. The combination of knowledge and information sharing between decision domains (Market, Product, Process and Resource) and information systems reflects a comprehensive application of the power of integration and coordination. It is an example of the logic and results that drove the development of the CAM-I SMP Model.

As suggested by Figure 18.2, three of the core SMPs were tightly intertwined during the Neon development process. Target Cost Management, deployed through QFD, served to identify key customer requirements and communicate them to the firm. Once defined by TCM, the Extended Enterprise SMP was engaged in the ongoing quest to find better ways to design the product and deploy technology to achieve design objectives within the tight cost constraints that discipline the product platform teams at DaimlerChrysler. As the design process developed, internal suppliers became essential partners in the knowledge-gaining and sharing effort. Reflecting the best features of Process Management, Target Cost Management, and the Extended Enterprise, this design effort illustrates the benefits that can be gained when a company leverages its information to create a competitive advantage.

Figure 18.2   The SMP Integration at DaimlerChrysler

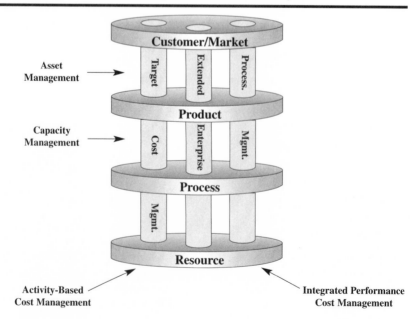

As the figure suggests, the seven SMPs played either a direct (the illustrated rods) or indirect (the hidden rods called out by name) role in the product design process used at DaimlerChrysler. The use of the SMPs, as did the design effort, spanned all four of the primary Decision domains. Illustrating the benefits as well as cultural implications of the CAM-I SMP Model, this case is one of today's best examples of how the power of information can be harnessed to create cross-organizational knowledge and competencies.

What are the lessons learned from the experiences at DaimlerChrysler? Just a few of these would include:

- Integration of the information available in the SMPs takes on a natural progression as the organization faces each incremental challenge in meeting customer requirements;

- No one SMP or one Decision domain dominates. Success requires the ongoing collaboration and sharing of information and expectations across the value chain;

- Information can be leveraged to gain improvements in customer value while reducing the cost and complexity of manufacturing;

- Teamwork requires a culture change which recognizes that critical information and learning can come from any source, including the line worker;

- Going beyond customer expectations is the basis for competitive advantage; and

- Achieving design goals can only be ensured if the design and development process itself is actively managed and structured.

Clearly, a DaimlerChrysler employee could provide an even greater list, including gains made on both a personal and professional level from the knowledge and skills honed through active integration of information and expertise across the boundaries of time and space. Information allows a company to turn to its past to inform its future, incorporate the external world in its internal activities, and drive toward the future with a reasonable assurance of success. It is a power, once harnessed, that can be turned to again and again as new challenges and opportunities arise.

In the end, the goal of the CAM-I SMP Model is to help more companies achieve the integration of information—to harness knowledge—to support their *Value Quest.*

It is a journey that you and your company have now begun.

Endnotes

---

[1] "Cost-cutting Crosses Atlantic, Both Ways," by Ralph Kisiel in *Automotive News*, March 8, 1999. In this article Tandem is described as a Daimler-Benz program with European suppliers that focuses on technology sharing among the automaker and its suppliers.

[2] "Making the Neon Fun to Drive," by J.E. Fernandez, J.L. Chamberlin, E.G. Kramer, J.H. Broomall, H.A. Rori, and R.L. Begley, delivered at the Sixth Symposium on Quality Function Deployment, June 13-14, 1994. This entire section draws very heavily from the paper prepared by these authors for the 1994 symposium.

[3] Ibid, pg. 15.

STRATEGIC MANAGEMENT PROCESS (SMP) TABLES

The intent of this appendix is to provide supplemental information regarding the information transfers between Strategic Management Processes (SMPs).

Each of the SMP Chapters contain a process flow which is organized by Decision domain. These flows depict the Decision domain(s) where the process step exerts influence as well as the interaction between the SMPs. The integrating mechanism is the flow of information, which for each SMP is depicted by arrows and data labels from each interacting SMP.

For simplicity in presentation, these data labels are intended to provide a broad characterization of the type of information required in the process, and provided by the supporting SMPs. This appendix will provide the reader with the next level of data descriptions.

There is a separate Strategic Management Process Integration Table for each SMP included in each SMP Chapter. The following supplemental tables first indicate the other SMPs that interact in the process. For each of the interacting SMPs, the information category (data label) is indicated along with a more detailed description of the information required by the SMP. The final column indicates the SMP process step where the information (or a subset of the information will be utilized.)

This addition breakdown of information exchange will assist the reader in further understanding the interaction between the Strategic Management Processes, and will provide the practitioner with the additional tools required to make these process interactions a reality.

SMP Tables
1.0 Target Cost Management - Integration Requirements

Interacting SMP	Information Category	Information Required	Process Step Impacted
Activity Based Cost Management	Activity/Product & Process Costs	• Product cost history • Process cost history • Component/Assemble level costing • Cost table formulation • Overhead rate structure • Benchmarking data • Trend analysis	1.4 Understand Customer Requirements 1.9 Compute Cost Gap
Capacity Management	Capacity Capability	• Industry capacity constraints • In-House capacity limits • Current capacity trends on cost	1.9 Compute Cost Gap
Asset Management	Investment Requirements	• Potential capital investment requirements • Capital investment options evaluation • Technology, commercial, economic risk anal. • Potential impact to performance metrics • Investment implementation risk & timing	1.9 Compute Cost Gap
Extended Enterprise Management	Make / Buy Assessment	• Supplier capability • Benchmarking assessment by work package • Economic indicators by supplier segment • Supplier cost assessment & risk analysis • Supplier quality/customer requirement evaluation matrix • Supplier ranking (by performance category) • Supplier performance conversion to in-house equivalent	1.9 Compute Cost Gap

SMP Tables
1.0 Target Cost Management - Integration Requirements (continued)

Interacting SMP	Information Category	Information Required	Process Step Impacted
Process Management	Current & potential process assessment	• Process benchmarking (internal and external) • Process cost capability • Potential current process cost improvement • Process cost leverage areas • Process re-engineering evaluations • Process re-engineering target leverage mapping matrix • Long range process cost reductions	1.9 Compute Cost Gap 1.12 Evaluate Process Re-engineering 1.14 Continuous Improvement
	Corporate Profit Plan	• Corporate profitability targets (by product/operating group) • Corporate/Shareholder profitability metrics	1.7 Develop Required Profit
Integrated Performance Management	Performance Assessment	• Evaluation of Key Performance Indicators (KPI) • Performance gap evaluations • Performance evaluation link to strategy • Critical Success Factor (CSF) evaluation • Current performance evaluations	1.9 Compute Cost Gap 1.12 Evaluate Process Re-engineering 1.14 Continuous Improvement

SMP Tables
2.0 Asset Management - Integration Requirements

Interacting SMP	Information Category	Information Required	Process Step Impacted
Target Cost Management	Product Portfolio Plan	• Product specifications • Forecasted volumes and mix • Delivery requirements (forecast) • Performance targets • Market share goals	2.1 Determine Product Portfolio Plan
Activity Based Cost Management	Activity, Product, Process Costs	• Activity costs • Product costs by mix • Process costs by type & grouping • Actuals vs plan • Driver information	2.2 Determine Core Competencies 2.5 Develop Technology & Process Capability Acquisition Plan 2.9 Perform Investment Post Audit 2.10 Continuous Improvement
Process Management	Current/Potential Process Assessment	• Process definition • Comparative process performance evaluation • Process responsibility matrix • Flow characteristics	2.2 Determine Core Competencies (including Knowledge Management) 2.4 Identify Process Requirements
Capacity Management	Capacity Requirements	• Bottlenecks • Internal/external capacity analysis • Volumes • Internal capacity utilization • Internal capacity constraints • Capital requirements for capacity	2.6 Establish Strategic Sourcing/Outsourcing Plan

SMP Tables
2.0 Asset Management - Integration Requirements (continued)

Interacting SMP	Information Category	Information Required	Process Step Impacted
Extended Enterprise Management	Supply Investment Plan	· Industry capacity · Make/buy analysis · Vendor capabilities · Core competency assessment · Competitive advantage strategy · Customer trends	2.5 Develop Technology & Process Capability Acquisition Plan 2.6 Establish Strategic Sourcing/Outsourcing Plan
Integrated Performance Management	Investment Performance Metrics	· Profitability goals and criteria · Quality, cost & responsiveness requirements · Quality, cost & responsiveness targets · Quality, cost & responsiveness actuals	2.7 Establish Internal/External Investment Performance Metrics 2.10 Continuous Improvement

SMP Tables
3.0 Capacity Management - Integration Requirements

Interacting SMP	Information Category	Information Required	Process Step Impacted
Target Cost Management	Market Timing and Quantity	• Forecasted market quantities • Optimal market introduction timing • Market timespread forecast • Competitive analysis information • Market constraint data • Market risk assessment • Market scenario analysis • Product diversion impact (market & current Portfolio)	3.1 Identify & Document Market Volume Requirements 3.5 Define Capacity
	Projected Demands	• Quantities • Options • Mix • Timing	3.7 Schedule/Prioritize Products in System
Asset Management	Existing vs . Potential Resource Availability	• Current asset availability • Available capital • Asset investment strategy • Required payback/returns	3.5 Define Capacity
	Constraints	• Current investment strategy • Investment performance requirements • Planned resource acquisitions • Planned resource disposals	3.9 Make Adjustments and Manage Capacity Backups
Extended Enterprise Management	Outsourcing Capability/ Strategies	• Supply chain capacity • Supply chain flexibility • Required lead times and commitments • Current agreements and constraints	3.5 Define Capacity
	Agreements	• Current outsourcing • Surge outsourcing	3.7 Schedule/Prioritize Products in System

SMP Tables
3.0 Capacity Management - Integration Requirements (continued)

Interacting SMP	Information Category	Information Required	Process Step Impacted
Extended Enterprise Management (cont.)	Delivery	• Lead times • Quality • Quantity limits • Surge capabilities	3.8 Identify Bottlenecks and Gaps Given System
	Constraints	• Resource lead times • Resource availability (quantity, timing, flexibility) • Optimal sourcing given supply chain strategy	3.9 Make Adjustments and Manage Capacity Backups
Process Management	Constraints/ Available capacity	• Throughput • Bottlenecks • Flexibility • Surge capabilities	3.5 Define Capacity
	Bottleneck Management	• Constraints • Schedule • Changeover times • Flexibility • Surge capacity • Quality limits	3.8 Identify Bottlenecks and Gaps Given Schedule
Activity Based Cost Management	Profitabilities & Costs	• Relative profit per unit of constrained resource used • Costs of easing bottlenecks • Projected costs & profits for given mix and sourcing	3.7 Schedule/Prioritize Products in System
	Costs	• Process costs/minute • Bottleneck costs • Outsourcing costs • Costs of using "off process" assets • Current vs. budgeted costs • Current vs. budgeted profits	3.8 Identify Bottlenecks and Gaps Given Schedule

SMP Tables
3.0 Capacity Management - Integration Requirements (continued)

Interacting SMP	Information Category	Information Required	Process Step Impacted
Activity Based Cost Management (cont.)	Costs	· Resource costs · Delivery costs (regular vs. expedited) · Inspection/quality costs · Make vs. buy analysis	3.9 Make Adjustments and Manage Capacity Backups
Integrated Performance Management	Required Results	· ROI · Profit goals · Quality goals · Delivery goals · Evaluation cycle · Evaluation weightings	3.7 Schedule/Prioritize Products in System
	Requirements	· Current vs. planned performance · Profit requirements · Delivery requirements · Quality requirements · Priorities	3.8 Identify Bottlenecks and Gaps Given Schedule
	History	· Vendor performance ratings · Resource yields/first pass performance ·Resource quality ratings	3.9 Make Adjustments and Manage Capacity Backups
	Performance Assessment	· Evaluation of Key Performance Indicators (KPI) · Performance gap evaluations · Performance evaluation link to strategy · Critical Success Factor (CSF) evaluation · Current performance evaluations	3.11 Continuous Improvement

SMP Tables
4.0 Process Management - Integration Requirements

Interacting SMP	Information Category	Information Required	Process Step Impacted
Activity Cost Management	Process Costs (Absolute, Trend & Comparisons)	• Process framework definition • Process decomposed to activities • Costs mapped to activities • Driver identification • ABC cost structure definition • Comparative cost data	4.7 Implement Process Performance metrics
Target Cost Management	Product Functionality & Current & Potential Process Cost Assessments	• Corporate strategy & objectives • Context assumptions • Product/process assumptions • Target Cost calculations • Target cost to "as-is" cost comparison	4.7 Implement Process Performance metrics
Integrated Performance Management	Performance Measurements	For any given process: • Customers of the process • Performance expectations • Customer's use of process outputs • Key Performance Indicators (KPI's) • Strategy alignment evaluation • Method of calculating metrics	4.7 Implement Process Performance metrics
	Performance Assessments	• Measures of performance • Comparison to expectations • Explanation of performance gaps • Evaluation of measurement effectiveness • Potential process change recommendations	4.10 Continuous Improvement

SMP Tables
4.0 Process Management - Integration Requirements (continued)

Interacting SMP	Information Category	Information Required	Process Step Impacted
Asset Management	Investment Requirements & Priorities by Process	• Corporate strategy & objectives • Product & non-product plans • Investment requirements • Spending limitations & priorities • Risks and opportunities • Performance required, relative to limitations/benchmarks/trends	4.8 Monitor Organizational Performance
Capacity Management	Capacity Capabilities & Bottlenecks by Process	• Market requirements • Evaluation of accepted capacities • Causal reasons for limitations • Bottleneck identification • Implications of breaking bottlenecks	4.8 Monitor Organizational Performance
Extended Enterprise Management	Supply Implications & Alternatives by Process	• Corporate priorities (strategic sourcing, capacity, trends) • Cost, quality & time measures • Benchmark evaluations • Extended enterprise metrics • Alternatives comparison	4.8 Monitor Organizational Performance

SMP Tables
5.0 Extended Enterprise Management - Integration Requirements

Interacting SMP	Information Category	Information Required	Process Step Impacted
Target Cost Management	Market Requirements	• Product description • Introductory schedule • Volumes • Target cost • Product performance criteria • Margin requirements • Distribution strategy	5.1 Identify & Document Market Requirements
	Target Cost Data	• Target cost • Cost gap analysis • Life cycle costs • Cost improvement goals • Competitor cost analysis	5.3 Perform Make or Buy Analysis
	Cost Gap Analysis	• Competitive intelligence • Alternative technologies • Leverage volumes • Waste reduction plan • Life cycle costs	5.11 Continuous Improvement
Process Management	Process Capability/ Manufacturability / Alternatives	• Recommended manufacturing processes • Process capability analysis • Reliability requirements • Critical-to-Function requirements • Performance criteria • Risk assessment • Next best alternative process	5.2 Write Product Specifications
	Process Capability	• Manufacturing process improvements • Business process improvements • Competitive Analysis • Alternative technologies • Product life cycle	5.11 Continuous Improvement

SMP Tables
5.0 Extended Enterprise Management - Integration Requirements (continued)

Interacting SMP	Information Category	Information Required	Process Step Impacted
Activity Based Cost Management	Make/Buy Assessment Data	• Internal manufacturing costs • Fixed vs variable costs • Cash flow analysis • Overhead cost analysis • Material handling costs • Tax impact analysis • Distribution cost analysis	5.3 Perform Make or Buy Analysis
Capacity Management	Capacity Analysis Make/Buy Analysis	• Capacity analysis • Life cycle analysis • Alternative capacity utilization • Marginal cost analysis	5.3 Perform Make or Buy Analysis
Asset Management	Investment Strategy Make/Buy	• Opportunity costs analysis • Global capacity plan • Regional capacity plan • Core competency strategy • Competitive advantage strategy	5.3 Perform Make or Buy Analysis
Integrated Performance Management	Performance Requirements	• Quality requirements • Reliability requirements • Cycle time requirements • Productivity improvement plan • Inventory turns • Logistics requirements	5.6 Define Performance Criteria (Suppliers)
	Performance Requirements	• Productivity goals • Volume forecasts • Life cycle costs • Competitive intelligence	5.11 Continuous Improvement

SMP Tables
6.0 Integrated Performance Management - Integration Requirements

Interacting SMP	Information Category	Information Required	Process Step Impacted
Asset Management	Investment Performance Objectives	· Business performance objectives · Revenue/profitability growth potential analysis · Return on Investment analysis (ROI, ROE, etc.) · Resource performance evaluation	6.1 Identify Strategic Objectives 6.6 Monitor Ongoing Performance
Capacity Management	Resource Analysis	· Market growth analysis · Resource capabilities analysis · Constraint analysis · Acquisition analysis	6.1 Identify Strategic Objectives
	Asset Utilization	· Physical assets utilization · (Non) Physical assets utilization · Constraint analysis	6.6 Monitor Ongoing Performance
Process Management	Core Process Definition	· Process stability performance · Process output performance (quality, time, cost) · Process design requirements · Manufacturing requirements	6.1 Identify Strategic Objectives
	Process Capability Current & Projected	· Performance gap analysis · Continuous improvement targets · Process benchmarking (internal, external)	6.6 Monitor Ongoing Performance 6.9 Continuous Improvement
Target Cost Management	Market/Customer Requirements	· Life cycle costs, customer value · Allowable target cost achievable, cost gap · Market/Customer requirements · Return on sales objective · Competitive offerings, benchmarking · Financial impact of meeting customer's needs analysis	6.1 Identify Strategic Objectives

SMP Tables
6.0 Integrated Performance Management - Integration Requirements (continued)

Interacting SMP	Information Category	Information Required	Process Step Impacted
Target Cost Management (cont.)	Market/Customer Requirements (cont.)	· Cost gap · Manufacturing costs · Total product costs · Life cycle costs	6.6 Monitor Ongoing Performance
		· Performance gap analysis · Continuous improvement targets · Cost, value analysis · Cost estimates	6.9 Continuous Improvement
Extended Enterprise Management	Extended Enterprise Performance Criteria & Data	· Customer satisfaction evaluation · Asset utilization · Vendor performance · Lead time · Due date performance · Product flexibility · Product introduction responsiveness	6.6 Monitor Ongoing Performance
Activity Cost Management	Cost Data & Driver Information	· Cost driver identification · Expenditures allocation to cost objects · Activity analysis · Value analysis · Process, product, market performance	6.6 Monitor Ongoing Performance

SMP Tables
7.0 Activity-Based Cost Management - Integration Requirements

Interacting SMP	Information Category	Information Required	Process Step Impacted
Asset Management	Capital Expenditure Data	• Capital equipment costs • Capital equipment usage pattern	7.3 Assess Existing Financial Structure & Data 7.4 Identify Activities and Processes 7.5 Analyze Activities and Processes
Process Management	Process Information	• Process flow charts / process maps • Cycle times	7.4 Identify Activities and Processes 7.5 Analyze Activities and Processes
Integrated Performance Management	Cost Driver Data	• Activity and cost drivers	7.6 Identify Drivers
	Performance Assessment	• Cost & performance trends	7.9 Continuous Improvement
Extended Enterprise Management	Supplier & Customer Performance Data & Potential Activity Cost Drivers	• Supplier performance data • Quality data • On-time delivery / responsiveness • Yields	7.6 Identify Drivers
Capacity Management	Capacity Data	• Capital equipment costs • Capital equipment usage pattern	7.7 Analyze Drivers

PART 1

- **VALUE QUEST DIAGNOSTIC FORMS**
  Input Sheets by Decision Domain
  Scoring Summary Worksheets
  Decision Domain Summary Sheets with
  Value Quest Reference Schedules

A PRACTITIONER'S DIAGNOSTICS

Perhaps one of the biggest obstacles to increasing the value of a company is in knowing where to start. To assist you in directing your *"Value Quest"*, the following diagnostic tool kit has been developed. The focus of the tool is to help your firm develop and integrate the Strategic Management Processes (SMPs) in a logical order based on a self-assessment of your company's needs. In this way the SMPs will blend into the Decision domains that determine how you provide your Customers and Markets with Product yielding the highest satisfaction by utilizing the best Processes with the most effective uses of Resources. By completing the diagnostic, you should be able to determine which decision domain requires your initial attention and which SMP within that domain is your most logical starting point.

The diagnostic has been developed in a manner that will allow you to understand your capabilities within a Decision domain from both a numeric and graphical perspective. You will also be able compare the four Decision domains, allowing you to better determine the area which will provide you the greatest leverage in your performance improvement efforts.

The diagnostic begins with a series of True/False statements concerning attributes within one of the Decision groupings discussed in the chapter for that Decision domain (Chapter 12-15). The statements provide an assessment of your firm's capabilities within a decision grouping. It is important that you answer these questions from a "black or white" perspective, in order to accurately assess your firm's capabilities. The diagnostic then utilizes a spider graphing technique to allow you to graphically display your relative strengths or weaknesses within the Decision domain. (The closer your plot is to the perimeter of the graph, the stronger your capability within the decision grouping.)

Completion of all the questions within a Decision domain allows you to determine your staring point within that decision domain. By graphing your relative position amongst the four Decision domains, you will be able to determine which Decision domain is your starting point. Finally, the diagnostics enables you to determine the SMP that you can begin to strengthen or develop to increase your capability within the Decision grouping/Decision domain.

Completion of the diagnostic can be accomplished either manually, by working through the formats at the end of the chapter, or electronically, through the use of the diskette included with the book.

MANUAL COMPLETION INSTRUCTIONS

To begin the diagnostic, answer the questions for each of the decision groupings within a Decision domain. Upon completion, refer to the scoring summary worksheet following the questions for that Decision domain. The worksheet asks that you indicate, by decision grouping the number of statements you answered "true". Multiple this number by five (5) and divide by the total number of questions within the Decision grouping (somewhere between 4 to 7 questions). This will give you a score (maximum score is 5) which can be plotted on the spider graph diagram, found on the appropriate Decision Domain Summary Sheet. (The closer your plot point is to the perimeter of the graph, the stronger your capability within this Decision grouping.) When you have completed the scoring for each of the Decision groupings, you can determine an average score for the Decision domain simply by adding the individual decision grouping scores and dividing by the number of Decision groupings within the domain. This will give you a numeric result that can be used in a comparison among the Decision domains. The Decision domain with the lowest average score would be a logical starting place.

Now that you have determined, numerically and graphically, your capabilities by each Decision grouping within the Decision domain, you are ready to determine your staring point for that particular Decision domain. The recommended starting point is the decision grouping where the plot point on the spider graph is closest to the center of the graph. By looking at the reference schedule, on the Decision Domain Summary Sheet, you will be able to determine the key SMP that will help improve your capability within a specific Decision grouping (in some cases, two key SMPs will be indicated). The reference schedule will direct you to the chapter where the key SMP is described. Supporting SMPs are also indicated in the reference schedule.

When you have completed answering and scoring all four Decision domains, you can use the reference schedule to determine your staring point based on which Decision domain reflects the greatest opportunity for improvement. The reference schedule indicates the key SMP for each Decision domain. The recommended approach to identifying your starting point is to determine the Decision grouping within the Decision domain where the greatest improvement opportunity exists.

ELECTRONIC COMPLETION INSTRUCTIONS

If you elect to utilize the diskette, which operates within Microsoft Excel (Version 7a), all you will need to do is answer the questions for each of the decision groupings by clicking on the appropriate True/False box. The program will automatically do the necessary calculations and plot your four spider graphs. A red "X" will highlight your lowest scoring Decision domain and decision grouping within a Decision domain. To determine your key SMP simply click on the red "X" and you will be referred to the proper reference schedule.

A sample of a completed diagnostic is provided at the end of the appendix. The sample indicates that, for this company, it scores the lowest within the Process Decision domain. Within this domain, its lowest score is for process design. The company should begin by developing its Process Management SMP and supporting its efforts in this area by developing its Extended Enterprise and Capacity Management SMPs. The company should then direct its effort to build its capabilities within the Customer/Market domain (its second lowest overall score) by developing a Target Costing Management SMP.

The authors of the book wish you a successful *Value Quest*.

Value Quest – Practitioner's Diagnostic
<u>CUSTOMER/MARKET DOMAIN</u>

Instructions: Check box as true or false. Input number of true answers on the summary sheet for the corresponding Decision domain.

T F

Value Creation

1) Processes and tools are in place and utilized for identifying customer's life cycle value expectations

2) Processes and tools are in place and utilized for determining the importance of differing value preferences between customers

3) Customer value preferences and be listed in order of importance

4) A reliable method exists and is utilized for evaluating the firm's current performance against customer expectations (versus that of key competitors)

5) A method exists to evaluate internal processes against customer value to determine process value and non-value added activities

6) Mechanisms exist to communicate customer value expectations to the internal stakeholders

Segment Strategy

1) A method is utilized to evaluate compatibility of Customer/ Market segment requirements with the firm's competencies and capabilities

2) Process and tools exist and are utilized for conducting price and value trade-off analysis for customer and market segments

3) The firm develops cost and profit projections for each viable customer and market segmentation strategy

4) Processes and tools exist and are utilized to assess investment and operational implications of various segment strategies

5) Processes and tools exist and are utilized to determine the compatibility and capability of the extended enterprise to effectively respond to different segmentation strategies

Value Quest – **Practitioner's Diagnostic**
<u>CUSTOMER/MARKET DOMAIN (cont.)</u>

Instructions: Check box as true or false. Input number of true answers on the summary sheet for the corresponding Decision domain.

Key Market Segment Dimensions
– Flexibility
– Responsiveness
– Capacity
– Technology
  Constraints
– Cost

T F

Positioning

1) Processes and tools exist and are utilized for assessing the firm/ extended enterprise's ability to meet key market segment dimensions (at right)

2) A method is utilized to benchmark the firm's capability to satisfy key market segment dimensions (at right) against those of major competitors

3) A process exists and is regularly utilized to solicit information from the firm's suppliers (and other members of the extended enterprise) regarding customer requirements within the market

4) Mechanisms exist to communicate the firm's segment position strategy to internal stakeholders

5) The firm utilizes a standardized process for linking market and customer strategies to management plans and daily work

Evaluation

1) Performance metrics are aligned with major customer segments

2) Customer/Market performance evaluations are made along key dimensions of cost, quality, profitability, delivery and customer satisfaction

3) A method exists to monitor performance metrics to Customer/Market segmentation strategy

4) Metrics exist to compare/contrast performance with competitors and to evaluate the relative success in the chosen customer market segment

5) A method exists to track and evaluate the progress and outcome of strategic investment decisions

Value Quest – Practitioner's Diagnostic
<u>PRODUCT DOMAIN</u>

Instructions: Check box as true or false. Input number of true answers on the summary sheet for the corresponding Decision domain.

T F

<u>Product Design</u>

1) Tools and processes are in place that effectively relate customer requirements to product and service bundle features

2) An effective measurement system exists that provides feedback on customer acceptance of the product/service features while still in the design phase

3) An effective measurement system exists that provides feedback on customer acceptance of the features after launch of the product/service

4) Tools and processes are in place to perform competitive analysis and translate results into future product/service design

5) A well defined process is in place to establish and monitor internal performance measures, such as return on investment, product cost, product reliability

6) An effective product development plan exists to determine when new products and/or services are required

7) A systematic method is in place, within the design process, to leverage internal competencies and supply chain capabilities

<u>Define Service Bundle</u>

1) A systematic process is in place to review and establish warranty programs (time periods, parts/products covered)

2) Responsibilities for support services are clearly defined and performance metrics are reviewed with effected parties on a regular basis

3) Service/spare parts levels are clearly defined for distributors; supported by an effective replenishment system

4) A performance measurement system is in place to evaluate the effectiveness and timeliness of support services and/or spare parts order fulfillment process

5) A well defined process is in place to determine technical publication requirements early in the development program

6) A systematic process is in place to update and distribute technical publications

Value Quest – Practitioner's Diagnostic
PRODUCT DOMAIN (cont.)

Instructions: Check box as true or false. Input number of true answers on the summary sheet for the corresponding Decision domain.

T   F

Strategic Partnering

☐ ☐ 1) Key vendors are considered "natural" extensions of the company and, as such, are involved in the product design process

☐ ☐ 2) Formal processes are in place to evaluate all sourcing decisions, ensuring that optimal utilization of resources is achieved

☐ ☐ 3) Tools and processes are in place that encourage vendors to offer cost improvement ideas in a mutually benefiting environment

☐ ☐ 4) Regular and frequent reviews of agreed performance measures are held with strategic partners and linked to improvement objectives

Managing Product/Service Bundle

☐ ☐ 1) A systematic method is in place to determine that the product and support services are meeting customer requirements

☐ ☐ 2) A continuous process improvement system is in place to drive
   – enhanced product performance   – product cost reduction
   – vendor performance   – life cycle cost reduction

☐ ☐ 3) A process exists that provides continuous feedback against competitive products

☐ ☐ 4) A systematic process is in place to assess the product/service features against changes in the environment and to effect changes to properly respond

Creating the Future

☐ ☐ 1) A formal product plan that extends beyond the current product life-cycle is in place

☐ ☐ 2) A regular and documented product review process is in place to compare development objectives against actual results Learnings are used in future projects

☐ ☐ 3) A documented process is in place to evaluate and determine when products or services are to be abandoned

☐ ☐ 4) A formal process is used and formally reviewed to ensure that product/service values are current and in line with customer requirements

☐ ☐ 5) A formal process is in place to ensure that service support is adequately maintained for products that are phased out

Value Quest – **Practitioner's Diagnostic**
<u>**PROCESS DOMAIN**</u>

Instructions: Check box as true or false. Input number of true answers on the summary sheet for the corresponding Decision domain.

T F

Creating Processes

1) Internal processes have been developed that allow an understanding of the way work is completed so that non-value added and wasteful activities are eliminated

2) Adequate time is spent in the design stage to ensure that excess capacity or waste is not embedded in the system

3) Early in the product cycle, a documented review of alternative processes is made to ensure that the most cost effective process is utilized

4) Process improvement targets are set and monitored

5) A formalized communication system ensures necessary linkage of individuals and activities across the organization

6) Tools exist and are utilized to ensure that standardization of processes help improve durability, reliability and process yields

Sourcing Decisions

1) Top management supports outsourcing, where appropriate

2) Tangible/intangible costs and benefits are agreed to and evaluated prior to making strategic sourcing decisions

3) A standardized, make/buy model is used throughout the firm

4) A formalized process links make/buy studies to the firm's investment plan

5) Process and tools exist and are utilized to monitor and assess changes in technology and process capabilities

6) A formal procedure is in place to monitor idle capacity for use in the sourcing decision process

Value Quest – Practitioner's Diagnostic
<u>PROCESS DOMAIN</u> (cont.)

Instructions: Check box as true or false. Input number of true answers on the summary sheet for the corresponding Decision domain.

Resource Choice

T F

1) Tools and systems exist and are utilized to analyze processes for deviations to desired performance levels

2) Process shortcomings of the firm's capabilities are constantly tracked and monitored

3) Following identification and assessment of performance gaps, a deployment process including responsible individuals is put in place to implement improvements

4) Gap analysis is converted into detailed action checklists, specifying tasks or activities needed to be addressed, that reviewed on a formal basis

5) Costing information on current and proposed processes is readily available

6) A measurement system, balanced between financial and non-financial measures is formally reviewed on a regular basis

Managing Processes

1) A formal system is utilized to rethink how work is managed in an organization which improves mindsets, methods and activities

2) Tools and systems exist and are utilized to ensure clarity and awareness of process vision throughout the organization

3) Procedures are in place to ensure a balance between functional-oriented and process-based organizational structure and policy

4) A process-based measurement system is in place and regularly reviewed to align goals and efforts across processes

5) As necessary, cross-functional teams are in place to manage and improve processes

6) Core processes are defined and documented to meet or exceed customer value

7) Formal processes are in place to evaluate the different capabilities within the extended enterprise

Value Quest – Practitioner's Diagnostic
RESOURCE DOMAIN

Instructions: Check box as true or false. Input number of true answers on the summary sheet for the corresponding Decision domain.

T F

Resource Choice

☐ ☐ 1) Processes and tools are in place and utilized to evaluate the utilization of resource alternatives to ensure maximum benefit across the organization

☐ ☐ 2) A process is in place for evaluating resource acquisition to ensure the proper balance of efficiency and effectiveness

☐ ☐ 3) A method exists and is utilized to evaluate resource acquisition against target cost objectives

☐ ☐ 4) A formal process is utilized to ensure that resource acquisitions are governed by sourcing policies in effect

Developing Sourcing Policies and Constraints

☐ ☐ 1) The organization has clearly defined sourcing strategy supported by published policies

☐ ☐ 2) The organization has a clearly defined inventory strategy supported by published policies

☐ ☐ 3) A formal project planning process is in place and utilized to manage shared resources effectively

☐ ☐ 4) Information regarding demand and forecast deliveries is shared with trading alliance partners through a formal process

Value Quest – Practitioner's Diagnostic
<u>RESOURCE DOMAIN (cont.)</u>

Instructions: Check box as true or false. Input number of true answers on the summary sheet for the corresponding Decision domain.

T   F

<u>Resource Flexibility</u>

□   □   1) A formalized process is in place and utilized to evaluate the organization's continuous improvement program

□   □   2) Formalized action plans to improve performance are developed and monitored to ensure timely implementation

□   □   3) A systematic method is in place for identifying and re-deploying idle resources

□   □   4) A formal plan exists to employ available capacity and services within trading alliances as required

<u>Developing Sourcing Policies and Constraints</u>

□   □   1) The organization uses a balanced scorecard performance management system that is reviewed on a regular basis

□   □   2) Formalized action plans to improve performance are developed and monitored to ensure timely implementation

□   □   3) Individual goals and objectives are formally tied to the goals and objectives of the organization

□   □   4) The performance measurement system monitors the entire extended enterprise, identifying and efficiently implementing improvement actions

□   □   5) An effective feedback process is in place to ensure that utilized resources are creating customer value

Value Quest – Scoring Summary Worksheet
<u>CUSTOMER/MARKET DECISION DOMAIN</u>

Decision Grouping	Number TRUE		Total Questions		Score	Maximum Score
Value Creation		out of	6	=		5.0
Segment Strategy		out of	5	=		5.0
Positioning		out of	5	=		5.0
Evaluation		out of	5	=		5.0
	INPUTS		Average			

Instructions: From the question sheets, enter the number of TRUE answers for each Decision grouping. Multiply the number of True answers by 5 and divide the result by the total questions for that decision grouping. Enter the result in the "score" box and plot on the "Spider Graph" on the appropriate Decision domain summary sheet.

Value Quest – **Scoring Summary Worksheet**
PRODUCT DECISION DOMAIN

Decision Grouping	Number TRUE		Total Questions		Score	Maximum Score
Product Design		out of	7	=		5.0
Define Service Bundle		out of	6	=		5.0
Strategic Partnering		out of	4	=		5.0
Managing Product/ Service Bundle		out of	4	=		5.0
Creating the Future		out of	5	=		5.0
				Average		

⇦ **INPUTS**

Instructions: From the question sheets, enter the number of TRUE answers for each Decision grouping. Multiply the number of True answers by 5 and divide the result by the total questions for that decision grouping. Enter the result in the "score" box and plot on the "Spider Graph" on the appropriate Decision domain summary sheet.

Value Quest – Scoring Summary Worksheet
<u>PROCESS DECISION DOMAIN</u>

Decision Grouping	Number TRUE		Total Questions		Score	Maximum Score
Process Design		out of	6	=		5.0
Sourcing Decisions		out of	6	=		5.0
Ongoing Process Management		out of	6	=		5.0
Performance Gap Management		out of	7	=		5.0
	INPUTS				Average	

Instructions: From the question sheets, enter the number of TRUE answers for each Decision grouping. Multiply the number of True answers by 5 and divide the result by the total questions for that decision grouping. Enter the result in the "score" box and plot on the "Spider Graph" on the appropriate Decision domain summary sheet.

Value Quest – Scoring Summary Worksheet
RESOURCE DECISION DOMAIN

Decision Grouping	Number TRUE		Total Questions		Score	Maximum Score
Resource Choice		out of	4	=		5.0
Policy Making		out of	4	=		5.0
Managing Flexibility		out of	4	=		5.0
Monitoring & Adjustment		out of	5	=		5.0
				Average		

INPUTS

Instructions: From the question sheets, enter the number of TRUE answers for each Decision grouping. Multiply the number of True answers by 5 and divide the result by the total questions for that decision grouping. Enter the result in the "score" box and plot on the "Spider Graph" on the appropriate Decision domain summary sheet.

Value Quest – Decision Domain Summary Sheet

Customer/Market Decision Domain

Low Score	Key SMP	Key SMP Chapter	Supporting SMPs
Overall	Target Cost Management	5	Extended Enterprise Integrated Performance Mgmt. Process Management
Value Creation	Target Cost Management	5	Extended Enterprise Integrated Performance Mgmt.
Segment Strategy	Target Cost Management	5	Extended Enterprise Capacity Management Process Management
Positioning	Target Cost Management	5	Extended Enterprise Integrated Performance Mgmt. Process Management
Evaluation	Integrated Performance Mgmt.	10	Asset Management Capacity Management Process Management

Instructions: From the Appropriate Scoring Summary Worksheet, plot the value of each Decision grouping score on the appropriate leg of the "Spider Chart" above. The center is "0" and the outer edge is "5". For the lowest scoring Decision groupings (nearest the center), use the reference schedule at the right for the guiding chapters.

Value Quest – Decision Domain Summary Sheet

Product Decision Domain

Low Score	Key SMP	Key SMP Chapter	Supporting SMPs
Overall	Target Cost Management	5	Integrated Performance Mgmt. / Extended Enterprise / Activity-Based Cost Mgmt.
Product Design	Target Cost Management	5	Extended Enterprise / Integrated Performance Mgmt.
Define Service Bundle	Target Cost Management	5	Extended Enterprise / Capacity Management / Process Management
Strategic Partnering	Target Cost Mgmt. Management / Extended Enterprise	5 / 9	Extended Enterprise / Integrated Performance Mgmt. / Process Management
Managing Product/Service	Integrated Performance Mgmt.	10	Asset Management / Capacity Management / Process Management
Creating the Future	Integrated Performance Mgmt. / Target Cost Mgmt.	10 / 5	Asset Management / Extended Enterprise / Activity-Based Cost Mgmt.

Instructions: From the Appropriate Scoring Summary Worksheet, plot the value of each Decision grouping score on the appropriate leg of the "Spider Chart" above. The center is "0" and the outer edge is "5". For the lowest scoring Decision groupings (nearest the center), use the reference schedule at the right for the guiding chapters.

Value Quest – Decision Domain Summary Sheet

Process Decision Domain

Low Score	Key SMP	Key SMP Chapter	Supporting SMPs
Overall	Process Management	8	Integrated Performance Mgmt. Extended Enterprise Capacity Management
Process Design	Process Management	8	Extended Enterprise Capacity Management
Sourcing Decisions	Extended Enterprise	9	Integrated Performance Mgmt. Process Management Activity-Based Cost Mgmt.
Ongoing Process Mgmt.	Extended Enterprise Process Management	9 8	Integrated Performance Mgmt. Capacity Management Process Management
Performance Gap Mgmt.	Process Management	8	Integrated Performance Mgmt. Extended Enterprise

Instructions: From the Appropriate Scoring Summary Worksheet, plot the value of each Decision grouping score on the appropriate leg of the "Spider Chart" above. The center is "0" and the outer edge is "5". For the lowest scoring Decision groupings (nearest the center), use the reference schedule at the right for the guiding chapters.

Value Quest – Decision Domain Summary Sheet

Resource Decision Domain	Low Score	Key SMP	Key SMP Chapter	Supporting SMPs
	Overall	Activity-Based Cost Management	11	Integrated Performance Mgmt. Extended Enterprise Capacity Management
	Resource Choice	Integrated Performance Management	10	Extended Enterprise Process Management Capacity Management
		Activity-Based Cost Mgmt.	11	
	Policy Making	Process Management	8	Activity-Based Cost Mgmt. Integrated Performance Mgmt.
	Managing Flexibility	Activity-Based Cost Management	11	Integrated Performance Mgmt. Extended Enterprise
	Monitoring & Adjustment	Integrated Performance Management	8	Extended Enterprise Capacity Management Process Management
		Activity-Based Cost Management	11	

Spider chart: Resource Choice (5.0, 0.0) — Policy Making — Managing Flexibility — Monitoring & Adjustment

Instructions: From the Appropriate Scoring Summary Worksheet, plot the value of each Decision grouping score on the appropriate leg of the "Spider Chart" above. The center is "0" and the outer edge is "5". For the lowest scoring Decision groupings (nearest the center), use the reference schedule at the right for the guiding chapters.

Appendix B

PART 2

- **COMPLETED DIAGNOSTIC SAMPLES**
    Input Sheets by Decision Domain
    Scoring Summary Worksheets
    Decision Domain Summary Sheets with
      Value Quest Reference Schedules

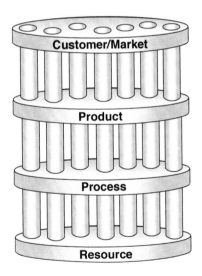

Customer/Market

Product

Process

Resource

Value Quest – Practitioner's Diagnostic
<u>CUSTOMER/MARKET DOMAIN</u>

Instructions: Check box as true or false. Input number of true answers on the summary sheet for the corresponding Decision domain.

T   F

<u>Value Creation</u>

[X] [ ] 1) Processes and tools are in place and utilized for identifying customer's life cycle value expectations

[ ] [X] 2) Processes and tools are in place and utilized for determining the importance of differing value preferences between customers

[X] [ ] 3) Customer value preferences can be listed in order of importance

[ ] [X] 4) A reliable method exists and is utilized for evaluating the firm's current performance against customer expectations (versus that of key competitors)

[ ] [X] 5) A method exists to evaluate internal processes against customer value to determine process value and non-value added activities

[ ] [X] 6) Mechanisms exist to communicate customer value expectations to the internal stakeholders

<u>Segment Strategy</u>

[X] [ ] 1) A method is utilized to evaluate compatibility of Customer/ Market segment requirements with the firm's competencies and capabilities

[X] [ ] 2) Process and tools exist and are utilized for conducting price and value trade-off analysis for customer and market segments

[X] [ ] 3) The firm develops cost and profit projections for each viable customer and market segmentation strategy

[ ] [X] 4) Processes and tools exist and are utilized to assess investment and operational implications of various segment strategies

[ ] [X] 5) Processes and tools exist and are utilized to determine the compatibility and capability of the extended enterprise to effectively respond to different segmentation strategies

Value Quest – **Practitioner's Diagnostic**
CUSTOMER/MARKET DOMAIN (cont.)

Instructions: Check box as true or false. Input number of true answers on the summary sheet for the corresponding Decision domain.

Key Market Segment Dimensions
- Flexibility
- Responsiveness
- Capacity
- Technology
- Constraints
- Cost

T F

Positioning

☒ ☐ 1) Processes and tools exist and are utilized for assessing the firm/extended enterprise's ability to meet key market segment dimensions (at right)

☐ ☒ 2) A method is utilized to benchmark the firm's capability to satisfy key market segment dimensions (at right) against those of major competitors

☒ ☐ 3) A process exists and is regularly utilized to solicit information from the firm's suppliers (and other members of the extended enterprise) regarding customer requirements within the market

☒ ☐ 4) Mechanisms exist to communicate the firm's segment position strategy to internal stakeholders

☐ ☒ 5) The firm utilizes a standardized process for linking market and customer strategies to management plans and daily work

Evaluation

☐ ☒ 1) Performance metrics are aligned with major customer segments

☒ ☐ 2) Customer/Market performance evaluations are made along key dimensions of cost, quality, profitability, delivery and customer satisfaction

☒ ☐ 3) A method exists to monitor performance metrics to Customer/Market segmentation strategy

☒ ☐ 4) Metrics exist to compare/contrast performance with competitors and to evaluate the relative success in the chosen customer market segment

☒ ☐ 5) A method exists to track and evaluate the progress and outcome of strategic investment decisions

Value Quest – Practitioner's Diagnostic
<u>PRODUCT DOMAIN</u>

Instructions: Check box as true or false. Input number of true answers on the summary sheet for the corresponding Decision domain.

T	F	Product Design
☒	☐	1) Tools and processes are in place that effectively relate customer requirements to product and service bundle features
☐	☒	2) An effective measurement system exists that provides feedback on customer acceptance of the product/service features while still in the design phase
☐	☒	3) An effective measurement system exists that provides feedback on customer acceptance of the features after launch of the product/service
☒	☐	4) Tools and processes are in place to perform competitive analysis and translate results into future product/service design
☐	☒	5) A well defined process is in place to establish and monitor internal performance measures, such as return on investment, product cost, product reliability
☒	☐	6) An effective product development plan exists to determine when new products and/or services are required
☒	☐	7) A systematic method is in place, within the design process, to leverage internal competencies and supply chain capabilities

T	F	Define Service Bundle
☒	☐	1) A systematic process is in place to review and establish warranty programs (time periods, parts/products covered)
☒	☐	2) Responsibilities for support services are clearly defined and performance metrics are reviewed with effected parties on a regular basis
☒	☐	3) Service/spare parts levels are clearly defined for distributors; supported by an effective replenishment system
☐	☒	4) A performance measurement system is in place to evaluate the effectiveness and timeliness of support services and/or spare parts order fulfillment process
☒	☐	5) A well defined process is in place to determine technical publication requirements early in the development program
☐	☒	6) A systematic process is in place to update and distribute technical publications

Value Quest – Practitioner's Diagnostic
PRODUCT DOMAIN (cont.)

Instructions: Check box as true or false. Input number of true answers on the summary sheet for the corresponding Decision domain.

Strategic Partnering

T F

[X] [ ] 1) Key vendors are considered "natural" extensions of the company and, as such, are involved in the product design process

[X] [ ] 2) Formal processes are in place to evaluate all sourcing decisions, ensuring that optimal utilization of resources is achieved

[X] [ ] 3) Tools and processes are in place that encourage vendors to offer cost improvement ideas in a mutually benefiting environment

[ ] [X] 4) Regular and frequent reviews of agreed performance measures are held with strategic partners and linked to improvement objectives

Managing Product/Service Bundle

[X] [ ] 1) A systematic method is in place to determine that the product and support services are meeting customer requirements

[X] [ ] 2) A continuous process improvement system is in place to drive
  – enhanced product performance   – product cost reduction
  – vendor performance   – life cycle cost reduction

[ ] [ ] 3) A process exists that provides continuous feedback against competitive products

[X] [ ] 4) A systematic process is in place to assess the product/service features against changes in the environment and to effect changes to properly respond

Creating the Future

[X] [ ] 1) A formal product plan that extends beyond the current product life-cycle is in place

[ ] [X] 2) A regular and documented product review process is in place to compare development objectives against actual results. Learnings are used in future projects

[X] [ ] 3) A documented process is in place to evaluate and determine when products or services are to be abandoned

[X] [ ] 4) A formal process is used and formally reviewed to ensure that product/service values are current and in line with customer requirements

[ ] [X] 5) A formal process is in place to ensure that service support is adequately maintained for products that are phased out

Value Quest – Practitioner's Diagnostic
PROCESS DOMAIN

Instructions: Check box as true or false. Input number of true answers on the summary sheet for the corresponding Decision domain.

Creating Processes

T	F	
☐	☒	1) Internal processes have been developed that allow an understanding of the way work is completed so that non-value added and wasteful activities are eliminated
☐	☒	2) Adequate time is spent in the design stage to ensure that excess capacity or waste is not embedded in the system
☐	☒	3) Early in the product cycle, a documented review of alternative processes is made to ensure that the most cost effective process is utilized
☒	☐	4) Process improvement targets are set and monitored
☐	☒	5) A formalized communication system ensures necessary linkage of individuals and activities across the organization
☐	☒	6) Tools exist and are utilized to ensure that standardization of processes help improve durability, reliability and process yields

Sourcing Decisions

T	F	
☐	☒	1) Top management supports outsourcing, where appropriate
☒	☐	2) Tangible/intangible costs and benefits are agreed to and evaluated prior to making strategic sourcing decisions
☐	☒	3) A standardized, make/buy model is used throughout the firm
☐	☒	4) A formalized process links make/buy studies to the firm's investment plan
☐	☒	5) Process and tools exist and are utilized to monitor and assess changes in technology and process capabilities
☒	☐	6) A formal procedure is in place to monitor idle capacity for use in the sourcing decision process

Value Quest – Practitioner's Diagnostic
PROCESS DOMAIN (cont.)

Instructions: Check box as true or false. Input number of true answers on the summary sheet for the corresponding Decision domain.

Resource Choice

T	F	
☐	☒	1) Tools and systems exist and are utilized to analyze processes for deviations to desired performance levels
☐	☒	2) Process shortcomings of the firm's capabilities are constantly tracked and monitored
☒	☐	3) Following identification and assessment of performance gaps, a deployment process including responsible individuals is put in place to implement improvements
☒	☐	4) Gap analysis is converted into detailed action checklists, specifying tasks or activities needed to be addressed, that reviewed on a formal basis
☐	☒	5) Costing information on current and proposed processes is readily available
☐	☒	6) A measurement system, balanced between financial and non-financial measures is formally reviewed on a regular basis

Managing Processes

T	F	
☐	☒	1) A formal system is utilized to rethink how work is managed in an organization which improves mindsets, methods and activities
☒	☐	2) Tools and systems exist and are utilized to ensure clarity and awareness of process vision throughout the organization
☐	☒	3) Procedures are in place to ensure a balance between functional-oriented and process-based organizational structure and policy
☒	☐	4) A process-based measurement system is in place and regularly reviewed to align goals and efforts across processes
☒	☐	5) As necessary, cross-functional teams are in place to manage and improve processes
☐	☒	6) Core processes are defined and documented to meet or exceed customer value
☐	☒	7) Formal processes are in place to evaluate the different capabilities within the extended enterprise

Value Quest – **Practitioner's Diagnostic**
RESOURCE DOMAIN

Instructions: Check box as true or false. Input number of true answers on the summary sheet for the corresponding Decision domain.

T F

Resource Choice

☒ ☐ 1) Processes and tools are in place and utilized to evaluate the utilization of resource alternatives to ensure maximum benefit across the organization

☐ ☒ 2) A process is in place for evaluating resource acquisition to ensure the proper balance of efficiency and effectiveness

☒ ☐ 3) A method exists and is utilized to evaluate resource acquisition against target cost objectives

☒ ☐ 4) A formal process is utilized to ensure that resource acquisitions are governed by sourcing policies in effect

Developing Sourcing Policies and Constraints

☒ ☐ 1) The organization has clearly defined sourcing strategy supported by published policies

☒ ☐ 2) The organization has a clearly defined inventory strategy supported by published policies

☒ ☐ 3) A formal project planning process is in place and utilized to manage shared resources effectively

☐ ☒ 4) Information regarding demand and forecast deliveries is shared with trading alliance partners through a formal process

Value Quest – Practitioner's Diagnostic
<u>RESOURCE DOMAIN (cont.)</u>

Instructions: Check box as true or false. Input number of true answers on the summary sheet for the corresponding Decision domain.

T F

<u>Resource Flexibility</u>

☒ ☐ 1) A formalized process is in place and utilized to evaluate the organization's continuous improvement program

☒ ☐ 2) Formalized action plans to improve performance are developed and monitored to ensure timely implementation

☐ ☒ 3) A systematic method is in place for identifying and re-deploying idle resources

☒ ☐ 4) A formal plan exists to employ available capacity and services within trading alliances as required

<u>Developing Sourcing Policies and Constraints</u>

☐ ☒ 1) The organization uses a balanced scorecard performance management system that is reviewed on a regular basis

☐ ☒ 2) Formalized action plans to improve performance are developed and monitored to ensure timely implementation

☐ ☒ 3) Individual goals and objectives are formally tied to the goals and objectives of the organization

☒ ☐ 4) The performance measurement system monitors the entire extended enterprise, identifying and efficiently implementing improvement actions

☒ ☐ 5) An effective feedback process is in place to ensure that utilized resources are creating customer value

Value Quest – Scoring Summary Worksheet
<u>CUSTOMER/MARKET DECISION DOMAIN</u>

Decision Grouping	Number TRUE		Total Questions		Score	Maximum Score
Value Creation	2	out of	6	=	1.7	5.0
Segment Strategy	3	out of	5	=	3.0	5.0
Positioning	3	out of	5	=	3.0	5.0
Evaluation	1	out of	5	=	1.0	5.0
	INPUTS			Average	2.2	

Instructions: From the question sheets, enter the number of TRUE answers for each Decision grouping. Multiply the number of True answers by 5 and divide the result by the total questions for that decision grouping. Enter the result in the "score" box and plot on the "Spider Graph" on the appropriate Decision domain summary sheet.

Value Quest – Scoring Summary Worksheet
<u>PRODUCT DECISION DOMAIN</u>

Decision Grouping	Number TRUE		Total Questions		Score	Maximum Score
Product Design	4	out of	7	=	2.9	5.0
Define Service Bundle	1	out of	6	=	0.8	5.0
Strategic Partnering	3	out of	4	=	3.8	5.0
Managing Product/ Service Bundle	1	out of	4	=	1.3	5.0
Creating the Future	3	out of	5	=	3.0	5.0
				Average	2.3	

INPUTS

Instructions: From the question sheets, enter the number of TRUE answers for each Decision grouping. Multiply the number of True answers by 5 and divide the result by the total questions for that decision grouping. Enter the result in the "score" box and plot on the "Spider Graph" on the appropriate Decision domain summary sheet.

Value Quest – Scoring Summary Worksheet
<u>PROCESS DECISION DOMAIN</u>

Decision Grouping	Number TRUE		Total Questions		Score	Maximum Score
Process Design	1	out of	6	=	0.8	5.0
Sourcing Decisions	2	out of	6	=	1.7	5.0
Ongoing Process Management	2	out of	6	=	1.7	5.0
Performance Gap Management	3	out of	7	=	2.1	5.0
	↑ INPUTS			Average	1.6	

Instructions: From the question sheets, enter the number of TRUE answers for each Decision grouping. Multiply the number of True answers by 5 and divide the result by the total questions for that decision grouping. Enter the result in the "score" box and plot on the "Spider Graph" on the appropriate Decision domain summary sheet.

Value Quest – Scoring Summary Worksheet
<u>RESOURCE DECISION DOMAIN</u>

Decision Grouping	Number TRUE		Total Questions		Score	Maximum Score
Resource Choice	3	out of	4	=	3.8	5.0
Policy Making	3	out of	4	=	3.8	5.0
Managing Flexibility	3	out of	4	=	3.8	5.0
Monitoring & Adjustment	2	out of	5	=	2.0	5.0
	INPUTS			Average	3.3	

Instructions: From the question sheets, enter the number of TRUE answers for each Decision grouping. Multiply the number of True answers by 5 and divide the result by the total questions for that decision grouping. Enter the result in the "score" box and plot on the "Spider Graph" on the appropriate Decision domain summary sheet.

Value Quest – **Decision Domain Summary Sheet**

| | X | = Concern Areas |

Customer/Market Decision Domain

<u>Low Score</u>	<u>Key SMP</u>	Key SMP <u>Chapter</u>	Supporting <u>SMPs</u>
Overall	Target Cost Management	5	Extended Enterprise Integrated Performance Mgmt. Process Management
Value Creation	Target Cost Management	5	Extended Enterprise Integrated Performance Mgmt.
Segment Strategy	Target Cost Management	5	Extended Enterprise Capacity Management Process Management
Positioning	Target Cost Management	5	Extended Enterprise Integrated Performance Mgmt. Process Management
X Evaluation	Integrated Performance Mgmt.	10	Asset Management Capacity Management Process Management

Instructions: From the Appropriate Scoring Summary Worksheet, plot the value of each Decision grouping score on the appropriate leg of the "Spider Chart" above. The center is "0" and the outer edge is "5". For the lowest scoring Decision groupings (nearest the center), use the reference schedule at the right for the guiding chapters.

Value Quest – Decision Domain Summary Sheet

X = Concern Areas

Product Decision Domain

Low Score	Key SMP	Key SMP Chapter	Supporting SMPs
Overall	Target Cost Management	5	Integrated Performance Mgmt. Extended Enterprise Activity-Based Cost Mgmt.
Product Design	Target Cost Management	5	Extended Enterprise Integrated Performance Mgmt.
X Define Service Bundle	Target Cost Management	5	Extended Enterprise Capacity Management Process Management
Strategic Partnering	Target Cost Mgmt. Management Extended Enterprise	5 9	Extended Enterprise Integrated Performance Mgmt. Process Management
Managing Product/Service	Integrated Performance Mgmt.	10	Asset Management Capacity Management Process Management
Creating the Future	Integrated Performance Mgmt. Target Cost Mgmt.	10 5	Asset Management Extended Enterprise Activity-Based Cost Mgmt.

Instructions: From the Appropriate Scoring Summary Worksheet, plot the value of each Decision grouping score on the appropriate leg of the "Spider Chart" above. The center is "0" and the outer edge is "5". For the lowest scoring Decision groupings (nearest the center), use the reference schedule at the right for the guiding chapters.

Value Quest – **Decision Domain Summary Sheet**

| X | = Concern Areas |

Low Score		Key SMP	Key SMP Chapter	Supporting SMPs
X	Overall	Process Management	8	Integrated Performance Mgmt. Extended Enterprise Capacity Management
X	Process Design	Process Management	8	Extended Enterprise Capacity Management
	Sourcing Decisions	Extended Enterprise	9	Integrated Performance Mgmt. Process Management Activity-Based Cost Mgmt.
	Ongoing Process Mgmt.	Extended Enterprise Process Management	9 8	Integrated Performance Mgmt. Capacity Management Process Management
	Performance Gap Mgmt.	Process Management	8	Integrated Performance Mgmt. Extended Enterprise

Process Decision Domain

Instructions: From the Appropriate Scoring Summary Worksheet, plot the value of each Decision grouping score on the appropriate leg of the "Spider Chart" above. The center is "0" and the outer edge is "5". For the lowest scoring Decision groupings (nearest the center), use the reference schedule at the right for the guiding chapters.

Value Quest – Decision Domain Summary Sheet

X = Concern Areas

	Low Score	Key SMP	Key SMP Chapter	Supporting SMPs
	Overall	Activity-Based Cost Management	11	Integrated Performance Mgmt. / Extended Enterprise / Capacity Management
	Resource Choice	Integrated Performance Management	10	Extended Enterprise / Process Management / Capacity Management
		Activity-Based Cost Mgmt.	11	
	Policy Making	Process Management	8	Activity-Based Cost Mgmt. / Integrated Performance Mgmt.
	Managing Flexibility	Activity-Based Cost Management	11	Integrated Performance Mgmt. / Extended Enterprise
X	**Monitoring & Adjustment**	Integrated Performance Management / Activity-Based Cost Management	8 / 11	Extended Enterprise / Capacity Management / Process Management

Resource Decision Domain

Spider chart with axes: Resource Choice, Policy Making, Managing Flexibility, Monitoring & Adjustment. Scale marked 5.0 (outer) and 0.0 (center).

Instructions: From the Appropriate Scoring Summary Worksheet, plot the value of each Decision grouping score on the appropriate leg of the "Spider Chart" above. The center is "0" and the outer edge is "5". For the lowest scoring Decision groupings (nearest the center), use the reference schedule at the right for the guiding chapters.